The Bonds of Trade:
Commerce and Community in the Liverpool Slave Trade, 1695–1775

by
Brian W. Refford

University Readers™
San Diego, CA

First published in the United States of America in 2008 by University Readers

Cover Image: © National Museums Liverpool, Walker Art Gallery
Cover design by Monica Hui Hekman

12 11 10 09 08   1 2 3 4 5

Printed in the United States of America

ISBN: 978-1-934269-25-1 (paper)

University Readers™
800.200.3908 | www.universityreaders.com

Acknowledgements

The preparation of a dissertation can be a soul-shredding experience. In my case, the support and kindness of two individuals made the completion of this work possible: Ian Duffy and Jean Soderlund. First, I would like to thank Ian Duffy, my dissertation director, for his kindness and support. A scholar of common sense, patience, and insight, Ian endured the various drafts of this study with good humor, a task I would not wish on anyone. Thank you Ian.

I would especially like to thank Jean Soderlund for her compassion and friendship. Without her on my side I could not have survived this ordeal. I respect few people more than Jean, both as a scholar and a person. She understood the many difficulties that disabled people must face in such a long-term undertaking. Thank you Jean.

A fellowship and other funds from the Lawrence Henry Gipson Institute at Lehigh University allowed me to complete research at the University of Liverpool, the Liverpool PRO at the Picton Library, and the Merseyside Maritime Museum. I would also like to thank all the members of my dissertation committee.

I would also like to thank two extraordinary women named Ann. My mother Ann Refford has always been there for me throughout my life. Thanks Mom. More than anyone else, however, I owe the most to Ann DeAngelis. She survived my bouts of ill-health and accompanied me on numerous trips to the hospital. She is my conscience, my best friend, and my partner. Without her love and support I could not have succeeded in this task. Ann, I owe you more than I can express in words.

Contents

List of Tables

List of Maps

Preface

The Bonds of Trade:
Commerce and Community in the Liverpool Slave Trade, 1695–1775

Brian W. Refford

The Atlantic slave trade fueled the rise of Liverpool. By 1750, Liverpool had supplanted Bristol as the leading slave port in Britain. In the process, a remarkable group of merchants formed a set of social and commercial relationships that served to underpin this growth. The rise of Liverpool is attributable to the character of the town's slave-trading community.

The liberation of merchants in the aftermath of the Glorious Revolution from centuries of aristocratic dominance was translated into political, social and commercial power in the decades after 1700. Merchants were the rulers of Liverpool throughout the eighteenth century, as trade became the *leitmotif* of town government. After 1700, newly influential merchants attempted to cast themselves as a new social and commercial aristocracy. This effort was short-lived, however, as a diverse group of men flocked to Liverpool in pursuit of profit in the African trade. Thus, migration to Liverpool had a transformative affect upon the social construction of the slave trade and the nature of the bonds that joined the slaving community together in common purpose.

A major feature of this study is an examination of the relatively open nature of the Liverpool trade for all who wished to sell slaves in the New World. This ease of access attracted would-be merchants to Liverpool and served to short-circuit any attempt to build a slave trading elite. Any investor with enough funds could trade for slaves in Africa, regardless of prior social position or place of origin.

Prominent merchant families did not monopolize the opportunities for profit in the slave trade. The involvement of new men in Liverpool trade after 1700 suggests that by the mid-eighteenth century a process of social and commercial liberalization had altered the social composition of the slave trading community.The openness of the Liverpool slave trade to outsiders can be traced to a general loosening of traditional social practices and institutions that had restricted access to trade before 1700. New entrepreneurs became the real powers in the Liverpool slave trade, if not in Liverpool society.

Introduction

In the first third of the eighteenth-century, Bristol emerged as the "metropolis of the west," an outport that grew rich on transatlantic trade.[1] Although a major center of the West Indian sugar trade, it is perhaps the West African slave trade that the port of Bristol is most closely associated.[2] Bristol had supplanted London as the leading slaving port in Britain by 1725. However, this dominance was short-lived. By 1750, Liverpool had eclipsed Bristol and remained the capital of the transatlantic slave trade until its abolition in 1807.[3] Bristol's failure to retain its share of the transatlantic traffic in slaves was largely the result of what Ralph Davis describes as "the tempestuous ascent of Liverpool, the eighteenth century's [greatest] success story."[4] From modest beginnings, Liverpool became the nation's second port after London, a prominence that flowed from the social and commercial character of the town's slave-trading community.

The struggles of the Glorious Revolution and its aftermath liberated the Whiggish merchants who came to dominate the Corporation of Liverpool for most of the eighteenth century.[5] The political emancipation of

---

[1] Walter Minchinton, "Bristol—Metropolis of the West in the Eighteenth Century," *Transactions of the Royal Historical Society* 4 (1953–4), 69–89.

[2] Kenneth Morgan, "Bristol and the Atlantic Trade in the Eighteenth Century," *English Historical Review* 107 (1992), 626–650.

[3] Minchinton, "Bristol—Metropolis of the West in the Eighteenth," 69–89; Seymour Drescher, "The Slaving Capital of the World: Liverpool and National Opinion in the Age of Abolition," *Slavery & Abolition* 2 (1988), 128–143; David Richardson, *The Bristol Slave Traders: A Collective Portrait* (1985), 1; Morgan, "Bristol and the Atlantic Trade in the Eighteenth Century," 637–641.

[4] Ralph Davis, *The Rise of the English Shipping Industry in the Seventeenth and Eighteenth Centuries* (1962) 38.

[5] *See*: Perry Gauci, *The Politics of Trade: The Overseas Merchant in State and Society, 1660–1720* (2001); Penelope Corfield, *The Impact of English Towns, 1700–1800* (1982); Sheila Marriner, *The Economic and Social Development of Merseyside* (1982); J.R. Harris, *Liverpool and Merseyside, Essays in the Economic and Social History of the Port and its Hinterland* (1969); Francis Hyde, *Liverpool and the Mersey: An Economic History of a Port, 1700–1800* (1971); C.N. Parkinson, *The Rise of the Port of Liverpool* (1952); Michael Power, "Councillors and Commerce in Liverpool, 1650–1750," *Urban History* 24 (1997), 302–323; Power, Politics and Progress in Liverpool, 1660–1740," *Northern History* 35 (1999), 119–138; Michael Mullett, "The Politics of Liverpool, 1660–1688," *Transactions of the Historical Society of Lancashire and Cheshire (THSLC)* 124 (1972), 31–56; Paul Clemens, "The Rise of Liverpool, 1665–1750," *Economic History Review* 29 (1976), 211–225.

Liverpool from the traditional dominance of aristocratic families permitted men of relatively common birth to assume control of the town and remove the feudal shackles that had long restrained commercial enterprise. Middling men of trade became the *de facto* lords of Liverpool. While many of them fought each other for control of the Common Council, they all viewed the promotion of trade as the primary goal of town government, and the council as the organ to achieve this goal. Newly influential town leaders such as Sir Thomas Johnson, Richard Gildart, William Clayton, and John Cleveland became the ruling oligarchs of Liverpool, merchants who charted a new course for the town that was widely accepted by many business-oriented townsmen of all political stripes. This liberation released a pent-up commercial energy that ultimately sped the town towards its dominance of the Atlantic slave trade. For an increasingly diverse group of men, this headlong pursuit of profit unlocked a world of commercial, political, and social opportunity that influenced how they viewed their place in Liverpool commerce and society.

Historians, however, have not always viewed the relationship between town and merchant as important and the role of merchants and merchant communities in the evolution of transatlantic trade has not been adequately explored. Of course, there have been exceptions: David Hancock explored the relationship between eighteenth-century London merchants and their place in the integration of the Atlantic economy, David Richardson examined the evolving role of slave merchants in the Bristol African trade, while Melinda Elder wrote a similar study of the Lancaster slave trading community.[6] These studies point towards a new appreciation of the role of social factors in the eighteenth-century expansion of the transatlantic slave trade. David Richardson's careful studies of the Bristol slave trading community between 1698–1807 suggests that it is possible to integrate larger questions concerning the nature and scope of the British slave trade with a more delimited focus on the community of slave traders that arose in Bristol, London, Liverpool, and elsewhere.[7]

Richardson has been important in fleshing out the relationship between society and trade. He argues, for instance, that the decline of the Bristol slave trade after the 1740s can be attributed, in part, to social changes within the city's slave trading community. By the 1740s, growing competition from Liverpool accelerated the already evident tendency for Bristol's principal slave traders to abandon the African trade and seek less risky investments for their capital, such as land and government bonds.[8] Thus, demographic factors served to undercut Bristol's commitment to the slave trade. Unlike Liverpool's slave traders, most of the leading Bristol traders of the first quarter of the eighteenth century failed to produce heirs to take their place, leaving the trade in the hands of former Guinea captains and lesser merchants.[9] As Richardson has found, five of the twenty leading managers of Bristol slaving ventures during this period died unmarried, and the ten who did marry failed to produce an heir.[10] As a result, the decline of the Bristol trade may have been as much a sociological phenomenon as it was an economic one.[11]

A different social dynamic was evident in Liverpool. From its start at the turn of the eighteenth century, new men flowed into the trade, and produced sons who followed in their footsteps. It was not unusual for three generations of a family to enter the trade in slaves. The purpose here is to demonstrate the ways in which these commercial and social bonds underpinned the growth of the Liverpool slave trade. This emphasis differs from traditional interpretations of the rise of the Liverpool slave trade in the eighteenth century. These arguments are many and varied. One attributes the rise of the Liverpool slave trade to ready access to the industrial products of East Lancashire and the Midlands, while others point to the construction of an unparalleled system of docks, an expansive regional trade in coal, salt, fish and Irish goods, the relative safety of the North Channel during wartime, the availability of investment capital, the low cost of Liverpool slaving

---

[6]David Hancock, *Citizens of the World: London Merchants and the Integration of the British Atlantic Community, 1735–1785* (1995); David Richardson, *The Bristol Slave Traders: A Collective Portrait* (1985); Melinda Elder, *The Slave Trade and the Economic Development of Eighteenth Century Lancaster* (1992).

[7]David Richardson, *The Bristol Slave Traders: A Collective Portrait* (1985) 1–5; *See also*: David Richardson, *Bristol, Africa, and the Eighteenth-Century Slave Trade to America, 1698–1807*, 4 vols., (1986–1996).

[8]Richardson, *The Bristol Slave Traders*, 27.

[9]Richardson, 27.

[10]*ibid.*

[11]*ibid.*

operations, and a long maritime tradition on Merseyside.[12] Important as these factors were, however, the rise of the Liverpool slave trade can also be attributed as much to the appearance of a diverse group of slave trading entrepreneurs after 1700, men whose commercial acumen, social relationships, business connections in the local merchant community, and wealth yielded a competitive advantage over their rivals in France, the Netherlands, Portugal, and elsewhere in Britain.

Not all slave traders arose from elite Liverpool families long involved in trade. After 1700, Liverpool became an increasingly inviting place to set up shop, and new arrivals benefited from the business climate of Liverpool. A major feature of the Liverpool slave trade was its openness, for unlike Bristol, any investor with sufficient funds could conceivably prepare a vessel for West Africa, regardless of social position. This was particularly true of ambitious Guinea captains, lesser merchants, tradesmen, and professionals, part-time investors who often became important slave merchants in their own right. Unlike the social exclusiveness which characterized both the Bristol slave trade during its heyday in the 1720s–1730s, and the Lancaster West Indian trade, the relative openness of the Liverpool slave trade shaped the social context of the local community of slavers, and ultimately the composition of slave trading partnerships.[13] The Liverpool slave trade was thus built upon the ingenuity and labor of both native-born and emigrant entrepreneurs.

In many ways, the openness of the Liverpool slave trade can be traced to a general loosening of traditional social practices and institutions; such as apprenticeship, trade guilds, religion, and the freedom; which had restricted access to Liverpool trade for many merchants. Although family connection remained important in the conduct of trade, kinship networks became increasingly attenuated as families grew in size over time. The slow weakening of traditional institutions after 1700 laid the groundwork for the openness that came to characterize the social construction of the Liverpool slave trade during the years of its greatest growth.

In exploring these and other questions, new sources of evidence have made it possible to approach the social context of the transatlantic slave trade with much greater confidence. The appearance of the *Trans-Atlantic Slave Trade Database* (*TSTD*) in 1999 has spurred scholarship on the slave trade, creating intellectual reverberations that promise to influence the field for decades to come.[14] Drawing together the available data on 27,233 British, French, Dutch, Portuguese, Danish, Spanish, and American slaving voyages that departed from both European and American ports between the early sixteenth and mid-nineteenth centuries, the *TSTD* makes available to scholars the raw, quantifiable evidence needed to clarify our understanding of such contentious issues as the volume and regional distribution of the European slave trade; the market structure and relative profitability of this trade; and the human cost to Africans and Europeans alike of slave trading in Africa and the New World.[15] The *TSTD* was intended to provide a common point of departure for slave trade studies, a readily available source of data with which to comprehend the extraordinarily complex and changeable commerce in African slaves over the course of three centuries. Indeed, the editors of the slave trade database project observe that a major aim of this undertaking had always been "to facilitate and stimulate new research on the slave trade, the implications of which reach far beyond the slave trade itself."[16]

Examining the social dimension of the Liverpool slave trade has also benefited from this resource. The editors of the database themselves suggest that the implications for new research on the socioeconomic envi-

---

[12]Jean Agnew, *Belfast Merchant Families in the Seventeenth Century (1996)*, 116–124; Frances Wilkins, *Manx Slave Traders (1999)*, 25, 29. *See also:* T.C. Barker, "Lancashire Coal, Cheshire Salt and the Rise of Liverpool," *THSLC* 103 (1951), 83–101; Maurice Schofield, "Shoes and Ships and Sealing Wax: Eighteenth Century Lancashire Exports to the Colonies," *THSLC* 135 (1986), 61–82; Schofield, "The Slave Trade from Lancashire and Cheshire Ports Outside of Liverpool," *THSLC* 126 (1977), 30–72; Marriner, *The Economic and Social Development of Merseyside*; Thomas Truxes, *Irish American Trade, 1660–1783* (1988); Thomas Truxes, ed., *Letterbook of Greg & Cunningham, 1756–1757: Merchants of New York and Belfast* (2001); ; Gomer Williams, *History of the Liverpool Privateers with an Account of the Liverpool Slave Trade* (1897); J.R. Harris, ed., *Liverpool and Merseyside;* C.N. Parkinson, *The Rise of the Port of Liverpool;* Francis Hyde, *Liverpool and the Mersey.*
[13]*See:* Richardson, *Bristol Slave Traders;* Elder, *The Slave Trade and the Economic Development of Eighteenth Century Lancaster;* Schofield, "The Slave Trade from Lancashire and Cheshire Ports..."
[14]David Eltis, Stephen Behrendt, David Richardson, and Herbert Klein, eds., *The Trans-Atlantic Slave Trade* on CD-ROM (1999).
[15]David Eltis, *et al*, eds., *The Trans-Atlantic Slave Trade.*
[16]User's Guide, in David Eltis, *et al*, eds., *TSTD*, 2.

ronment of the slave trade in those regions which participated in it are "obvious."[17] This general observation, however, has not always borne fruit. Although a steady scholarly output testifies to the increasingly important role that the *TSTD* has assumed in interpretations of the Atlantic slave trade, this resource has yet to be employed in any meaningful way to examine the structure and composition of slave trading partnerships in Liverpool.[18] This reflects the fact that the formation and composition of Liverpool slaving partnerships has not been a central focus of recent scholarship. "Surprisingly little is known," David Richardson notes, "about the size, composition, and character of the Liverpool slave trading community at any stage of the eighteenth century," and despite the "abundant literature" on the Liverpool slave trade, "knowledge of its practical operation remains imperfect."[19]

Perhaps the primary reason for this neglect lies in the fact that while many aspects of Liverpool slave trade has been examined in exhaustive detail by a succession of noteworthy scholars, the questions most frequently asked center upon more general interpretations of the slave trade, such as the scale of the trade, its regional distribution, the evolution of the trade in the Americas, and slave mortality. These broader questions have not borne directly upon the composition of slave trading community Liverpool, or how patterns of partnership influenced their commerce in African slaves. This study attempts to remedy this deficiency. When used in conjunction with other types of evidence—for instance, the extant papers of prominent Liverpool slave traders such as William Davenport, William Earle, John Tarleton, John Knight, and Christopher Hassell—the *TSTD* can provide insight into the familial, commercial, and social composition of slaving partnerships and the men who made them. A notable feature of the database is an extensive listing of the partners in slaving ventures, which in the case of the Liverpool slave trade runs to almost 1,000 names for the period 1695–1775 alone. It is necessary to know the identity of these Liverpool slave traders to make possible an understanding of the types of men—and women—involved in the trade, and how they organized this trade.[20] These comprehensive partnerships lists, which are far more complete for Liverpool than any other eighteenth century British slaving port after 1747, indicate that slaving partnerships did indeed change over time, in terms of size, longevity, social composition, and regional orientation. This suggests that throughout the eighteenth century the Liverpool slave trade served a variety of commercial purposes for those investors willing to assume its risks.

---

[17]User's Guide, 2.

[18]The best example of scholarship based upon the TSTD is the collection of essays contained in David Eltis and David Richardson, eds., *Routes to Slavery: Direction, Ethnicity and Mortality in the Atlantic Slave Trade (1997)*. Among the best essays in this collection include: David Eltis and David Richardson, "West Africa and the Transatlantic Slave Trade: New Evidence of Long Term Trends," 16–35; Herbert Klein and Stanley Engerman, "Long Term Trends in African Mortality in the Transatlantic Slave Trade," 36–48; and Stephen Behrendt, "Crew Mortality in the Transatlantic Slave Trade in the Eighteenth Century," 49–71.

[19]David Richardson, "Profits in the Liverpool Slave Trade: The Accounts of William Davenport, 1757–1784," in Roger Anstey and P.E.H. Hair, eds., *Liverpool, the African Slave Trade, and Abolition: Essays to Illustrate Current Knowledge and Research*, (1976), 81; *See also*: Richardson, *The Bristol Slave Traders*, 11; David Hancock, *Citizens of the World:*.

[20]*TSTD*. The database reveals that four women—Elizabeth Crosbie, Mary Roberts, Elizabeth Rigby, and Mary Rigby—invested in eight different Liverpool slaving partnerships after 1760. All of these women were related to established Liverpool slave traders in some way.

Chapter 1

The Rise of Liverpool

In 1688, fourteen-year-old John Earle left his father's house in Warrington, Lancashire, and made his way towards the small but bustling port of Liverpool and the merchant apprenticeship that awaited him there. Like many enterprising young Lancastrians in late Stuart England, John Earle set forth on the well-trod road to Liverpool in pursuit of opportunity, wealth, and social status, benefits that increasingly came to be associated in the popular imagination with the flourishing Merseyside town. This perception attracted young men into both prestigious skilled trades and professions, such as Earle's, and far less distinguished and remunerative vocations in the lesser craft trades and semi-skilled and unskilled laboring trades. In either case, the flood of young apprentices and other indentured labor was vital to the early growth of Liverpool's commerce and population, attracting financial resources, labor, and new mercantile talent to the town's overseas trade that grew after 1670. Men of business eagerly sought the service of able young apprentices in building their trades. "Wants a Clerk's Place," ran an ad in a Liverpool newspaper, "A Young M A N, of good Character, who writes a fair Hand, and would be willing to contract for a Term of Years. Apply to R. Williamson, at his Office near the Exchange, in Liverpool."[21] This chapter examines the reasons for Liverpool's rise in the late seventeenth-century. It deals in turn with the rise to political power of a merchant class, the slow expansion of the Irish, salt, and overseas trades, and the arrival of new men in Liverpool after 1700.

I

Migration to Liverpool had been common for a long time. Many men arrived as tradesmen, laborers, or mariners and moved into overseas trade. The emergence of Liverpool as a leading port of the transatlantic slave trade can be traced back to this migration in the late-seventeenth century. The Williamson and Tarleton families, for instance, and a number of other merchant families that later rose to prominence in overseas trade, were already established in Liverpool by this time. As early as Elizabeth's reign, the Williamsons arrived in Liverpool as leather workers, tanners, and shoe makers, who, by the end of the sixteenth century, "embarked

---

[21] *Williamson's Liverpool Advertiser*, No Date (1761?).

their capital in overseas trade, bringing back hides and skins from Irish, French, and Spanish ports."[22] Before the Restoration, however, the migration of merchant-apprentices, and more established merchants, to Liverpool was an intermittent, leisurely demographic process that noticeably quickened only after 1700, when the town began to cast off the economic stranglehold of its feudal past. Such migration increased in the late seventeenth and early eighteenth centuries when many young men journeyed to Liverpool as apprentices from Lancashire, Cheshire, Yorkshire, Suffolk, and elsewhere in Britain.[23] By this time, the migrants also included skilled merchants in pursuit of overseas trade. This exodus of merchants was an important factor in the rise of Liverpool.

By the advent of the seventeenth century, the pioneering ambition and industry of the town's nascent merchant community in exploring new lines of trade in Lancashire, Cheshire, and the Irish Sea, had set it apart from most of its neighbors, with the exception of the larger port of Chester.[24] Residents of a sparsely populated village, Liverpool merchants had not always been pioneers, or even particularly industrious. Rising from a nearly inaccessible village in the mid-sixteenth century, Liverpool rose steadily in wealth and population in the decades leading to the outbreak of civil war in 1641. As the graph on the next page demonstrates, Liverpool had grown from a village of 700 in 1565 to a bustling port city of nearly 40,000 by 1775. A quaint country town surrounded by mills, orchards, and pasture lands, it remained an overwhelmingly manorial community rooted in the pastoral rhythms of the medieval past, where agriculture remained the foremost pursuit of its denizens. The inward-looking perspective characteristic of many Liverpudlians had deep historical roots. However, a few men looked beyond these limited horizons to a wider realm of overseas trade. Although the Atlantic Ocean was easily accessible *via* the Irish Sea, Liverpool's small fleet of ships seldom ventured far from shore, and the town had a truly circumscribed maritime heritage before 1600. With a mere 200 resident mariners, only twelve ships were registered in Liverpool in 1555, each vessel averaging only 20 tons.[25]

The emergence of Liverpool as a major international port was a lengthy, conflicted, ambiguous, and often erratic process of interconnected economic, social, and political change. Between 1660 and 1725, a "critical mass" of commercial development took shape in Liverpool, comprised in equal parts of merchant and maritime talent, investment opportunities, available financial resources, civic outlay upon commercial infrastructure, active merchant-politicians operating within a commercialized political climate, as well as a dense network of regional and overseas trading connections.[26] Before John Earle ever set foot in Liverpool, a small group of native-born, would-be merchants pioneered Liverpool's first limited forays into seaborne trade, probably sometime before the reign of Elizabeth I. These men were seldom professional merchants, and most were not actively involved in the ventures in which they invested. Varied in skill and background, they were more often ship's captains, ship-owners, gentlemen and elite landowners; professional men, small manufacturers and skilled craftsmen; than they were experienced overseas merchants. The participation of ordinary men and women in trading ventures was typical of the outports. As Kathleen Wilson points out, in Bristol in the first three quarters of the seventeenth century, individuals who extended credit to merchants in the colonial trade, or invested in colonial trading vessels and/or their cargoes, were frequently "ordinary men and women…convinced of [the] profitability [of] buying and selling commodities aimed at colonial

[22]Francis Hyde, *Liverpool and the Mersey: An Economic History of a Port, 1700–1970* (1971), 3.

[23]John Tyler, "Foster Cunliffe and Sons: Liverpool Merchants in the Maryland Tobacco Trade, 1738–1765," *Maryland Historical Magazine*, 78 (1978), 249, *International Genealogical Index;* Michael Power, "Councillors and Commerce in Liverpool, 1650–1750," *Urban History* 24 (1997), 306–308; Lt. Col. Fishwick, "Notes on the Hardman Family," *The Transactions of the Historical Society of Lancashire and Cheshire*, 42 (1890), 78; Thomas Baines, *History of the Commerce and Town of Liverpool, and of the Rise of Manufacturing Industry in the Adjoining Counties,* (1852), 413–414, Will of Roger Brooke, merchant of Liverpool, Wills and Inventories, Chester Probate Registry, 1753; T. Algernon Earle, "Earle of Allerton Tower," *Transactions of the Historical Society of Lancashire and Cheshire*, 42 (1890), 39.

[24]Jarvis, "The Head Port of Chester," 69–71*f*; Parkinson, 30-2.

[25]Parkinson, 26; Peter Aughton, *Liverpool: A People's History* (1990), 31.

[26]Kathleen Wilson, *The Sense of the People: Politics, Culture, and Imperialism in England, 1715–1785* (1998), 151.

Table 1.1   *Population of Liverpool, 1565–1851 (in thousands)*

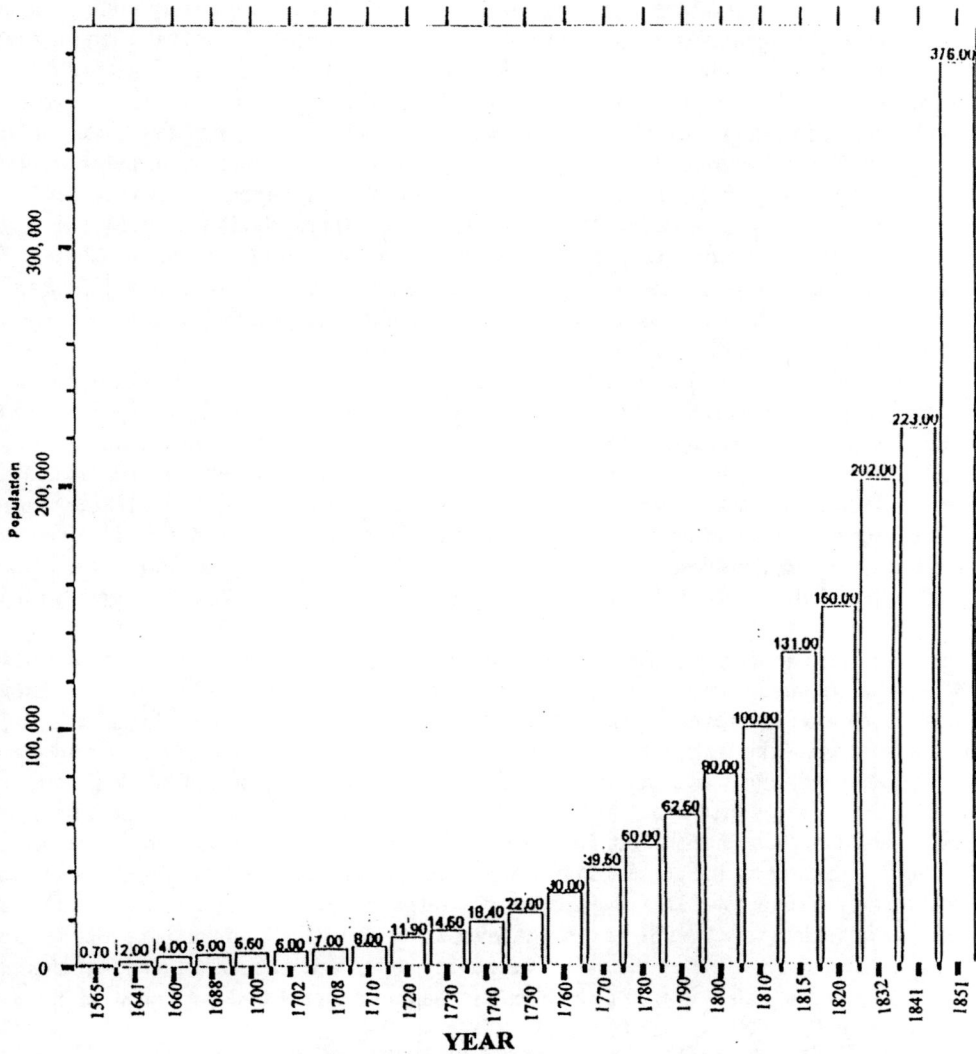

YEAR	Population
1565	0.70
1641	2.00
1660	4.00
1688	6.00
1700	6.60
1702	6.00
1708	7.00
1710	8.00
1720	11.90
1730	14.60
1740	18.40
1750	22.00
1760	30.00
1770	39.50
1780	60.00
1790	62.60
1800	90.00
1810	100.00
1815	131.00
1820	160.00
1832	202.00
1841	223.00
1851	376.00

Source: Penelope Corfield, *The Impact of Towns* (1982); François Vigier, *Change and Apathy* (1970)

and foreign markets, or distributing imported goods at home."[27] This tendency for a large proportion of the working population to launch into ventures by sea was repeated in many smaller English ports throughout Britain.[28] Although late seventeenth century men of means dominated trade to the colonies from the outports, it was still open to any investor who possessed the will and the means to pursuit it, regardless of his occupation or status.

---

[27]Wilson, *The Sense of the People*, 159.

[28]Roger North, *Life of Lord Guilford* (1742), quoted in Wilson, 159; Nigel Tattersfield, *The Forgotten Trade: Comprising the Log of the Daniel & Henry of 1700 and Accounts of the Slave Trade from the Minor Ports of England, 1698–1725* (1991), 15, 195–201.

The rise of Liverpool to the second port after London by 1775 is one of the great socio-economic developments of eighteenth century British history. Its remarkable expansion, especially after 1660, set it apart from neighboring towns in Lancashire and Cheshire, whose development it had largely mirrored prior to that date. Liverpool's transformation was all the more noteworthy for its suddenness, as Liverpool had changed little for centuries after its emergence as a chartered town in the early thirteenth-century. Lying astride a spit of land at the juncture of the restless, windswept Mersey River and the low, marshy banks of the tidal inlet known simply as the Pool, Liverpool was the very definition of a provincial backwater prior to the seventeenth century, and a most unpromising site for an oceangoing port. Connecting Manchester and east Lancashire with the Irish Sea and beyond, the Mersey, a mere seventy-miles in length from source to mouth, has been described as a "gurgling mud-bottomed waterway" for most of its length, a body of water whose only saving grace was that it became a broad, well-protected harbor as it approached Liverpool.[29] This harbor was a crucial factor in the rapid rise of Liverpool, particularly when compared to the fate of Chester. The largest port in northwest England before the rise of Liverpool in the late-seventeenth century, the trade of Chester declined as its outlet to the sea, the River Dee, silted up and became impassable.[30] As a result, a considerable portion of Chester trade was redirected to Liverpool.

Although gifted by geography, Liverpool's overseas trade scarcely existed before the sixteenth century, and grew only slowly from the mid-sixteenth century to the early eighteenth century, in part, because the village's commercial development was hampered by an almost total lack of wharves, docks, and other basic harbor facilities. These deficiencies made the loading and unloading of merchant ships a hazardous affair, and forced vessels to be careened, or run aground, on the low, muddy banks of the Mersey in order to effect even the simplest of repairs. As a harbor the Mersey River had great potential, but required a substantial commitment of political influence in Westminster, organizational talent in Liverpool, and above all financial resources, to be developed adequately; valuable assets which Liverpool did not possess in great measure before 1700.

Liverpool has often been described by historians as a simple fishing hamlet for much of the nearly five centuries between its reputed founding by King John in 1207, and the Glorious Revolution. However, this simplistic characterization ignores the varied nature of the town's early economic life. Liverpool was never simply a fishing village. Like Warrington, and other nearby towns in eastern and southern Lancashire, Liverpool was a market town, albeit an insignificant one. On market days, a range of goods produced in Liverpool were offered to visiting merchants, and a wide array of goods were carted into Liverpool from nearby farms, mills, and manufactories in both Lancashire and Cheshire. The occupational diversity and complexity of the town increased as the centuries passed, and by the seventeenth century, men and women plied a host of occupations in Liverpool. This diversity demonstrates that, even before overseas trade became important to Liverpool in the late seventeenth century, the town's economic development had embarked upon a trajectory of slow but steady growth after the mid-sixteenth century. As will be shown later, occupational diversity was a response to a broadening web of local enterprise and regional trade, which was, in turn, a response to a rise in regional population after 1600.[31]

The few men who entered trade at this time brought a traditional outlook to the new world of trade. An evolving commercial *mentalité* was inhibited by the ingrained habits of thought and action which feudal attitudes continued to impress upon Liverpudlians after the passing of the Middle Ages. Legally, historically, and politically, the town of Liverpool existed to serve the manorial interests of powerful aristocratic families such as the aggressively royalist Stanleys, Molyneauxs, and Moores. During the reign of Henry VIII, the crown awarded the valuable lordship of Liverpool to the Molyneaux family, whose fee farm encompassed various feudal rights including;

---

[29]Mark Kurlansky, *Salt: A World History* (2002), 179.

[30]R.C. Jarvis, "The Head Port of Chester; and Liverpool, its Creek and Member," *Transactions of the Historical Society of Lancashire and Cheshire* 102 (1950), 70f; Hyde, *Liverpool and the Mersey*, 3; C.N. Parkinson, *The Rise of the Port of Liverpool* (1952) 29.

[31]F.A. Bailey and T.C. Barker in "The Seventeenth-Century Origins of Watchmaking in South-West Lancashire," in *Liverpool and Merseyside: Essays in the Economic and Social History of the Port and its Hinterland*, ed. J.R. Harris (1969), 1–15.

[The] Passage over the Water of Mersey…the meat shambles in the said Towne or Lordship of Liverpool, And also all the stallage and Toll of the Market there and fairs with the Perquisites of Courts…and all Customs Anchorage and Key Toll of the Water of Mersey aforesaid…and all the singular farms, messuages, cottages, mills, houses…barns, stables, dovecotes, orchards, gardens…lands, tenements, ponds, meadows, pastures…commons, demesne lands, customary lands, gleb lands, assart lands, wastes, heaths…moors, marshes…paths, easements, woods… and [all] trees whatsoever; and all the lands and soil of the same…tithes of corn, grain, and hay, wool, linseed, and lambs and all other tithes great and small, also…fruits, profits, commodities, gulfs, banks, rivers…fishings, fowlings, huntings…mines, quarries, pensions, portions, rents, reversions, and services…rents of assize…works of tenants, yearly rents…. fee farms, annuities, wards, marriage escheats, reliefs, herriotts…common fines [of] courts Leet…hundred courts…and [other] perquisites and profits of courts [such as] waived goods and Chattels of felons [and] outlaws.[32]

This seemingly all-encompassing "bundle of feudal rights," which the Lords Molyneaux shared with the town's other grand *seigneurs* and prominent families, allowed a "proprietary manorial element" to influence and control both the tempo and complexion of socio-economic and political life in Liverpool well into the seventeenth century.[33] These rights of lordship proved particularly onerous for Liverpool's merchants. Filing claims in local and regional courts, leasing land, traversing the Mersey, anchoring a ship, participation in markets, and other activities incidental to the ordinary conduct of trade, required Liverpool's merchants to pay a customary fine or fee to Lord Molyneaux, Lord Derby, or some other aristocratic fee farmer. The enforcement of increasingly obsolete feudal exactions continued to fuel political conflict in early seventeenth century Liverpool. Michael Mullett argues that "ominous tensions" arose between resentful townsmen and grasping landlords over the continued legitimacy and extent of these feudal rights in the years of bitter strife leading to the English Civil War in the 1640s, and during the four decades after the Stuart Restoration.[34] The anticlimactic ending of this struggle between Liverpool's declining feudal proprietors and its rising merchants in the early 1670s decided the town's future, and set it on a course towards political independence, undreamt of prosperity, and national commercial greatness.

In the more favorable political and economic environment of the 1650s and 1660s, Liverpool merchants joined to promote their common interests. Taking short, halting steps at first, Liverpool's merchants drew upon a recent history of political conflict before the war to achieve self-awareness in the 1650s–60s, coalescing as a distinct political group to resist the long-standing dominance in Liverpool politics of the proprietary element. The struggle against the proprietors was furthered by the acceleration of economic growth after 1660, which served to enrich the merchant group and strengthen them politically.

For the titled landlords, holding public office in Liverpool was not merely a prestigious symbol of rank and status, it was a long-established, and inalienable political right. This conviction was upheld most intractably by the noble families with the most to lose from the rise of a whiggish merchant group determined to run the town in its own interest. As perhaps the dominant lords of Liverpool, the Earls Derby selected many of the men who ultimately served Liverpool both as Lord Mayors and members of Parliament, with several members of the family holding these offices themselves. The last member of the Stanley family, and the last noble lord, to serve as Lord Mayor of Liverpool was James, Earl of Derby, who had the misfortune of dying in office in 1734 after an unsuccessful attempt to reassert his family's once dominant role in Liverpool politics. The Catholic Viscounts Molyneaux served as constables of Liverpool Castle, stewards of the Hundred of West Derby, Lord Mayors, and members of Parliament for Liverpool, while the Moore family, great landholders and loyal clients of Lord Derby, also attended Liverpool as Lord Mayors and members of

---

[32]*Lord Molyneaux's Fee Farm Release to the Corporation of Liverpool, May 27, 1672*, cited in Ramsay Muir and Elizabeth Platt, *History of the Corporation of Liverpool*, (1906), 386.

[33]The phrase "proprietary manorial element" belongs to Mullett. Michael Mullett, "The Politics of Liverpool, 1660–1688," *Transactions of the Historical Society of Lancashire and Cheshire*, 124 (1972), 31.

[34]Mullett, "The Politics of Liverpool", 31; Parkinson, 19.

Parliament. Because all three of these powerful families clung to archaic feudal rights and held large tracts of land in Liverpool, they stood to profit enormously from the town's commercial growth, especially in view of the marked rise in property values and rents after 1660.[35] The fact that Liverpool's traditional leaders and landlords were growing rich on the labors of the town's expanding mercantile community created an enormous store of resentment among the ever more powerful and numerous merchants.

This animus was well founded. Royal grants of overlordship in Liverpool had never been intended to convey full ownership rights to their noble recipients, but over time, as Cecil Parkinson observes, these grants passed "by degrees into…perpetual lease and finally into the private ownership of their custodians."[36] As might be expected, the merchant-authors of Liverpool's new prosperity maintained that they had the right to govern the town since they could guide it through the travails of commercial development more effectively than hidebound landlords. As Mullett says, "much of the content" of the political contests of post-Restoration Liverpool is directly attributable to a struggle between the merchants and landlords over which group would profit most from Liverpool's accelerating growth.[37]

Despite the discontent of Liverpool's merchants, the proprietary interest continued to claim a superior position within the town's polity after 1660, but with diminishing returns. As they entered trade themselves, the proprietors became a less distinct and coherent social group, merging with the larger trading community in the late seventeenth century. Almost anticlimactically, the triumph of the merchants took the prosaic form of a business deal, a lop-sided real estate transaction that overtly favored the merchants. This occurred after a lengthy and acrimonious dispute between Caryl, Lord Molyneaux and the Corporation of Liverpool regarding a plan to build a road and bridge across the Pool. In light of the "suits and controversies [that] have been stirred up," the Common Council of Liverpool instructed Mayor Lawrence Brownlowe on April 26, 1671 to open discussions with the representatives of Lord Molyneaux and attempt to negotiate a settlement that would be binding on both parties.[38] It turned out that both factions were eager to settle—for very different reasons—and an agreement was quickly concluded in May 1671. In this settlement, the Corporation purchased the fee farm of Liverpool from Lord Molyneaux for the trifling sum of £30 *per annum*, and with it all rights of overlordship in perpetuity. This agreement effectively ended the feudal encumbrances which had for so long been a source of frustration for Liverpool merchants, obstacles to both local and regional commercial development. In exchange, the myopic Lord Molyneaux was permitted to build his road and bridge, paying the Corporation, "as lords of the soil," a mere pittance—a symbolic annual rent of 20p.[39]

While both sides to this dispute won their respective points, in the long run the interests of the Corporation of Liverpool, increasingly dominated by wealthy merchants, were best served. Although a largely unheralded chapter in the rise of Liverpool, the 1671 purchase of the fee farm by the Corporation brought forth momentous changes in the town's governance, population, socio-economic base, appearance, size, and commercial infrastructure. As a result of this agreement, the Corporation obtained unhampered access to both sides of the Pool, an advantageous development that assured it control of the lands upon which the town's unparalleled system of docks was later constructed. In addition, the town acquired the right to collect a host of feudal fines, fees, dues, customs, and taxes, which became an ever more important source of revenue for the Corporation, amounting to an annual income of over £100,000 by 1850.[40] Finally, the purchase of the fee farm brought nearly 1,000 acres of borough land suitable for building into the hands of freemen, valuable land-holdings managed by the Lord Mayor and Common Council. "They were thus enabled to introduce the plan," the Liverpool historian Thomas Baines observed in 1852,

[35]Mullett, 32.

[36]Parkinson, 19.

[37]Mullett, 32. Mullett makes the sensible point that the opposition between "land and business must not be overdrawn." Many members of the landlord interest supported, and participated in, the commercial development of Liverpool, and many arranged for younger sons to serve apprenticeships with Liverpool merchants.

[38]Thomas Baines, *History of the Commerce and Town of Liverpool, and of the Rise of Manufacturing Industry in the Adjoining Counties*, (1852), 332; J.M. Neeson, *Commoners: Common Right, Enclosure, and Social Change in England, 1700–1820* (1993), 158–63.

[39]Muir and Platt, *History of the Corporation of Liverpool*, 385–391; Baines, 332.

[40]Baines, 333.

of letting [this land] on building leases, first for three lives, and then for three lives and twenty one years, renewable on easy and well-ascertained terms; a plan which secured to the tenants land, without any great outlay of capital, and to the Corporation a revenue, without the risk of building.[41]

The income earned by the Corporation from these leases rose from a few hundred pounds in the latter part of the seventeenth century to some £50,000 by the mid-nineteenth century.[42] Most importantly, the Corporation acquired the means to finance an enormous program of public works and infrastructure development after 1700.

II

This political liberation was the cumulative result of the slow expansion of Liverpool's maritime trade since the mid-sixteenth century. Previously, the village of Liverpool had been little more than a simple haven in which passing ships took refuge during storms, and through which a number of medieval campaigns against Ireland passed, but from which little trade actually originated. Before 1500, Liverpool's limited maritime trade was centered upon small-scale exchanges along the coast of northwest England. Liverpool ships are also known to have voyaged even further out to sea at an early date, with a few sailing as far as Calais and Bordeaux in the 1360s.[43] Venturing sporadically into surrounding seas since the later Middle Ages, Liverpool's earliest merchants were largely homegrown coastal traders dealing in a varying number of locally produced commodities. After the accession of Elizabeth, Liverpool's mercantile isolation began slowly to change, as a profitable trade with Ireland and the Isle of Man, commerce that eventually introduced Liverpool merchants to the transatlantic trade, became ever more important.

However, when it did occur, intermittently after 1600, Liverpool's transformation into first an insignificant local anchorage, and thereafter a major national port, was based upon two regional trades of national significance: the Irish trade and the Cheshire salt trade. Previously, these trades had been of limited importance when compared to the town's traditional coastal trade. Specializing in the importation of linen yarn, Liverpool's Irish trade had remained small throughout the reign of Elizabeth, but rose markedly in volume between 1600 and 1660. Its only serious downturn occurred because of the Irish Rebellion of 1641. Recovering quickly after 1650, the trade became larger and more varied by 1660, and included the export of malt, hardware and cutlery from Sheffield, Lancashire coal, Cheshire salt, soap, alum, cowhides and finished leather goods, woolens from Yorkshire, copper, iron, pewter, wine, dried fruit, hops, and grain to Belfast, Dublin, Dundalk, Drogheda, Carrickfergus, Carlingford, and Waterford.[44] Return cargoes included raw flax and linen yarn, fresh and salt herring, finished textile goods, ship's provisions such as butter and salt pork and beef, as well as tallow, wool, and sheepskins.[45] "Irish merchants come much thither [to the Mersey] as a good haven," English merchant John Leland noted during the reign of Henry VIII, "[as] Good merchandise [is available] at Liverpool."[46] As Leland suggests, this preference was due to the availability of trade goods in Liverpool, particularly Lancashire textiles, a commodity that Liverpool merchants were exporting as early as 1590–1600. Paul Clemens notes that after 1660 Liverpool merchants "extended…traditional Irish connections into a triangular pattern [of trade] circumscribing the West Indies [and] by the last quarter of the seventeenth century, Cork and Dublin had become stopping-points for almost three-fourths of the West

---

[41]*ibid.*

[42]*ibid.*

[43]Parkinson, 15. Parkinson notes that the Liverpool ship *Peter* was detained at Calais on August 28th, 1364 by English authorities for loading wool without paying the required duties.

[44]Hyde, *Liverpool and the Mersey*, 3.

[45]Hyde, 3.

[46]*Calendar of State Papers, Ireland, 1606–08*, 488; cited in Parkinson, 29.

Indian shipping of the outports."[47] Thus, the Irish trade provided Liverpool merchants with an invaluable lesson in the rewards of trade on the Atlantic periphery.

Perhaps one of the most important lessons that Liverpool merchants learned in the Irish trade was the value of religious ties, personal affiliations, business friendships and kinship in the ordinary conduct of trade. After the sixteenth century, the rising Irish trade led to the formation of many close contacts between Liverpool and Irish merchants. Liverpool merchant-freemen enjoyed reciprocal trading rights with several ports in eastern Ireland, and throughout the Irish Sea. As many of these Irish and Liverpool trading men were Protestant dissenters, common religious faith was also a point of connection. Coleraine, Londonderry, and Belfast in the northern counties, the Pale around Dublin, and to a lesser extent the environs of the busy southern port of Cork, were all home to varying populations of Presbyterians and other dissenters. Similarly, in Liverpool, a large number of Presbyterians and other dissenters lived and traded descendants of Scots-Irish settlers.[48] While the natal origin and background of many Liverpool merchants is frequently unclear, a significant number were either of Irish or Manx-Irish roots, coreligionists, or both.[49]

For many merchants of Irish descent, the formation of trading connections was often difficult. Several Irish merchants settled on the Isle of Man during the early years of the seventeenth-century Guinea trade, although, as Frances Wilkins suggests, "their presence was not [always] welcomed by...native Manx merchants."[50] Two such Irish-born merchants, Patrick and Andrew Savage, were major figures in the early depot trade on the Isle of Man in the 1710s–1720s, and supplied visiting slave ships with trade goods imported from the continent. These Irish-Manx merchants were kinsmen, sons of Patrick Savage, a Belfast mariner who died in 1695.[51] Richard Savage was probably a grandson of the elder Patrick Savage and, while it is unclear which of this Belfast mariner's sons was his father, it is likely that Richard arrived in Liverpool as a merchant-mariner, following his father's footsteps in the Manx depot trade. Within a few years of his first slaving venture in 1745, Savage rose to become a prominent figure in his adopted town, serving with the elite of Liverpool society as an original trustee of the Liverpool Infirmary at its founding in March 1749.[52] As both a ship's husband and a casual investor, Richard Savage formed a great variety of slaving partnerships with a wide range of prominent Liverpool slave merchants. As some of his partners were Presbyterians, Savage shared with them a common faith, while with others he shared little more than a common desire for profit.[53] Among these partners were such important slave traders as John Crosbie, Arthur Heywood, Jonathan Blundell, Samuel Shaw, John Knight, William Gregson, all of whom had extensive trading contacts with Irish and Manx merchants, were of Irish descent, or had themselves been born in Ireland.[54] In a thirty-year slaving career, Richard Savage was a partner in nearly 80 Liverpool slaving ventures, from the voyage of the *Blundell* in 1745 to the *Richard* in 1774.[55]

Like Richard Savage, Captain Patrick Black had roots in both Northern Ireland and the Isle of Man. A slave-ship captain and African trader, Black was, by the mid-1760s, an extremely well-connected Liverpool slave merchant with a prestigious Hanover Street address.[56] Son of John Black of Belfast, and brother of Robert Black, a partner in the prominent firm of *Ross, Black & Christian* of Castletown, Isle of Man, Patrick

---

[47]Paul G.E. Clemens, "The Rise of Liverpool, 1665–1750," *Economic History Review* 29 (1976), 214.

[48]*Liverpool Directory of 1766;* Frances Wilkins, *Manx Slave Traders* (1999), 9, 25; Anne Holt, *Walking Together: A Study in Liverpool Nonconformity, 1688–1938* (1938), 134; *The Liverpool Memorandum Book;* George McLoughlin, *A Short History of the Liverpool Infirmary, 1749–1824* (1978), App. V, 94–97; Brooke, *Liverpool as it was..."* 239; Will of Patrick Savage, October 29,1695, PCC: PROB 11/427239, Will of Richard Savage of Liverpool, esquire, Wills and Inventories, Chester Probate Registry, 1793.

[49]Thomas Truxes, ed., *Letterbook of Greg & Cunningham, Merchants of New York and Belfast* (2001), 41ff; Thomas Truxes, *Irish-American Trade, 1660–1783* (1988), 72–106, 147–212.

[50]Wilkins, 25.

[51]Will of Patrick Savage, October 29,1695, PCC: PROB 11/427.

[52]McLoughlin, App. V, 94–97.

[53]Holt, 134; *The Liverpool Memorandum Book of 1753;* Richard Brooke, *Liverpool as it was..."* 239.

[54]*TSTD*, Wilkins, 34, 55.

[55]*TSTD*.

[56]*Liverpool Directory of 1766.*

Black was an experienced transatlantic entrepreneur who used his maritime experience as a slave-ship captain, together with his commercially advantageous kinship ties, to build a long and profitable career as a slave merchant.[57] Black was a captain and/or partner in 30 slaving ventures between 1753–1774, one solely as captain in 1753, three as captain and partner in 1754, 1756, and 1757, and 26 as a partner between 1759–1774.[58] However, important as kinship ties and maritime experience were in advancing his career, perhaps the most important factor in his success as a slave trader was the close business and personal relationships he formed with prominent English-born merchants as captain of the 130-ton snow *Chesterfield* during four voyages to the Bight of Biafra between 1753 and 1757.

When Black first captained the *Chesterfield* in 1753, the owners included not only the significant Liverpool merchants John Clayton, Edward Lowndes, John Williamson, and William Whalley, but also Whaley's former apprentice William Davenport, an up-and-coming slave merchant in only his sixth slaving venture.[59] Between the return of the *Chesterfield* from Old Calabar and Barbados in April 1754, and her next departure for Old Calabar in June 1754, the ship's ownership group underwent a fundamental change in composition. Absent from this reformulated partnership were the elderly ship's husband William Whalley, John Clayton, Peers Legh, and Edward Lowndes; they were replaced by the shipbuilders John Gorell and William Pownall, the merchant Thomas Moseley, and Captain William Earle, third and youngest son of Alderman John Earle, and former commander of the *Chesterfield*. The brewer John Williamson and William Davenport remained in the partnership, and Patrick Black, doubtless having prospered from his voyage to Africa, invested in the *Chesterfield* himself. As the friend and partner of both Davenport and Earle, Black had the good fortune to form close business connections with two of the most prolific slave traders operating from Liverpool between 1750–1775. The closeness of the relationship between Davenport, Earle, and Black is suggested by the facts that, between 1753 and 1774, Davenport was a partner in 90% of the slaving ventures in which Black was also a partner, Earle was a partner in 70%, while 72% of ventures featured both Earle and Davenport.[60]

Although Irish-born merchants did not comprise a significant proportion of the business community of Liverpool until the nineteenth-century, a few merchants, such as Richard Savage and Patrick Black, used wealth and close personal contacts to join Liverpool's transatlantic merchant elite. While Patrick Black, Richard Savage, or such Irish-born Liverpool merchants as Hugh Pringle, Edward Forbes, Millington Eaton, Maurice Melling, Isaac Blackwood, and others, shared a common Presbyterian faith, their slaving partnerships suggest, that while a common religion was a source of strength for these strangers in an alien town, as they grew more successful their religious affiliation became less important. Savage, for instance, attracted a large number of investors in his first decade as a slave trader—35 between 1745–1750, and 40 between 1751–1755—but only a third were co-religionists.[61] After 1756, however, Savage typically partnered with a smaller but more discrete group of larger slave traders, few of whom shared his religious faith. Many of these men, great slave traders such as William Gregson, John Knight, William Boates, and William Trafford, were significant figures in Liverpool society, men whose friendship was a crucial foundation of Savage's commercial success after 1760. Capable and wealthy men, Irish-born merchants such as Savage succeeded in establishing themselves both as fixtures in the merchant community of Liverpool by 1750, and as members of Liverpool's Presbyterian chapels, despite the often-difficult relations that existed between Irish and Liverpool merchants.

---

[57]Wilkins, 19–20, 25, 56, 58, 60.

[58]*Liverpool Directory of 1766; TSTD;* Wilkins, 56–58; Will of Patrick Black, mariner of Liverpool, Wills and Inventories, Chester Probate Registry, Admon., 1776.

[59]David Richardson, "Profits in the Liverpool Slave Trade: The Accounts of William Davenport, 1757–1784," in *Liverpool, the African Slave Trade, and Abolition*, eds., Roger Anstey and P.E.H. Hair (1976), 61.

[60]*TSTD.*

[61]*TSTD.*

III

In addition to this commerce with Ireland, a trade in salt emerged as a crucial factor in orienting Liverpool merchants towards a wider world of overseas trade. At the time that Liverpool merchants first became significant participants in the Irish trade during the sixteenth century, they also entered upon a high-volume trade in salt. This trade continued to fill Liverpool bottoms for decades, and remained a profitable staple of Merseyside commerce long after the abolition of the British slave trade in 1807. Salt had been mined in northwest England, primarily at Northwich and Nantwich in Cheshire, since Roman times, and, by the ninth century, Cheshire had become the major salt-producing region for all of Anglo-Saxon England.[62] The fates of war, however, changed this reality for Chester for some long centuries. The last fortified city to fall to William the Conqueror, Chester was destroyed by the Normans in 1070 in retribution, and, as a result, the center of English salt production shifted southwards to Droitwich for most of the Middle Ages.[63] Although by the sixteenth century Bristol was a more important center for the importation of higher quality French and Portuguese rock salt, Liverpool merchants had entered the lucrative bilateral trade in Breton rock salt by 1566, re-exporting small amounts of it to the Isle of Man, Ireland, and North Lancashire for agricultural purposes.[64] By the 1570s, however, as the Cheshire salt industry slowly recovered, Liverpool merchants turned to local supplies of brine, rather than dealing in salt imported from distant French sources.[65] By 1600–10, Liverpool merchants were filling barrels with unrefined salt brine for shipment to cod fisheries in Newfoundland, as well as lyng-fish and salmon fisheries in Scotland, Ireland, and the Isle of Man.[66] Liverpool industry and shipping received a further stimulus in the late seventeenth century from the development of higher quality deposits of rock salt near the River Weaver at Marbury, Cheshire that were exported *via* Liverpool to Ireland, and later to the Baltic, Germany, and Flanders.[67]

In response, Liverpool entrepreneurs established a large-scale, capital-intensive industry for the first time. To a greater extent than the traditional Irish or coastal trades, this forced Liverpool merchants to deal with a complex trade that required new technical skills, technological innovations, reliable partnership groups that permitted a systematic mobilization of capital, and a functional commercial infrastructure. Like the later slave trade, the salt trade grew slowly, and was limited, at first, to the shipping of raw salt, not its processing, and there is little evidence that salt refineries were erected on or near the Mersey until after 1690.[68] In 1696, the brothers John and Jonathan Blackburn of Hale, Lancashire petitioned the Liverpool Common Council for permission to build a salt refinery within the town's borders.[69] In the following year, the Dungeon works, a salt refinery south of Liverpool near Hale on the Mersey, was established by a group of investors headed by Thomas Johnson the younger. The opening of these refineries made Liverpool a center for not only the export of salt but also its refining, a capital intensive industry that attracted new men and resources to Liverpool. Like the Irish trade, the commerce in salt demonstrated the importance of personal affiliations, business connections and kinship ties in building a profitable trade.

In the first half of the eighteenth century the heirs of Jonathan Blackburn I dominated the Liverpool trade in salt. Son of Jonathan Blackburn I, nephew of John Blackburn I, brother of Jonathan Blackburn II, John Blackburn II (died-1766) was a scion of this important local family from Hale, Lancashire, across the River Weaver from the Cheshire salt-mines. The family became well-established in Liverpool in the early eighteenth century, and the salt refinery which John and Jonathan Blackburn inherited from their father Jonathan

---

[62]Mark Kurlansky, *Salt: A World History* (2002), 181.

[63]Kurlansky, *Salt: A World History*, 181.

[64]Kurlansky, 181; Hyde, 2.

[65]Hyde, 2–3.

[66]Clemens, "The Rise of Liverpool, 216–217, Hyde, 2–3.

[67]Davis, *The Rise of the English Shipping Industry... "* 38; T. C. Barker, "Lancashire Coal, Cheshire Salt, and the Rise of Liverpool," *The Transactions of the Historical Society of Lancashire and Cheshire*, 111 (1951), 85–87.

[68]Barker, "Lancashire Coal, Cheshire Salt, and the Rise of Liverpool," 86.

[69]*ibid*, 86.

Blackburn I was constructed on a valuable site near where Liverpool's second wet dock, the Salthouse or South dock, which opened in 1753. Like his forbears, John Blackburn II saw himself primarily as a salt merchant and refiner, but like many Liverpool men of business he was active in many lines of trade, including the transatlantic slave trade. Partnering such major Liverpool West Indian and African merchants as John Tarleton, Joseph Manesty, Richard Savage, Richard Powell, William Earle, James Crosbie, John Crosbie, William Dobb, Peter Leay, Maurice Melling, and others, John Blackburn II was involved in thirteen slaving ventures between 1748–1761.[70] Although these investments were primarily inspired by a remorseless search for profit, Blackburn, like many other contemporary Liverpool men of business, was also motivated by overtly political and social considerations. Blackburn stood shoulder to shoulder with the entire community of merchants in Liverpool when he signed the 1750 petition to King George II in support of the African trade, and, by becoming a freeman of the Liverpool Company of Merchants Trading to Africa, Blackburn expressed his solidarity with fellow investors in support of a trade that had become vitally important to the financial well-being of the whole town by the mid-eighteenth century.[71]

While this confirmed his social and political status within Liverpool's all-important body of merchant-princes, Blackburn also garnered support for his own trade in salt. The expansion of the salt trade in the early eighteenth century was hampered by expensive, and inadequate connections between the coalfields around St. Helens, Lancashire, which supplied the bulk of the fuel required to refine rock salt, and the Cheshire salt fields to the south.[72] The construction of the Weaver River Navigation southwards into the salt fields of Cheshire in the early 1730s did indeed improve transportation, but it was only a partial, and at best, temporary solution. "The opening of the Weaver," T.C. Barker observes,

> was followed by a rapid expansion in salt production. Shipments down the river totaled 14,000 tons in the first year 1732–3. Twenty years later they were twice as great…all of which [was] boiled at the salt field, consuming some 9,000 tons of coal. This was a great weight of fuel to be carried by packhorse from the [coal] pits down to the Mersey, and it was by no means the total that was being carried to the south and the west of the collieries, for there were the Mersey refineries and the considerable domestic and industrial requirements of Liverpool to be supplied. Despite the Turnpiking of the road from Liverpool to the coalfield, the needs neither of port nor saltfield could be adequately met by land transport [and thus] the scale and scope of the salt industry was in danger of being restricted by a fuel crisis.[73]

The looming logistical crisis which Barker describes compelled John Blackburn and his brother and partner Jonathan, to join forces with the well-connected John Ashton (1711–1759), a Liverpool merchant who had acquired the Dungeon salt-works by auction in December 1746, in order to contrive a solution.[74] John Ashton was born at Woolton Hall, Liverpool in 1711, and in 1728 married Elizabeth Brooks, daughter of prominent Liverpool merchant John Brooks (1681–1730) of Middlesex.[75] In resolving this crisis, kinship and religious ties proved to be a great advantage to John Ashton, who was related by marriage to the prominent Liverpool merchants John Brooks II (died-1779), Jonathan Brooks (1708–1787), and Joseph Brooks (1706–1788), sons of John Brooks I; and joint congregants with the Brooks brothers at the Presbyterian Chapel on Key Street, Liverpool.[76] Not surprisingly, Ashton also materially benefited from the business connections of his brothers-in-law. The three Brooks brothers were active in the West Indian and African trades, and were co-partners in one voyage of the slaver *Pretty Peggy* in 1748, one voyage of the *Three Sisters* in 1748, together with

---

[70]Will of John Blackburn of Blakelyhurst, Lancashire, Esquire, Wills and Inventories, Chester Probate Registry, Admon., 1766.

[71]*The Liverpool Memorandum Book.*

[72]Barker, 92–94.

[73]*ibid*, 93.

[74]Arthur Wardle, "Some Glimpses of Liverpool during the First Half of the Eighteenth-Century," *The Transactions of the Historical Society of Lancashire and Cheshire*, 97 (1937), 35–37.

[75]Brooke, 239; Holt, 143.

[76].

brother-in-law John Ashton, and four voyages of the *Neptune* in 1749, 1751, 1752, and 1754.[77] Because John Ashton frequently partnered his brother-in-laws, he was confident that he could rely upon them when it came time to secure financial backing for the construction of the Sankey Brook Navigation.

By the early 1750s, Ashton and the Blackburn brothers were deftly using their well-developed network of connections to secure financing for improving river transportation. These salt dealers used friendly persuasion to win support in the Council, and ultimately to achieve parliamentary approval for their scheme. Ashton's close tie with his brother-in-law John Brooks II was of particular importance. For as a former Lord Mayor of Liverpool (1743) he was an alderman, and thus a ranking member of the Common Council. Brooks thus possessed the political stature within the council that Ashton needed to win the Council's support. Ashton and the Blackburns appealed to the self-interest of the town's leading merchants when promoting the improvement of Sankey Brook, much as they had the River Weaver Navigation project two decades before. This project, they asserted, was vital not only for the further development of the Cheshire salt and Lancashire coal industries, but also the future commercial prosperity of Liverpool.[78] The fact that both the council and a significant portion of the merchant community stood to profit by these improvements ensured that their arguments were quickly accepted.[79]

On June 5, 1754, the Common Council ordered Henry Berry, chief engineer of the docks, to study the feasibility of improving the navigation of Sankey Brook, and to determine whether it could be made to connect the coalfields at St. Helens in southwest Lancashire with the Mersey, and hence, the salt-fields that lay beyond in Cheshire.[80] In the end, this persistent campaigning paid off for Ashton and the Blackburns, and the Council agreed to petition Parliament in 1755 for an act sanctioning the construction of a canal at Sankey Brook. Together with merchants James Crosbie, Charles Goore, and Richard Trafford, Ashton and the Blackburns provided half the capital for the project. After the rapid completion of the Sankey Brook Canal in 1757, Barker concludes,

> the Liverpool-dominated salt interest had called into being a most efficient water transport system [creating] an internal triangular trade between Liverpool, the St. Helens coalfield, and the Cheshire salt field which played, perhaps, as significant a part in the prosperity of the port as that other triangular trade which has gained so much publicity.[81]

Like the Blackburn brothers, Ashton had strong connections within the Liverpool slave trade, and was a vocal supporter of the African trade. Like many merchants whose primary business was not the slave trade, Ashton was a freeman of the Liverpool Company of Merchants Trading to Africa, and was a signatory of the 1750 petition to King George II.[82] This support was more than a *quid pro quo*, although Ashton himself was far less invested in the slave trade than other freeman of the Liverpool Company or the great merchants who supported the Sankey Brook petition. Ashton himself partnered in two slave ships with his three Brooks brothers-in-law, the *Pretty Peggy* and the *Three Sisters*, both of which departed Liverpool for Angola in 1748. After Ashton's death in August 1759, the Dungeon salt works passed to his son Nicholas Ashton, a nephew of John, Jonathan, and Joseph Brooks.

[77]*TSTD;* Will of John Brooks of Liverpool, gentleman, Wills and Inventories, Chester Probate Registry, 1779; Will of Jonathan Brooks of Liverpool, Lancashire, February 9, 1787, PCC: PROB 11/1150; Will of Joseph Brooks of Liverpool, Lancashire, May 6, 1788, PCC: PROB 11/1165; TSTD.

[78]John Langton, "Coal Output in South-West Lancashire, 1590–1799," *Economic History Review*, 25 (1972), 42.

[79]Barker, 92–94.

[80]*ibid.*

[81]*ibid.* This trade was, of course, the commerce in West African slaves.

[82]*The Liverpool Memorandum Book* (1753); McLoughlin, App. V, 94–97.

IV

Like the Irish trade, the traffic in salt became an important element in the slow expansion of Liverpool's overseas trade. English overseas trade tripled between 1650–1733, with much of this growth after 1700 being concentrated in provincial ports like Bristol, Plymouth, and Liverpool.[83] The growth enabled Liverpool to burst through the confines of its trade in salt and Irish goods. In addition to a growing trade with Northern Europe, especially Sweden and Russia, the Mediterranean littoral, and other parts of the continent, Liverpool merchants began to develop a keen interest in transatlantic trade after 1660, particularly the West Indian sugar and Chesapeake tobacco trades. These trades had long been dominated by London and Bristol.[84] The earliest involvement of Liverpool merchants in transatlantic trade flowed naturally from a desire to expand beyond traditional venues of overseas commerce, such as the Irish and Spanish trades, and enter profitable, new branches of exchange in a commercial world where trading opportunities were delimited by government-sanctioned monopolies such as the East India Company, Levant Company, Royal African Company, and others.[85] The mercantilistic enactments of the crown also occasionally operated to the advantage of merchants from Liverpool and other British outports. The *Navigation Act of 1660*, for instance, opened Atlantic trade to England, Ireland, and the American colonies on an equal basis, and "made no distinction between their ships and seamen, nor did it offer advantages to one that were not available to all."[86] The overall commercial effect of English mercantilism, combined with the survival of the great monopolies, was to funnel the commercial energies of outport merchants towards Atlantic trade. As the Crown permitted unrestricted trade with the West Indies and the Chesapeake to all comers, many Liverpool merchants eager to gain a foothold in a lucrative line of overseas trade found themselves edging towards and participating in the legal and open trade in sugar, tobacco, and other American colonial produce.[87]

These merchants, however, were also driven by a sense of grievance, resenting their "restriction to these two [American] trades [preferring instead] to poach in forbidden waters."[88] This ill-will was especially palpable in the one branch of the transatlantic trade that was expressly denied Liverpool's avid merchants, the trade in West African slaves. In 1709, the Commissioners of Trade reported to Parliament that the monopoly of the Royal African Company was extremely unpopular and all but impossible to uphold, and that,

> Several Complaints [had been lodged] against the [Royal Africa] Company and a general Dissatisfaction that so profitable a Trade should be confined to an Exclusive joint-stock [company] soon brought on an interloping trade; during that time several Private ships with their Cargoes were seized on the Coast of Africa and in the Plantations for Trading contrary to the Company's Charter whereby such private Trade was in a manner crushed. But upon the late Revolution [of 1688–9] it revived again and was carried on for some years to a much greater degree than formerly [until] in 1698 an Act…was passed for settling that trade, whereby Liberty is given…to any of her Majesty's subjects to trade within the limits of the Company, paying the Duties in the said Act mentioned, viz. 10.p.c. *ad valorem* on all Exports and Imports.[89]

Self-interested advocates of free trade, Liverpool's first slave traders were interlopers who often employed chicanery and customs fraud to bypass the lawful monopoly of the Royal African Company.[90] After 1698,

---

[83]Wilson, *The Sense of the People*, 159.

[84]Wilson, 159.

[85]Parkinson, 52.

[86]Truxes, *Irish-American Trade*, 8–9

[87]Ralph Davis, "English Foreign Trade, 1700–1774," *Economic History Review* 15 (1962), 285–303.

[88]Parkinson, 52.

[89]*Report by the Commissioners of Trade* (1709), quoted in Parkinson, 86.

[90]K.G. Davies, *The Royal African Company*, (1957), 111–119; Ann M. Carlos and Jamie B. Kruse, "The Decline of the Royal African Company: Fringe Firms and the Role of the Charter," *Economic History Review*, XLIX, 2 (1996), 293.

Liverpool slave traders often misrepresented the destination of their voyages in order to evade payment of the 10%.[91] Even before the few remaining restrictions imposed by the act of 1698 were lifted in 1712, Liverpool merchants were smuggling African trade goods from the continent to the Isle of Man to evade the payment of customs duties in Liverpool, and employed agents and factors in Jamaica to sell slaves to Spanish middlemen.[92] Efforts by such men to evade the monopolistic restrictions imposed by the crown led to pervasive corruption, and the continued cooptation of town officials and Customs Collectors alike.[93]

The removal of the Royal African Company's monopoly in 1712 led to explosive growth in the British traffic in slaves. Liverpool's rising merchant class had much to gain from circumventing the law. Smuggling, for instance, made Liverpool's earliest slavers competitive in the American slave markets, often allowing them to deliver slaves at lower prices than the Royal African Company could manage. The huge profits which Liverpool's slave smugglers often realized from dealing in contraband slaves formed a ready source of capital which was used to finance further smuggling ventures, invest in legitimate commercial undertakings, or lend out at interest to American slave factors and purchasers of slaves. While the lifting of restrictions for separate traders in 1712, and thus the effective end of the Royal African Company's monopoly, led to explosive growth in the British traffic in slaves, the Liverpool slave trade remained miniscule for many years thereafter. Although Liverpool's slave traders did not pose a serious threat to their Bristol competitors before 1740, a decade later, by 1750, Liverpool had eclipsed both Bristol and London to become the premier slaving port in the Atlantic world.[94] This dominance became even more marked between 1757 and 1776, when 1,540 slave ships cleared from Liverpool for West Africa, while only 691 ships departed for Africa from London, 457 from Bristol, and 86 from Lancaster.[95]

In many ways, the expansiveness of Liverpool commerce after 1750 can be attributed to the steady rise of industry in Manchester, Birmingham, and Sheffield during the course of the eighteenth century. A harbinger of future developments, Liverpool ships first began exporting Manchester textiles in about 1600. Thus, long before the emergence of the great Lancashire textile industry of the nineteenth century, a symbiotic relationship between Manchester manufacturers and Liverpool exporters had taken root. "While Manchester created Liverpool by giving it goods to export," Parkinson observes, "Liverpool created Manchester by finding markets for all it made."[96] Manchester and Liverpool faced a rapidly growing demand for goods employed in transatlantic trade, supplying the cheap textiles widely to purchase West African slaves, and clothe the slave populations of the Americas.[97] Liverpool's dominance of the British slave trade relied, in great measure, upon the industrial output of Lancashire and the Midlands.

IV

Thus, in a few short years after the Restoration, and long before Liverpool's merchants ventured to Africa in a systematic way, a multiplying commerce with the Americas, Ireland, and continental Europe combined to make Liverpool a boom town—the entrepreneurial capital of western England. As an increasingly important *entrepôt* of English regional trade after 1725, Liverpool emerged as Britain's second port after London by 1800. As early as the later seventeenth century, Liverpool's frantic commercialism was visible to visitors as

[91]David Galenson, *Traders, Planters, and Slaves: Market Behavior in Early English America* (1986), 13–21; K.G. Davies, *The Royal African Company*, 135–151; Parkinson, 87–9.

[92]Rupert C. Jarvis, "Illicit Trade with the Isle of Man, 1671–1765," *Transactions of the Lancashire and Cheshire Antiquarian Society* 58 (1945–6), 246–248, Parkinson, 95.

[93]Parkinson, 94; Michael Power, "Councillors and Commerce in Liverpool, 306–7; Arthur Wardle, "The Customs Collection of the Port of Liverpool," *Transactions of the Historical Society of Lancashire and Cheshire*, 99 (1949), 38f; Wilkins, 17–24.

[94]Averil Mackenzie-Grieve, *The Last Years of the English Slave Trade: Liverpool, 1750–1807* (1941), 3–6.

[95]*TSTD*; Maurice Schofield, "The Slave Trade from Lancashire and Cheshire Ports outside Liverpool, c. 1750–1790," *Transactions of the Historical Society of Lancashire and Cheshire* 126 (1977), 33.

[96]Parkinson, 58

[97]Davis, 38

well. When he visited Liverpool in 1673, the eminent English cartographer Richard Blome found an active town full of,

> divers eminent merchants and tradesmen, whose trade and traffic, especially unto the West Indies, made it famous: its situation affording in greater plenty, and at reasonable rates than most places in England, such exported commodities proper for the West Indies; as likewise a quicker return for such imported commodities; by reason of the sugar bakers, and great manufacturers of cottons in the adjacent parts; and the rather for that it is found to be the convenient passage to Ireland, and divers considerable counties in England, with which they have intercourse of traffic.[98]

Similarly, the famed diarist Celia Fiennes, wrote in 1698, that,

> Ships from all over the Atlantic world were berthed in the Mersey, coastal ships, Scottish, Irish & Manx merchantmen as well as Norwegian, Dutch, Danish, Flemish, Spanish, French, Portuguese, Baltic & Hamburg ships, and ships trading with the American colonies…its London in miniature as much as ever I saw anything.[99]

The rapid rise of Liverpool trade by 1750, however, did not beggar the merchants of London, for they "began to act as commission agents, bankers, and insurers for provincial ports."[100] London remained the principal port in British transatlantic trade throughout the eighteenth century, increasing its colonial imports by 277% and exports by 474% between 1699/1701–1772/1774.[101] However, the volume of colonial imports reaching outports such as Liverpool, Bristol, and Whitehaven during these years grew at an even greater rate, by 479%, while exports departing the outports grew by an astonishing 873%.[102]

For Liverpool, the socio-economic repercussions of these dramatic developments were immediate and far-reaching. In the late seventeenth century, colonial trade both attracted a flood of new men to town, such as the young apprentice John Earle, and tempted long-established residents to consider venturing their limited resources. Between 1665 and 1709, the proportion of Liverpool merchants making ten or more voyages rose fourfold, from eleven to forty.[103] Moreover, half of this latter group of forty merchants made over thirty shipments in 1709, which, as Gauci suggests, "that there was an elite tier within the upper echelons of the trading fraternity."[104] Certainly, there are strong indications that by 1730 a small group had arisen to form a distinct elite. This group included prominent old Liverpool families with strong ancestral connections to Liverpool and the surrounding villages and towns of Lancashire and Cheshire. As in all trades, some merchants had greater financial resources, extensive social and commercial networks, social rank, political connections prospered more in the transatlantic trades than men lacking these advantages. In the first quarter of the eighteenth century, prominent men such as Sir Thomas Johnson Jr., Bryan Blundell Sr., Samuel Ogden, George Tyrer, and John Pemberton Sr., translated the high position they enjoyed within Liverpool society into practical commercial advantage. A similar dynamic was also evident in Bristol, Liverpool's great commercial rival in the west of England. In Bristol's slave trade, for instance, what mattered most to a merchant in achieving commercial success were the correct local credentials and connections especially the formation of close

---

[98]Richard Blome, *Blome's Britannia*, 134, quoted in Baines, 335.

[99]Celia Fiennes, *The Journeys of Celia Fiennes* ed. Christopher Morris (1947) 183–4; Aughton, 48.

[100]P.J. Cain and A.G. Hopkins, "Gentlemanly Capitalism and British Expansion Overseas: The Old Colonial System, 1688–1850," *Economic History Review*, 39 (1986), 519; Christopher J. French, "Crowded with Traders and Great Commerce: London's Domination of English Overseas Trade, 1700–1775," *London Journal*, 17 (1992), 27.

[101]French, "Crowded with Traders and Great Commerce," 30; Nuala Zahedieh, "Making Mercantilism Work: London Merchants and Atlantic Trade in the Seventeenth Century," *Transactions of the Royal Historical Society*, 9 (1999), 158.

[102]French, 30; Zahedieh, "Making Mercantilism Work," 158.

[103]Power, "Councillors and Commerce in Liverpool," 313.

[104]Perry Gauci, *The Politics of Trade: The Overseas Merchant in State and Society, 1660–1720* (2001), 60.

contacts with elite Bristol families.[105] Such "inside" contacts, often formed as a result of marital alliances between influential commercial families, were crucially important for an aspiring merchant in achieving commercial respectability and prominence, offering valuable access to Bristol's closed commercial society.[106] Merchants who lacked such connections, Richardson maintains, "largely failed to penetrate the higher echelons of social and political life in Bristol [which] to a large extent probably reflected the relatively closed and elitist structure of Bristol society at that time."[107] In Liverpool, as in Bristol, the advantages of birth, kinship, and connection made it possible for a privileged few to pursue the African trade with confidence, and hopefully, profit.

In the eighteenth-century Liverpool slave trade as a whole, however, birth, kinship, and social status alone were not sufficient to insure a hopeful merchant's ultimate success. Fathers and sons such as Thomas Johnson Sr., Sir Thomas Johnson Jr., Richard Gildart Sr., James Gildart, and James Gildart Jr., represented successive generations of merchants who made effective use of family connections and political influence to grow wealthy in Liverpool's slave trade, men whom Perry Gauci refers to as "the new breed of Liverpool merchant."[108] Such families did constitute a merchant elite in the first quarter of the eighteenth century. However, they did not monopolize the opportunities for profit that transatlantic commerce in tobacco, sugar, or slaves offered. As pioneers in Liverpool's first ventures in the slave trade, these social-*cum*-economic elites were in a far better position to benefit from the African trade—or any other trade—than were lesser merchants, tradesmen, mariners, or other would-be investors in overseas trade. Many of Liverpool's greatest slave traders between 1695–1775—John Welch, Robert Green, Thomas Rumbold, Richard Savage, William Dobb, Felix Doran, Miles Barber, and others—were neither native to Liverpool, nor did they arise from socially or occupationally prestigious backgrounds. By 1709, the year that John Earle, son of a Warrington brewer, served as Lord Mayor of Liverpool, the benefits of the expanding transatlantic commerce of Liverpool were widely shared over a broad stratum of the port's trading community. These men included merchants, ship's captains, grocers, tradesmen, manufacturers, and professionals.[109] The growth of Liverpool trade had been preceded by the emergence of a distinct cadre of overseas merchants whose prominence reflected both the evolution of a broadly-based commercial *mentalité* in Liverpool in the seventeenth century, as well as a growing specialization in transatlantic trade that became the basis of their wealth and power in the eighteenth century.[110]

---

[105]David Richardson, *The Bristol Slave Traders: A Collective Portrait* (1985), 17–22.

[106]Richardson, *The Bristol Slave Traders*, 17–22.

[107]*ibid*, 22.

[108]Power, "Councillors and Commerce in Liverpool..." 305–309; Gauci, *The Politics of Trade*, 60.

[109]Gauci, 60; Muir, *A History of Liverpool*, 194.

[110]Gauci, 60–1

Chapter 2

Merchant Patriarchs

The three-quarters of a century between 1695 and 1775 witnessed the rise of a wealthy and powerful merchant oligarchy in Liverpool. The old aristocratic political order of Liverpool had been overturned at the end of the seventeenth century. Grown rich in the Irish, salt, and overseas trades, middling men of trade transcended their modest origins to supplant the old aristocratic elite as the real powers in Liverpool. Between the 1720s and 1750s, their claim to social and political authority was effectively realized. This chapter will examine the ways in which the transformation of middling men of trade into merchant oligarchs altered Liverpool politics and society.

These merchants were would-be patriarchs whose claim to high social status and political authority was based upon wealth, rather than birth or tradition. Prominent early merchants demonstrated a patriarchal *persona* that was redolent of the stern but fatherly political demeanor of the old landed elites. Although they assumed the role of patriarch, they governed Liverpool in their own interest. This resulted in a concerted policy to better the appearance of Liverpool by building churches, public buildings, streets, and homes. To further the expansion of trade, they created a infrastructure of docks, wharves, canals, and roads. After 1695, town government became more exclusive in composition, and more devoted to the interests of larger, overseas merchants. An ever-smaller group of merchant-oligarchs came to monopolize political power and public office. By the mid-eighteenth century, this narrow merchant oligarchy had become disconnected from the average run of Liverpool traders, as social position came to reflect birth and not necessarily wealth.

A host of demographic, social, and political developments after 1750 also made it more difficult for merchants to fulfill older notions of the social obligations of wealth. The expansion of Liverpool commerce attracted new men of trade to Merseyside, many of whom had little interest in the traditional structure of town society. These men did not come to Liverpool to become town fathers, but rather to make a fortune in trade. Many of the new men were considered outsiders by the merchant elite, and were denied a role in town government. This was acceptable to many outsiders who wished only to trade without assuming a social or political role. After 1750, new men were welcomed to trade in Liverpool, but were not permitted a place in society.

I

The Liverpool that greeted young John Earle in 1688 was in the throes of unprecedented change. For centuries, the outward appearance of Liverpool had changed little. Beginning in the late seventeenth century, the reclamation of the wasteland beyond the inlet known as the Pool opened this area to development.[111] By 1715, the Pool was filled in, and wet and dry docks and streets replaced the muddy inlet.[112] Churches and public buildings were built on this new land, and a functional commercial infrastructure was developed. Liverpool's pragmatic and farsighted merchants underwrote the construction of an elaborate system of docks and wharves, served on the Turnpike Trusts that planned and funded the building of a regional network of turnpike roads, and helped to finance and organize the construction of a much-needed system of canals.[113]

Although crucial to the expansion of Liverpool commerce, these capital improvements took place very slowly. The leisurely pace was especially evident in the construction of roads. While regularly scheduled stagecoaches traversed the abysmal roads between London and Liverpool long before 1750, the first dedicated coach road was not opened until 1760.[114] The high cost of overland transport, particularly for bulky items such as coal and salt, led Liverpool's merchants to turn to other forms of transport, such as canals. The improvement of local rivers and the construction of canals between 1750–1775, such as the Weaver navigation, Mersey-Irwell, and Douglas river navigations, the Sankey Brook canal, the Bridgewater canal, the Trent-Mersey canal, and the much delayed Leeds-Liverpool canal, meant that goods such as Cheshire salt, Lancashire coal, textiles produced in the mills and factories of Manchester, and other manufactured goods from Leeds, Birmingham, Sheffield, and other points in the Midlands, could be shipped to Liverpool in increasingly large quantities and at a lower cost.[115] Once shipped to Merseyside, goods bound for Africa, the Americas, and Europe were loaded aboard Liverpool's fleet of merchant ships, which grew from only 70 vessels in 1700, to some 220 by 1750.[116]

The initiative for these changes came from merchants. These building projects were promoted as commercial necessities, as the public weal increasingly came to be defined in narrow, self-interested terms. In the minds of the town's expanding community of merchants, it was the responsibility of the Corporation of Liverpool, which they themselves controlled, to support the expansion of trade by planning and financing such improvements and obtaining the necessary permissions from Parliament. As one historian has argued, the parliamentary acts which sanctioned the building of commercial structures such as docks, turnpikes, and canals became "essential building blocks" in the development of ocean-going ports such as Liverpool.[117] As the ancient face of Liverpool changed in the decades after 1660, and the muddy medieval town grew into a fashionable center of trade, the Corporation of Liverpool made the economic prosperity of the town's merchants a civic responsibility.

As the map on the next page demonstrates, Liverpool centered upon seven ancient streets fronting the River Mersey west of the Pool. These narrow alleys, Castle Street, Bonke or Bank Street (later Water Street), Dale Street, Juggler Street (later High Street), Chapel Street, Moor Street (later Tithebarn Street), and Mill or Whitacre Street (later Oldhall Street), were arrayed in a distinctive "H" pattern on the peninsula that formed the medieval village, and comprised the heart of old Liverpool.[118] A far from fashionable town, Liverpool retained the appearance of a muddy riverside settlement as late as 1719, when the Lord Mayor ordered

[111]Ronald Stewart-Brown, "The Pool of Liverpool," *Transactions of the Historical Society of Lancashire and Cheshire*, 82 (1930), 90.

[112]Stewart-Brown, "The Pool of Liverpool," 91.

[113]Sheila Marriner, *The Economic and Social Development of Merseyside* (1982), 5, 15-6

[114]*Liverpool Memorandum Book of 1753*; John Hughes, *Liverpool Banks and Bankers* (1906), 36; Mackenzie-Grieve, 6.

[115]Penelope Corfield, *The Impact of English Towns, 1700–1800* (1982) 11, 34, 42-4; Rosemary Sweet, *The English Town, 1680–1840: Government, Society, and Culture* (1999), 11, 100; Hughes, *Liverpool Banks and Bankers*, 36.

[116]Ramsay Muir, *History of Liverpool*, 181. According to Ramsay Muir, the number of seamen in Liverpool kept pace with the rising number of Liverpool merchants, growing from 800 in 1700, to 3,319 in 1751.

[117]Sweet, *The English Town, 1680–1840*, 100-1.

[118]Arthur Black, *et al*, *The Changing Face of Liverpool, 1207–1727* (1981), 6–7.

Map 2.1   *Liverpool c. 1207–1485*

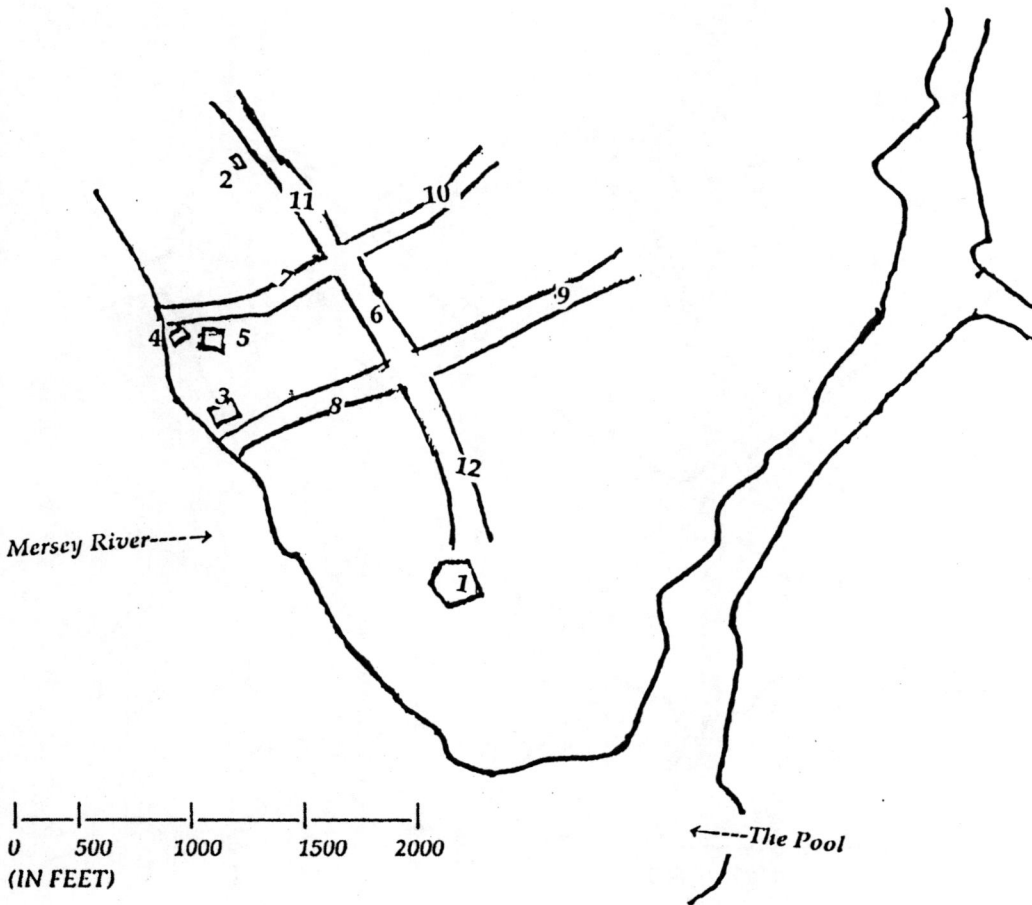

Mersey River----→

←----The Pool

|—|———|———|———|———|
0   500   1000   1500   2000
(IN FEET)

1) Castle
2) Moore Hall (Old Hall)
3) Tower
4) St. Mary del Key Chapel
5) St. Nicholas Chapel
6) Juggler Street (High Street)
7) Chapel Street
8) Bank Street (Water Street)

9) Dale Street
10) Moor Street (Tithebarn Street)
11) Mill Street/Whiteacre Street (Old Hall Street)
12) Castle Street

Source: Arthur Black, *et al*, *The Changing Face of Liverpool, 1207-1727* (1981), 12.

that carts be provided twice weekly "to take away all the muck and dirt in the streets and passages of this town."[119] Although most of its structures were made of wood, thatch, and daub, five stone buildings, symbols of authority in the medieval community, had long dominated Liverpool: the castle, the chapel of St. Mary

---

[119]Order of Thomas Fillingham, Esq., Mayor of Liverpool, October 24, 1719, Corporation Minute Books, MF2/2–5.

Map 2.2   *Liverpool c. 1485–1660*

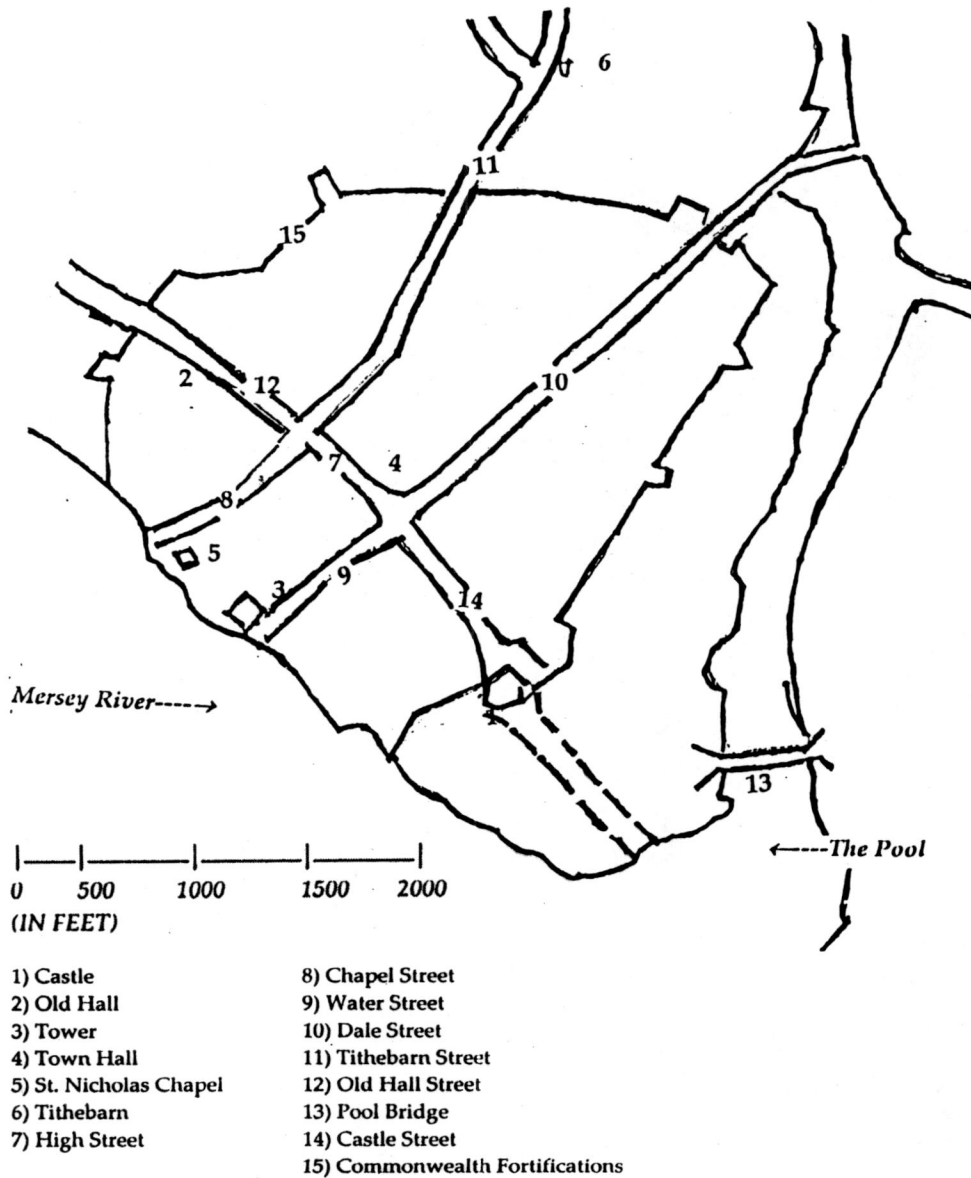

6

11

15

2 12

10

7

8

4

5

3 9

14

Mersey River----→

|—|————|————|————|————|
0   500   1000   1500   2000
(IN FEET)

←----*The Pool*

13

1) Castle
2) Old Hall
3) Tower
4) Town Hall
5) St. Nicholas Chapel
6) Tithebarn
7) High Street

8) Chapel Street
9) Water Street
10) Dale Street
11) Tithebarn Street
12) Old Hall Street
13) Pool Bridge
14) Castle Street
15) Commonwealth Fortifications

*Source: **Arthur Black**, et al, The Changing Face of Liverpool, 1207-1727 (1981), 12.*

del Key, the church of St. Nicholas, Old Hall, and the Tower of Liverpool.[120] These buildings symbolized the medieval primacy of church and manor in local civic life, the timeless social, economic, religious, and

---

[120]Arthur Black, *et al*, 10; Ramsay Muir, *A History of Liverpool* (1907), 6–7; Ronald Stewart-Brown, "The Tower of Liverpool, with some notes on the Clayton Family of Crooke, Fulwood, Adlington, and Liverpool," *Transactions of the Historical Society of Lancashire and Cheshire* 61 (1909), 46f. The castle was built between 1232 and 1237, St. Mary del Key some time before 1257, and St. Nicholas in 1355. Old Hall, long the seat of the Moore family, was built along Mill Street in 1388–89 by Thomas Moore.

Map 2.3   *Liverpool c. 1660–1714*

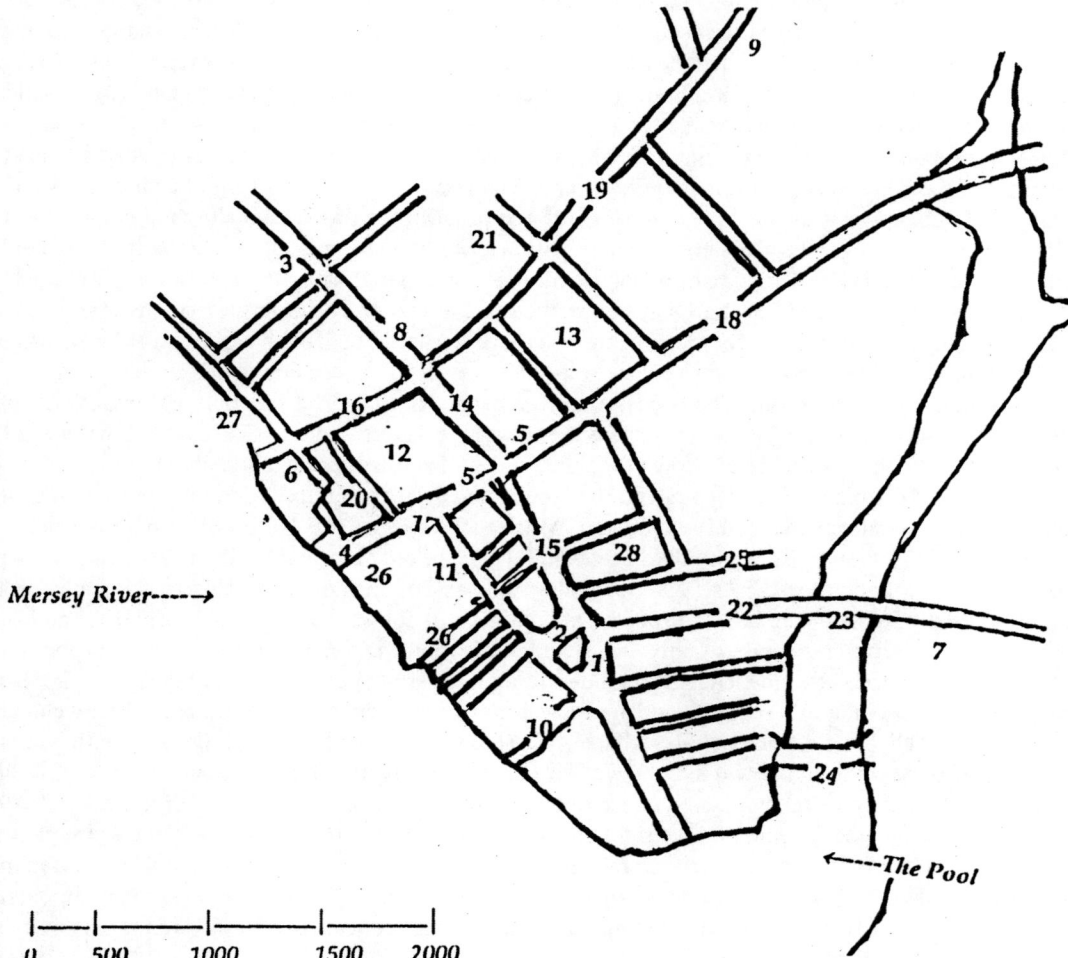

Mersey River---->

<----The Pool

|—|———|———|———|———|
0   500   1000   1500   2000
(IN FEET)

1) Castle
2) Castle Hill
3) Old Hall
4) Tower
5) Town Hall
6) St. Nicholas Chapel
7) St. Peter's Church
8) Old Hall Street
9) Tithebarn
10) Redcross Street
11) Fenwick Street
12) Common Garden
13) Hackins Hey
14) High Street

15) Castle Street
16) Chapel Street
17) Water Street
18) Dale Street
19) Tithebarn Street
20) Chapel Yard
21) Key Street Presbyterian Chapel
22) Lord Street
23) Lord Street Bridge
24) Pool Bridge
25) Harrington Street
26) Custom House
27) Lancelot's Hey
28) Castle Hey

Source: **Arthur Black**, *et al*, *The Changing Face of Liverpool, 1207-1727* (1981), 20.

political realities which had shaped the outward aspect of Liverpool for centuries. With the emergence of independent and wealthy merchants after 1660, however, new kinds of public and private construction began to fill the town lands and field-lots that surrounded old Liverpool, as the village became a town. Ambitious merchant-speculators, grown rich in transatlantic trade, built stylish, well-furnished town houses set upon wide thoroughfares and spacious public squares, lavish municipal buildings, impressive corporation churches, and an advanced commercial infrastructure. Exuberant entrepreneurs, Liverpool's great merchants systematically reinvented old Liverpool to serve them better in a burgeoning new world of transoceanic trade.[121]

A few substantial civic buildings were erected in the century and a half before 1660, such as the stone tithe-barn, and the West Derby courthouse. However, the construction of the most significant civic buildings, churches, and public works awaited the rise to power and prominence of these wealthy merchants. In 1673, the first of these buildings, the Exchange, a combination town hall and merchant's exchange, was built on the site of the medieval High Cross near the intersection of Water and Castle Streets. This new structure was designed to replace the crumbling building bequeathed to the mayor and aldermen of Liverpool in 1515 by John Crosse. The Exchange became the centerpiece of mercantile life in Liverpool until 1754, when an elegant new town hall was opened, and the old building was demolished. For three quarters of a century, Liverpool's merchants met to conduct business at the Exchange "flags," the stone courtyard laid down before the pillars of the old Exchange. Buildings such as the Exchange, taverns, and coffee houses had replaced the parish church as the meeting place of choice for Liverpool's upwardly mobile merchant elites.

The parish church remained a potent symbol of social and political authority in late seventeenth century Liverpool. This remained unchanged for 350 years. Much to the chagrin of Liverpool's rising merchants, the growing town of 1700 remained what it had been since 1399, an out-sized part of the nearby rural parish of Walton-on-the-Hill, Lancashire.[122] As Power suggests, this lack of an independent parish indicates of how unimportant Liverpool had been before 1700.[123] The total lack of church-building for nearly three and a half centuries resulted from the secondary status under which Liverpool labored. After 1695, the Corporation of Liverpool, now dominated by independently-minded Whig merchants such as Thomas Johnson Jr., applied to Parliament for the creation of a separate parish of Liverpool, as well as permission to build a new church to supplement the small, obsolete St. Nicholas Chapel.[124] To meet the demands of Liverpool's mounting population, and under pressure from the two members of Parliament for Liverpool, Sir William Norris and William Clayton, Parliament responded by passing an act that created the independent parish of Liverpool in 1699, at the same time granting the Corporation the right to appoint two rectors, and sanctioning the construction of a new corporation church. Liverpool's striving merchants saw elaborately constructed churches, located more conveniently in the outlying neighborhoods where merchants increasingly lived, as a central component in their grand vision for Liverpool's future, testimonials in brick and stone of Liverpool's rapid prosperity and their own newfound importance.

The first of these new churches to be built, St. Peter's at the foot of Lord Street, was completed in 1704, the earliest significant building to rise on the wastelands across the Pool from the old town center. Designed by Scottish architect John Moffat, this squat, brick-clad church, with its distinctive octagonal tower, St. Peter's was reputedly the first church built in England since the 1540s, the height of the Henrician Reformation, and served as the pro-cathedral of Liverpool between 1880 and 1922 when it was pulled down.[125] The construction of the next corporation church, St. George's, began in 1726 on the site of the recently-demolished Liverpool Castle. Perhaps more than any other episode in the eighteenth-century transformation of Liverpool, the fate of this once-grand castle is symbolic of the reconstruction of the squalid medieval village into a substantial, well-built commercial town by 1700. The castle, long the stronghold of the aristocratic Molyneaux family,

[121]John Brewer, "Commercialization and Politics," in *The Birth of a Consumer Society: The Commercialization of Eighteenth Century England*, ed., Neil McKendrick, John Brewer, and J.H. Plumb, (1982), 197–262.

[122]Peter Borsay, *The English Urban Renaissance: Culture and Society in the Provincial Town, 1660–1770* (1989), 104–110.

[123]Power, "Progress and Politics," 128; Baines, *History of the Commerce and Town of Liverpool*, 339–40.

[124]Edith M. Platt, "Sir Thomas Johnson," *Transactions of the Historical Society of Lancashire and Cheshire*, 52 (1900), 152.

[125]Janet Gnosspelius and Stanley Harris, "John Moffat and St. Peter's Church, Liverpool," *Transactions of the Historical Society of Lancashire and Cheshire* 130 (1981), 1–2f.

Map 2.4   *Liverpool c. 1714–1727*

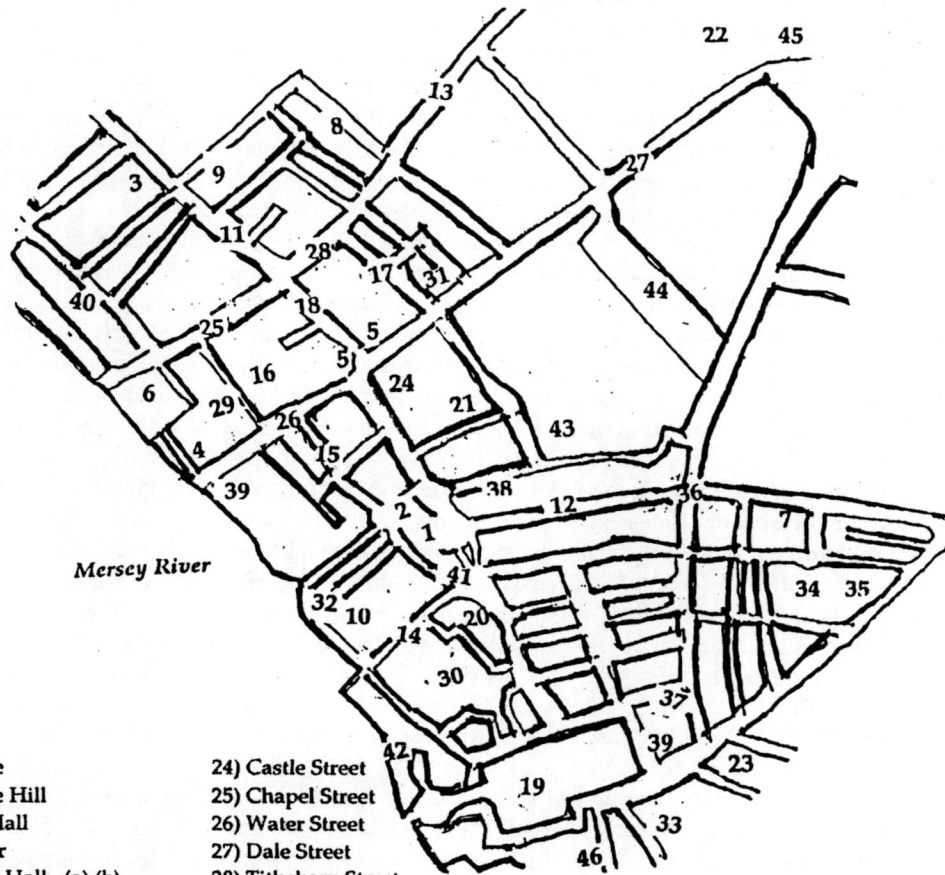

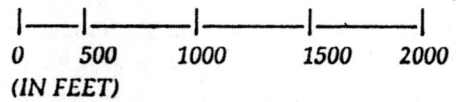

Mersey River

1) Castle	24) Castle Street
2) Castle Hill	25) Chapel Street
3) Old Hall	26) Water Street
4) Tower	27) Dale Street
5) Town Hall (a) (b)	28) Tithebarn Street
6) St. Nicholas Chapel	29) Chapel Yard
7) St. Peter's Church	30) Benn's Garden Chapel
8) Key Street Chapel	31) Friends' Meeting House
9) R.C. Church	32) Baptist Meeting House
10) Baptist Chapel	33) St Thomas Church (*site*)
11) Old Hall Street	34) Blue Coat School
12) Lord Street	35) Charity School
13) Tithebarn	36) Lord Street Bridge
14) Redcross Street	37) Pool Bridge
15) Fenwick Street	38) Harrington Street
16) Common Garden	39) Custom House (a) (b)
17) Hackins Hey	40) Lancelot's Hey
18) High Street	41) Castle Hey
19) Wet Dock	42) Dry Dock
20) Sugar Refinery	43) Sugar Refinery
21) Sugar Refinery	44) Rope Yard
22) Pot Works	45) Pot Works
23) Glass Works	46) Mersey Street

0   500   1000   1500   2000
(IN FEET)

Source: Arthur Black, *et al*, *The Changing Face of Liverpool, 1207-1727* (1981), 32.

had become an eyesore in the middle of old Liverpool by the eighteenth century. A hated symbol of feudal overlordship, the castle had long been targeted for destruction by the merchants who dominated the Liverpool Corporation by 1700, especially Thomas Johnson Jr. who oversaw the project.[126] For decades, schemes were discussed to convert this prime property to better uses, with the result that by 1704 the Corporation had obtained a license from the crown to pull down the old castle and build a church that would form the centerpiece of the projected Derby Square development scheme.[127] Although the demolition of the castle began in earnest by 1709, it was delayed several times as Lord Molyneaux and his family appealed the granting of this license in crown court. Finally by 1718, the Corporation of Liverpool surmounted the final legal challenges, and secured clear leasehold. The largest portion of the old castle was pulled down between 1718 and 1725, and the construction of St.George's began on the site in 1726, and was completed in 1734.

These construction projects, as well as the creation of an independent parish, signified the rise of the new masters of Liverpool. In 1747, the Corporation of Liverpool once again applied to Parliament for official permission to build a new church, as the "buildings and inhabitants of the said town…are of late years so greatly increased, that the said three churches…are not sufficient to contain one-third part of the inhabitants… professing the doctrine of the Church of England."[128] After ship-builder, timber merchant, and transatlantic trader John Okill (1687–1773) donated land near his home on Park Lane to build the projected church of St. Thomas, a public subscription campaign was undertaken which raised a total of £2,300.[129] The planning, authorization, and building of this church was promoted by a cohort of merchants and shipbuilders, politically prominent men who formed a remarkably cohesive leadership group that shared numerous close personal, political, and commercial connections. In addition to John Okill, the men named as overseers of the 1747 parliamentary enabling act for the new church formed a litany of town leaders. They included Bryan Blundell Sr. (1674–1756), Joseph Bird (died-1767), James Crosbie (died-1755), Thomas Seel (died-1755), Charles Goore (1702–1783), John Gorell (died-1761), Richard Golightly (died-1779), John Seddon (died-1759), John Parke, William Shaw, and Bryan Blundell's former brother-in-law, Thomas Shaw.[130] Of these twelve men, five served Liverpool between 1721–1767 as either Lord Mayor or bailiff, or both. The best-known figure of this group, Bryan Blundell Sr., attended Liverpool as Lord Mayor in 1721 and 1728, while Joseph Bird held office as bailiff in 1738, and Lord Mayor in 1746, and Thomas Shaw served as bailiff in 1738, and Lord Mayor in 1747, James Crosbie served as bailiff in 1748, and Lord Mayor in 1753, and Charles Goore served as bailiff in 1747, and was selected Lord Mayor in 1754, and 1767, and was chosen to complete term of office of Lord Mayor William Pownall upon his death on March 12, 1767.[131] The social, commercial, and political interconnectedness of these men was pronounced in other ways as well. In addition to overseeing the construction of St. Thomas, Park Lane, within a few years eight of these men served as trustees of the Liverpool Infirmary at its founding in March 1749, eight were investors in the Greenland whaler *Golden Lion* in 1749, and seven were freemen of the Liverpool Company of Merchants Trading to Africa in 1750.[132] The overseers of St. Thomas, Park Lane, were close allies in a Liverpool that was very much a merchant town.

---

[126]Edith Platt, "Sir Thomas Johnson," 153–154.

[127]Ramsay Muir, Henry Young, and Harold Young, *Bygone Liverpool* (1913), introduction, xviii.

[128]Baines, *History of the Commerce and Town of Liverpool*, 415. These churches are, of course, Our Lady and St. Nicholas's, St. Peter's, and St. George's.

[129]Will of John Okill, timber merchant of Liverpool, Wills and Inventories, Chester Probate Registry, 1773; *Liverpool Directory of 1766*, Baines, *History of the Commerce and Town of Liverpool*, 415.

[130]Baines, *History of the Commerce and Town of Liverpool*, 415. Two other less significant men, anchorsmith Samuel Irlam, and Reverend William Martin, also served as administrators of the 1747 parliamentary act.

[131]Baines, *History of the Commerce and Town of Liverpool*, 355–6.

[132]George McLoughlin, *A Short History of the Liverpool Infirmary, 1749–1824* (1978),App. V, 94–97; Brooke, *Liverpool as it was…*," 239–40; *The Liverpool Memorandum Book* (1753); *The Humble Petition of the Mayor, Aldermen, and Bailiffs, and Common Council of Liverpool in Council Assembled, to the Right Honorable, The Lords Spiritual and Temporal in Parliament Assembled, May 14, 1750*, Committee Book of the African Company of Merchants Trading from Liverpool, 1750–1820, Charles Goore was the manager and primary investor in the Greenland whaler *Golden Lion*.

While these weighty men pursued various primary occupations, most were, at one time or another, either merchants or investors in a regular pattern of overseas trading ventures. A legendary founder of the Blue Coat School and Hospital in 1708, Bryan Blundell was originally a mariner by trade, but gave up the sea to pursue the lucrative trade in tobacco, sugar, and slaves shortly after 1700.[133] These Atlantic trades were also the primary focus in the mercantile careers of Joseph Bird, James Crosbie, and Thomas Seel, men who were, above all, professional merchants.[134] Like most eighteenth-century British merchants, these men were involved in a wide variety of economic pursuits, from shop keeping, manufacturing, and brokerage, to such professional vocations as law and medicine. Charles Goore, for instance, began his career as a captain for the tobacco merchants *Foster Cunliffe & Sons*, eventually entering transatlantic trade himself as a merchant, and becoming, thereafter, a whaler, and a manufacturer of merchant supplies such as barrels and rope, and an importer of flagstones, ironware, and hemp.[135] Like Bird, Crosbie, and Seel, John Okill, John Gorell, John Parke, Richard Golightly, and William Shaw were also professional merchants. But unlike them, they were principally shipwrights whose primary trade in timber was ancillary to their ship building business.[136] These men, rivals and partners in the competitive business of building and fitting out ships in Liverpool, were also, like the anchorsmith John Seddon, significant investors in transatlantic trade. John Gorell and John Parke, for instance, were partners in the ship-building firm of *Gorell & Parke* as well as in eight slaving ventures, primarily to Bonny and Calabar, between 1749 and 1756.[137] Such investments were far from atypical, as every one of the overseers of St. Thomas, Park Lane, with the exception of Lord Mayor Thomas Shaw, eventually invested in the transatlantic slave trade. Even so, most of them were followers rather than leaders in the Liverpool slave trade, since their participation in the Guinea trade was sporadic, short-lived, and highly variable.

In a few cases, however, involvement in the slave trade was considerable and persisted over long periods of time. This involvement ranged from the 41 slaving ventures of John Gorell between 1748–1764, and the 23 of James Crosbie between 1745–1761, to one venture each for Richard Golightly (1749) and William Shaw (1748).[138] Excluding these four outliers, the average number of slaving ventures for the group was nine, including thirteen ventures for John Parke (1749–1756), twelve for John Okill (1747–1756), ten for Thomas Seel (1714–1743), nine for Bryan Blundell Sr. (1718–1739), eight for John Seddon (1755–1758), seven for Joseph Bird (1748–1768), and four for Charles Goore (1748–1755).[139] While they all sought to prosper in the promising trade in West African slaves, these men were not great slave merchants, and lacked the resources, expertise, market knowledge, or interest to manage a long cycle of slaving ventures on their own. For all except Gorell and Crosbie, slave trading represented little more than a series of opportunistic investments, rather than a primary trade. Small slave merchants like Bird, Parke, and Seddon depended upon the commercial *entrée* afforded them by a good reputation, social position, close friendships, kinship ties, religious bonds, political connections, and economic self-interest to find the investment opportunities they needed to prosper in the risky world of the West African slave trade.

---

[133]Harry Hignet, "Extracts from Bryan Blundell, his Journal," http://www.cronab.demon.co.uk/hig.htm, p. 1. Blundell provided 1/4 of the funds for the Blue Coat School at its founding, a share that rose to half.

[134]Hyde, 17. According to Francis Hyde, a Thomas Seel was also an important land developer in Liverpool who built up "the area from the bottom of Seel Street to Colquitt Street."

[135]Stanley Chapman, "British Marketing Enterprise: The Changing Roles of Merchants, Manufacturers, and Financiers, 1700–1860," *Business History Review*, 53 (1979), 209; Alexander Grant, "The Cooper in Liverpool," *Industrial Archeology Review*, 1 (1976), 28–30; *Liverpool Directory of* 1766. Despite Chapman's contention that Charles Goore was a Guinea captain, Goore is not listed in the *TSTD* as a captain of any slave ship.

[136]Ronald Stewart-Brown, *Liverpool Ships in the Eighteenth Century: Including the King's Ships Built there, with Notes on the Principal Shipwrights*, (1932), 117–19.

[137]Stewart Brown, *Liverpool Ships in the Eighteenth Century*, 117–19; *TSTD*.

[138]*TSTD*.

[139]*TSTD*; D. Anderson, "Blundell's Collieries, The Progress of the Business," *Transactions of the Historical Society of Lancashire and Cheshire*, 116 (1965), 75; *International Genealogical Index*; Will of Thomas Seel, merchant of Liverpool, Wills and Inventories, Chester Probate Registry, 1755; Will of John Seddon, anchorsmith of Liverpool, Wills and Inventories, Chester Probate Registry, 1759.

II

Property holding also became a major investment and source of wealth, and legitimized the growing political power and social standing of Liverpool's affluent and aspiring merchants and tradesmen.[140] Like many English merchants, they translated commercial prosperity into material possessions and land, with the wholesale purchase of homes, yards, warehouses, manufacturing facilities, and town lots. This created a pattern of land holding that was intended to be intergenerational. For example, property ownership was an important element in the business careers of John Renshaw and Peter Rigby, men who also enjoyed modest success in the Liverpool slave trade. Son of an old but undistinguished Liverpool family, John Renshaw was listed in the *Liverpool Directory of 1766* as a roper of Ranelagh Street, Liverpool, the son of the Liverpool roper John Renshaw whose will was proven at Chester in 1742.[141] The elder John Renshaw was a significant property owner in Liverpool at the time of his death, with land-holdings that included houses and warehouses on Moorfields, Dale Street, and Cheapside, a leased ropery yard on Dale Street, and houses on Water and Bickesteth Streets.[142] By 1766, the younger Renshaw was a wealthy roper himself, residing on the newly laid-out Ranelegh Street, near modern-day Renshaw Street.

Similarly, the will of Liverpool merchant and ironmonger Peter Rigby reveals that he had extensive property holdings in Liverpool, especially on Lord and Atherton streets and in Derby Square. Like Renshaw, Rigby was the son of a successful father whose prospects were enhanced by a family legacy of wealth and commercial success. Son of ironmonger Edmund Rigby, bailiff in 1741 and Lord Mayor in 1751, Rigby succeeded in establishing himself as an ironmonger, and is described in his 1795 will as "a merchant and ironmonger of Liverpool."[143] By taking up the occupations of their middling fathers, both Renshaw and Rigby built upon a considerable landed inheritance to establish themselves as leading members of Liverpool society. Although Renshaw and Rigby both held significant land holdings in Liverpool, and were counted among the town's merchant elite as trustees of the Infirmary in 1749, neither was ever a major merchant or political figure.[144]

Some of Liverpool's greatest merchants and political figures were also instrumental in pushing land development past the confines of the old village. Power notes that the post-1695 generation of "trader politicians" were much more heavily invested in real estate than their merchant predecessors had been, a development which suggests that their growing commercial prominence was beginning to be expressed in more traditional ways in Liverpool society.[145] In the thirty years before 1695, great tracts of land in Liverpool town center had became available for purchase from the Molyneaux and Moore families, and merchants were the largest purchasers. This acquisition of land was rapid, and a few prominent merchant-councilors quickly assembled sizeable real estate portfolios. Power argues that the parish rate assessment of 1708 reveals the true extent of this ownership of property by town councilors.[146] Among the largest merchant-landowners were Sir Thomas Johnson, who held 27 properties, Alderman George Tyrer, who held 23, and Aldermen Thomas Bickesteth, William Clayton, and Richard Houghton, who held 15 properties each.[147] Land ownership among merchants was much more widespread in 1708 than it had been in 1670, when a great swath of the town was still held by titled magnates such as the Earl of Derby, Sir Edward Moore, John Crosse, and Caryl, Lord Molyneaux.[148]

---

[140]Sir Edward Moore, *The Moore Rental, 1667–1668*, ed., Thomas Heywood (1847), introduction.

[141]*Liverpool Directory of 1766*; Will of John Renshaw, roper of Liverpool, Wills and Inventories, Chester Probate Registry, 1742.

[142]*Rate Assessment Book for the Parish of Liverpool* (1743), Liverpool PRO, 920/PLU/pt. 51.

[143]*Liverpool Directory of 1766*; Will of Peter Rigby, merchant and ironmonger of Liverpool, Lancashire July 4, 1795, PCC: PROB 11/1264.

[144]McLoughlin, App. V, 94–97.

[145]Power, "Politics and Progress in Liverpool," 127–128.

[146]*ibid*, 127–128.

[147]*ibid*.

[148]*Plan of the Ancient Town and Harbour of Liverpool, with the Ownership of Property, about 1670*, Macdonald & Macgregor, Liverpool, (No Date), Public Record Office, Central Library of Liverpool .

These newly acquired lands could thus be used to advance the long-term economic interests of Liverpool's mercantile elite.

After 1715, speculative property development was particularly evident in the lands east of Liverpool's new wet dock, on commons formed from the reclamation of the Pool, and the surrounding heath-covered wastes. With hopes of fostering development in this thinly settled area, Alderman Richard Gildart had laid out a street by 1750, subsequently known as Gildart Street, upon land he owned northeast of the old town center of Liverpool. Guided by similarly entrepreneurial motives, merchant Richard Kent, Customs Collector John Colquitt Jr., Engineer Thomas Steers, timber merchant Edward Mason, and other would-be developers, built streets on former wasteland they owned across the old Pool.[149] In addition to the wide streets, ornate churches, and majestic public buildings planned and built by Liverpool's great merchant-developers in the first half of the eighteenth century, other more ostentatious development projects, such as Ranelagh Gardens, Wolstenholme Square, Cleveland Square, Faulkner Square, Pownall Square, Rainford's Gardens, Clayton Square, and the Theatre-Royal on Williamson's Square, were laid out in order to provide suitable neighborhoods for Liverpool's wealthy elites, as well as a gloss of refinement to the still narrow and rude town of Liverpool.[150]

III

As Liverpool merchants grew wealthy, prosperity acted as a solvent to the old order, empowering Liverpool's community of merchants in the process. By 1700, a new merchant elite had come to dominate Liverpool's polity, as great merchants largely supplanted the old landed elites in both the communal market stalls and the councils of town government. However, the political conflict which heralded the coming of the new commercial order proved short-lived. In Liverpool socially ambitious men of trade sought to form marital alliances with well-born families when they could, occasionally for themselves but more often for their children, while the younger sons of the gentry often entered trade. The process of social amalgamation was repeated throughout the length and breadth of eighteenth-century England. In London, for instance, Penelope Corfield has found that by the early eighteenth century the leading merchant families of the City "moved on relatively easy social terms with—and married into—the ranks of English landed society."[151] In Liverpool, such advantageous marital alliances bolstered the claim of mercantile families to social and political authority. Over the course of the eighteenth century, Liverpool's great transatlantic merchants, often aided by such marriages, erected a self-perpetuating, but often loosely defined, commercial oligarchy, which became, in time, every bit as closed and exclusive as the old aristocratic order had been. Within the "close" corporation of Liverpool, these merchants served on the Common Council for life, co-opting men of similar wealth and social standing to fill vacancies as they occurred.[152] However, not every Liverpool merchant—or those who flocked to Liverpool from elsewhere—who grew rich in overseas trade after 1660 was accepted as a member of this mercantile oligarchy, nor did all desire to become "made men."

In the first half of the eighteenth century, the great opportunities for commercial success that were available in Liverpool trade, and the resulting fortunes that were built up trading West Indian sugar, Chesapeake tobacco, and African slaves, were more frequently translated into elevated social position and political office

---

[149]Arthur Wardle, "The Customs Collection of the Port of Liverpool," *Transactions of the Historical Society of Lancashire and Cheshire*, 99 (1949), 38–9; *Gore's Liverpool Directory of 1766*. John Colquitt Jr. succeeded his father, John Colquitt Sr., as Collector of Customs for Liverpool in 1749, and served until 1773. Mayor of Liverpool in 1739, the Kentish-born engineer Thomas Steers (1672–1750) originally came to Liverpool from London in 1710 to oversee the construction of the town's first wet dock, which was completed in 1715.

[150]Richard Brooke, *Liverpool as it was During the Last Quarter of the Eighteenth, 1775–1800* (1853), 80-5, 86-8, Arthur Wardle, "Some Glimpses of Liverpool during the first half of the Eighteenth Century," *Transactions of the Historical Society of Lancashire and Cheshire*, 93 (1941), 157.

[151]Corfield, *The Impact of English Towns*, 130-1; Harold Perkin, *The Origins of Modern English Society, 1780–1880* (1969), 62.

[152]H. T. Dickinson, *The Politics of the People in Eighteenth-Century Britain* (1994), 99–106.

than they would be by the time of the American Revolution. The merchant-elite of Liverpool learned, as their landed predecessors had earlier, that a socially exclusive and politically restrictive oligarchy was difficult to maintain in the midst of disruptive socioeconomic change, particularly when this oligarchy had not established its *bona fides*. As Peter Borsay suggests, the rise of urban oligarchy in early modern Britain, and the mounting pressures promoting social "uniformity and rigidity" which this implies, is "belied by the local context and the swift pace of change."[153] While the structure of social hierarchy, status, and power in the urban environment was often inflexibly established, the human element remained supremely changeable. "In urban society," Peter Clark and Paul Slack observe,

> wealth might be fairly quickly won—though more so at some periods than others—and even more quickly lost. Whereas those who rose to wealth through urban employments have had their achievements chronicled in the histories of many towns, those who failed to make their fortunes and sank back into obscurity were undoubtedly much more common.[154]

As Clark and Slack suggest, eighteenth-century overseas trade was very much a slippery slope, especially for young merchants just starting out and would-be traders with meager resources.[155] During the first half of the eighteenth century, rapid commercial growth had a transformative impact upon the old landed social order of Liverpool. This tended to break down long-accepted political and commercial verities, thereby preparing the ground for the rise of an altogether new kind of civic leader, the merchant patriarch.

Liverpool merchants differed more than merely in generational terms from their heirs and successors, and from their rivals in Bristol and London. Those trading between 1695 and 1740, sought to emulate the social position of the old landed elites in order to create an easily comprehensible political authority that was not simply a social manifestation of the great riches that they were earning in the Atlantic trades.[156] These prosperous merchants were self-styled communal fathers, would-be patriarchs whose claim to high social status was based upon the tangible reality of wealth. Men of business were viewed as natural leaders not because they were pious men or members of elite families. Rather, the wealth of such merchants, and other middling men, came to be associated with *de facto* social and political authority.[157] This authority was well understood in Liverpool society, and was reflected in the ways merchant patriarchs comported themselves in public. Prominent early merchants evinced a patriarchal *persona* that was evocative of the stern but fatherly political demeanor of the old landed elites. Because their claims to social and political legitimacy lacked the authenticity of aristocratic bloodlines and long usage, politically ambitious merchants understood that they had to recreate the role—and image—of the patriarch for themselves.

---

[153]Borsay, *The English Urban Renaissance*, 10.

[154]Peter Clark and Paul Slack, *English Towns in Transition, 1500–1700* (1976), 111.

[155]Sweet, *The English Town*, 163.

[156]*TSTD*; This older generation of prominent merchants included John Pemberton Sr. (1668–1744), Samuel Powell (died-1745), Richard Gildart Sr. (1671–1770), John Earle (1674–1749), Bryan Blundell Sr. (1674–1756), Foster Cunliffe (1682–1758), Samuel Ogden (1689–1752), Thomas Tarleton (1685–1730), James Crosbie (died-1755), Edmund Rigby (died-1758), and Edward Trafford (1692–1763); while their sons and sons-in-laws included such men as John Pemberton Jr. (1690–1740s), John Powell (died-c.1776), Richard Powell (died-1793) Folliott Powell (1734–1791), James Gildart (1711–1790), Johnson Gildart (died-1740), George Gildart (born-1716), Richard Gildart Jr. (died-1771), Christopher Whytell (died-1755), Spencer Steers (died-1765), Ralph Earle (1715–1790), Thomas Earle (1719–1781), William Earle (1721–1788), William Blundell (1714–1774), Bryan Blundell Jr. (1720–1790), Richard Blundell (1722–1760), Jonathan Blundell (1723–1800), Sir Ellis Cunliffe (1717–1767), Sir Robert Cunliffe (died-1778), Edmund Ogden, Arthur Heywood (1717–1795), Benjamin Heywood (1723–1795), John Tarleton (1718–1773), John Crosbie (died-1791?), William Crosbie (1718–?), Peter Rigby (died-1795), William Trafford (died-1767?) Richard Trafford (1732–1783), and Henry Trafford (died-1798).

[157]Corfield, 131–2; Sweet, 56–9; Michael Mullett, "The Politics of Liverpool, 1660–88,"*Transactions of the Historical Society of Lancashire and Cheshire*, 124 (1972), 55–56; W.G. Hoskins, "English Provincial Towns in the Early Sixteenth Century," in *The Early Modern Town*, ed. Peter Clark (1976), 94–5.

Although wealth had long determined relative levels of social status and political power in market and port towns like Liverpool prior to 1670, class distinctions arising from growing disparities in wealth had yet to create an insurmountable divide of power and status between rulers and the ruled. While overseas merchants ascended to new levels of power and prominence in many port towns in late Stuart England, the rise of merchants to power in Liverpool, which Power likens to a *coup d'etat*, was especially pronounced and sudden.[158] The involvement of self-promoting merchants in Liverpool politics and government resulted from a collective perception within the town's mercantile community that public service should support private interest.

Individually, Liverpool's great merchants sought political office for diverse reasons, ranging from a sense of obligation to a love of pomp and prestige. Collectively, however, they strove to safeguard their own vested economic interests by grasping the reins of town government and setting public policy. In this way, the Common Council became the exclusive preserve of rich merchants by the second half of the eighteenth century.[159]

The political victory of whiggish merchants over their landed opponents after 1695 made the process of patriarchalization easier. It liberated the Corporation of Liverpool from the unquestioned domination of a landed, aristocratic elite and opened the doors of the Common Council, and thus the mayoralty, to most men with the will and the means to play the role of civic patriarch. Before 1660, Liverpool's Lord Mayors and bailiffs—the two leading officers in town—rarely came from the ranks of the town's merchants, as most officeholders were affiliated with the landed elite. Nevertheless, the rapid rise of transatlantic trade after 1660 served to change the outlook and influence of Liverpool's merchants in a remarkably short period of time. In his study of three generations of the Johnson–Gildart family of Liverpool between 1650–1750, Power observes that their rapid rise after 1660, provided them with an unparalleled degree of influence over the economic and political life of Liverpool. Merchant-oligarchs such as Thomas Johnson, Richard Norris, and William Clayton, increasingly came to monopolize public office in Liverpool after 1695, a phenomenon that was particularly characteristic of Liverpool's increasingly slave traders. At least nine Liverpool slave traders—Thomas Johnson Jr., John Cleveland, William Cleveland, Charles Pole, William Pole I, Richard Gildart, John Hardman, Sir Ellis Cunliffe and William Pole II—served Liverpool in Parliament between 1701 and 1770; while five of the seven men who held the extremely important local post of Corporation treasurer between 1716–1775 were significant slave merchants.[160]

However, the Common Council was the most important seat of political power, and became the virtual preserve of slave traders after the 1720s. By 1753, ten of fourteen aldermen, influential former Lord Mayors who together served as a sort of executive committee within the Council, were slave merchants, as were 26 of the 40 members of the council in 1753.[161] The number of slave merchants in the Council continued to increase after 1753, and by 1775, thirteen of sixteen aldermen were slave merchants, while 29 of 36, including aldermen, were African traders of various size.[162] Power argues that the establishment of the generational dominance of a select group of elite merchants is most clearly reflected in the changing composition of the Common Council after 1700.[163] Even more tellingly, between 1700–1780, slave traders held the office of Lord Mayor for 55 of 81 years, or 69% of the entire period, a proportion that rose to an astonishing 93% for

---

[158]Power, 311.

[159]Peter Clark and Paul Slack, *English Towns in Transition, 1500–1700* (1976) 111–125.

[160]*TSTD*; Brooke, 207; *Liverpool Memorandum Book* (1753). Liverpool's treasurers between 1716–1775 included: Sylvester Moorcroft, August 31, 1716; Peter Hall, October 13, 1720; slave merchant Henry Trafford, March 20, 1721(*resigned*); slave merchant William Pole I, September 20, 1734; slave merchant Edward Forbes; December 24, 1759; slave merchant Matthew Strong, April 21, 1760; and slave merchant John Crosbie, November 3, 1773.

[161]*TSTD*; Brooke, 195; *Liverpool Memorandum Book* (1753). In these calculations, the mayor and two bailiffs were included; as were the aldermen and councilmen, but not the recorder or town clerk, who held office on good behavior, and served upon the council on an *ex officio* basis.

[162]*TSTD*; Brooke, 195; *Liverpool Memorandum Book* (1753).

[163]Michael Power, "Councillors and Commerce in Liverpool…," 306–13.

the period between 1750–1780 alone.[164] (See appendix 2.1) The emerging office-holding monopoly of slave traders was even more pronounced in the office of bailiff, a secondary position filled annually to assist the Lord Mayor in his many duties. Between 1700–1780, 75% of Liverpool's bailiffs were also slave traders, and between 1750–1780, slavers served as one of the two bailiffs chosen annually—or both—for 29 of 30 years during this period.[165] (See appendix 2.2) The preponderance of slave traders is particularly noteworthy because, among the 162 men who served as bailiff between 1695–1775, 70—or 43%—went on to become Lord Mayor. For politically active merchants, serving a term as bailiff was the next step—after admission to the Common Council—on a career path that often led to selection as Lord Mayor by the freemen or ultimately selection as a member of Parliament for Liverpool.[166] For example, Yorkshire-born merchant Richard Gildart was elevated to the Common Council in 1707, the same year that he wed Sir Thomas Johnson's daughter, was elected a bailiff in 1712 and Lord Mayor in 1714, 1731 and 1736, and finally a member of parliament between 1734–1754.[167] Selection as an M.P. was perhaps the greatest vote of confidence that Liverpool's community of merchants could give to one of their fellows. On July 18th, 1767, a group of influential town fathers and slave traders led by three powerful alderman—William Gregson, James Gildart Sr., and John Crosbie—approached Alderman John Tarleton, or "Great T" as he was known in Liverpool's elite social and political circles, and proposed that he offer himself as a candidate for parliament. "From your knowledge of trade in general," the delegation wrote Tarleton,

> and more particularly what relates to the interest and welfare of this town[,] We think you a very proper person to represent us in Parliament, and if you will declare yourself a candidate, we now make you a tender of our votes and interest, and doubt not your success at the next General Election.[168]

At a meeting five days later, 120 prominent merchants, over half of whom were slave traders, declared their support for him.[169] However, the hesitant Tarleton's hopes of elevation to Westminster were dashed when Liverpool's other sitting member, Sir William Meredith, declined to endorse him, and after a near riot between Tarleton supporters and opponents—including hostile whalers brandishing long blubber knives—cost him backing in Liverpool's all-important assembly of freemen.[170] While slave merchants and their allies did indeed run the eighteenth-century town of Liverpool, not even John Tarleton—"Great T" himself—or other rich, powerful, and privileged slave traders got their way all the time.

While John Tarleton never served as a bailiff before his term as Lord Mayor in 1764, this ancillary office continued to grow in importance after the later seventeenth century, although it had not always played such an significant role as a jumping-off point to the mayoralty. Between 1604–1659, for example, only 27% of bailiffs (25 of 94) rose to become Lord Mayor, a figure that remained relatively constant—28%—over the course of the next forty years (1660–1700).[171] The proportion, however, rising to 43% between 1701–1750, before declining somewhat to 40% between 1751–1780.[172] While the time it took for a bailiff to become Lord Mayor declined sharply. Between 1606–1637, on average, it took 10.5 years between a man's first election as bailiff and his ultimate election as Lord Mayor, falling to 7 years between 1637–1663, rising to 8.2

---

[164]TSTD; Baines, 355–6; Brooke, 207.

[165]TSTD; Baines, 355–6; Brooke, 207.

[166]Mark Kishlansky, *A Monarchy Transformed: Britain, 1603–1714* (1996), 59–60.

[167]Power, "Councillors and Commerce in Liverpool," 306, 308.

[168]Letter to John Tarleton, July 18th, 1767, Letters relating to the Candidacy of John Tarleton for Parliament, *Tarleton Papers*, 920 TAR (2)

[169]Declaration of Support for John Tarleton, July 23rd, 1767, Letters relating to the Candidacy of John Tarleton for Parliament, *Tarleton Papers*, 920 TAR (2)

[170]Declaration of Support for John Tarleton, July 23rd, 1767; Averill McKenzie-Grieve , 16.

[171]Baines, 355–6; Brooke, 207. Overall, in the half-century between 1730–1780, 81 of the 100 men who served as bailiff went on to become mayor, while every bailiff but one who served between 1760–1771 became mayor.

[172]Baines, 355–6; Brooke, 207.

years between 1663–1700, and 9.8 years between 1701–1750, before declining sharply to 5.7 years between 1751–1780.[173] After 1750, a term as bailiff became virtually a requirement for higher office.

While political conflict erupted periodically throughout the seventeenth century between a fervently royalist landed interest and shifting groups of whiggish merchants and tradesmen, more often than not the landed elite controlled the mayoralty between 1600 and 1695. The landed magnates seldom served as Lord Mayor themselves, relying instead upon others to safeguard their economic and political interests. Between 1603 and 1734, for instance, the Earls of Derby held the office of Lord Mayor only five times, in 1603, 1666, 1677, 1707, and 1734. The Earl's eldest son, Lord Strange, served as Lord Mayor only twice in 1625 and 1668, while other sons and close kin of the Earl held the office an additional four times in 1612, 1639, 1662, 1667. In addition to the Earls of Derby, other titled landowners also served as Lord Mayor between 1615 and 1684, including the powerful Sir Richard Molyneaux in 1618. Many of these aristocrats were either allies of the Earls of Derby, the greatest landed family in the northwest, or his employees and retainers. For the most part, however, this ascendancy was indirect, and the magnates maintained their political primacy in Liverpool through a small group of trusty lieutenants, such as Edward Moore, four-times selected Lord Mayor of Liverpool in 1604, 1611, 1620, and 1626, and John Walker, also a four-time Lord Mayor in 1622, 1628, 1632, and 1641. However, the representatives of the landed elite were also confronted by middling men who stood for the interests of small merchants, tradesmen, and their allies in town government. Men such as John Williamson, Lord Mayor of Liverpool in 1623, 1630, 1638, and 1643, and other members of his family, who together served a combined total of eleven terms as Lord Mayor between 1623–1659, struggled for dominance with the old elites.[174] Because the Earls of Derby, the Molyneaux family, and other elites chose to rule through a few long-serving deputies, a clearly defined pattern of promotion did not emerge in town politics until after Liverpool's commercial rise, and the emergence of a public political culture which followed by 1700 and after. Many of Liverpool's merchants sought a term as Lord Mayor to celebrate their new wealth and social status, and, most importantly, publicly to proclaim their identity as eminent men. In such direct ways, the great merchants edged their former overlords from power, and established themselves as the symbolic successors to Liverpool's landed elite. Between the 1720s and 1750s this claim was effectively realized, as the great merchants became the real powers in Liverpool affairs, establishing the generational dominance of a select group of elite merchant families in the process. As late as 1755, a troika of senior merchant-oligarchs, 84 year-old Richard Gildart, 70 year-old Foster Cunliffe, and 81 year-old Bryan Blundell Sr., traders in tobacco and slaves, and founding members of Liverpool's ruling merchant oligarchy, remained as firmly in control of Liverpool's Common Council as they had been three decades before. As a consequence, the wealth and eminence of these men of trade firmly established their children as successful merchants, and more importantly, as their presumptive heirs in Liverpool society and government.

IV

While Foster Cunliffe and Bryan Blundell Sr. were largely the authors of their own success, Richard Gildart built upon a legacy of commercial accomplishment and political power founded by two members of the prominent Johnson family, Thomas "Baly" Johnson Sr. and his son Sir Thomas Johnson Jr., which Gildart had the good fortune of marrying into in 1707. "The Johnson family biography," Power argues,

> could be viewed as an illustration of the progress of a merchant family from first generation small-scale merchant and political rebel, to second generation large-scale merchant and property owner breaking into political power, to third generation merchant turning increasingly to property and conservative political establishment.

---

[173]Baines, 355–6; Brooke, 207. For the entire period between 1606–1663, the average length of time between a man's first election as bailiff and his first election as mayor was 8.6 years, a figure which fell to 8 years between 1660–1780.

[174]Baines, 355–6; Brooke, 207. This includes the period during the English Civil War, and the Commonwealth period that followed, when supporters of the parliamentary cause controlled Liverpool.

Thomas "Baly" Johnson Sr. (1630?–1700) left a small Lancashire village—Bedford Leigh—as a young man and migrated to Liverpool sometime between 1645–1648. In Liverpool Johnson was apprenticed to Thomas Hodgson, scion of an old Lancashire family, a leading merchant, and Lord Mayor in 1649. He became a freeman in October 1655 after completing his apprenticeship, and, after being admitted to the Common Council in October 1659, held a succession of corporate offices, ultimately serving as a bailiff in 1663, and Lord Mayor in 1670.[175] A provincial man of decidedly middle-class attitudes, Johnson was a merchant of the High Street, a small man of business who possessed no special claim to social deference or political authority. A grocer by training, Johnson was only sporadically involved in overseas trade, investing in fewer than five such trading ventures in his entire career, all in the mid-1660s and all to Ireland.[176]

However, only a minority of Baly Johnson's colleagues on the Common Council between 1663–1677 were wealthy overseas merchants trading to exotic climes, and most pursued far less exalted, less capital in-tensive, and less prestigious vocations. Within the confines of the Corporation of Liverpool, most Councilors, like Baly Johnson himself, were part of the humble majority of men who dominated Liverpool society until the end of the seventeenth century. While these men were ambitious and eager to make their fortunes, their world extended little further than the counting houses and market stalls of Liverpool.

However as Liverpool grew into a great port, the responsibilities of town government increasingly became the sole prerogative of a wealthy merchant elite that emerged by 1700, many of whom were the descendants of the modest men who had served their community in the preceding decade. This was because town government became both smaller in size and more exclusive in composition, and more devoted to the interests of larger, overseas merchants.[177]

However, a few wealthy merchants already enjoyed a large measure of authority in the Common Council prior to 1700 that was not justified by their small numbers. Power has found that in the 1660s councilors com-posed 3% of the total population of Liverpool, a figure which declined to only 0.7% in the 1700s, and 0.2% in the 1740s, a development that, Power argues, was "intensified" by restrictions imposed by the Whiggish, merchant-friendly Charter of 1695.[178] Prior to 1695, the body of freemen, assembled in the increasingly feeble Port Moot or Assembly of Freemen, retained the right to elect one of the two bailiffs who waited upon the Lord Mayor. While most bailiffs invariably became councilors, before 1695 not all bailiffs were councilors prior to their election. The Charter of 1695 not only reduced membership of the Common Council to 40 from the 60 prescribed in the royalist Charter of 1677, it also provided that only sitting councilors could serve as bailiff or Lord Mayor.[179] While councilors had long been drawn from among town elites, the Charter of 1695 allowed merchants to join forces and dominate the Council for the first time. Less affluent Liverpool freemen were thus denied a voice in town government unless first elevated to the Common Council, an institution that grew smaller and more privileged as the population of Liverpool steadily increased.

Thus, in a relatively short space of time, wealth, status, and political influence enabled Liverpool's merchants to wrest control of the Common Council from their less affluent neighbors. While merchants occupied only 40% of Council seats between 1649 and 1699, this proportion doubled to 82% in the first half of the eighteenth century, or 70% if one omits professionals such as attorneys-at-law, men closely allied to the evolving merchant elite.[180] As the Council became less occupationally after 1700, it increasingly became a self-perpetuating political oligarchy of merchants. This development was probably inevitable after the promulgation of the Charter of 1695. For merchants eager to plumb the connections required to break into transatlantic trade, membership in the Council was an invaluable asset that multiplied possible trading con-nections and thus increased the range of business prospects to eager, would-be investors.

[175]Sir Edward Moore, *The Moore Rental, 1667–1668*, ed., Thomas Heywood (1847), appendix, 143.

[176]Power, "Councillors and Commerce in Liverpool," 305–307.

[177]*ibid*, 309, 320.

[178]Power, 309–310.

[179]Muir, *A History of Liverpool*, 152–172.

[180]Power, "Councillors and Commerce in Liverpool," table 2, 311; Barry Coward, *Social Change and Continuity: England, 1550–1750*, (1997), 64–66.

It is noteworthy that all of Baly Johnson's trading ventures to Ireland took place only after he was admitted to the Common Council in 1659, and his strongly Whiggish opinions and evident leadership abilities aided him in forming personal connections and business contacts with wealthy merchants of like mind, men who regularly traded to Ireland and elsewhere. However, Johnson did not embrace the calling of professional overseas merchant, or turn the business opportunities in transatlantic trade that were available to him into a sustained involvement in overseas trade. Although he became a prominent figure in Liverpool government and society, Johnson remained a small merchant-grocer who lacked the connections, experience, and capital resources to exploit fully the profitable new markets that were then emerging in overseas trade. Johnson's advancing age, traditional trading interests, and intervening political crises, best explain his failure to join his fellow councilors in a head-long pursuit of profit in foreign trade.

After the imposition of an unpopular charter by Charles II in 1677, political issues came to dominate Johnson's attention. Faced with the prospect of a Common Council controlled by Tories and loyal to the King, Johnson refused to take the oath required of councilors in the new charter, and withdrew from the Common Council in protest. Even before he left, however, Johnson had abandoned his small and short-lived Irish trade. It is possible, therefore, that these Irish ventures represented the profitable fruit of close friendships or political relationships between Johnson and his whiggish merchant allies on the Council. After an absence of six years, the Tory majority stymied Johnson's bid for readmission to the council in November 1683. Johnson's fortunes improved after 1689, as William III named him acting-mayor, a position he soon yielded to his son Thomas Johnson Jr.[181] Thus, Johnson's rise in Liverpool politics resulted from his whiggish opinions, abilities, and social connectedness, not from wealth.

Although landowner Sir Edward Moore referred to Baly Johnson as "one of the hardest men [of business] in town," self-interest alone did not motivate him and other early town leaders.[182] Even more than great merchants who controlled the Common Council after 1700, the outlook of these modest town fathers was informed by traditional paternalism and enthusiastic commercialism. After 1695, the commercial ambition of merchants on the Common Council fueled a vast movement to build the docks, wharves, canals, and other facilities deemed necessary to transform Liverpool into a first-rate port. This ambition—a form of patriarchal urban boosterism—was an economic and political constant in Liverpool in the late seventeenth and eighteenth centuries. The traditional town fathers of 1670, and the merchant-patriarchs who dominated town government by 1740, understood the profitable uses of civic self-promotion. Town fathers were comfortable with their unabashed material self-interest, a blatant commercialism that coexisted with their responsibilities as civic leaders. Sanctified by royal charter, urban corporations such as Liverpool's were originally conceived as private bodies whose founding purpose was to promote and regulate commerce, but came to be imbued with numerous public functions over time.[183]

These expanding functions were byproducts of the reigning *ethos* of patriarchalism, a concatenation of paternalistic attitudes and beliefs that shaped the context and structure of English town life before the nineteenth century. Within the larger community of responsible, rate-paying men and women, and their lesser neighbors, councilors fulfilled both practical and symbolic social and political roles. Generally, the "better sort" fulfilled these roles," respected men of wealth and social status within the community. Consequently, Liverpool's Common Councilors, men who emerged from the council's ranks to serve as mayor and bailiff, were widely perceived in Liverpool as the natural masters of town society for the simple reason that they were able—and often willing—to fulfill a vital social role, that of town father. In this respect, they supplanted the former aristocratic elite, many of whom became merchants themselves. Because of the social expectations that often attached to wealth, the role of town father was often thrust, unbidden, upon eminent but middling merchants, tradesmen, and professionals with sufficient leisure time to participate in town affairs.[184]

---

[181]Power, "Councillors and Commerce in Liverpool," 320; Michael Mullett, "The Politics of Liverpool, 1660–88," *Transactions of the Historical Society of Lancashire and Cheshire*, 124 (1972), 55–56.

[182]Sir Edward Moore, *The Moore Rental, 1667–1668*, 47.

[183]Averill Mackenzie-Grieve, *The Last Years of the English Slave Trade: Liverpool, 1750–1807* (1941), 17–35; Halliday, *Dismembering the Body Politic*, 41.

[184]Friedrichs, *Urban Politics in Early Modern Europe*, 18.

Christopher Friedrichs suggests that because municipal office holding was usually unsalaried and voluntary, not all men could afford to serve. Merchants, in particular, had sufficient freedom from the daily grind of work to allow them to hold public office.[185] While many merchants relished the role of town father, and avidly sought office, others did not. Some saw office holding as an inconvenience that distracted them from business, and could not, or would not, spend inordinate amounts of time serving as public officials. England's rising class of overseas merchants increasingly came to possess the financial wherewithal, and the social status, to determine when, or if, they would serve their communities in any political capacity.

Although some merchants chose to opt out of political life, most agreed that deference was owed town leaders by lesser men and women, and, in turn, the men so honored had an obligation to promote the welfare of the town, including in theory, that of its lowliest of inhabitants.[186] In 1702, the oath taken by Liverpool Common Councilmen required that each "shall do [his] reasonable Endeavours from time to time for the furtherance & advancem't of the comon proffit."[187] Although this notion of "common profit" remained essentially patriarchal in meaning at the dawn of the eighteenth century, an important change in emphasis began to transform what it meant to be a Common Councilor in the years that followed, and ultimately the larger purposes of town government. For the Corporation of Leicester in the 1660s, for instance, Paul Halliday maintains that "the 'weale public' was [a] surprisingly…private concern, promoted largely by the corporation's own revenues."[188] Similarly, for Liverpool's merchant-oligarchs after 1700, the primary purpose of public service had to do less with the betterment of the common weal than with commercial development, political power, and private wealth.[189]

In Liverpool, a traditional conception of patriarchal governance still had a strong hold on the mentality of town rulers long after the great merchants rose to power. Claiming full legal powers to "carry out all the services required of an enlightened regime," Liverpool's merchant-patriarchs saw it as their duty not only to encourage the town's trade and regulate commerce, but also to enforce the king's law, hold elections, conduct corporate business, oversee parish affairs, maintain streets, bridges, churches, and other public facilities, and provide charitable relief for the poor when needed.[190] All these undertakings involved duties that had been fully a part of the town father's calling for centuries.[191] Within this *repertoire* of paternal responsibility, providing charity was perhaps the public duty most freighted with patriarchal symbolism. Receiving and answering petitions from the town's desperate poor remained a major responsibility of Liverpool mayors, aldermen, and common councilors for generations. For these merchants, aping a style of lordly leadership practiced by the great landowning aristocrats, the provision of charity was a visible sign of power if not gentility, a symbolic duty that confirmed the place and status of these trading men within the traditional frameworks of society.[192] The 1729 letter of supplication addressed to Lord Mayor Foster Cunliffe, a leading tobacco and slave merchant, by the wife of a local man imprisoned for debt in Lancaster is perhaps typical of the appeals for justice, mercy, or assistance that town fathers often received from less fortunate neighbors.[193] "To the Right Worshipful Foster Cunliffe, Esq., Mayor In Liverpoole," the supplicant wife, Susannah Turner, wrote on December 8, 1729,

[185]Weber, quoted in Friedrichs, *Urban Politics in Early Modern Europe*, 18.

[186]Nicholas Rogers, "The Middling Sort in Eighteenth Century Politics," in *The Middling Sort of People: Culture, Society, and Politics in England, 1550–1800*, eds., Jonathan Barry and Christopher Brooks (1994), 167.

[187]Oath of a Comon Coucellman, 1702, *Liverpool Town Book*, 352 CLE/TRA/2/1/8, Liverpool PRO, Picton Library, Liverpool.

[188]Halliday, 45.

[189]John Brewer, "Commercialization and Politics," in *The Birth of a Consumer Society: The Commercialization of Eighteenth Century England*, ed., Neil McKendrick, John Brewer, and J.H. Plumb, (1982), 197–262.

[190]Paul Langford, *Public Life and Propertied Englishman, 1689–1798*, (1991), 223.

[191]Gordon Schochet, *The Authoritarian Family and Political Attitudes in Seventeenth Century England: Patriarchalism in Political Thought* (1988), 201.

[192]Julian Hoppitt, *A Land of Liberty? England, 1689–1727* (2000), 81.

[193]John W. Tyler, "Foster Cunliffe and Sons: Liverpool Merchants in the Maryland Tobacco Trade, 1738–1765," *Maryland Historical Magazine*, 78 (1978), 249.

May it please your worship, with humble submission [that] I make bold to acquaint your worship that necessity compels me to become…your poor petitioner; this day having received advice from Lancaster that my poor husband is just famished to Death [where] they…keep him [imprisoned]…he is not guilty of any crime whatsoever…and I myself am just lost for want… and left [with] no moneys…which drives me almost to the brink of despair, now I humbly beg that your Worship, for the sake of Almighty God, would be pleased to Send for me…and I will upon my solemn Oath relate unto you the whole cause of …my husband's imprisonment, for I am so [much] in pain in all my limbs through [this] cold and long imprisonment that before I will endure it longer I will put a final end to all my misery; with humble submission I desire your worship with mature deliberation to take pity of me and consider my case, [my husband] having been in prison above three quarters of a year.[194]

Although it is not known how Foster Cunliffe responded to this plea for assistance, Liverpool's merchant-oligarchs were generally sensitive to the plight of the less fortunate, in both their corporate capacities as councilors, and individually as well-meaning benefactors. Pious townsmen, tender fathers, affectionate husbands, and employers and mentors who managed large households of servants and apprentices, town fathers like Foster Cunliffe employed a traditional rhetoric of compassionate paternalism modeled on the felicities of family life.[195] This heart-felt compassion was as much a part of the attitudinal and intellectual clothing of Liverpool's town fathers as was their blood-red robes of office, but even this fatherly sensitivity had its limits.

The number of inhabitants receiving poor relief or assistance directly by act of the Common Council grew significantly between the later seventeenth and early eighteenth centuries.[196] In response, the Common Council ordered the construction of a workhouse in 1731 and an infirmary for the poor in 1744. At the same time, prominent men made bequests to the needy, and sponsored the erection of almshouses. Almshouses appeared on Shaw's Brow in 1682, Dale Street in 1684 and 1724, Hanover Street in 1706, School Lane in 1723.[197] The men who governed Liverpool after 1700 evinced a newfound attitude of *noblesse oblige* when dealing with powerless beggars, servants, sailors, apprentices, and journeymen.[198] "Whereas, it hath been represented to the Worshipful, the Mayor, Aldermen, Bailiffs, and the rest of the Common Council of this Corporation," Lord Mayor Thomas Steers declared in December 1739,

> that Great Numbers of the inhabitants of this town are in great Distress for Want of work which they are deprived of by and thro' the severity of the season, and Reduced to great Misery, and that thro' the Dearness of the Markets, are not able to Subsist themselves and [their] families and must inevitably perish if not timely Relieved and that it hath been proposed by the principal Merchants and inhabitants to contribute thereto and that if a collection be made thro' the town amongst the better sort of the Inhabitants, A competent Relief for such poor miserable persons might be raised and distributed amongst them and that several persons having undertook such Collection and Distribution which this Council taking into consideration

[194]Susannah Turner to Foster Cunliffe, December 8, 1729, *Papers relating to the Mayoralty of Foster Cunliffe, 1729–1731: Petitions to Foster Cunliffe as Mayor from debtors in Prison, 8 December 1729–20 June 1730*, MD72/116, Liverpool PRO, Picton Library, Liverpool.

[195]Christopher Brooks, "Professions, Ideology, and the Middling Sort in the Late Sixteenth and Early Seventeenth Centuries," in *The Middling Sort of People: Culture, Society, and Politics in England, 1550–1800*, eds., Jonathan Barry and Christopher Brooks (1994), 123–5.

[196]Paul Slack, *The English Poor Law, 1531–1782* (1990), 17-26; G.W. Oxley, "The Permanent Poor in South-West Lancashire under the Old Poor Law," in *Liverpool and Merseyside: Essays in the Economic and Social History of the Port and its Hinterland*, ed., J.R. Harris, (1969), 16–49.

[197]George McLoughlin, *A Short History of the Liverpool Infirmary, 1749–1824* (1978), 8–10.

[198]Friedrichs, *Urban Politics in Early Modern Europe* (2000), 19–21, 23.

Doe Agree that the Treasurer Do advance the sum of £50 out of the Corporation stock for and towards such charitable contribution.[199]

In that same month, Steers proposed that the Council fund the construction of houses on wasteland owned by the corporation for the benefit of "poor decayed seamen and such [others] as shall happen to be maimed in the public service."[200] For Liverpool's merchant-oligarchs, trading men whose rise to authority was of recent vintage, such displays of kindly public-mindedness served to establish their *bona fides* as rulers, and demonstrate their practical credentials as town fathers.

However, in Liverpool and other towns of comparable size, the body of respectable men available to uphold the duties of a Common Councilman was exceedingly variable in number, as high mortality rates, commercial and residential transience, and financial reverses whittled away at their numbers.[201] The class-ridden character of the early modern town placed restrictions upon the men who could attend to public business, and not every man was socially acceptable. "[These] day laborers [and] poor husbandmen," Sir Thomas Smith argued in 1583,

> [and] yea merchants or retailers which have no free land, copyholders, all artificers, and tailors, shoemakers, carpenters, brick-makers, bricklayers, masons, Etc. These have no voice nor authorities in our common wealth, and no account is made of these but only to be ruled, not to rule others, and yet they be not altogether neglected. For in cities and corporate towns for default of yeomen, they are faine to make their inquests of such manner of people. And in villages they be commonly made Churchwardens, alecunners, and many times constables.[202]

Participation in civic affairs by socially and politically available men could be extremely sporadic and infrequent, and only a few men were actively involved in everyday town business in any given year. The charters and by-laws of many towns required suitable men to serve on the council and share the responsibilities of governance, to attend the mayor or his deputy upon lawful summons, and provided fines for those who refused to serve or attend.[203] To town fathers such as Richard Gildart, holding Council sessions was deemed a "great necessity…in order to dispatch the publick & necessary Business of the…Burrough, which without a sufficient Number [of councilors] canot be held & that it often happens [that] such number [of councilors] canot be gott to attend in councill."[204] Those who did serve, however, did not allow differences of political opinion to divide them when issues of importance to the town's trade were contested. Despite the "rage of party" which periodically afflicted Liverpool between 1694 and 1740, its merchant-politicians were notable for their willingness and ability to put aside differences, political or otherwise, when mutual interest, and the possibility of common profit, required.

Regardless of their place of birth, many merchants expressed exasperation over the amount of time that public service often consumed. Jasper Maudit (1634–1714), an attorney and merchant from Devonshire who served as Lord Mayor in 1693 and as a Member of Parliament for Liverpool between 1689 and 1698, complained in 1700 that he had spent forty weeks "absent from my [private] concerns in the service of the town."[205] John Cockshutt, prominent Whig politician and Lord Mayor in 1702, was equally loath to spend any more time in the service of the town than was necessary. However, he saw no reason why other merchants should not bear the burdens of office in his stead. In October 1703, the Whig-dominated Common Council,

---

[199]Order of Thomas Steers, Esq., Mayor, December 10, 1739, *Extracts from Liverpool Town Books, 1727–1755*, 352 CLE/TRA 2/1/9, Liverpool PRO, Picton Library, Liverpool.

[200]Order of Thomas Steers, December 10, 1739, *Extracts from Liverpool Town Books, 1727–1755*, 352 CLE/TRA 2/1/9.

[201]Clark and Slack, *English Towns in Transition*, 117–118.

[202]Sir Thomas Smith, *De Republica Anglorum*, quoted in Halliday, *Dismembering the Body Politic*, 77.

[203]*ibid*, 77.

[204]Order of Richard Gildart, Esq., Mayor, October 18, 1731, in *Extracts from the Liverpool Town Book, 1727–1755*, vol. 9., 352 CLE/TRA 2/1/9, 48, Liverpool PRO, Picton Library, Liverpool.

[205]Perry Gauci, *The Politics of Trade: The Overseas Merchant in State and Society, 1660–1720* (2001), 152.

with Mayor Cockshutt at its head, elevated three Tory merchants—John Cleveland, William Hurst, and John Earle—as members. Although the three were normally associates of the Tory magnate William Clayton, they were temporarily allied to the Whig leader Thomas Johnson Jr. While selection to the Common Council was much sought after, an honor and a great mark of distinction, all three refused to serve, but not for partisan political reasons. "Now we do resolve to Elect Mr. Cleaveland, Mayor [and] Mr. Earl, one Bailiff," Mayor Cockshutt's ally Thomas Johnson Jr. advised former Whig mayor Richard Norris of Speke, "and if they refuse us…they may be indicted, and [there] after fined, or a *Mandamus* brought against them to show cause."[206] Arguing that allowing anyone to refuse service on the Common Council, or as mayor or bailiff, would bring shame and discredit upon the council, and diminish the town's limited reserve of political leadership, Johnson and Cockshutt were prepared to make examples of the recalcitrant Cleveland and his Tory associates. Among the leaders of Liverpool's political community, it was generally accepted that the many burdens of office shouldered by "Mr. Mayor" and other town leaders should be evenly distributed among Liverpool's merchant elite, regardless of political affiliation. It was feared, particularly within Liverpool's dominant Whig faction, that if such a refusal to serve went unpunished, many prominent men, Whigs included, would opt out of public service altogether. Thomas Johnson felt confident that his ally Mayor John Cockshutt would continue in office if necessary, if "we make a return of this election."[207] However, Cockshutt was concerned about the effects that a delay in selecting his successor would have upon his business interests, and informed Richard Norris that he would not stand for re-election, "for I fear [I] shall be continued [as] Mayor."[208]

Mercantile success bore a price in communal expectation. Wealthy Liverpool merchants were expected to serve the community in which he lived and/or prospered. Once he became well-established within the local fraternity of merchants, the affluent Liverpool trader was frequently pressured to assume the public duties required by wealth and rank within the tradition-bound urban polities of late Stuart England.[209] In London and York it was possible to avoid holding public office by the payment of a hefty fine, which, in the case of London, became a valued source of income for the perpetually strapped city.[210] In London fines could reach several hundred pounds, but in Liverpool they were generally much less. In 1710, Mayor George Tyrer ordered that James Halsall, a merchant who had refused to serve in the minor office of sub-bailiff, be fined £10.[211] Regardless of their desire to serve, holding office was, for most Liverpool merchants, a small price to pay, for the profits to be made in Liverpool's expansive transatlantic trade far outweighed the possible inconveniences that might encountered in public office. Masters of civic promotion, the merchant town fathers of Liverpool also had no desire to taint the town's welcoming reputation, or to place obstacles in the way of any merchant wishing to relocate to Liverpool, and relatively few men were ever prosecuted and forced to hold office against their will.

Perhaps the greatest sin of Cleveland, Earle, and Hurst, however, was that their refusal to hold office threatened to disturb the carefully cultivated solidarity that joined together Whigs and Tories in the common cause of Liverpool trade. As Power suggests, the commercial ties that drew Liverpool's merchant community together, "usually loomed larger than political differences."[212] Tory stalwarts such as William Clayton and John Cleveland understood that all roads to political preferment led to Thomas Johnson and the Whigs, and both eventually succumbed to Whig political blandishments and temporarily left the Tory faction. As Johnson warned his fellow councilors in 1703, the importance of trade to the future prosperity of Liverpool required that "we must not be [so] angry with one another that we differ in judgment."[213] However, this preference

---

[206]Thomas Johnson Jr. to Richard Norris, Liverpool, October 15, 1703, *The Norris Papers*, ed., Thomas Heywood, in *Remains Historical and Literary Connected with the Palatine Counties of Lancaster and Chester*, vol. 9, (1846), 131.

[207]Thomas Johnson Jr. to Richard Norris, October 15, 1703, *The Norris Papers*, 131.

[208]John Cockshutt to Richard Norris, October 15, 1703, *The Norris Papers*, 132.

[209]Gauci, 95; Richard Wunderli, "Evasion of the Office of Alderman in London, 1523–1672," *London Journal* 15 (1990), 11-5.

[210]Joan Kirby, "Restoration Leeds and the Aldermen of the Corporation, 1661–1700," *Northern History*, 22 (1986), 138–9; Richard Wunderli, "Evasion of the Office of Alderman in London," 10–13.

[211]Order of George Tyrer, Esq., Mayor of Liverpool, October 1710, *Corporation Minute Books*, MF2/2-5.

[212]Power, "Politics and Progress," 133.

[213]Power, 133.

for easy commercial relationships among partisans may have only partly been a conscious choice. Power suggests that the ability of Liverpool merchants to avoid the partisan rancor that afflicted many other English towns in the later seventeenth and early eighteenth centuries arose from the fact that the victory of the Whigs in 1695 had not created a "monolithic Whig establishment...and High and Low church parties existed in Liverpool as they existed elsewhere."[214] Johnson and the Whigs feared that imposing a litmus test of political and religious orthodoxy would affect trade adversely. They understood that influential Tories such as Clayton and Cleveland were effective spokespersons for Liverpool trade in Westminster. Whatever their religious or political stripe, the talents of such men could not be denied the town.[215]

Johnson's self-interested collegiality and enforced *bonhomie*, and more importantly the evident desire of a large segment of Liverpool's merchant community to paper over partisan political differences, frequently extended to business relationships. More specifically, this influenced the composition of business partnerships. While it cannot be said that partisan affiliation had no influence, other factors were of equal or greater importance. In the Liverpool slave trade between 1695 and 1775, varying patterns of kinship, friendship, and even religious affiliation were more important.[216] Partnerships formed among Liverpool slave merchants before 1750, were often limited in membership to a select group of handpicked familiars, men who tended to be relatives, business associates, and co-religionists, but not necessarily political *confreres*. Throughout this period, religious and political commonalities between groups of merchants had an inconsistent influence upon the formation of partnerships, as purely commercial considerations more often took precedence. For instance, while the Tory political allies John Cleveland and John Earle partnered in the slave ship *Peace* in 1714, Cleveland and his Whig rival Richard Gildart were co-investors in the slaver *Elizabeth* in the same year.[217]

The changing nature of the African trade influenced the formation of partnerships as well. Although family ties remained the most important factor in the formation of Liverpool slave trading partnerships throughout the eighteenth century, the expansion and changing character of the West African slave trade after 1730 greatly increased the capital requirements of slaving. In part, this was a result of the shifting *locus* of the Liverpool slave trade southwestward towards the greater volume and higher cost slave ports of the Bight of Biafra.[218] For many potential merchant-investors, the resultant increase in capital costs raised a substantial bar to entry in the slave trade, while, for others, it inspired a regular search for partners and credit outside their normal circles of commercial association. A burgeoning volume of credit was extended by the producers and purveyors of African trade goods to subsidize the sale of these items, thus providing the capital necessary for roughly half of the African cargoes purchased by Liverpool slave merchants after 1750.[219] Some of these lenders were motivated solely by market factors in advancing a greater volume of credit, while others simply increased the volume of credit they were already lending to relatives and other close associates. As a result, the growth in available credit had the contradictory effect of making family and personal trade connections more important for some regular Liverpool slave traders, at least through the 1760s, and less important for others. "As a merchant's fortune grew," Kenneth Morgan observes, "he found it easier...to borrow from outside his family [and his] ability to borrow ever larger sums of money [was] a measure of [his] advancement in the world."[220] While the ties of family and friendship supported the ventures undertaken by most Liverpool slave traders before 1740, for many other small investors with fewer such valuable family connections, the speculative impulse at the heart of Liverpool's expanding slave trade called forth the support of willing investors.

---

[214]*ibid*, 130.

[215]Gauci, *The Politics of Trade*, 152–155; Power, "Politics and Progress...," 132.

[216]*TSTD*.

[217]*TSTD*.

[218]David Richardson, "Slave Exports from West and West-Central Africa, 1700–1810: New Estimates of Volume and Distribution," *Journal of African History*, 30 (1989), 11–22.

[219]David Richardson, "Profits in the Liverpool Slave Trade: The Accounts of William Davenport," in *Liverpool, the African Slave Trade, and Abolition*, eds., Roger Anstey and P.E.H. Hair (1976), 72.

[220]Kenneth Morgan, *Slavery, Atlantic Trade, and the British Economy*, 79

After 1700, the expansion of Liverpool commerce attracted new men of trade to Merseyside. However, many these men were not bred as sons of Liverpool, and had little interest in the traditional structure of town society. These men did not come to Liverpool to become town fathers, but rather to make a fortune in trade. Moreover, the requirement that men of trade become freemen of the Corporation of Liverpool before they would be permitted to trade was enforced less and less frequently after the mid-eighteenth century, gradually becoming a virtual dead letter by 1775. Nevertheless, freeman status remained a legal requirement for trade for much of the eighteenth century, and comprised a normal first step in the pursuit of status and power. Attitudes towards office-holding within the merchant community changed over the course of the eighteenth century as the merchant oligarchy became ever more deeply entrenched in control of the Corporation of Liverpool. By 1750 and after, many of Liverpool's greatest merchants viewed freeman status, and hold-ing office, as a much prized honor. This, however, was not shared by all great merchants. While many of Liverpool's great merchants saw themselves as gentlemen and natural leaders, many simply went about their business with little thought of politics or office holding, devoting themselves to everyday concerns and the singular acquisition of wealth. Thus, by the 1750s - if not earlier - many great merchants no longer felt com-pelled to enter upon a life of public service simply because they were commercially successful, nor were all Liverpool merchants preoccupied with political aspirations or the accumulation of social prestige. Between 1660 and 1730, expectant merchants, mariners, and manufacturers continued to migrate to Merseyside from throughout the British Isles, although Liverpool was still a rough, provincial backwater, an overgrown vil-lage lacking the full range of trading opportunities that a merchant could find in London or Bristol. What Liverpool did have, many merchants understood, was a future. In Liverpool, commercial opportunities were available to non-freemen that were unavailable elsewhere. It was the relative openness of Liverpool trade to outsiders that attracted young men like John Earle, as well as older, more experienced traders, to Merseyside in the first place.[221] As Liverpool grew apace, what it meant to be a town father changed, as did the perception of the social obligations that prosperous merchants owed society. After 1750, Liverpool merchants, and their heirs, continued to assay the role of civic patriarch, but did so in a far more superficial manner that reflected the fact that the promotion of overseas commerce had largely supplanted the preservation of older notions of patriarchal leadership - ideas rooted in English social memory and the Old Testament - as a guiding principle of public governance.[222] Commerce became the *leitmotif* of town government, a common interest of Liverpool's merchant governors which promised to make their town an important and prosperous mart to the world.[223]

VI

Increasingly, men of wealth opted out of public life with little fear of retribution. A host of demographic, social, and political developments after 1750 also made it more difficult for merchants to fulfill older notions of the social obligations of wealth. After 1750, the merchant community of Liverpool expanded at the same time that political power was becoming more tightly held within an ever-smaller cadre of inbred, merchant elites. Many of the new merchants doing business in Liverpool after 1750 were considered outsiders by the port's evolving merchant elite, and were denied a political role by an increasingly exclusive Common Council that was jealous of its official and ceremonial prerogatives. This was acceptable to many outsiders who wished only to invest in Liverpool trade, without assuming a prescribed social or political role. Although the old aristocratic political order of Liverpool had been overturned in the seventeenth century, after 1700 a nascent commercial oligarchy arose in its stead. By the mid-eighteenth century, this narrow merchant oligarchy had become disconnected from the average run of Liverpool traders, as social position came to reflect birth and not necessarily wealth.

---

[221]Gauci, 95, Estabrook, 110–12.

[222]Gordon Schochet, *The Authoritarian Family and Political Attitudes in Seventeenth Century England: Patriarchalism in Political Thought,* (1988), 6–7, 117.

[223]John Brewer, "Commercialization and Politics," in *The Birth of a Consumer Society,* 197–262.

Chapter 3

The Most Intimate Bonds

A siren call of possibility, the promise of wealth and security drew John Earle to Liverpool. The opportunities that had opened up in transatlantic trade after the Restoration attracted growing numbers of merchants and migrants to upstart Liverpool.[224] Earle arrived at a town whose merchants derived from diverse backgrounds. His experience as a merchant-apprentice in the last decade of the seventeenth century illustrates that, though declining, traditional methods of apprenticeship continued to play an important role in the business life of the merchant. Kinship, marriage, friendship, as well as the fraternal relationships forged during long years of apprenticeship, all influenced the shape and pattern of the commercial partnerships available in the eighteenth-century Liverpool slave trade.[225] Most young migrants were solitary figures apprenticed to complete strangers, and, although towns and cities were full of masters and apprentices, admission into the trained labor force was no "assurance of widespread social interaction."[226] While some were blessed by ties of kith and kin that aided their entry into the African trade, apprentices like Earle, and others who lacked such ties of blood, had first to establish a reputation for competence and fair-dealing, find well-connected partners, and then build a network of regular commercial relationships before *bona fide* opportunities became routinely available.[227] While the leap from poor apprentice to wealthy merchant was more than many young men could ever hope to make alone, some sons of the English countryside were better placed to succeed in the urban sprawl that was eighteenth century Liverpool than were others. This chapter will examine the ways in which young migrants from diverse backgrounds established themselves as merchants in Liverpool after 1660. The first section will deal with the importance of apprenticeship as an entry point into the world of trade for would-be merchants. Later sections will look at other connections that provided *entrée* for migrants, such as kinship, religious affiliation, and business friendship, and how apprenticeship complemented these ties.

---

[224]Perry Gauci, *The Politics of Trade: The Overseas Merchant in State and Society, 1660–1720*, (2001), 14; Paul Clemens, "The Rise of Liverpool, 1665–1750," *Economic History Review* 29 (1976), 212–13.

[225]Peter Mathias, "Risk, Credit, and Kinship in Early Modern Enterprise," in *The Early Modern Atlantic Economy*, eds., John McCusker and Kenneth Morgan (2000), 18–19.

[226]Carl Estabrook, *Urbane and Rustic England: Cultural Ties and Social Spheres in the Provinces, 1660–1780* (1998), 110.

[227]Peter Clark and Paul Slack, *English Towns in Transition, 1500–1700* (1976), 14f.

I

The rising tide of internal migration in seventeenth-century England was spurred both by intense rural poverty and by the commercial ambitions of a more affluent middling sort. The common poor of many English towns and villages, whom local authorities were often glad to be rid of, departed meager village homes in ever-greater numbers after 1600 for London, the larger provincial centers of trade and industry, and the New World. Before the merchants and mariners of Liverpool discovered the profitability of the African slave trade in the first decades of the eighteenth century, 28 Liverpool ships are known to have transported indentured servants to North America between 1697 and 1707.[228] Many servants did not leave voluntarily, however, and the crown, as well as many urban corporations, sought to end the criminal practice of "Inveigling, purloining, carrying and Stealing away Boys, Maidens and other persons and transporting them beyond Seas and there selling or otherwise disposing of them for private gaine and profitt."[229] Town fathers commonly employed such brutal tactics when it was adjudged expedient or convenient. In 1648, perhaps under pressure from rate paying townsmen, the Liverpool Common Council gathered all the beggars and poor children it could find on the streets, and forcibly shipped them to Barbados.[230]

In the case of John Earle, however, poverty and a lack of prospects did not compel him to leave home at an early age, nor was his Lancashire birthplace a declining community bereft of opportunity for a middling young man. Had Earle followed in the footsteps of his father, brewer John Earle Sr. (1627–1709), and remained in Warrington, he would have achieved a modicum of success as a brewer, grocer, or small merchant, and perhaps a great deal more. Rising in the world meant leaving home in search of opportunity, marriage, and a secure future. For John Earle's family this search for opportunity was not new. Originally from Cheshire, the Earle family had lived in Warrington for more than 60 years by 1688, and the younger John Earle was the second generation of the family to call Lancashire home.[231] His father, John Earle Sr., was the son of Gregory Earle (1600–1650) of Stockton, Cheshire, who moved to Warrington as a young man, probably as an apprentice to a Warrington tradesman, merchant, brewer, or grocer.[232] At the outset of the seventeenth century, the busy markets of Warrington offered the young Gregory Earle the alluring promise of wealth and social distinction. Some half-century later, the growing port of Liverpool held a similar promise of fame and fortune for Gregory Earle's grandson.

"Large, populous, [and] old built," Warrington was an important crossroads town of modest standing long before the rise of Liverpool as an overseas port.[233] Site of a strategically important bridge across the upper Mersey River, Warrington was situated less than twenty miles upriver from Liverpool near the northern frontier of Cheshire. "Full of country tradesmen," it was a prosperous market town, the location of a regional trade fair that dated back to the thirteenth-century.[234] As Daniel Defoe noted in the 1720s, Warrington was especially renowned as the site of notable markets for flannel and linen, where "there are…as many pieces

---

[228]Doreen M. Hockedy, "Bound for a New World: Emigration of Indentured Servants Via Liverpool to America and the West Indies, 1697–1707," *THSLC* 144 (1995), 130; Farley Grubb and Tony Stitt, "The Liverpool Emigrant Servant Trade and the Transition to Slave Labor in the Chesapeake, 1697–1707: Market Adjustments to War," *Explorations in Economic History* 31 (1994), 376–405; Marianne S. Wokeck, *Trade in Strangers: The Beginnings of Mass Migration to North America* (1999).

[229]Bristol City Archives, Tolzey Book, frontispiece of emigrant lists, 29, Sept. 1654; quoted in Hockedy, "Bound for a New World," 120.

[230]George Chandler, *Liverpool under Charles I* (1965), 411–412.

[231]T. Algernon Earle, "Earle of Allerton Tower," *The Transactions of the Historical Society of Lancashire and Cheshire*, 42 (1890), 35f; *See also*: Gordon Reed, *Introduction to the Earle Collection*, D/EARLE/1, Merseyside Maritime Museum, Liverpool.

[232]In her article on the Earle Papers, Dawn Littler suggests that before John Earle left Warrington in 1688 the Earle family "had been resident in south Lancashire for four centuries." Littler, "The Earle Collection: Records of a Liverpool Family of Merchants and Shipowners," *Transactions of the Historical Society of Lancashire and Cheshire* 146 (1996), 94; T. A. Earle, "Earle of Allerton Tower," 35f.

[233]Daniel Defoe, *A Tour Through The Whole Island of Great Britain* (1724–6) ed., Pat Rogers (1978), 544.

[234]Defoe, *A Tour Through The Whole Island of Great Britain*, 544.

of…linen sold…every market day as amounts to £500 value, sometimes much more, and all made in the neighborhood of the place."[235] While the commercial rise of Liverpool in the century after 1660 was more visible than that of Warrington, or the host of other "mere villages" in the English Midlands and Northwest, this expansion was not *sui generis*.[236] In an extensive hinterland that encompassed much of Northern England, Liverpool's rise fueled an explosion of economic development in large and small towns alike. For regionally minded merchants in Chester, Leeds, Birmingham, and Manchester, Liverpool now provided an indispensable outlet to local, national, and world markets not only for their own local goods, but also for the products of Lancashire, Cheshire, the Midlands, North Wales, Yorkshire, and Staffordshire in which they dealt. Specifically, the emergence of Liverpool quickened the economic life of Warrington, calling forth latent entrepreneurial energies which benefited new industries such as the production of canvas sacking and sailcloth, pins, hinges, and other metalware, and later copper goods. As was the case in other English towns, Defoe remarked, this rapid economic growth was fast changing the face of Warrington by the turn of the eighteenth century. "Let the Curious examine," Defoe observed in 1728,

> the great Towns of *Manchester, Warrington, Macclesfield, Hallifax, Leeds, Wakefield, Sheffield, Birmingham, Froom, Taunton, Tiverton*, and many Others, Some of these are mere Villages; the highest magistrate in them is a Constable, and few or no Families of Gentry among them; yet they are full of Wealth, and full of People, and daily increasing in both; all of which is occasioned by the mere Strength of Trade, and the growing Manufactures established in them.[237]

Despite this widespread urban growth, Liverpool's emergence as an international port monopolized public attention and overshadowed the very real growth in manufacturing and commerce that was altering life in neighboring small towns.

Warrington could not contain the expansive commercial ambitions of upwardly mobile provincial apprentices like John Earle. Often strangers with little in their pockets, expectant but penniless apprentices were a common feature of late seventeenth-century Liverpool. The most unfortunate apprentices were little more than charity cases, orphans in need of bed, board, and schooling. Motivated in part by a desire to be rid of their expensive charges, parish officials in coastal towns like Liverpool often apprenticed orphaned and pauper children in the most likely maritime trades.[238] Parliamentary legislation in 1704 gave local Overseers of the Poor the power to apprentice any pauper boy over 10 years of age to the sea until he reached 21 years of age, and masters of ships were obliged to take these boys, or pay a penalty of £10 for refusal.[239] In November 1716, the overseers of the poor of West Derby village apprenticed eleven year old Michael Grigson to Liverpool merchant Thomas Dale "for tenn yeares…till he be 21 ys of age."[240] By the mid-eighteenth century, apprenticeship was increasingly associated with poor children, who generally benefited far less from the experience than the sons of wealthy merchants and professionals.[241]

---

[235]Defoe, 544.

[236]*ibid.*

[237]Daniel Defoe, *A Tour Through England & Wales,* quoted in Penelope Corfield, *The Impact of English Towns, 1700–1800* (1982) 23.

[238]E.G. Thomas: "The Old Poor Law and Maritime Apprenticeship," *Mariner's Mirror* 63 (1977),153. Thomas notes that by the terms of the *Settlement Act of 1662* this was the accepted way for an apprentice to establish residence, which was a further incentive for parish officials to apprentice orphans and paupers outside their parish. In the case of apprenticeships at sea, it was the parish in which a ship was registered which became the parish of settlement. (154)

[239]E.G. Thomas: "*The Old Poor Law and Maritime Apprenticeship,*" 154

[240]Indenture of Michael Grigson or Gregson, A poor child of West Darby, November 21, 1716, *Apprenticeship Enrollment Book,* 352/CLE/REG/4/1, Liverpool PRO, Picton Library, Liverpool.

[241]Christopher Brooks, "Apprenticeship, Social Mobility, and the Middling Sort, 1550–1800," in Jonathan Barry and Christopher Brooks, eds., *Middling Sort of People: Culture, Society, and Politics in England, 1550–1800* (1994), 68; E.G. Thomas, "The Old Poor Law and Maritime Apprenticeship," 153. First conceived in the Tudor Poor Laws of the sixteenth century, Thomas notes that the practice

Other apprentices were more fortunate, and could rely upon wealth and family business connections to establish themselves as merchants, professionals, artisans, or tradesmen. Those not similarly blessed were forced to assemble, if they could, a personal network of commercial and political connections *de novo*.[242] A Liverpool apprenticeship had advantages over those to be found in the English metropolis, such as, for example, a relative lack of guild regulations. In London, it was necessary for a merchant to become a member of a guild before he could be admitted as a freeman of the city, a requirement for taking up trade.[243] A powerful force in metropolitan commerce and society for centuries, restrictive guilds made it difficult for provincial migrants to establish themselves in London trade. By 1700, however, the authority of these medieval holdovers, which varied throughout England, was on the wane nationally. "[While] trade guilds survived the Reformation," Peter Clark observes,

> and retained significant social functions…they were increasingly regulated by…town authorities, and their social ambit narrowed with the growing dominance of leading masters, marginalizing ordinary members from the social and cultural life of guilds. After 1700 they were in decline in many English towns.[244]

Thus, for a provincial apprentice setting up in business in Liverpool was less difficult than setting up in London, because it required far fewer financial resources.

Whether in London or Liverpool, an apprentice had to be "just as careful to cultivate contacts both at home and abroad in order to make his way in the business world."[245] The apprenticeship itself provided a useful venue for forming commercial contacts, preparing a new merchant for the next phase of life, freeman status, partnership, and marriage. It was necessary to be a freeman to trade in Liverpool, and legal presentments continued to be made against offending merchants "for exerciseing their respective Trades… within this Corporation not being free."[246] In addition to conferring the right to trade in Liverpool, freeman status held enormous symbolic importance as well. Emblematic of a merchant's coming of age, admission to the freedom of the town was perceived as a necessary first step towards wealth, status, and political office. However, obtaining freeman status was more a *pro forma* legal requirement than a guarantee of success. In both London and Liverpool, merchants understood that getting ahead in the world of trade was frequently a result of not only admission to freedom status, commercial judgment, financial resources, and favorable kinship ties, but also the friendships formed in their youth as apprentices and later as active men of trade.

Migrants like John Earle who lacked kin in Liverpool often turned to close friendships or propitious marriages in order to establish themselves as merchants. Better-connected friends, especially former masters, often provided novice merchants with the access they needed at the tentative beginnings of a mercantile career. In an occupational sense, such associations compensated a former apprentice for a shortage of kin in town. John Earle received some degree of financial and moral support from his family in Warrington, but they

---

of apprenticing poor boys at the expense of the parish was "viewed…as the best method to prepare poor children [for work] with a reasonable means of earning a living, thus avoiding one source of poverty."

[242]Peter Borsay, "The London Connection: Cultural Diffusion and the Eighteenth Century Provincial," *London Journal* 19 (1994), 24; Susan Whyman, "Land and Trade: The Case of John Verney, London Merchant and Baronet, 1660–1720," *London Journal* 22 (1997), 19–21. *See also*: Susan Whyman, *Sociability and Power in Late-Stuart England: The Cultural Worlds of the Verneys, 1660–1720* (1999).

[243]Rosemary Sweet, *The English Town, 1680–1840: Government, Society and Culture* (1999), 37–39; Penelope Corfield, 86–90; Charles Phythian-Adams, "Ceremony and the Citizen: The Communal Year at Coventry, 1450–1550," in *The Early Modern Town*, ed., Peter Clark (1976), 106–128. *See also*: Ronald Hutton, *The Rise and Fall of Merry England: The Ritual Year, 1400–1700* (1994).

[244]Peter Clark, *British Clubs and Societies, 1580–1800: The Origins of an Associational World* (2000), 35; J.A. Sharpe, *Early Modern England, A Social History, 1550–1760* (1987), 88.

[245]Gauci, *The Politics of Trade*, 95.

[246]Order of John Earle, Esq., Mayor of Liverpool, October 1709, *Corporation Minute Books*, MF2/2–5.

were not in a position to aid him in the incestuous world of Liverpool commerce at the end of the seventeenth century. "Modest capital and…personal connections," Peter Mathias says,

> were usually preconditions for success and overcoming the initial risks of establishing a business, [risks] minimized by following one's father in trade, or being introduced into a partnership by patrimony. Access to a prosperous business…career depended greatly upon family wealth and connections, despite well-published individual instances to the contrary. [247]

John Earle had chosen not to follow his father's trade, or even to take advantage of the older Earle's commercial patrimony. For Earle, leaving the safety of Warrington for the uncertainties of Liverpool was not only an act of hope and courage, it was a demonstration of a conviction that he could succeed in a world of privileged merchant families.

II

Before the rise of the slave trade, Liverpool commerce was already very much a family affair in which kinship connections played an important role in the social construction of partnerships. Similarly, as David Richardson notes, in the Bristol slave trade the sons of merchants enjoyed clear advantages in establishing themselves, since they were "born into established commercial networks" and were better positioned to follow their fathers into the trade.[248] Correspondingly, the important Clayton family connection in Liverpool demonstrated that the intermarriage of merchant families often served to expand a novice merchant's network of commercial contacts many-fold. However, this was not always the case with all connections formed with mighty trading families. Important Liverpool merchant families were often composed of large, loosely connected clusters of distantly related kin, families whose subaltern branches often varied greatly in wealth and social stature from other, more privileged branches. In some cases, these lesser branches were still deeply involved in far less prestigious occupational pursuits than their wealthier kin. In the early eighteenth century, branches of the Williamson, Tarleton, Parr, Seel, Aspinall, Shaw, Gregson, and other well-known merchant families, were still engaged in honest but less esteemed work.[249] Moreover, the wealth and status of many leading families was of recent vintage, and unlike the eastern port of Hull, where, few "men… made good from nothing," rags-to-riches stories were not uncommon in Liverpool.[250] Marrying into a wealthy family with a wide experience of trade was undoubtedly the preference of most new merchants, but perhaps it was easier to add an impressive name to the family tree. A struggling young merchant who could claim a connection to a branch of a great merchant family such as the Claytons or Tarletons, no matter how tenuous the link, had a better chance of gaining access to the inner circle of the merchant elite than men who lacked

---

[247]Mathias, "Risk, Credit, and Kinship in Early Modern Enterprise," 17.

[248]David Richardson, *The Bristol Slave Traders: A Collective Portrait* (1985), 23

[249]Averill Mackenzie-Grieve, *The Last Years of the English Slave Trade*, (1941), 20–21.

[250]Gordon Jackson, *The Trade and Shipping of Eighteenth Century Hull* (1975), 40–41. A particularly well-known rags-to-riches story in Liverpool involves the slave trader Captain William Boates (1716–1794). Although the origins of "Billy Boats" were legendary in eighteenth century Liverpool, the circumstances of his birth were actually quite commonplace. In his classic study, Gomer Williams noted that "the story of Captain Boates is a strange one [and] his real name will never be known, as he was a waif, found in a boat, hence the peculiar surname." Gomer Williams suggests that the orphaned Boates was "brought up by the person who found him, placed in the Blue Coat School…and afterwards [was] apprenticed to the sea," later rising to become the commander of slave ships and becoming "one of the leading merchants and ship owners of Liverpool." The record, however, reveals that William Boates was the son of James Boates, and was christened on September 11, 1716 at St. Nicholas, Liverpool. In about 1760, Boates married Elizabeth Bridson, daughter of Paul Bridson (1694–1772), merchant and Collector of Custom's at Douglas, Isle of Man. Gomer Williams, *History of the Liverpool Privateers and Letters of Marque with an Account of the Liverpool Slave Trade* (1897), 484–5; *International Genealogical Index*, Derek Jarrett, *England in the Age of Hogarth* (1986), 88–92; Kathleen Wilson, *The Sense of the People: Politics, Culture and Imperialism, 1715–1785* (1995), 3–26, 315–75.

Table 3.1   *A Sample of Family Relationships in the Liverpool Slave Trade*

Name of Slave Trader	Type of Relationships
1. Foster Cunliffe, Ellis Cunliffe, Robert Cunliffe	*Father-Son*
2. Charles Pole I, Wm. Pole I, Charles Pole II, Wm. Pole II *(Charles Pole I was the son-in-law of Foster Cunliffe)*	*Brothers, Father-Son* *Nephew-Uncle*
3. Richard Gildart I, Thomas Gildart, Johnson Gildart, Richard Gildart II, George Gildart, Christopher Whytell, James Gildart I, James Gildart II, Spencer Steers	*Father-Son, Sons-in-law, Grandson, Nephew-Uncle, Brothers-in-law*
4. Samuel Ogden, Edmund Ogden, Arthur Heywood, Benjamin Heywood	*Father-Son, Son-in-law Brothers, Brothers-in-law*
5. Captain Thomas Tarleton, Captain John Tarleton, John Tarleton Sr., John Tarleton Jr., Edward Falkner	*Brothers, Son, Son-in-law, Nephew-Uncle, Cousins*
6. John Earle, Captain William Earle, Ralph Earle, Thomas Earle, William Earle Jr., Thomas Earle, Captain John Copeland	*Father-son, Brothers, Grandson, Brothers-in-law*
7. James Crosbie, Captain John Crosbie, William Crosbie I, William Crosbie II	*Father-son, Brothers, Nephew-Uncle, Grandson*
8. Henry Trafford, Edward Trafford, Richard Trafford, William Trafford, Henry Trafford	*Brothers, Father-Son, Nephew Uncle*
9. Captain Bryan Blundell I, Jonathan Blundell, Bryan Blundell II, William Blundell, Richard Blundell, Samuel Shaw I, John Shaw, Christopher Shaw, Samuel Shaw II	*Father-Son, Brothers, Cousins*
10. Samuel Powell, Richard Powell, Folliott Powell, John Powell	*Father-Son, Brothers*
11. Alexander Nottingham I, Alexander Nottingham II, James Bryning	*Father-Son, Cousins, Nephew-Uncle*
12. John Goad, Christopher Hassell	*Father, Son-in-law*
13. George Campbell I, Captain George Campbell II	*Father-Son*
14. Thomas Lake, Richard Lake, William C. Lake	*Brothers*
15. Thomas Galley, John Galley	*Brothers*
16. John Touchet, Peter Touchet, Samuel Touchet, Thomas Touchet	*Brothers*
17. Thomas Newbould I, Thomas Newbould II	*Father-Son*
18. Captains John Simmons I, John Simmons II	*Father-Son*
19. Captains Thomas Kewley, Philip Kewley, William Kewley	*Father-Son, Brothers*
20. Thomas Clare, Joseph Clare, Captain John Clare	*Brothers*
21. Captain William Ford, Matthew Ford	*Brothers*
22. Captain Patrick Black, Robert Black	*Brothers*
23. Thomas Crook, Nicholas Crook	*Brothers*
24. Captain Michael Finch, Hugh Cosnahan	*Brothers-in-law*
25. Clayton Case, Thomas Case	*Brothers*
26. John Hodgson, Thomas Hodgson Jr.	*Brothers*
27. Roger Fisher, John Fisher, Peter Hunt	*Father-Son, Son-in-law, Brothers-in-law*
28. Francis Ingram, William Ingram	*Brothers*
29. John Penketh, William Penketh	*Brothers*

Table 3.1   *A Sample of Family Relationships in the Liverpool Slave Trade (Continued)*

Name of Slave Trader	Type of Relationships
30. Owen Pritchard, John Pritchard	*Father-Son*
31. Edmund Rigby, John Rigby, Peter Rigby	*Father-Son*
32. Miles Barber, Miles Barber Jr.	*Cousins*

such *entrée*.[251] Ubiquity and complexity characterized the connections between elite merchant families in the late seventeenth and eighteenth centuries. Intermarriage in the generations before and during the rise of Liverpool resulted in the formation of a dense cousinhood of merchants, a tight network of related traders who generally shared a common social status and knew each other well, and whose close family relationships greatly influenced both the configuration of partnerships and the everyday conduct of trade.[252] In Liverpool a select few merchant families prospered together, intermarried, and generally dominated social and political life between the 1660s and 1740s.[253]

A few family networks emerged in the seventeenth century that were especially extended, overlapping, and influential. The following list demonstrates the complexity of these networks. In part, the origins of the great Clayton family connection can be traced to the prolific William Clayton (1651–1715) of Liverpool and Fullwood, Lancashire. Son of Liverpool merchant Robert Clayton (born 1627), and nephew of a former mayor of Liverpool, William Clayton moved to Liverpool from London in 1669, and quickly established himself as a leading transatlantic merchant, trading in West Indian sugar and Chesapeake tobacco, often in partnership with his brothers Richard and John Clayton. In August 1690, Clayton married Elizabeth Leigh (1670–1745) daughter of Cheshire squire George Leigh. Over the course of the next decade and a half, Elizabeth Clayton bore her husband fifteen children, many of whom married into significant Liverpool merchant families. The marital ties formed by Clayton's children were often extraordinarily complex. In January 1713, for instance, two years before her father's death, Eleanor Clayton (1694–1827) married Richard Houghton II (1690–1752), scion of another important local family of merchants. The family's next generation greatly thickened this web of connection. In November 1740, daughter Margaret Houghton (1717–1752) married William Blundell (1714–1774), the eldest son of Alderman Bryan Blundell I (1674–1756) and Elizabeth Livesley Blundell (died-1725).[254] Like Houghton II, Blundell was a major Virginia merchant, slave trader, and political figure, and a marital link to him was both socially and commercially advantageous. This Houghton-Clayton-Blundell connection was further broadened by Blundell's already extensive network of familial ties within the Liverpool commercial community, which added branches of the important Shaw and Crosbie families to the collective family tree. Brother of Hannah Blundell Shaw, Bryan Blundell was the uncle of slave trader

---

[251]Richardson, *The Bristol Slave Traders*, 17–22.

[252]A number of recent works comment upon the close relationships between merchant families found in a number of English and Irish ports, including: Jacob Price, "The Great Quaker Business Families of Eighteenth Century London," in *Overseas Trade and Traders: Essays on some Commercial, Financial, and Political Challenges Facing British Atlantic Merchants, 1660–1775*, (1996); David Sacks, *The Widening Gate: Bristol and the Atlantic Economy, 1450–1700* (1991); Madge Dresser, *Slavery Obscured: The Social History of the Slave Trade in an English Provincial Port* (2001); and Jean Agnew, *Belfast Merchant Families in the Seventeenth Century* (1995).

[253]James Horn, *Adapting to a New World: English Society in the Seventeenth Century Chesapeake* (1994). In terms of their interconnectedness, seventeenth and eighteenth century Liverpool merchant families bear a superficial resemblance to the so-called "tangled cousinry" that ruled colonial Virginia in the seventeenth, eighteenth and early nineteenth centuries.

[254]D. Anderson, "Blundell's Collieries, The Progress of the Business," *Transactions of the Historical Society of Lancashire and Cheshire*, 116 (1965), 75; *International Genealogical Index*.

and insurance broker Samuel Shaw II (1718–1781).[255] These complex ties were invariably reflected in the patterns of trade undertaken by the Blundell, Shaw, and Crosbie families. Between 1745 and 1760, James Crosbie, and his son John, as well as the younger Samuel Shaw, became frequent slaving partners with their cousins William, Bryan, Richard, and Jonathan Blundell, the sons of Alderman Bryan Blundell.

Two other daughters of William Clayton also married well. First, in 1719, Anne Clayton (born-1697) married Banastre Parker of Cuerden Hall, Briarcliffe, Lancashire, father of Jane Parker (1726–1797), who later became the wife of Liverpool slave trader John Tarleton in 1751, and the mother of General Banastre Tarleton, a controversial figure of the American Revolution.[256] The Tarleton connection to the Clayton family was especially tortuous. In May 1715, John Tarleton's father, Captain Thomas Tarleton (1685–1730) had married Bridget, a daughter of Liverpool merchant Richard Houghton I (1660–1712), and sister-in-law of Eleanor Clayton Houghton.[257] Among Richard and Eleanor Houghton's seven children was Elizabeth Houghton (1714–1810), wife of Liverpool merchant William Williamson (1710–1762). They, in turn, had seven children. William Williamson and his wife, however, were both related to the Tarleton family before their marriage. In July 1705, his mother Anne Tarleton had married Ralph Williamson.[258]

Second, in 1722, another of William Clayton's daughters, Margaret (1698–1769), married the important Liverpool merchant Thomas Case I (1692–1748) of Red Hazels, Huyton, Lancashire. Two sons of this union, Thomas Case II (1731–1790) and Clayton Case (died-1779) were partners and active participants in the Liverpool slave trade in the 1760s and 1770s, jointly investing in some thirty ventures.[259] In 1775, the younger Thomas Case wed Anna Ashton, granddaughter of John Ashton of Woolton Hall, Liverpool, daughter of Nicholas Ashton, and niece of John, Joseph, and Jonathan Brooks.

However, it was one of William Clayton's youngest surviving children who made perhaps the best match. In 1726, Jemima (born-1704) wed George Tyrer II (born 1700), an affluent merchant twice selected mayor of Liverpool in 1726 and 1730. His father, George Tyrer I, had served as mayor in 1710, and was a close political ally of William Clayton and his anti-Whig circle of merchant-politicians.[260] For several generations, these elite families seldom married outside a well-defined group of associated merchant families. Anne Houghton (born 1691), for instance, sister of Bridget Houghton Tarleton and Richard Houghton II, cousin of Anne Tarleton Williamson, sister-in-law of Eleanor Clayton Houghton, Jemima Clayton Tyrer, Margaret Clayton Case, and Anne Clayton Parker, and aunt of Elizabeth Houghton Williamson and Margaret Houghton Blundell, wed an uncle of George Tyrer II in September 1712. By the mid-eighteenth century, Thomas and William Tyrer, the two sons of George and Jemima Tyrer, could claim a relationship, by either marriage or blood, to most of the first families of Liverpool commerce.[261]

---

[255]Samuel Shaw and Hannah Blundell were married on February 28, 1717, *Selected Marriage Records of the Parish of Liverpool at Our Lady and St. Nicholas; The Liverpool Directory of 1766*; Maurice Schofield, "The Virginia Trade of the Firm of Sparling and Bolden, of Liverpool, 1788–99," *Transactions of the Historical Society of Lancashire and Cheshire* 116 (1964), 122; Will of Samuel Shaw, December 10, 1781, PCC: PROB 11/1085.

[256]*Selected Burial Records of the Parish of Liverpool at our Lady and St. Nicholas, March 26, 1705—October 1725; Selected Marriage Records of the Parish of Liverpool at Our Lady and St. Nicholas, April 1705-January 1725,* in *The Cheshire Sheaf, History of Cheshire* (1882), vol. 11, 60; Ronald Stewart-Brown, "Tarleton of Fazakerley, Aigburth, Liverpool, and Bolesworth Castle," in *The Cheshire Sheaf* (1930), 1f; W.R. Serjeant, "The Tarleton Papers: A Merchants Accounts," *The Liverpool Libraries, Museums, and Arts Committee Bulletin,* 6 (1956), 29–31; R.D. Bass, *The Green Dragon,* (1957), 11–13. John Tarleton, merchant of Water Street, is frequently confused with his cousin John Tarleton the mercer, who also invested in slaving ventures.

[257]Lord Mayor of Liverpool in 1691, *Richard Houghton I (1660–1712)* married *Margaret Richmond (1663–1737)*, daughter of *Dr. Sylvester Richmond (1645–1692)*, on October 23, 1683 at Walton-on the-Hill, Lancashire. Their children included: *Anne Houghton* (born 1691/2), wife of *Thomas Tyrer*, and *Richard Houghton II (1690/1–1752)*, husband of *Eleanor Clayton (1694–1727)*. *Cheshire Sheath,* 60f.

[258]Agreement of Anne Tarleton, daughter of Capt. John Tarleton, and Ralph Williamson: July 16, 1705, 920 TAR 1/3.

[259]*TSTD*; Will of Clayton Case, merchant of Liverpool, Wills and Inventories, Chester Probate Registry, 1779.

[260]Michael Power, "Politics and Progress in Liverpool, 1660-1740," *Northern History* 35 (1999), 119–138.

[261]The Case Family of Prescott & Liverpool, Pedigree of Case of Thingwall, Lancashire, Wakefield MSS, 2 of 3, 942/WAK33/103/10, Liverpool PRO; *Our Old Families*, (no date, no author given, but presumed to be William H. Wakefield, Wakefield MSS, 2 of 3, 942/

III

An apprenticeship in the house of so prominent a man as William Clayton of Fulwood opened doors for John Earle, exposing him to a world of wealth and privilege unavailable in Warrington. Although a marital connection with a major merchant family seemed out of his reach when he arrived in Liverpool, both Earle and his children were able to form useful marital bonds. In December 1700, shortly after the conclusion of his apprenticeship, the 26-year old Earle married Eleanor Tyrer (1674–1702), took up the freedom of the town, and entered trade on his own account as a shipper dealing primarily in wine, but also iron, tobacco, and sugar.[262] As the Tyrer and Clayton families were connected by marriage, it is possible that Earle's relationship with William Clayton provided him an introduction to Eleanor Tyrer *via* George Tyrer II. By 1710, if not earlier, Earle had his own apprentices, accepting into his service the sons of important men such as the Rector of Walton and merchant John Atherton.[263] In addition, Earle was quickly admitted to the merchant elite of Liverpool. He was invited to join the Common Council in 1703, and was selected bailiff in 1705 and Lord Mayor in 1709. Although Eleanor Tyrer Earle had died in July 1702, Earle waited until 1709, the year he was selected Lord Mayor, to remarry. Like his first wife, Earle's second wife, Mary Finch, was well connected. The only daughter of the prominent Ralph Finch of Chester, Mary was an heiress of the Finches of Watford, Cheshire.[264] Of the seven children of John and Mary Earle, only sons Ralph, Thomas, and William, and daughter Sarah survived into adulthood.

Eldest son Ralph (1715–1790) married Dorothy Aldersay, the second daughter of Richard Aldersay, a collector of customs in Liverpool, and had two sons, Richard and Willis Earle.[265] Bailiff in 1761, and Lord Mayor in 1769, Ralph Earle was primarily a timber merchant, but like his father and brothers, he was also a general merchant dealing in a variety of goods, as well as a partner in nine slaving ventures with his brothers between 1761–1771.[266] In 1766, Ralph and his brothers broadened their involvement in the African trade by joining William Davenport, John Copeland, Peter Holme, and Thomas Hodgson, in a partnership "for carrying on [a] trade of selling beads, arrangoes, etc."[267] Although the sons of John Earle frequently joined in various ventures throughout their respective business careers, they were only peripherally involved in each other's core businesses.

A wealthy Levant merchant by the mid-1750s, Earle's second surviving son, Thomas (1719–1781) in 1754 wed Mary Mort (1726–1785), the only daughter and heiress of Adam Mort of Wharton Hall, Lancashire, who was closely connected to the Clayton, Leigh, and Hardman families of Liverpool.[268] Unlike his brothers, Thomas Earle spent much of his early business career away from Liverpool. Based in Livorno, Italy, Thomas was the managing partner in a trading firm, which included his brothers, which shipped Mediterranean goods to Liverpool.[269] While in Italy, Thomas Earle had three children by Mary Mort Earle, a son Adam, who died in infancy, and two daughters, Elizabeth Jane and Maria.[270] Thomas Earle returned to Liverpool in 1766, taking

---

WAK33/10, Liverpool PRO.

[262]T.A. Earle, 35*f.*

[263]*Apprenticeship Enrollment Book, 1707–1757*, 352 CLE/REG/4/1, Liverpool PRO, Picton Library, Liverpool, July 7, 1710, Richard Richmond, son of Reverend Richard Richmond, Rector of Walton, apprenticed to John Earle, Esq., August 24, 1714, John Atherton, son of John Atherton, Lancashire, apprenticed to John Earle, Merchant.

[264]T.A. Earle, 35f.

[265]*ibid*, 38.

[266]*TSTD.*

[267]*Partnership Agreement between Thomas Earle, Peter Holme, Thomas Hodgson, Ralph Earle, William Davenport, William Earle, and John Copeland, in a firm for carrying on trade of selling beads, arrangoes, etc.*, July 24, 1766, D/EARLE/2/2.

[268]The connections between the Earle and Hardman families were distant but provided the Earle family with a claim to Hardman's estate at Allerton Hall, which later became the Earle family seat. T. A. Earle, 39.

[269]T. A. Earle, 39.

[270]*ibid*, 42.

an active part in the commercial and public life of his hometown, entering the Common Council in 1770, and serving as bailiff the following year.[271]

John Earle's fourth and youngest surviving son, William Earle (1721–1788) was a Guinea captain and slave trader, ship-owner, general merchant, Levant trader, and ironmonger of Redcross Street, Liverpool, and the Brick House in West Derby Village.[272] Although William Earle became a major figure in the business community of Liverpool, it cannot be said that he married particularly well. In 1753, he wed Anne Winstanley (died-1789) daughter of Thomas and Mary Hosken, and widow of Samuel Winstanley, an ironmonger of Liverpool who had died in the late 1740s. When she wed Earle, Anne Winstanley had two married sisters, Catherine Jennings and Elizabeth Copeland, both of whom were already married to future business associates of her new husband. The two surviving sons of William and Anne Earle, married within the family. Eldest son Thomas Earle of Spekelands (1754–1822) married cousin Maria Earle in 1786, daughter of uncle and namesake Thomas Earle. Second son Ralph Earle (1756–1767) died as a child, and never married. Third son William Earle of Everton (1760–1839) also married a cousin, Anne Copeland (1769–1819) in 1797. However, daughter Mary Earle (1758–1831) broadened the family web of connection the most when she wed Richard Heywood, eldest son of the renowned slave trader, merchant, and banker Arthur Heywood.[273]

John Earle retired from an active business career in 1737 at the age of 63, and moved to nearby Prescott, Lancashire during his final years before his death in 1749. "On John Earle," family historian T. Algernon Earle observed in 1890, "we may look as one of the small handful of men whose active brains molded the rising destinies of [Liverpool], and whose watchful eye and energetic hands laid the solid foundation upon which it stands today."[274] When Earle arrived in town in 1688, Liverpool had a population of only a few thousand, and was essentially an overgrown market town with one church, a few muddy streets, and an inadequate harbor. By the time of his death, Liverpool's population had grown four-fold, churches, docks, and public buildings had been built, and the customs collected by the crown were second only to London in all of Britain. In May 1753, his great success was visibly but posthumously proclaimed with the marriage of his daughter Sarah (1717–1809) to the Rev. John Stanley (1693–1781), brother of the 11th Earl of Derby, and a member of the greatest noble family of northwest England.[275]

Even more importantly, John Earle bequeathed a legacy of commercial success, a valuable inheritance which his surviving sons used to increase the family's wealth and improve its social standing. T.A Earle notes that his ancestor was purported to have bequeathed £100,000 to his three sons, an enormous inheritance for the time, comparable to what the much greater merchant Foster Cunliffe left to his two sons at his death in 1758.[276] However, it is clear that Earle's commercial success did not benefit his sons equally. Elder sons Ralph and Thomas entered elite trades with high entry costs, requiring the investment of significant capital. Much of this capital undoubtedly came from John Earle himself. Son William, however, was not so favored. Like many younger sons of merchant families, he was apprenticed to the sea, eventually rising to the command of a slave ship by 1748. Many slave traders began as mariners after being apprenticed to the sea, training that was far less costly than an elite merchant apprenticeship. Like many contemporary slave merchants such as Ambrose Lace, John Crosbie, and William Boates, Earle rose in trade largely by his own exertions to become "one of the leading merchants and ship owners of Liverpool."[277] Thirty years of age in 1748, Earle was some-what older than most new slaving captains, and was constrained in his career choices by a lack of funds. The

[271]ibid, 43.

[272]Liverpool Directory of 1766; T. A. Earle, 45; D. Anderson, 69, 71. In 1774, William Earle joined in a partnership with Jonathan Blundell, Samuel Warren, and Edward Chaffers to mine coal at Wigan, Lancashire.

[273]T. A. Earle, 45.

[274]ibid, 36.

[275]ibid, 35-36.

[276]John W. Tyler, "Foster Cunliffe and Sons: Liverpool Merchants in the Maryland Tobacco Trade, 1738–1765," Maryland Historical Magazine, 78 (1978), 270–271. Although T. A. Earle suggests that his ancestor "left his family settled…in prosperous circumstances," he also states that "his fortunes were [often] chequered, [and while] he was [sometimes] successful…towards the close of his life…he seems to have suffered considerable losses and disappointments [and] died a comparatively poor man." T. A. Earle, 36

[277]Williams, History of the Liverpool Privateers, 484–485.

death of his father in 1749 almost certainly provided William with an inheritance that permitted him to pursue more lucrative opportunities, and he soon made the transition from mariner to merchant. As his father had not been involved in the slave trade since 1718, Earle could scarcely rely upon his father's mercantile contacts in the African trade in his early career as a slave captain and merchant. After his father's death, however, Earle took a while to arrange his personal business affairs before he returned to the sea, this time in command of a "better" ship with wealthier, more substantial partners. As captain of the slaver *Chesterfield* in 1750 and 1751, Earle formed relationships with a number of important merchants, most notably William Davenport, one of the greatest British slave traders of the later eighteenth century. In 1753, the year he married, Earle joined Davenport and several other merchants as investors in the slave ship *Grampus*, his first slaving venture as an owner.[278] Thereafter, Earle's responsibilities grew rapidly. Not only did he inherit the management of his father's iron-mongering business on Redcross Street, he became an owner of the *Chesterfield* in 1754, and before long had established himself as an important slave merchant, with eighty ventures between 1748 and 1775.[279] By 1775–1780, the aging William Earle was in a better position than his father had been to provide equally for his surviving sons Thomas and William, making them partners in the family firm at an early age. After brother Thomas Earle died in April 1781, William Earle amalgamated his firm with his own and allowed his son Thomas to take control of the combined business at age 27.[280] Soundly managed, the firm of *T&W Earle & Co.*, became one of the largest slaving concerns of late eighteenth-century Liverpool. As wealthy young men, both sons moved from Liverpool town center to estates in the surrounding Lancashire countryside, Thomas at Speke, and William II at Everton. With the family business in good hands, The elder William Earle went into comfortable semi-retirement in 1781, dying seven years later at age 67.

IV

For other Liverpool merchant families, bonds of faith and religious affiliation further reinforced kinship and business connections. Before the African slave trade took root in Liverpool in the 1720s and 1730s, religion often formed a clannish badge of association for many merchants. However, in Liverpool doctrinal differences between dissenters and Anglicans did not impede the conduct of trade. Dissenters were important merchants in Liverpool, and tolerance characterized their social and commercial relationships with Anglicans.[281] While religion was often a thorn of political contention before 1725, pragmatism ultimately guided Liverpool's merchants in the conduct of their trade. In a town were dissenters outnumbered Anglicans, the religious identity of a prospective partner was seldom an issue in the construction of business partnerships.[282] For Anglicans, men whose trade would have been jeopardized by a rejection of dissenters as suitable partners, it could be no other way, and even before 1740 sectarian issues were largely rendered moot. However, religion did influence the shape of eighteenth-century Liverpool trade in other ways. At a time when a few families of dissenters stood at the center of the city's trade, religious affiliation played an important but largely invisible role in the organization of the early Liverpool slave trade, most especially in the composition of slaving partnerships.

Because the partnership records of the early Liverpool are incomplete, it is not possible to determine the religious affiliations of all slave traders.[283] However, it is reasonable to assume that dissenters never formed more than a fraction of the total number of slave traders, a proportion that declined over the course of the eighteenth century. Religious identity was a more important factor in the formation of slaving partnerships prior to 1740 than in the decades thereafter. This was especially the case for dissenters. In the early

---

[278]*TSTD.*

[279]*TSTD.*

[280]T.A. Earle, 45f.

[281]Power, "Politics and Progress," 131.

[282]Morris, ed., *The Journeys of Celia Fiennes*, 183. During her brief stop in Liverpool in 1698, Fiennes noted that "there are a great many Dessenters in…town."

[283]*TSTD.*

slave trade, a number of prominent slave merchants were Presbyterians and members of Benn's Garden chapel. The group exclusiveness of these slave-trading dissenters was notable.[284] For instance, when the prominent Virginia merchant and Presbyterian John Pemberton II (1668–1744), and his son John Pemberton III (1690–1740s), participated in more than twenty slaving ventures between 1713 and 1739, they dealt with few known investors from outside the small community of Benn's Garden.[285] In twenty-one slaving ventures between 1713 and 1739, John Pemberton II joined ten men, six of whom were congregants at Benn's Garden chapel.[286] Similarly, multiple bonds of religious affiliation, marriage, and commercial association linked the families of John Pemberton II and Samuel Ogden, important Presbyterian merchants who co-partnered in seven voyages of the Hardman slaver between 1730 and 1739.

Although perhaps less intricate than the extensive Clayton family connection, close kinship circles also linked the families of other merchant-dissenters. A resident of Mossley Hill near Liverpool, merchant Samuel Ogden (1689–1752) was born in Liverpool in September 1689, the son of Edmund Ogden and Phoebe Buxton Ogden.[287] As a newly minted merchant, Ogden married Sarah Pemberton, a daughter of fellow dissenter and merchant John Pemberton II (1668–1743) at Castle Hey chapel in July 1715.[288] This union with the Pemberton family solidified Ogden's future as a merchant and town father. Over time, his patriarchal and mercantile ambitions were greatly advanced by his father-in-law's high social standing and extensive trade connections in Liverpool, Africa, and the Chesapeake. Samuel Ogden had risen high in his native Liverpool by his thirtieth birthday, emerging as a leader in both the close universe of the chapel and the larger merchant community of his home town.

Despite his nonconformist beliefs, or perhaps because of them, Samuel Ogden was a successful slave merchant in the decades after his marriage in 1715. In a career stretching from 1720 to 1751, Ogden engaged in over fifty slaving ventures with 17 different partners. Of these men, nearly two-thirds were dissenters known to be members of Benn's Garden chapel.[289] Although the number of co-religionists involved in his slaving partnerships varied over time, their importance was perhaps greatest at the beginning of his career than at its end. Between 1720 and 1745, nearly 70% of his partners were members of Benn's Garden chapel, including his two sons-in-law, Arthur and Benjamin Heywood.[290] Although the proportion of co-religionists partnering with Samuel Ogden declined to 58% between 1745 and 1751, they remained central to his trade in slaves.

At first Ogden traded exclusively with his father-in-law John Pemberton II, and his close business associates John Hardman, Captain Arthur Hamilton, and Richard Hampson, all members in good standing of Benn's Garden. Among Ogden's known slaving partners between 1720 and 1745, only the Virginia merchant Foster Cunliffe was not a member of Benn's Garden chapel.[291] In three slaving ventures in 1745, however, several new men became partners with Ogden, including John Bridge, John Goodwin, Thomas Ball, and Richard Cribb, all partners in the slaver *Nancy*, and Samuel Reid, Edward Forbes, William Williamson, partners in the *Sea Nymph* and the *Postilion*. Of these men, Reid and Williamson were members of Benn's Garden chapel; Thomas Ball may have been related to John Ball, a known member of the chapel, while

---

[284]Anne Holt, *Walking Together: A Study in Liverpool Nonconformity, 1688–1938* (1938), 177-25, 132, 155. These slave merchants included John Pemberton II, John Pemberton III, Samuel Ogden, Edmund Ogden, John Hardman, Richard Hampson, Samuel Reid, Robert Reid, Joseph Manesty, Robert Law, Richard Goulding, Matthew Goulding, Edward Cropper, John Armstrong, David Agnew, Thomas Williamson, Thomas Cockshutt, John Williamson, William Williamson, Thomas Ball, Nathaniel Bassnett, Arthur Heywood, Benjamin Heywood, John Kennion, Peter Holme, Arthur Hamilton, John Bostock, Samuel Smith, Richard Savage, Nathaniel Litherland, George Campbell, James Crosbie, Thomas Rumbold, James Percival, and others.

[285]Holt, *Walking Together,* 123, 150–162.

[286]Holt, 117–125.

[287]*International Genealogy Index.*

[288]Holt, 123.

[289]*TSTD*, Holt, 117–125.

[290]TSTD.

[291]John Tyler, "Foster Cunliffe and Sons…," 249.

the religious affiliation of Richard Cribb, Edward Forbes, John Goodwin, and John Bridge is unclear.[292] Returning to the partnership patterns of his earliest slaving ventures, Samuel Ogden partnered with kinsmen and close associates in his last four slaving ventures prior to his death in 1752. These included the four voyages of the *Sarah Frigate* in 1747 and 1751, and the *Phoebe* in 1748 and 1751, all conducted in partnership with a kinsman and co-religionist, Ogden's eldest son-in-law Arthur Heywood.

A similar pattern of association is evident in the slaving partnerships formed by other dissenters and slave traders. Co-partner with Pemberton and Ogden in the *Hardman* slaver, John Hardman of Allerton Hall (1698–1755) was a pew-holder at Benn's Garden chapel, and briefly a member of Parliament for Liverpool after the retirement of Richard Gildart in 1754.[293] John Hardman and his brother James had arrived in Liverpool in 1732 from Rochdale, Lancashire, and quickly established themselves in Liverpool mercantile circles.[294] In the overlapping commercial worlds of Anglicans and dissenters, marital connections helped pave the way for the Hardman brothers. James Hardman's wife Jane was a daughter of George Leigh of Oughtrington, Cheshire, and was thus related to the Claytons, Houghtons, and other important merchant families.[295] Like Samuel Ogden, but unlike his brother James, John Hardman married the daughter of a co-religionist, in his case the daughter of John Cockshutt, Lord Mayor in 1702 and an important figure in early eighteenth-century Liverpool politics. Unlike Ogden, however, Hardman partnered many investors from outside the chapel in numerous slaving ventures at various times throughout the course of his trading career. Hardman invested primarily with co-religionists during his early years as a slave trader between 1728 and 1737. In his 24 slaving ventures during these years, he partnered ten men, of whom seven were dissenters and members of Benn's Garden chapel, including his step-father Richard Hampson.[296] However, in his later slaving career, between 1737 and 1761, the proportion of co-religionists known to have partnered with him declined precipitously. While the religious affiliation of a significant number of Hardman's slaving partners is difficult to determine, 25% are known to have belonged to Benn's Garden, and another 15% may have been dissenters. Religious affiliation may well have been the most important factor in Hardman's early slaving partnerships but had ceased to be so by 1740. Overall, John Hardman partnered some 53 men in 73 slaving ventures between 1728–1761, of whom only 19, or 36%, worshipped at Benn's Garden chapel.[297]

These dissenters all belonged to a religious community characterized by a benign sectarianism that was more a manifestation of a commitment to a larger spiritual family than of hostility to Anglicans. Ogden's devotion to his church is suggested by the fact that when the congregation outgrew its cramped quarters at Castle Hey, where it had met since at least 1689, he sold his fellow worshippers a potentially valuable tract of land for the construction of a new chapel in 1726 for the paltry sum of £1. 7s.[298] This gift permitted the growing congregation to build a new meeting house which opened in 1727 as Benn's Garden chapel. Ogden's status within his congregation, and ultimately his great success as a tobacco, sugar, and slave merchant, rested most firmly upon a foundation of family connection in the bounds of the chapel. Within the context of his religious community, marriage had marked him out as an up-and-coming man long before he became a successful merchant.

The value of a judicious marriage as a building block in a successful trading career was well understood within Liverpool's mercantile families, dissenters and Anglicans alike. With the exception of their only son, the children of Samuel and Sarah Ogden all married within the close community of Benn's Garden. Daughters Elizabeth and Phoebe Ogden wed two eligible brothers born in Ireland of Lancashire stock,

---

[292]Holt, 118.

[293]Lt. Col. Fishwick, "Notes on the Hardman Family," *The Transactions of the Historical Society of Lancashire and Cheshire*, 42 (1890), 78f; T. A. Earle, 39; Will of Christopher Whytell, merchant of Liverpool, Lancashire, July 3, 1755, PCC: PROB 11/817; Will of Richard Gildart of Liverpool, February 23, 1770.

[294]Fishwick, "Notes on the Hardman Family," 78F.

[295]Fishwick, 78f; T. A. Earle, 39–40.

[296]Holt, 121.

[297]*ibid*, 117–125.

[298]*ibid*, 39, 106; Arthur Black, *et al*, *The Changing Face of Liverpool, 1207–1727*, 20, 23, 35.

Arthur and Benjamin Heywood.[299] Arthur Heywood departed Ireland in 1731 to begin a five-year merchant apprenticeship with merchant John Hardman, a member of Benn's Garden Chapel, while Benjamin followed his older brother to Liverpool in 1741 to serve his own apprenticeship with the merchant James Crosbie, Lord Mayor in 1753, and also a member of Benn's Garden. Not only were the Heywood brothers partners, they married sisters who shared their Presbyterian faith and lived in adjoining houses on fashionable Hanover Street for many years. Son Edmund Ogden II, however, married outside the chapel, exchanging vows with Mary Gildart, daughter of Liverpool merchant Richard Gildart, and granddaughter of Sir Thomas Johnson, both Anglicans and former Lord Mayors.[300] Although intermarriage between Christian denominations was increasingly common in late seventeenth- century English cities and towns, marriage remained an important spiritual and social bond that united dissenters more than Anglicans, many of whom were latitudinarian in belief and lax in practice.[301] In Benn's Garden, marriage was celebrated not only as a form of friendship, or a "mixture of hierarchy and equality infused with a significant degree of mutuality," but also as a concomitant of group identity and religious distinctiveness.[302]

As Liverpool emerged as a prosperous center of commerce and industry after 1700, and wealthy merchants from many backgrounds came to dominate Liverpool society, religious identity became less important as a bond of alliance between important merchant families. The individualistic impulses of the entrepreneur proved antithetical to the collective bonds of faith. Whether Edmund Ogden II remained a congregant at Benn's Garden chapel after his marriage or not, his religious affiliation had little impact upon the partnerships he formed in the slave trade, his success as a merchant, or his social standing in Liverpool. For the Ogden family, the financial consequences of building marital connections with wealthy merchant families gradually supplanted purely religious considerations in choosing mates for their children. In the hierarchical world of the eighteenth-century English town, elevating the social station of one's family was a major aim of matrimony.[303] "In the early modern period," Margaret Hunt observes, "who and how one married directly and decisively affected one's place in the social, cultural, and economic hierarchy."[304] For Samuel Ogden and Richard Gildart alike this was as it should be, because children were, in part, a precious resource to be utilized for the greater benefit of he family.[305]

V

In many trades, advantageous kinship or religious ties alone were not sufficient to assure a merchant's success. Traders could also rise by dint of hard work, skill, good fortune, and the establishment of close associations within a highly personalized circle of "business friends." Increasing in importance during the course of the eighteenth century, such business connections were crucial to a merchant's ability to conduct trade, and his ultimate commercial success. Outsiders such as Earle, however, were often able to make use of declining institutions like guilds, livery companies, apprenticeship, and civic freedom "as formal mechanisms easing

[299]ibid, 123.

[300]Will of Richard Gildart of Liverpool, Lancashire, February 23, 1770, PCC: PROB 11/955; Margaret Hunt, *The Middling Sort: Commerce, Gender, and the Family in England, 1680–1780* (1996), 48–49.

[301]Hunt, *The Middling Sort*, 48–49.

[302]Holt, 123f; *See also*: Katharine W. Swett, "The Account Between Us: Honor, Reciprocity and Companionship in Male Friendship in the Later Seventeenth Century," *Albion*, 31 (1999), 24, Hunt, *The Middling Sort*, 155–157.

[303]Hunt, *The Middling Sort*, 150–155; Lloyd Bonfield, "Affective Families, Open Elites, and Strict Family Settlements in Early Modern England," *Economic History Review* 29 (1986), 344f. Brooks notes that while fathers made money available for marriage portions for their daughters, "matrimony was considered the primary objective for most girls." C. Brooks, "Apprenticeship, Social Mobility, and the Middling Sort," in Barry and Brooks, eds., *Middling Sort of People*, 53.

[304]Hunt, 150.

[305]Ann Gildart wed merchant Spencer Steers, son of Alderman Thomas Steers, Ellen Gildart married merchant Christopher Whytell (died-1755), while Lydia and Elizabeth Gildart remained unmarried at their father's death in 1770. Will of Richard Gildart of Liverpool, Lancashire, February 23, 1770, PCC: PROB 11/955.

their entry into urban society," although many found it difficult or impossible, to surmount the range of impediments erected by town oligarchies to bar their way.[306] Newcomers often had difficulty establishing themselves because they lacked connections. Although Earle did not have kin to watch after him in this new town, neither did he necessarily require such attentive kinsman or family friends to safeguard him or promote his interests. While guilds provided avenues of advancement in some towns, they had never been well established in Liverpool. One alternative was apprenticeship, as the career of John Earle demonstrates. Apprenticeship was an important venue in which business friendships were formed. In many cases, these connections later gave rise to business partnerships. This created an associational nexus that connected men, expanding the possibilities of trade and sources of investment capital.[307] Large numbers of apprentices arrived in Liverpool after 1660, bolstering the rise of Liverpool commerce.[308] As a newcomer in town, John Earle lacked a network of family and business relationships.

Although he held little real property, Earle's father was not without means or influence. John Earle Sr. (1627–1709) secured a merchant apprenticeship for his son with one of the greatest Liverpudlians of the age, William Clayton.[309] To the elder John Earle, arranging such a coveted apprenticeship for his son was more than merely an expression of paternal devotion. It was an investment in his son's future, a calculated attempt to enrich his son and improve his marriage prospects. For parents who had to work for their livings, a child's future was a major concern. "For the majority of parents," Brooks observes, "finding a niche for their children which would eventually enable them to set up and maintain a household, to provide for a wife and children, and keep poverty at bay, was the overriding imperative."[310] Diligent fathers such as the elder Earle took great care to find their sons suitable employments with suitable masters, a task they saw as both a practical necessity as well as a moral responsibility.[311] As one English judge observed in 1620, ensuring a child's future became a parental responsibility that assumed the force of law, because "The putting of an apprentice is a matter of great trust for his diet, for his health, [and] for his safety."[312] After 1700, Liverpool trade promised rewards for the sons of anxious parents that were unavailable in the sleepy market towns and villages that dotted the surrounding landscape of Lancashire, and elsewhere in the north of England.

The apprenticeship indenture was a legal agreement that set a specified term of service, and established the process by which young men acquired the knowledge and skills necessary to set themselves up in trade. In addition, the provisions of the apprenticeship indenture, typically composed of legalistic boilerplate, established the material obligations that the master owed the apprentice, employing stylized language to specify the care to be given the apprentice within the master's household. In return, the apprentice agreed to serve his master faithfully, and comply with his instructions. The *Statute of Artificers* of 1563 established a seven-year apprenticeship as a necessary requirement for apprentices entering a number of specified trades. Over time, however, apprenticeship terms declined significantly from the traditional seven years to five or even three years, although paupers apprenticed to sea often served ten years or more. By the early eighteenth century, seven-year apprenticeships at sea were something of a rarity, averaging closer to 3-5 years, while conditions for apprentices varied enormously.[313] The primary rationale behind apprenticeship was pedagogical, and teaching apprentices basic literacy and numeracy was viewed as a sacred responsibility of the master. As business grew ever more complex in the late seventeenth and eighteenth centuries, the demand for apprentices who could read, maintain accounts, master the intricacies of currency exchange, insurance, and law,

---

[306]Peter Clark and Paul Slack, *English Towns in Transition, 1500–1700*, 94.

[307]Sweet, *The English Town, 1680–1840*, 37–38; C. Brooks, 55.

[308]E.A. Wrigley, "Urban Growth and Agricultural Change: England and the Continent in the Early Modern Period," *Journal of Interdisciplinary History*, 15 (1985), 684–695; C. Brooks, 55. In early modern England, Wrigley suggests that the ratio of urban to national population increased nearly threefold, from 5.25% in 1520 to 13.5% in 1670.

[309]Gauci, *The Politics of Trade*, 60–62, 95.

[310]C. Brooks, 52.

[311]*ibid*, 74; Lawrence Stone, *The Family, Sex, and Marriage in England*, (1977), 167.

[312]*The Reports of That Learned Sir Henry Hobart Knight: Late Chief Justice of his Majesties Court of Common Pleas at Westminster* (1641), 134; quoted in C. Brooks, 74.

[313]Davis, *The Rise of the English Shipping Industry*, 120.

increased many fold.[314] While acquiring skills and knowledge was the *raison d'etre* of apprenticeship, it was only part of the learning process of the apprentice.

Stock characters in early modern urban history, apprentices were long characterized as hot-blooded, debauched youths who indulged in drink and sexual escapades at every opportunity, and all too often participated in street riots, plunder, and political disorder.[315] To keep such youthful enthusiasms in check, the indenture of apprenticeship enshrined a traditional code of moral conduct designed to guide the unruly apprentice during his term of service in order to inculcate proper business values, such as sobriety, honesty, and thrift.[316] *The Apprentice's Monitor; or, INDENTURES IN VERSE, shewing what they are bound to do,"* proclaimed that,

> Each young Apprentice, when he's bound to Trade,
> This solemn Vow to GOD and MAN has made,
> To do with joy his Master's just commands,
> Nor trust his secrets into other hands,
> He must no damage to his substance do,
> And see that others do not wrong him too,
> His Master's goods he shall not waste or lend,
> But all his property with care defend,
> He shall not buy nor sell without his leave,
> Nor lie, nor injure, nor at all deceive,
> Taverns and ALE-HOUSES he shall not haunt,
> Those snares to youth, those scenes of vice and want,
> At CARDS and DICE he shall not dare to play,
> But fly from such temptations, far away,
> O Youth! remember thou to this art BOUND,
> See that no breach of this in thee be found.[317]

Both a customary method of instruction and an initiation to urban society, Brooks argues, "apprenticeship was [also] a social device which instilled commercial ideas as well as skills."[318] In this respect, the common experience of apprenticeship in seventeenth- and eighteenth-century English commercial towns helped to maintain the bonds of sociability and fellowship that were necessary both to promote a town's trade, and unify its cadre of merchants.

Merchant apprenticeships did not come cheap, however, and required the payment of an often-substantial fee, or premium, to a master willing to undertake the training of an apprentice in the arts of trade. In Liverpool, an apprenticeship became a valuable commodity, a means of establishing a son in a lucrative trade, such as the booming transatlantic trade after the 1670s. Prominent merchants such as William Clayton could command a high fee, because apprenticeship premiums depended not only on the repute of the master but also the prestige and potential profitability of his trade or profession.[319] Placing a son in a suitable apprenticeship was a major factor in his future career as a merchant, often significantly influencing his ultimate success in trade. "It is clear," Brooks argues, "that the [payment of an] apprenticeship premium meant that…the financial position of a father had a direct influence on the point at which his son would be able to enter the

---

[314]Hunt, 56, C. Brooks, 76, Whyman, 43.

[315]Clark and Slack, *English Towns in Transition*, 94; Hunt, 47; C. Brooks, 77.

[316]Hunt, 47. Arguing that it brought dishonor on their sober and decorous fraternity of men, Hunt notes that theft, riotous behavior, licentiousness, and quarrelling were often severely punished by masters and others leaders of guilds.

[317]S. Hazard, J. Marshall, R. White, *The Apprentice's Monitor; or, INDENTURES IN VERSE, shewing what they are bound to do* (1795) No, 27 Queen-Street, Cheap-Side, and No. 4, Aldermary Church Yard; Piccadilly, London.

[318]C. Brooks, 77–78, Whyman, 42*f.*

[319]R.G. Wilson, *Gentlemen Merchants: The Merchant Community in Leeds, 1700–1830* (1971), 23; C. Brooks, 60; Ralph Davis, *Aleppo and Devonshire Square: English Traders in the Levant in the Eighteenth Century* (1967), 10, 66–67.

urban hierarchy."[320] In London, these premiums reflected the perceived importance of a range of trades, perceptions that gave rise to a strict occupational hierarchy. The disparity between the premiums paid for apprenticeships in the lesser crafts and manual trades and the more prestigious mercantile and professional apprenticeships widened substantially in the first half of the eighteenth century. Increasingly dominated by wealthy families by the late seventeenth century, elite professional and mercantile apprenticeships often cost in excess of £100, an immense sum for the time. [321] The situation was similar in Liverpool. The apprenticeship of William Davenport to merchant grocer William Whalley in 1741, for instance, cost his family and guardians £120.[322] Although Levant and East Indies merchants in London often asked as much as £500 to take on apprentices by the 1670s, the average premium was far less for most of the period before 1750.[323] In fact, apprenticeship premiums in most centers of commerce, particularly for the prestigious manual and crafts trades, were ordinarily a great deal less than £100. In 1715, for instance, two-thirds of premiums paid to masters in Birmingham in 1715 were £10 or less, while in London between 1715 and 1718, the average premium paid for all apprenticeships was only £28.[324]

The rising cost of apprenticeship premiums after 1700, however, affected the social and demographic complexion of elite apprenticeships, as less affluent rural and urban families were excluded and largely supplanted by wealthier merchant and gentry families better able to pay the higher premiums. Even for wealthy families, suitable apprenticeships steadily rose beyond their reach after 1700. Paul Langford notes that two-thirds of the premiums paid in Surrey between 1711 and 1731, for example, were valued at £20 or more, "sums which would have eaten quite heavily into the annual incomes of most members of the affluent middling sort …those worth between £40 and £100 a year."[325] In his *Complete English Tradesmen*, Defoe argued that the increase in premiums was a result of the willingness of gentry parents to pay higher premiums in order to ensure that their children received preferential treatment in the households in which they were placed.[326] This unquestionably gave the sons of wealthy merchants and gentry a decided advantage in the market for elite apprenticeships. The payment of an often hefty apprenticeship premium limited the possibilities of entry into more privileged occupations such as law, medicine, and the more profitable mercantile trades for the "30% of the population which lived by wages alone…[and]…not surprisingly, the more elite trades tended to attract richer, better born recruits."[327] For a young merchant just starting out, a wealthy family meant not only a better chance of entry into much sought-after trades but also readier access to the capital necessary to set up in business once the apprenticeship term was completed. The expenses of setting a son up in a suitable trade or profession could be significant, and families often sacrificed a great deal to help their sons get a good start in business, including signing large bonds as surety against theft for sons apprenticed in particularly lucrative trades.

In the first half of the eighteenth century, a large proportion of apprentices came from the rural countryside or from small towns, where a majority of Englishmen still lived and the social status of a young man did not determine the types of apprenticeships that were available to him. Although an imperfect source, the Liverpool *Apprenticeship Enrollment Book*, which covers the period between 1707 and 1757, provides some indication of the humble origins of many of the new apprentices arriving in town, and the far more elevated status of others. Between 1707 and 1727, approximately 25–30% of apprentices came from families where the father practiced a trade that varied in prestige from apothecary and silversmith, to porter and wheelwright,

---

[320]C. Brooks, 70.

[321]*ibid.*

[322]David Richardson, "Profits in the Liverpool Slave Trade: The Accounts of William Davenport, 1757–1784," in *Liverpool, the African Slave Trade, and Abolition*, eds., Roger Anstey and P.E.H. Hair (1976), 61–62. *See also*: Bruce Anderson, "The Lancashire Bill System and its Liverpool Practitioners: The Case of a Slave Merchant," in *Trade and Transport: Essays in Economic in Honor of T.S. Willan*, ed., W.H. Chaloner and Barrie Ratcliffe (1977)

[323]Whyman, 42.

[324]C. Brooks, 67–68.

[325]*ibid*, 68.

[326]Daniel Defoe, *Complete English Tradesmen*, (1738 edition), cited in C. Brooks, 68.

[327]C. Brooks, 60.

Table 3.2	*Occupations of Fathers in the* **Apprenticeship Enrollment Book,** *1707–1727*
Occupation of Father	Number Listed
1. Gentleman	15
2. Yeomen Farmer	5
3. House Carpenter	2
4. Clergy	1
5. Landwaiter	1
6. Apothecary	1
7. Glassmaker	1
8. Wheelwright	1
9. Slater	1
10. Silversmith	1
11. Ironmonger	1
12. Porter	1
13. Linen draper	1
14. Innkeeper	1
15. Clerk	1
16. No Occupation Listed:	30
Total:	64

while 23% were the sons of gentlemen or merchants.[328] In most cases, the social eminence of the father, and his chosen trade or profession, had a noticeable correlation with the types of apprenticeships he could secure for his son. The sons of the Lancashire yeomen Myles Troughton, John Cross, and Richard Pope, for instance, were all apprenticed in Liverpool between 1713 and 1718 to humble masters practicing modest trades such as ship's carpenter.[329] Similarly, the son of Robert Walsh, house carpenter of Ormskirk, Lancashire, was apprenticed in 1719 to John Livesley, a bricklayer, while in1724, the son of Henry Leatherbarrow, an Ormskirk innkeeper, was apprenticed to the blacksmith James Harvey.[330] While an apprenticeship with a bricklayer or a blacksmith held the promise of moderate success and self-sufficiency for middling sons, it was not the road to great riches desired by the more ambitious or affluent.

For wealthier fathers eager to establish their sons in Liverpool society, apprenticeships in such unglamorous minor trades was not an option. The wealth, social status, and political eminence that well-born and successful men sought for the next generation of their families required the expansive opportunities that were only available in more profitable mercantile pursuits such as the Levant and transatlantic trades, or elite professions such as medicine and law. The objective of many ambitious fathers was the acquisition of sufficient wealth to permit sons and daughters to marry into prominent gentry and mercantile families, and ultimately to move from Liverpool to landed estates. A son of the great Liverpool merchant John Tarleton,

[328]*Liverpool Apprenticeship Book*, 352/CRE/REG/4-1, Liverpool PRO. For the period 1707–1727, the occupations of nearly half of the fathers listed in the *Apprenticeship Book* are not specified.

[329]*Liverpool Apprenticeship Book*, December 9, 1713, Andrew Troughton, son of Myles Troughton, yeomen of Lancashire, [apprenticed] to Richard Aspinwall; February 8, 1717, Samuel Cross, son of John Cross, yeomen of Rainhill, Lancashire, [apprenticed] to Robert Litherland, ship's carpenter of Liverpool, "for 7yrs. From the 25th—March 1715 by Indenture dated 28th of March 1714; May 10, 1718;" Richard Pope, son of Richard Pope, yeomen of the parish of Leyland, Lancashire, [apprenticed] to Robert Litherland, shipwright of Liverpool.

[330]*Liverpool Apprenticeship Book*, May 13, 1719, William Walsh, son of Robert Walsh, house carpenter of Ormskirk, Lancashire, to John Livesley, bricklayer of Liverpool; 8/10/1724, Robert Leatherbarrow, son of Henry Leatherbarrow, innkeeper of Ormskirk, Lancashire, to James Harvey, blacksmith of Liverpool.

as well as the sons of Foster Cunliffe, William Earle, and William Boates retreated to landed estates in Lancashire, Cheshire, Middlesex, and Wales after they had retired from active commerce.[331] Over time, the developing nexus between gentle birth, family ambition, wealth, and kinship ties gave more affluent families a growing advantage in the competition for elite apprenticeships. Even before 1700, there was a tendency for apprentices entering privileged trades to rely upon family connections to ease their entry, as many had wealthy and influential relatives and family friends who were well established in specific trades and professions. While the apprenticeship market in Liverpool remained socially diverse well into the eighteenth century, this changed decisively after 1740, as a chasm opened in the types of apprenticeships that were available for wealthy families, and those for families lacking significant financial resources. As a result, the vast majority of "lesser" apprenticeships, those which held few prospects of wealth and social advancement, went to the less privileged sons of urban tradesmen, artisans, minor professionals, and yeomen.

The influx of gentry sons into Liverpool in the eighteenth century reinforced the growing social stratification of apprenticeship, a development which had become increasingly commonplace throughout England by the seventeenth century. In London, for instance, the proportion of apprentices who described themselves as gentlemen increased steadily, from 5% in 1530–1 to 18% in 1630–60, an increase that was most pronounced in the four Inns of Court and the more prestigious trades.[332] This, Brooks argues, indicates that apprenticeship had become a much more socially acceptable career option for the gentry, promoting "a significant, and increasing, degree of mobility between the gentry and trade during the sixteenth and seventeenth centuries."[333] In London, many members of elite guilds were the children of established freemen, as both apprenticeship and guild membership became "increasingly inbred."[334] Although apprenticeship was in decline by 1700, for the sons of the wealthy and well born it remained the only way to enter many elite trades and professions, gradually evolving into a heredity social perquisite that was reserved for elite families.[335] For middling sons, however, apprenticeship increasingly lost its significance as means of social advancement after 1700.

In both London and Liverpool, apprenticeship shared many similarities. As in London, the sons of landed gentlemen flocked to Merseyside by the 1690s to train as merchants. During her visit to Liverpool in 1698, Celia Fiennes observed that "many gentlemen's sons from the counties of Lancashire, Yorkshire, Derbyshire, Staffordshire, Cheshire, and North Wales [were being] put [as] apprentices in the town."[336] The sons of a number of gentlemen remained in the city for the balance of their business careers. As these wealthy families could afford to pay the high premiums charged by the most illustrious of merchants, their sons generally apprenticed in some of Liverpool's greatest trading houses. In April 1715, for instance, Roger Brooke (c.1700–1753), son of Sir Thomas Brooke of Norton, Cheshire, was apprenticed to Alderman John Earle, later becoming a prominent merchant in his own right, and participating in some 24 slaving ventures between 1733 and 1754.[337] Another prominent Liverpool merchant and political figure, Charles Pole, the son of Samuel Pole Esq., of Radbourne, Derbyshire, entered a merchant apprenticeship with Richard Gildart in 1712, eventually serving as an M.P. for Liverpool after a profitable career as a slave trader.[338] The son-in-law of Foster Cunliffe, Pole joined his father-in-law in several slaving ventures prior to Cunliffe's death

---

[331]*Cheshire Sheaf*, 60; Will of Sir Ellis Cunliffe of Saint George Hanover Square, Middlesex, November 28, 1767, PCC: PROB 11/933; Will of Sir Robert Cunliffe of Chester, Cheshire, November 27, 1778, PCC: PROB11/1047; Tyler, 250.

[332]Paul Lucas, "A Collective Biography of Students and Barristers of Lincoln's Inn, 1680–1804: A Study in the 'Aristocratic Resurgence' of the Eighteenth Century," *Journal of Modern History* 46 (1974), 227–261; C. Brooks, 61.

[333]C. Brooks, 61.

[334]W.F. Kahl, "Apprenticeship and the Freedom of the London Livery Companies, 1690–1750," *Guildhall Miscellany*, 7 (1956), 17–19; C. Brooks, 61, 65, 71.

[335]Paul Langford, *A Polite and Commercial People: England, 1727–1783* (1989), 180; C. Brooks, 54; Sweet, 38.

[336]Celia Fiennes, *The Journeys of Celia Fiennes* (1698); quoted in Aughton, *Liverpool: A People's History*, 49.

[337]*Liverpool Apprenticeship Book*, April 7, 1715, Roger Brooke, son of Sir Thomas Brooke of Norton in Cheshire, Baronet, [apprenticed] to Alderman John Earle, Esq., of Liverpool, merchant; Will of Roger Brooke, merchant of Liverpool, Wills and Inventories, Chester Probate Registry, 1753, *TSTD*.

[338]*Liverpool Apprenticeship Book*, May 22, 1712, Charles Pole, son of Samuel Pole Esq., of Radbourne, Derbyshire, [apprenticed] to Richard Gildart, merchant of Liverpool.

in 1758.[339] Likewise, William Bulkeley (1691–1760), the son of a landed gentleman from Anglesey, North Wales, was apprenticed to Cunliffe in September 1731, and joined him in all eleven of his slaving ventures between 1745–1756.[340] A later transplant to Liverpool, Christopher Hassell (1739–1773), was the fourth son of Squire Edward Hassell (1698–1781) of Dalemain Hall, Cumberland, and the maternal grandson of Sir Christopher Musgrave, baronet, of Edenhall, Penrith, Cumberland.[341] A man of means, Edward Hassell paid a premium of £100 to apprentice his son to merchant and salt refiner John Blackburn in 1759, a prominent figure in Liverpool who was selected Lord Mayor the following year. Soon after the younger Hassell became a freeman of Liverpool in 1763, his father gave him £1,000 to set up business, a sum which eased his entry into the lucrative slave trade, and permitted him to marry the daughter of wealthy slave trader John Goad (1707–1772) in 1765.[342] Families from throughout North England and the Midlands contributed to this steady influx of gentry sons into Liverpool trade.[343]

While the social backgrounds of Liverpool merchant apprentices became increasingly less diverse after 1700, their regional origins remained consistently narrow throughout the seventeenth and eighteenth centuries, most coming from neighboring Lancashire and Cheshire. For the well-to-do family, the question of where to apprentice a son was influenced not only by a town's propinquity and importance, but also by family wealth and stature, the perceived value of particular types of apprenticeships in specific towns, and by the ability of fathers to contract appropriate arrangements with suitable masters. For many nearby families after 1660, the pull of Liverpool became irresistible. A sample of entries in the *Apprenticeship Enrollment Book* indicates that for the period between 1707 and 1755, over half of all entering apprentices whose place of origin is identified came from Lancashire and Cheshire, with far fewer coming from Yorkshire, Derbyshire, Berkshire, Wales, Ireland, Scotland, and North America.[344] This contrasts sharply with London, where about 40% of the estimated 20,000 apprentices in London in 1650 came from outside the city, many traveling long distances, mostly from North England and the Midlands, to take up their apprenticeships.[345] As entry into the elite trades in London became progressively more circumscribed in the eighteenth century, the regional origins of apprentices shifted southward and became less diverse. A larger proportion now came from London itself and fewer from small towns and rural precincts.[346]

As might be expected in a port such as Liverpool, a significant number of middling sons were apprenticed as sailors with local merchants and mariners. While an apprenticeship at sea was the starting point for many of Liverpool's great slave traders, it was an occupational dead-end for many others. Some apprenticeships at sea were simply introductions to the hard life of the able seamen, what Ralph Davis describes as the lower ranks of sailing, and by the mid-eighteenth century, such apprenticeships were becoming less popular with families of even moderate means.[347] Increasingly, apprentice sailors were simply paupers forced into a mari-

---

[339]*TSTD*; C. Brooke, 297. Charles Pole was a partner in approximately 27 slaving ventures between 1747–1774, and died in 1779.

[340]*Liverpool Apprenticeship Book*, September 1731, William Bulkeley, son of Thomas Bulkeley, of Anglesey, in North Wales, Gent., [apprenticed] to Foster Cunliffe, Esq., merchant of Liverpool; *International Genealogy Index, The Liverpool Memorandum Book of 1753; TSTD*.

[341]Maurice Schofield, "A Good Fortune and a Good Wife: The Marriage of Christopher Hassell of Liverpool, Merchant, 1765," *The Transactions of the Historical Society of Lancashire and Cheshire* 138 (1989), 85.

[342]Schofield, "A Good Fortune and a Good Wife…," 85.

[343]*Liverpool Apprenticeship Book*, September 19, 1713, William Whalley, son of Ralph Whalley of Croston, Lancashire, [apprenticed] to Foster Cunliffe in August 24, 1714, John Atherton, son of John Atherton, of Lancashire, [apprenticed] to John Earle in September 1738, John Blackburn, son of John Blackburn Esq. of Hale, Lancashire, [apprenticed] to Foster Cunliffe. Will of John Blackburn of Blakelyhurst, Esquire, Wills and Inventories, Chester Probate Registry, Admon., 1766; *The Liverpool Memorandum Book; TSTD*. Scion of a long-established Lancashire family, and cousin of Richard Houghton II, John Blackburn II was primarily a salt merchant and refiner, although he was active in many lines of trade, including the slave trade. Blackburn served as a bailiff in 1755, and Lord Mayor in 1760, and is listed in the *TSTD* as a partner in thirteen slaving ventures between 1748–1761.

[344]*Liverpool Apprenticeship Book*; Gauci, *The Politics of Trade*, 100–102.

[345]Clark and Slack, *English Towns in Transition*, 65.

[346]C. Brooks, 63–64, Kahl, 17–20, Lucas, 227f.

[347]Davis, *The Rise of the English Shipping Industry*, 120.

time career under an *Act of 1704*, legislation designed to augment the recruiting of seamen.[348] Initially, some middling families sought out these maritime apprenticeships in the late seventeenth and early eighteenth centuries, hoping to heighten a son's career prospects by apprenticing him to a major Liverpool merchant. The prospects for a profitable career in trade for Edward Whalley, the son of a wheelwright apprenticed as a sailor to prominent merchant Richard Norris, were brighter than those of John Greenwood, a porter's son apprenticed as a sailor to Edward Rathbone, a little known Liverpool mariner.[349] As real wages rose in England in the decades before 1750, a flood of young men eager for work poured into urban centers, and merchants and ship's masters took advantage of this shifting mass of labor to hire only the sailors they needed, while still adhering to the superficial legal niceties that had long governed indentured apprenticeship. Paid by either the family or the local Overseers of the Poor, the premiums charged for these apprenticeships, when they were paid at all, were generally in the range of £10 or £20.[350] In many cases, the payment of a premium was wholly replaced by wages. Motivated purely by market factors, such arrangements evolved into a bastardized form of apprenticeship that no longer provided young men with the possibility of one day becoming a prosperous ship owner and merchant.[351]

While kinship ties and privileged relationships remained the essential building blocks of many merchant fortunes, the involvement of less-rooted men in Liverpool trade after 1700, men who were neither freemen nor residents, suggests that by the mid-eighteenth century an ongoing process of social and commercial liberalization had altered the composition of the Liverpool mercantile community.[352] Langford notes that the decline of apprenticeship resulted from a general weakening of the "ancient framework of regulation," a restrictive social regime that, many market-oriented reformers argued, had long impeded the free flow of labor.[353] However, the changing face of apprenticeship also affected the sons of wealthy tradesmen, merchants, and gentry, as the relative openness of Liverpool trade drew wealthy new men to Merseyside, and multiplied opportunities for trade. Driven, in part, by an unceasing search for new sources of investment, Liverpool's privileged merchants-*cum*-entrepreneurs willingly partnered these newcomers.

The Yorkshire historian Francis Drake observed in 1736 that a major factor in the growth of Liverpool trade was the cultivation of trading contacts by the ruling merchant oligarchs with non-resident merchants, a farsighted policy that attracted many men of means to Liverpool in the decades that followed.[354] This migration of new blood countered a fundamental obstacle to the further expansion of overseas trade after 1700, a lack of local merchants with the necessary resources and experience to take advantage of the trading opportunities which Liverpool's rise increasingly made available. As growing numbers of young men migrated to towns, many did so without first having entered into formal apprenticeships, and former apprentices entered trades for which they had not been trained.[355] In the slave trade this meant that the occupational backgrounds of investors were fairly diverse. Slave traders had trained as sailors, tradesmen, artisans, or professionals, while others served merchant apprenticeships in commercial centers prior to moving to Liverpool. Over time, this resulted in a loosening of long-established requirements for trading in Liverpool. A significant number of Liverpool's greatest slave traders, often *nouveaux riches* with few connections to the town, did not follow the typical career path that began with a Liverpool merchant apprenticeship.

For aspiring young men of business, the ultimate goal of a Liverpool apprenticeship was to secure the rights of a freeman. At the end of his term of service, an apprentice was typically admitted to the freedom of the town, gaining potentially lucrative trading privileges. The freedom of Liverpool could be obtained

---

[348]*ibid*, 120.

[349]*Apprenticeship Enrollment Book*, October 11, 1711, Edward Whalley, son of James Whalley, wheelwright of Walton, Lancashire, apprenticed as a sailor to Alderman Richard Norris, Esq., merchant of Liverpool.; September 24, 1714, John Greenwood, son of John Greenwood, porter, apprenticed as a sailor to Edward Rathbone, mariner of Liverpool.

[350]Davis, 120.

[351]C. Brooks, 72, 68; Corfield, 84; Langford, 180.

[352]Gauci, 100. Gauci use the value-laden term "democratization."

[353]Langford, 182.

[354]Francis Drake, *Eboracum: Or the History and Antiquities of the City of York* (1736) 240; cited in Gauci, 100.

[355]C. Brooks, 63, Kahl, 17.

in three well-established ways: by virtue of birth or patrimony, which required a payment of 3s. 4d. to the Liverpool Common Council; by servitude or apprenticeship, which required a payment of 6s 8d; and finally, *via* purchase, which required the payment of various sums as established in negotiations between the Common Council and petitioners, men who were often prominent merchants from other cities.[356] For many elite Liverpool merchant families, the freedom was viewed as a generational birthright. The sons of merchant-freemen John Earle, Bryan Blundell, Foster Cunliffe, Richard Gildart, Samuel Shaw, Richard Golightly, and Thomas Galley, for instance, were all admitted to the freedom by birth, allowing them to trade in Liverpool, manage the family businesses they inherited, and assume an elevated social and political standing within the town and Corporation.[357]

Before 1600, the freedom was simply a legal acknowledgement of a man's right to carry on a craft or trade but, by the early eighteenth century, it had become a mark of social prestige much coveted by wealthy and socially ambitious artisans, merchants, and professionals alike.[358] In addition to its social distinction, the freedom carried with it the franchise, corporate voting rights which provided men with the all-important privilege of entering the Freeman Assembly, possibly even the Common Council itself, a role in the selection of the Lord Mayor and bailiffs, and the right to hold high office. Although becoming a freeman did not guarantee selection as a Councilman, it was the generally accepted first step in entering the ranks of the town's ruling merchant-oligarchs. However, the freedom, like apprenticeship itself, was a declining institution in many places by 1700, an institution for which membership requirements were inconsistently enforced. Municipal corporations throughout England tried to halt their decline by redoubling efforts at enforcing corporate restrictions. These restrictions denied non-resident outsiders the valuable trading rights that were reserved for *bona fide* freemen alone.[359]

Like many English towns, Liverpool was eager to defend the economic privileges of its freemen. For Liverpool's economic and political leaders, this defense of privilege was not motivated by mere altruism. In defending their own trading rights, they reasoned that the town would continue to benefit from the wealth, expertise, and influence of merchant-freemen. Despite this, in the decades before and immediately after 1700, the Liverpool Common Council took strong action against outsiders attempting to do business in Liverpool, fining merchants not approved by council, and issuing presentments against resident freemen "for Entertaining inmates."[360] Efforts in the late seventeenth century to relax trading restrictions for non-freemen were decisively rejected by the freemen assembly, the Portmoot. Not surprisingly, one such gathering in October 1676 upheld the trading monopoly of freemen, as Mayor Robert Williamson, voicing the consensus of the town's freemen, declared,

> That by the custome and usage of this Corporation, any person intending to get his living by buying and selling in a way of traffick, trade or merchandize not having served an apprenticeship seven years to a freeman of this burrow, not being the son of a domestick freeman and borne within this burrow, ought not be made free without speciall order of the Councell of this Corporation.[361]

Although the Corporation was frequently sued by neighboring municipalities to end these trading restrictions, Liverpool nearly always won in court, and unapproved merchants continued to be fined for violating

---

[356]Holt, 118*n.*

[357]*Liverpool Directory of* 1766, Stewart-Brown, 114–115; Will of Thomas Galley, boat-builder of Liverpool, Wills and Inventories, Chester Probate Registry, 1770.

[358]Kahl, 17.

[359]Langford, 181.

[360]*Liverpool Town Book, Corporation Minutes*, 135, MF2/2-5, Liverpool PRO. A non-resident merchant was termed an "inmate."

[361]Order of Mayor Robert Williamson, October 18, 1676, cited in Sir James Picton, *Selections from the Municipal Archives and Records, from the 13th to the 17th Century Inclusive* (1883), 295.

the trading monopoly of Liverpool freemen.[362] While the Corporation most often proceeded against outsiders attempting to trade in Liverpool, a case in 1709 involved two presentments made against prominent merchant Richard Gildart for conspiring to allow inmates to exercise "their respective Trades following within this Corporation [while] not being free."[363]

Recent research has demonstrated that the importance of apprenticeship as a mode of admission to the freedom of Liverpool varied in the period between 1660 and 1750. Gauci has found that, for all merchants admitted to the freedom between 1660 and 1719, service was the most important method of entrance, particularly after 1690. Between 1660 and 1719, 41% of all new freemen were admitted through service, a method that had superseded admission by purchase or birth by 1710.[364] However, as apprenticeship declined after 1730, a larger number of traders gained admission to the freedom by purchase and patrimony than by service. The importance of purchase after 1740 suggests that many new traders relocating to Liverpool sought the freedom simply to acquire trading privileges, not to establish themselves as resident merchants and tradesmen. In addition, it became increasingly clear that a significant number of former Liverpool apprentices never intended to become freemen, since many failed to establish permanent residences in Liverpool and returned home at the end of their apprenticeship term while remaining active in Liverpool trade.[365] In the slave trade, former Liverpool apprentices who returned home continued to participate in slaving ventures from Liverpool, as did established slave traders who retreated to country estates. Young men seldom entered apprenticeships specifically to train as slave traders, and the absence of a recognized career path allowed not only merchant-apprentices to acquire the freedom and enter that trade, but also men who had trained as craftsmen, professionals, mariners, and tradesmen.

Although prominent merchant-freemen often participated in the slave trade, this emergent trade was not bound by the same types of restrictions that limited membership in the prestigious craft trades and professions, or the more elite trading companies, such as the East India and Levant Companies. Ilana Ben-Amos suggests that in Liverpool by 1700 it was possible for a migrant to set up in trade in London, Bristol or Newcastle "without ever having obtained formal qualifications."[366] Liverpool slave traders often began their careers as mariners, eventually becoming great slave merchants by effectively exploiting both their earnings and expertise. Many, like the Lancaster-born merchant mariners John Goad (1707–1772) and James Strangeways (died-1770), never became freemen.[367] Although Strangeways was a partner in five Liverpool slaving ventures between 1748 and 1754, at his death in 1770 he described himself in his will as a merchant of Lancaster.

While the sons of affluent families continued to enjoy advantages that aided their rise in Liverpool commerce, these became less important in the slave trade after the 1740s. What mattered most to the organizers of ventures was neither the social status nor kinship ties a potential investor possessed, but rather the commercial connections and financial resources he could bring to the partnership. In the decades after 1730, the Liverpool slave trade became an open, fluid, and profitable trade that attracted great numbers of would-be participants. The capital requirements of this trade, however, led slave merchants effectively to ignore the restrictions upon the trade of non-freemen in order to attract investment from outside Liverpool. By at least 1730, Liverpool

---

[362]Picton, *Selections from the Municipal Archives and Records,* 298. For instance, Carlisle, Lancaster, and Wigan all unsuccessfully sued the Corporation of Liverpool in 1663 in an attempt to secure trading rights in Liverpool for their own freemen.

[363]*Liverpool Town Book, Corporation Minutes,* 120, 135, MF2/2-5, Liverpool PRO.

[364]Gauci, 56.

[365]*ibid,* 56.

[366]Ilana Krauseman Ben-Amos, "Failure to Become Freemen: Urban Apprentices in Early Modern England," *Social History* 16 (1991), 156–159.

[367]Schofield, "A Good Fortune and a Good Wife," 89; Maurice Schofield, "The Slave Trade from Lancashire and Cheshire Ports Outside Liverpool, c. 1750–c.1790," *Transactions of the Historical Society of Lancashire and Cheshire* 126 (1977), 46–47; *Liverpool Directory of 1766. See also:* Maurice Schofield, "Shoes and Ships and Sealing Wax: Eighteenth-Century Lancashire Exports to the Colonies," *Transactions of the Historical Society of Lancashire and Cheshire* 135 (1986), 61–82; F. J. Singleton, "The Flax Merchants of Kirkham," *Transactions of the Historical Society of Lancashire and Cheshire* 126 (1977), 73–108.

slave traders had fashioned a partnership system in which the overall management of a slaving venture was retained by merchant-freemen, while non-free investors became owners but not operators.

The experience of one merchant demonstrates the investment options that were available to non-freemen. Son of a poor yeomen family from the Furness region of North Lancashire, John Goad had settled in Liverpool by 1738 and became a captain in the Virginia tobacco trade, later partnering in over 40 slaving ventures between 1752 and 1774.[368] Although he never became a freeman of Liverpool, Goad overcame his trading disabilities by investing with major slave traders such as John Welch, also a native of North Lancashire, who became a freeman of Liverpool by purchase in 1744.[369] Major slave traders like Welch welcomed the entry of experienced merchant-investors such as Goad into the African trade, regardless of their lack of freeman status. Although the freedom of Liverpool remained commercially desirable until 1777 when the right of freemen to import goods into Liverpool free of town-dues was abolished, it had become difficult, even impossible, to enforce the trading monopoly of freemen while at the same time attempting to encourage non-free investors to participate in Liverpool trade.

The slow collapse of the ancient occupational structure of English trade gradually altered the manner in which many Liverpool merchants formed the business relationships that were the lifeblood of the slave trade. Even during the heyday of traditional apprenticeship practices in the mid-seventeenth century, the social construction of an apprenticeship weighed more heavily in the formation of a commercial career than did its pedagogic or occupational features.[370] Although affluent men continued to pay extremely large premiums to bind their sons to well-known and prominent merchants, the key to success in trade was not so much the apprenticeships themselves, important though they were in preparing a young man for the rigors and uncertainties of trade, but rather the social universe which merchants in particular trades inhabited. In terms of apprenticeship and the bonds of partnership, Carl Estabrook observes that "the performance of a job or the transmission of occupational skills were important bases of long-term personal associations in early modern England."[371] For many merchants, but not all, the years spent as an apprentice were the most important of their professional life, as they formed personal and business connections that influenced the whole course of their mercantile career.

The relationship between master and apprentice could be especially close and long-lived if the master and apprentice were relatives. For many slave merchants, the personal bonds formed between masters and apprentices often laid the foundation for a profitable career in slave trading. While most apprentices did not enjoy the types of personal relationships with their masters that might ultimately lead to close friendships, business partnerships, or even marriage into a masters family, some masters did assist former apprentices in raising the capital necessary to enter into business for themselves, while others took apprentices on as partners, eventually passing the business on to them when they retired.[372] William Earle took great pains to assist his former apprentice Isaac Dove during his first few independently managed ventures to the West Indies, providing advice, soliciting business for him, making the necessary introductions, and recommending him to his business associates as "an honest, industrious, and sober man."[373] "As Mr. Dove served his time with Mr. William Earle," Earle and his business partner Nehemiah Holland wrote to Captain John Hogan in Virginia, "[and] is a young man of good character, [we] will be obliged to you to countenance him & if he stands in need of your advice & of assistance, you will assist him, which [we] shall take…as a favor

[368]TSTD; Maurice Schofield, "Lancashire Shipping in the Eighteenth Century: The Rise of A Seafaring Family," *Transactions of the Historical Society of Lancashire and Cheshire* 140 (1991), 9f; Schofield, "A Good Fortune and a Good Wife," 89.

[369]TSTD; Schofield, "A Good Fortune and a Good Wife," 92; Will of John Goad, merchant of Liverpool, Wills and Inventories, Chester Probate Registry, 1773; Will of John Welch, merchant of Leck, Lancashire, March 16, 1780, PCC: PROB 11/1063; Melinda Elder, *The Slave Trade and the Economic Development of Eighteenth-Century Lancaster* (1992), 78.

[370]Davis, *The Rise of the English Shipping Industry*, 120; C. Brooks, 60f.

[371]Estabrook, *Urbane and Rustic England*, 110.

[372]C. Brooks, 74.

[373]William Earle to Isaac Dove, December 8, 1760, *Daybook of William Earle*, D/EARLE/2/2, Merseyside Maritime Museum; William Earle to Richard Bradshaw & Co., January 8, 1761, *Daybook of William Earle*, D/EARLE/2/2; Captain Nehemiah Holland & William Earle to John Hogan, [No Date], D/EARLE/2/2.

conferred."[374] Increasingly, Liverpool slave traders were drawn together by a growing variety of bonds in the pursuit of profitable trade that drew upon, and transcended traditional commercial connections arising solely from kinship ties and/or master/apprentice relationships. By 1750, Liverpool slave traders routinely forged commercial ties with traders with whom they had no personal history, men with whom they shared little besides a common desire for profit.

VI

The rapid growth of Liverpool trade after 1700 attracted a diverse group of men eager to establish themselves on Merseyside as merchants, mariners, professionals, tradesmen, and craftsmen. Unlike Bristol where an elite group of merchants monopolized the slave trade for much of the eighteenth century, in Liverpool that trade was much more open, and represented commercial opportunity for a range of expectant men from throughout Britain, men with often diverse social and occupational backgrounds. The Liverpool slave-trading community was thus an amalgam of long established merchant families and new men in search of both profit and social connection. While a number of slave traders were able to utilize close family ties with resident kin to ease their introduction to Liverpool and launch successful mercantile careers, many, if not most, had small connections in Liverpool prior to their arrival. A fortunate few, men like John Earle and later Arthur Heywood, came to Liverpool as apprentices bound to elite merchants, prosperous and influential gentlemen like William Clayton and John Hardman who could provide access and open doors for their former apprentices. Most newcomers, however, could not rely upon an elite apprenticeship to establish them in trade, and were thrown upon their own devices to get ahead in Liverpool. Forging a prosperous career became far easier for such aspiring merchants after 1750 as both apprenticeship and the freedom fell into desuetude. Although most lived in town or nearby Lancashire or Cheshire, an increasing number of active merchants, new men who never served apprenticeships in Liverpool or established permanent residence, were illegally engaged in trade. While many of these new men were merely investors in the slave trade, migrants who did not assume an active role in the preparation or management of slaving ventures, some of the largest, most important slave traders to emerge after 1740 were also migrants who quickly established themselves as masters of their chosen trade.

---

[374]Captain Nehemiah Holland & William Earle to John Hogan, [No Date] D/EARLE/2/2.

Chapter 4

Merchant Friends

It is usually assumed that non-market factors have been less important in the conduct of commerce than impersonal market forces. Liberal thinkers such as Adam Smith, and more recently Karl Polanyi, have argued that rational impersonality characterized the operation of modern markets, thus creating, in effect, a price-driven economic system of mutually beneficial exchange in which participants sought their own advantage at the expense of others.[375] This posited impersonality has often been discounted by more recent writers who have championed the importance of non-market social and personal factors in early modern market exchange.

Also crucial were friendships. Mathias argues that non-economic imperatives, such as respect, reputation, and reciprocity might well be honored "at the expense of economic rationality, narrowly considered," but this could hardly be otherwise in a society held together by close personal relationships.[376] Naomi Tadmor maintains that while friendship has been defined most often "as a voluntary sentimental attachment between people that lacked any practical economic benefits," there has always been an instrumental economic dimension to friendship, particularly among merchants and tradesmen.[377] As Hancock says of London, personal associations formed a major point of contact among London merchants in the formation of business relationships.[378] Non-market varieties of exchange have persisted into modern times, and in fact continue to exist. As the enormous number and variety of commercial relationships evident in the eighteenth-century Liverpool slave trade indicates, market exchange was far from impersonal, or even rational.

---

[375]Adam Smith, *The Theory of Moral Sentiments*, eds., D.D. Raphael and A.L. Macfie (1976) 1, chap., ii. 50; Karl Polanyi, *The Great Transformation: The Political and Economic Origins of our Time* (1944), cited in Offer, 450.

[376]Mathias, 31–32.

[377]Tadmor, 168–169.

[378]David Hancock, *Citizens of the World: London Merchants and the Integration of the British Atlantic Community, 1735–1785* (1995); *See also*: Richardson, *The Bristol Slave Traders: A Collective Portrait*, (1985).

I

The eighteenth century Liverpool slave trade was influenced far more by connections of friendship between men of trade than has been heretofore recognized. Closely interrelated families of merchants were only part of the *dramatis personae* of eighteenth century Liverpool trade, and kinship played a variable role in the formation of commercial partnerships. For many merchants the ties that connected them with non-related friends and business associates were often as important as blood relationships in the conduct of their trade. Merchants formed business networks that consisted, in large part, of multiple and overlapping circles of friends, intense and enduring relationships based on bonds of mutuality and reciprocity.

Merchant friendships contributed significantly to the expansion of the Liverpool slave trade in the decade and a half between 1748 and 1763. Satisfying, efficient, and useful, merchant friendships were founded upon a multitude of personal bonds, connections that emphasized mutual respect, personal reputation, and friendly sociability. The personal interactions were animated by what Avner Offer terms "the pursuit…[of]… regard, " a sense of acceptance which spurred cooperation between merchants, thereby making trade more effectual.[379] Cooperation was founded on trust, which Offer argues was efficient because "it economizes on the transaction costs of monitoring, compliance, and enforcement, and may be viewed as transaction [as a] benefit."[380] Friendship and sociability thus acted to promote commercial expansion because merchants needed to form dependable, trustworthy connections with potential trading partners in order to form partnerships, raise capital, and effectively pursue the economic opportunities that were available to them.

In the eighteenth-century market place, merchants generally knew what to expect from the varied relationships they formed with each other in the ordinary pursuit of trade and profit. Their understanding of friendship was far broader and more inclusive than today, and included not only relationships based upon personal attachment and sentiment, but also ties that ranged in intimacy from the closest kinsmen and religious brethren to political allies and distant business associates. In theory, true friendship was a rare and valuable blessing, especially in business, where merchant friendships were properly motivated by both affection and common interest in pursuit of mutual commercial gain. In practical commercial terms, however, friendship was ideally a mutual exchange that was advantageous to all parties within a network of association, a bond that was "both sentimental in inspiration and instrumental in effects."[381] Largely, merchant behavior and comportment was regulated by an unofficial code of conduct that enshrined commonly held attitudes and expectations regarding personal interactions between merchants, and the mutual requirements of respect, reciprocity, and reputation.[382] These attitudinal and behavioral expectations made possible the formation of close, often intimate relationships between merchants, an interpersonal dynamic that was essential to the normal conduct of trade. The bonds which informed merchant friendships, however, were not based solely upon mutual respect, generosity, or affection, but rather upon an admixture of motivations that ran the gamut from selfishness to selflessness. To a gentleman, the only thing worse than a selfish friend was not having friends at all, for "there [was] no greater wilderness than to be without true friends."[383]

Eighteenth-century conceptions of friendship served many purposes in early modern England. However, little has been written about the almost invisible bonds of friendship and affiliation that often drew merchants and their associates together in common pursuit of profit in the West African slave trade. Of course, many different degrees and types of connection and familiarity existed between slavers and other men of trade, ranging from mere business connections, to sociability and conviviality, to friendship and kinship. Katherine

---

[379]Avner Offer, "Between the Gift and the Market: The Economy of Regard," *The Economic History Review* 50 (1997), 451; Naomi Tadmor, *Family and Friends in Eighteenth Century England: Household, Kinship, and Patronage* (2001), 204; Katharine Swett, "The Account Between Us: Honor, Reciprocity and Companionship in Male Friendship in the Later Seventeenth Century," *Albion*, 31 (1999), 4.

[380]Offer, 454. *See also*: Jacob Price, "Transaction Costs: A Note on Merchant Credit and the Organization of Private Trade," in *The Political Economy of Merchant Empires: State Power and World Trade, 1350–1750*, James Tracy, ed., (1991), 276–297.

[381]Julian Pitt-Rivers, "The Kith and Kin," in Jack Goody, ed., *The Character of Kinship* (1973), 89–105

[382]Offer, 451.

[383]Richard Braithwaite, *The English Gentlemen* (1630); quoted in Swett, 1.

Swett notes "friendship was both chosen and given, a fortunate accident or a tie strenuously worked for and assiduously cultivated [as well as] ubiquitous and vital…an act as much as a state of mind."[384] While the word 'friend' was perhaps a common term of social identification between individuals, it was a mutable word with innumerable meanings that encompassed a broad spectrum of relationships in both theory and practice.[385] Arising from variegated patterns of connection, merchant friendships served to personalize the reciprocal relationships that were a necessary component in the world of seventeenth- and eighteenth -century English trade.[386] Together with kinship ties, the sociable bonds that linked merchant friends in common cause helped to shape the social construction of the eighteenth-century Liverpool slave trade, especially after 1763, forming vital ingredients in the configuration of slaving partnerships.

II

Two points of contact between merchants—written correspondence and sociability—evidence the importance of friendship in eighteenth-century English trade. Although merchant friendships were often based upon common activities such as club membership, drinking, or common commercial pursuits, letter-writing itself was a form of sociability which proclaimed the social connectedness of the correspondents.[387] As is typically reflected in their correspondence, many merchants greatly valued close connections with select friends and business partners as both personally satisfying and commercially beneficial. As result, the letters of many eighteenth-century merchants are frequently a mish-mash of seemingly unrelated topics that demonstrate the degree to which personal and business interests were often intertwined. Merchant correspondents engaged in a superficial discourse with one another that was larded with polite pleasantries, expressions of friendship and obligation, market news and commercial observations, complaints, assessments of other men, offers of service, and gossip. In even the most sharply worded letters, however, social convention was honored and a strict etiquette of civility was observed throughout. Swett notes that the language of friendship used in commercial letters was often highly stylized, and was "indistinguishable not only from the language of courtship but also from much elite business correspondence between patron and client, ties often described by elite men as friendships."[388] The language employed in these letters expressed a desire to cultivate useful relationships with a wide range of possible business friends and partners, as well as deepening purely sentimental friendships. For the most part, this discourse between merchants was designed to avoid any suggestion of rejection in written communications, as well as face-to-face meetings between friends and strangers.[389] For a young merchant, building a useful network of merchant correspondents often required a veritable campaign of friendly solicitousness, a circle of friends that was evidence of his arrival as both an adult and a merchant.

The business correspondence of William Earle reveals an identifiable circle of merchant friends with whom he conversed, complained, commiserated, argued, importuned, and exchanged flatteries. Outwardly, these letters were models of polite discourse, friendliness, and gentility which often masked self-interested. Earle was capable of applying the same superficial friendliness and good humor to both distant business associates and close kin, employing a standardized geniality that became a common theme in many of his letters. "Mrs. Earle & my best respects to Peter, your son," Earle wrote Hamburg merchant Joachim Koch in November 1760, "We have 3 boys and a girl, all in good health."[390] Earle never met this German supplier, but was eager to maintain his friendship and confidence. "I am much obliged to you for [your] inquiry after my

---

[384]Swett, 1.

[385]Tadmor, 167; Swett, 16; Randolph Trumbach, *The Rise of the Egalitarian Family: Aristocratic Kinship and Domestic Relations in Eighteenth-Century England* (1978), 64.

[386]Swett, 2–3.

[387]Swett, 6–7.

[388]Linda Levy Peck, *Court Patronage and Corruption in Early Stuart England* (1990), cited in Swett, 2.

[389]Offer, 454.

[390]William Earle to Joachim Henry Koch (Hamburg), November 5, 1760, D/EARLE/2/2.

family," Earle replied to a sea captain in February 1761, "who are all well & join with me in best respects."[391] Earle's correspondence routinely featured reciprocal exchanges of personal information between partners, families, friends, and often strangers, communications that built a bond of familiarity and trust. In August 1761, Earle wrote a short note to John Baillie, captain of the overdue slaver *Elizabeth*, which expressed friendship, concern, and a degree of familiarity. "Dear Sir," Earle wrote Baillie,

> This [note] serves only to enclose a letter from your mother. I hope it will meet you well, which will give me great pleasure to hear after your long & tedious purchase [in Africa], which I dread to hear of, fearing your mortality will be very great. Mrs. Earle joins with me in best respects & believe me to be truly your assured friend & very humble servant.[392]

Earle's solicitousness in this case is attributable to his desire to establish good relations with Baillie, a capable and experienced captain in the slave trade, in order to lure him away from the slaving firm of *Crosbies & Traffords*, Earle's rivals and Baillie's current employers. The conclusion of a June 1760 letter to his close friend, partner, and brother-in-law Captain John Copeland, as well as a letter to a former apprentice Isaac Dove in April 1761, differed very little in either form or meaning from those written to relative strangers like John Baillie, or Hamburg merchant Joachim Koch. "Mrs. Earle joins me in best respects," Earle wrote to Captain Copeland at sea aboard the slaver *Industry*, "[and offer] my service to [West Indian slave factors] Mr. Jones & Mr. Crewdson & believe me, Dear Sir, [I am] your assured friend." In a similar vein, Earle wrote Dove in April 1761 that "Your mother is very well, she was here today [and] Mrs. Earle & the children are well & desire their love & service."[393] At times, it is difficult to determine what Earle actually thought of the men with whom he corresponded, or how intimate many of his business friendships really were. Adhering to the expected etiquette of merchant communications, Earle's often ingratiating letters demonstrate that he sought to create a pseudo-sentimental connection with many of his correspondents in order to multiply his future business prospects.

The bond of friendship between merchants was also expressed in the exchange of personal favors, intimate personal exchanges, and gifts within a well-developed personal network of associates. Because a gift was frequently not a selfless gesture but rather an attempt to create reciprocal obligations between business friends and well-disposed correspondents, it was not without cost, regardless of the value of the gift. "Reciprocity is not all pleasure," Offer observes, "[as] giving gives rise to obligation...a burden, which can only be relieved by means of a return gift...[as]...an unreciprocated gift...vexes both giver and receiver... [and]...can be rejected or misconstrued."[394] Earle made every reasonable effort to return the friendly gestures and gifts presented to him by his business associates. In January 1761, Earle responded to an unknown favor or gift proffered by Captain James Littley with the promise of a return gift. "My wife waits on opportunities of sending you some triffle," Earle wrote Littley, "[although] she has been very much indisposed, but is now better."[395] Similarly, Earle wrote his friend and partner John Joseph Bacon in February 1761 that "I return you my best thanks for the fine codfish & claret [and] will send you, as soon as ready, some ale of my own brewing. I remain, Sir [Your humble servant]."[396] Earle was not shy about asking for favors either. In November 1760, for instance, he sent a bill of exchange for £70 to London to be credited to his account with the merchants *Harrison & Wilson*, requesting that they debit this account the price of two lottery tickets "not [to] cost above £5–10 each."[397] While such minor interactions between business associates were typical of

---

[391]Earle to Captain Sherwell, February 14, 1761, D/EARLE/2/2.

[392]Earle to John Baillie, August 2, 1761. The *Elizabeth* was captured by the French after disembarking slaves in Guadeloupe in 1760. *TSTD*.

[393]Earle to Isaac Dove, April 30, 1761.

[394]Offer, 455.

[395]Earle to Captain James Littley, January 26, 1761, D/EARLE/2/2.

[396]Earle to John Joseph Bacon, February 12, 1761, D/EARLE/2/2.

[397]Earle to Messrs. Harrison & Wilson (London), November 29, 1760.

the many small favors exchanged by friends, they often lacked the emotional connection characteristic of true friendships.

Additionally, Earle sought to build a reserve of good-will and obligation with his merchant correspondents by undertaking inquiries on their behalf, or by doing personal favors. He occasionally went out of his way to assist his friends and their extended families. In February 1761 Earle wrote his close business associate Joseph Wimpey, a prominent London merchant, financier, and broker, requesting that he inquire after the whereabouts of Captain William Robinson, at the behest of Robinson's mother. "If it would not be too much trouble to inquire," Earle wrote Wimpey,

> for the mother of Captain William Robinson…[who]…keeps a slop shop on Execution dock… to know where Captain Robinson of the [ship] *Loyalty*, arrived from Guadeloupe, now is & whether he left any directions with her to pay the wages of William Taylor, a servant of mine who came with him from Guadeloupe…I will readily pay any expense upon the inquiry [that is] required.[398]

A fortnight later, Earle apologized to Wimpey for the difficulties he had encountered in locating Captain Robinson, suggesting that the inquiry had come to naught.[399]

Earle also requested that his friends undertake inquiries that were more directly related to the conduct of his business. In April 1761, Earle asked his associate Thomas Jordan, a Birmingham ironmonger and gun merchant, "to order [an] inquiry to be made at the Inns in your town for Captain John Sachaverell of the ship *Rumbold* & deliver [to him] the enclosed [note from Mr. Thomas Rumbold] who [has] ordered me to write him [in order] to give him the preference of what heavy Angola muskets you can."[400] Earle's note, written on behalf of Liverpool slave merchant Thomas Rumbold, was to be delivered to Sachaverell upon his arrival in Birmingham from London. "Mr. Rumbold," Earle's note to Sachaverell explained,

> desired me to write you to call upon Mr. Thomas Jordan of Birmingham to look at his heavy Angola muskets. He has been pleased to promise us the order for the *Rumbold* if you approved of them when [you] saw them…Mr. [Peter] Leay, Mr. [Nehemiah] Holland & myself are concerned in the commission, who will be equally obliged to you for your interest. [401]

A complex web of association connected Earle to Rumbold, and hence to both their respective commercial partners, and enabled him to supply Rumbold with the muskets that he required for an upcoming slaving venture to Angola.[402]

Although most business was conducted by letter, merchants often chose to travel, frequently great distances, in order to socialize with their business correspondents and solidify reciprocal trading relationships. These visits, or more accurately business tours, could cover a great deal of ground, and be quite time-consuming. The reciprocal exchange of letters between merchants served to fix the general commercial rationale for such tours, and set the groundwork for individual business trips. Tadmor notes that Thomas Turner, a shopkeeper of East Hoathley, Sussex, traveled much in his "near neighborhood transacting business, settling parish affairs, visiting and socializing."[403] Overseas merchants liked William Earle, however, traveled much farther afield. As the British Empire expanded, business travel became an indispensable and common part of commercial life, as young merchants toured widely on business.[404] British merchants traveled throughout England, Ireland, Scotland, the continent, the Baltic, the Levant, Africa, the West Indies, and North America

---

[398]Earle to Messrs. Joseph Wimpey & Co. (London), February 10, 1761.

[399]Earle to Messrs. Joseph Wimpey & Co., February 25, 1761.

[400]Earle to Mr. Thomas Jordan (Birmingham), April 1, 1761, D/EARLE/2/2.

[401]Earle to Mr. Thomas Jordan, with enclosed letter to Captain John Sachaverell, April 1, 1761.

[402]*TSTD*. This ship, the *Rumbold*, departed Liverpool for Angola on June 1, 1761.

[403]Tadmor, 173.

[404]Peter Clark, *British Clubs and Societies, 1580–1800: The Origins of an Associational World* (2000) 159.

in order to establish a physical presence in new markets, build overseas networks of business friends and solicit their custom, and to support relationships with British suppliers. In the burgeoning transatlantic trade, such business travel was not a "one-way affair," as colonial, English, Irish, and Scots merchants crisscrossed the Atlantic to promote their trade.[405] Young Quaker merchants from the colonies, for instance, often traveled in Britain in order to form important connections within the community of British Quaker merchants, and to gain knowledge of the types of British goods that were available.[406] The far-flung travels of eighteenth-century British merchants strengthened mutual ties of trust and reputation that connected traders, bonds that served to integrate the larger imperial trading community.[407]

The perambulations of William Earle between March and July 1760, for instance, took him from Liverpool to the Isle of Man, London, Manchester, Bury, Sheffield, Yorkshire, Birmingham, and back to Liverpool, and revealed the pains Earle took to maintain personal ties with business associates and friends. Earle wrote Joseph Wimpey in London on March 28, 1760, his partner in a Highland-fishing venture, that he had returned from the Isle of Man on March 20 after arranging an upcoming voyage to the waters off Shetland.[408] Less than two months later, Earle departed for London both to confer with the firm of *Carter & Woodhouse*, London merchants who had contracted with Earle for a shipment of fish, concerning the purchase of a vessel suitable for the Highland fishing trade, and to purchase cargoes of trade goods for the upcoming voyages of the slaver *Minerva* to Old Calabar in the Bight of Biafra, and the *Seahorse* to the Windward Coast of Africa.[409] Nehemiah Holland, a partner of Earle in both the *Minerva* and the *Seahorse*, probably accompanied him for at least a part of this trip, for as Earle reported to a correspondent in Sheffield, Holland "got everything he could wish for at London & Manchester & says he now has a completer cargo than ever he had."[410] Earle and his friend Holland, and on other occasions his associate Patrick Black, formed a veritable mercantile embassy to the suppliers of African trade goods in London and elsewhere, coordinating their efforts to fulfill their obligations in trade goods that were apportioned to them by their fellow partners in both the *Minerva* and *Seahorse*.

Earle, however, could not visit all of his many correspondents on his various business trips. With an air of regret, and eager to clarify his reasons for not having visited him, Earle explained to this Sheffield correspondent, Joseph Kitchingham, that he "had almost a mind to have called on you when in Sheffield but my wife being but very indisposed obliged me to hurry home [and] she is now very well."[411] Similarly, Earle took pains to explain to his close associate John Humphreys, a Manchester ironmonger, why he had not been able to visit him in Manchester while he was there on business. "Sir," Earle informed Humphreys,

> I wrote [you] from Bury That I was going to Sheffield from whence I returned on [May] 14th & found [your letter] of the 5th. We came down the Derbyshire Road on account of going to Manchester so that I received yours in London [but] it would not have been in my power to have had the pleasure of seeing you...I am on all occasions, Sir, Your...[humble servant]... William Earle.[412]

---

[405]Kenneth Morgan, "Business Networks in the British Export Trade to North America, 1750–1880," in *The Early Modern Atlantic Economy*, eds., John McCusker and Kenneth Morgan (2000), 44.

[406]Kenneth Morgan, ed., *An American Quaker in the British Isles: The Travel Journals of Jabez Maud Fisher, 1775–1779* (1992), cited in Morgan, "Business Networks...," 41–42. Morgan argues that "the movement of merchants between Britain and America represented an attempt at more aggressive marketing techniques than had been the norm earlier in the export trade." Morgan, "Business Networks...," 45.

[407]Morgan, "Business Networks...," 47; David Hancock, *Citizens of the World*, 14–19, 81–84.

[408]Earle to Messrs. Joseph Wimpy & Co. (London), March 28, 1760.

[409]Earle to Messrs. Joseph Carter & John Woodhouse (London), May 18, 1760, D/EARLE/2/2; Earle to Joseph Kitchingham (Sheffield), May 16, 1760.

[410]Earle to Joseph Kitchingham, May 16, 1760.

[411]Earle to Joseph Kitchingham.

[412]Earle to John Humphreys (Manchester), May 17, 1760.

Upon his return to Liverpool in late May 1760, Earle also wrote John Darbyshire, a Birmingham ironmonger, to apologize for having forgotten to leave an insurance policy with him while he was in Birmingham, a policy that Earle had contracted for Darbyshire in Liverpool to cover his 1/8th share in the slaver *Calypso*.[413] Fearing that his correspondents would discover that he had visited their respective towns without personally presenting his regards, Earle penned several such apologies when he returned home in late May 1760. Although his apologies often seem contrived and insincere, Earle understood that such calculated acts of contrition were necessary in order to reassure his merchant friends, however superficially, that his failure to visit them did not signify any unfriendliness or estrangement on his part.

In addition to touching bases with them periodically, overseas traders like William Earle also relied upon their established friends to provide them with introductions to potential trading partners with whom they had no connection. In order to expand his network of commercial contacts, Earle actively sought such introductions, and provided them to traders with whom he hoped to do business at a future date. A statement of approbation and trust, an introduction from a reputable man of trade was a great advantage to a merchant, as it was a valued pledge of confidence in his character and abilities. Although letters of introduction were not always accepted by their intended recipients, and were occasionally disregarded, they provided traveling merchants, as well as respectable migrants, with the means of acquiring acceptance of their communal status away from home, recognition that was essential in establishing local trading connections.[414] It was not always easy for a newly arrived merchant who lacked local connections to gain *entrée* into the business community of a strange town. Such merchants ordinarily carried letters of introduction that they presented to prominent local individuals from mutual friends or well-known patrons but, more often than not, these newcomers were forced to frequent coaching inns, coffeehouses, taverns, and other drinking houses to initiate social contacts, venues that "acted as clearinghouses for regional flows of migration into the towns."[415] While an aristocratic pedigree or an established business reputation might ease a new migrant's entry into the social *milieu* of a great port like Liverpool, it was still no guarantee of his acceptance or ultimate commercial success. As Whyman says, "city contacts were casual [and were] based upon *rôle* as well as status."[416] In a competitive business like the slave trade, what counted most was not so much who a new merchant was, but rather the wealth and expertise he could bring to a prospective slaving venture.

Requests for letters of introduction between established merchants were firmly based in the reciprocal expectations underlining mercantile exchange, and often took the form of *quid pro quo* promises of favors in return. In June 1760, for instance, William Earle, hoping to sell dried fish *en route* from Liverpool or Africa to the New World, asked a correspondent in Jamaica to ease his introduction with a merchant on Madeira, "at which place I know nobody, and as I am in the fish trade, something may be done in the way to the West Indies... [and I] Shall be glad to render you any service and remain with great esteem, Sir, Yours, etc., William Earle."[417] Besides service, Earle offered nothing material to his Jamaican friend in return for his assistance. Although Swett describes the offers of service often found at the end of a letter as simply "reflexive hierarchalism," they were valuable in their own right, and in effect amounted to a personal debt that could be redeemed at some future date of the Jamaican's choosing.[418]

Although William Earle was not hesitant to redeem the promises of his trading partners, he took the golden rule as a guiding principle in his relationships with other merchants. "I shall advise you by all opportunities as anything occurs," Earle wrote a fellow partner in the slaver *Calypso*, "& I shall do in every respect for you as I should wish you to do for me.[419] Pledges of future service were especially useful in meeting the material requirements of slaving ventures. "As you were so obliging to offer to render the owners of the *Prince Vada* any service, especially in the article of cushtais," Earle wrote merchant Folliott Powell in October 1760,

---

[413]Earle to John Darbyshire (Birmingham), May 24, 1760.

[414]Clark, *British Clubs and Societies*, 160.

[415]*ibid*, 160; Corfield, 105.

[416]Whyman, 64.

[417]Earle to Robert Pooley (Jamaica), June 12, 1760.

[418]Swett, 16.

[419]Earle to Richard Rabone, January 24, 1761.

"I must now claim your promise & have to beg the favor [that] you would [send] 200 pieces of cushtais... This will be a great obligation conferred [upon me]."[420] Given the great distances and slow communications involved in the transatlantic trades, such vague and often attenuated promises of service between merchants were a functional necessity in the ordinary conduct of business. A Liverpool merchant such as William Earle could not hope to attend to every aspect of his trade in Britain, the continent, Africa, the West Indies, and North America, and relied upon resident merchants, and other surrogates, to look after his local interests. Such reciprocal obligations created what Offer called an "economy of regard" that was mutually advantageous to both parties in a business transaction, "even if its modes could be subtle, delicate, and oblique as well as direct."[421] Hancock argues that both parties in a commercial endeavor entered a relationship founded upon mutual obligation, suggesting, for instance, that if a tobacco planter in Virginia requested supplies from his contact in Britain, he would consign his crop to this merchant-factor because "obligations ought to be mutual.[422] The exchange of reciprocal favors, letters of introduction, and commercial services between merchants greatly expanded the possibilities of overseas trade by both strengthening the bonds of mutual obligation that connected a far-flung network of traders, manufacturers, agents, and investors, and introducing an element of predictability into a complex and erratic system of trade. In short, mercantile reciprocity mobilized the resources necessary for sustained commercial growth.[423]

These mutual obligations were particularly useful in the African trade, since slave merchants in Britain had to rely upon a wide assortment of suppliers, financiers, insurance underwriters, and slave factors in order to bring cargoes of slaves to market in the New World. William Earle's offers of service to the merchants he dealt with were not lightly given and represented promises to act on behalf of correspondents, as the need should arise. Preserving such promises was very much in Earle's interest as well, for he understood that he too might have occasion to request assistance at some future date.

Because business friendships were based upon underpinnings of personal closeness and mutual respect, a perceived failure of reciprocity, such as blatant self-promotion or a simple lack of mutuality, could seriously damage the often-tenuous relationship that existed between trading men.[424] Reputation and honor were crucial elements in conceptions of mutual obligation, and any action that acted to impugn the honor of an associate, such as dishonesty, profligacy, or sharp practice, could have a deleterious effect upon a merchant's trading relationships, and hamper his ability to do business in the future. However, the obligation of reciprocity had its limits as well, and the mutual obligations and expectations inherent in friendship meant that a trading partner could not be expected to provide support that would damage him, either financially or socially.[425] Operating within clearly delineated and well understood limits, the obligations of reciprocity not only offered merchants practical benefits, but infused their discourse with an equally important element of social connection and personal satisfaction.

Another common feature of merchant correspondence was the information that was exchanged regarding the reputation of other trading men, assessments that influenced the scope and character of both their trade and partners. Merchants took pride in their associations with reputable businessmen as such connections bolstered their social and commercial standing. Because these friendships had a well-understood, almost instinctive, moral dimension, merchants expected friends to be sober, pious, moderate, and upright men.[426] A merchant who willfully transgressed the boundaries of acceptable conduct could easily find himself ostracized as word of his misdeeds spread throughout the society of traders. William Earle's letters, for instance, are littered with references to the reputation of the men with whom he traded. In late January 1761, Earle informed two important London merchant firms that his friend John Darbyshire, a minor investor in his slaver *Calypso*, "is

---

[420]Earle to Folliott Powell, October 31, 1760. In addition to his trade in African slaves, Folliott Powell, a Liverpool and Manchester textile merchant-middleman, supplied other slavers with the imported fabrics used to trade for African slaves.

[421]Offer, 450f; Mathias, "Kinship...," 31.

[422]Hancock, 125.

[423]Offer, 450.

[424]Tadmor, 179, 198–99.

[425]*ibid*, 179.

[426]*ibid*, 205.

become a bankrupt," and that he, as the ship's husband, would take responsibility for Darbyshire's unpaid share of the ship.[427] Although Earle was sympathetic to his friend's plight, fiduciary obligations to his London friends required that he reveal to them Darbyshire's financial predicament. On another occasion a short time later, Earle wrote his Manx partner John Joseph Bacon that he did not like the behavior of James Crisp, their mutual associate in the Highland fishing trade, suggesting that he would never have any more to do with him.[428] Such assessments could be a devastating setback for a struggling merchant like Darbyshire, bringing into questions not only his integrity and worth as a man, but also his abilities as a merchant.

William Earle's correspondence was usually framed as sociable discourse that served pragmatic ends, as he frequently offered favors and services to business associates that served his own purposes as well. An ironmonger as well as a merchant, Earle at times manipulated some of his closest trading associations in order to sell his ironwares. "Mr. [John] Maine [will] no doubt…acquaint you [of] the *George & Betty* being took," Earle told his friend John Joseph Bacon, "[and] if you replace your vessel, I shall be obliged to you for the installation of the ironmongery & smiths [work]. I will make a point to oblige you.[429] In pursuing his trade in slaves, Earle made similar use of his wide web of commercial connections to sell his human cargoes in the West Indies. "Gentlemen," Earle wrote the firm of *Turner, Hilton & Briscoe* in London,

> I take the liberty of addressing myself to you by recommendation of Mr. James Clemens. I am ship's husband for ship *Calypso*, Captain Copeland, who sailed from hence [on] 18th March last for Bonny, who [I] have ordered to Barbados for further orders. [Mr. Clemens]…informs me you will [stand as] security for a cargo of Negroes that may be consigned to your friends *DeGoy, Boscawen & Co.* of Guadeloupe & that you will Take up any of [said] Gentlemen's drafts that may not be duly honored. You will please to Signify the same to me & desire your friends to Lodge letters at Barbados with the Terms they can propose.[430]

Two weeks later, Earle wrote directly to *DeGoy, Boscawen & Co.* in Guadeloupe and requested their assistance. "I have been recommended to your correspondence," Earle noted,

> [by] Messrs. [Turner,] Hilton & Briscoe of London. I have to acquaint you: Expect the ship *Calypso*, Captain Copeland, to arrive at Barbados with a cargo of Negroes from Bonny about the month of October next or sooner & have to desire you will, from time to time, as any alteration may happen in the market, advise captain Copeland at the house of Messrs. Wood & Simmons the price of the slaves at & the value of your produce for the captain's government & doubt not him having a choice good cargo & that you will give him suitable encouragement to come down [to Guadeloupe].[431]

Thus, in order to request assistance from a firm of prominent slave factors on Guadeloupe, Earle parlayed a personal recommendation from his friend and fellow slave trader James Clemens into an opening to a prominent firm of London merchants with connections in Guadeloupe. While such convoluted chains of communication made trade extremely complex, they permitted men like Earle to build a store of useful acquaintances throughout the transatlantic trading world.

Earle, however, did not always seek a commercial advantage when offering to assist a friend. In March 1761, Earle responded to a request for assistance from merchant James Patterson by directing him to other merchants who could fulfill his particular trading needs, promising to vouch for him when he ordered goods from them. "Mr. Thomas Hetham in this town," Earle informed Patterson, "has a mug warehouse in

---

[427]Earle to Messrs. Tennant & Massenbird, (London), January 30, 1761; Earle to Messrs. Sargeant, Aufrere & Co., (London), January 30, 1761.

[428]Earle to John Joseph Bacon, February 16, 1761.

[429]Earle to John Joseph Bacon, (Isle of Man), April 7, 1760; Earle to Messrs. Smith, Knox & Co. (Ireland), March 22, 1760.

[430]Earle to Messrs. Turner, Hilton & Briscoe (London), July 7, 1760.

[431]Earle to Messrs. DeGoy, Boscawen & Co. (Guadeloupe), July 20, 1760.

Staffordshire [and] Messrs. John Knight & Co. have a glass house & sugar house here. These are worthy gentlemen & can serve you with those articles on the best terms…[and]…You may recommend yourself to me when you write for goods to the above gentlemen."[432] Imbued with an understanding of the importance of an expanding web of correspondence and connection, William Earle was more than glad to offer his good offices to men such as Patterson.

III

In addition to the circles of correspondence maintained by merchants, face-to-face conviviality played an important role in joining merchants together in friendship and common interest. A period of flourishing expansion for many English towns, the eighteenth century witnessed the construction of numerous streets, squares, parks, playhouses, homes, shops, taverns, inns, and coffee-houses centered around the market place and the high street.[433] Merchants freely mingled with each other on these newly constructed public spaces, establishing and maintaining relationships with business friends, gathering commercial intelligence, and conducting business.[434]

Although the cultural institutions of polite society multiplied rapidly in London and the provinces after 1660, enriching the lives of merchants and their families, "the real seat of intellectual delights," Borsay argues, "was the coffee-house."[435] Centers of business and conviviality, coffeehouses were "talk shops," where merchants socialized and conducted business over a bowl of coffee, and read newspapers in often well-equipped libraries and reading rooms.[436] Growing in popularity after 1660, the coffeehouse largely supplanted the drinking house in London and the larger provincial towns as the preferred meeting place for gentlemen, brokers, underwriters, ship-owners, and overseas merchants by 1700, when some 2,000 coffee-houses were operating in London alone.[437] The social environment of associational venues such as coffeehouses was open and communicative, an openness that Borsay argues was "encouraged by the cultural message of sociability that coffee drinking carried."[438] A sober alternative to the drunken revelries that frequently erupted in taverns and inns, the far more polite sociable gatherings at coffee houses, a contemporary observed, acted to "improve arts, merchandise, and all other knowledge."[439] This shift to what Stephen Copley has termed "newly moralized centers of daily social life," was, in part, a consequence of a general campaign against all forms of anti-social behavior that was a common feature of the popular press by 1700.[440] The polite sociability which coffeehouses promoted softened the sharp edges of a competitive and unforgiving marketplace by improving the quality of civil discourse among merchants. In the Liverpool slave trade, this helped to create bonds of fraternity and friendship among slave merchants, thus giving rise to a widely shared sense of equanimity and civility that strengthened both personal and commercial relationships.

Several important coffeehouses appeared in Liverpool during the early eighteenth century, quickly emerging as important centers of civil discourse, literacy, leisure, and commerce for the local merchant community.

---

[432]Earle to James Patterson, March 28, 1761.

[433]Corfield, 21.

[434]Jurgen Habermas, *The Structural Transformation of the Public Sphere* (1989), cited in Whyman, 64.

[435]Borsay, 145.

[436]Borsay, 145–146; A.H. John, "The London Assurance Company and the Marine Insurance Market…," 129; Stewart-Brown, "The Early Coffee Houses of Liverpool," 1; Clark, *British Clubs and Societies*, 163. Although the first English coffee-house opened in Oxford in 1650, it reached fullest development in London, where the first coffee-house opened on St. Michael's Lane, Cornhill, in 1652.

[437]Clark, *British Clubs and Societies*, 160, 162; Whyman, 64; Corfield, 142; Wright and Fayle, *A History of Lloyd's from the Founding of Lloyd's Coffee House to the Present Day* (1928), cited in Joseph Inikori, "Measuring the Unmeasured Hazards of the Atlantic Slave Trade: Documents Relating to the British Trade," *Cahiers D'Etudes Africaines* 36 (1996), 55–56.

[438]Borsay, 269.

[439]John Houghton, *Husbandry and Trade Improved*, (London, 1727 edition), iii. 132, quoted in Clark, *British Clubs and Societies*, 178.

[440]Stephen Copley, "Commerce, Conversation, and Politeness in the Early Eighteenth-Century," *The British Journal for Eighteenth-Century Studies* 18 (1995), 66–69.

The first, the *Exchange Coffee-house* in Water Street, was established around 1707, at a time when travelers and residents of all types most often frequented traditional inns like the *Woolpack*, near the Exchange, and later the *Cross-Keys*, the *Golden Fleece*, the *Angel*, and the *Bull and the Punch Bowl*, establishments that had changed little since the sixteenth century.[441] Subsequently, a number of other important coffee-houses appeared, including *Pontack's Coffee-house* on the north side of Water Street, the *Neptune Coffee-house* fronting Water and High Streets, *George's Coffee-house* on the west side of Castle Street, the *Merchant's Coffee House* in the Old Churchyard and later Dale Street, the *Bath Coffee-house* also in the Old Churchyard, the *St. James Coffee-house*, or *Mount Coffee-house*, on St. James's Walk, and the *Cave Coffee-house* to the northward of the Old Shambles.[442] The two most important of these coffee-houses were the *Merchants' Coffee-house*, "a neat-looking white tavern…of considerable antiquity…much frequented by respectable persons," and the *Neptune*, one of the oldest coffee-houses in the town.[443] The *Merchants' Coffee House* was mentioned in the *Bee, or Universal Weekly Pamphlet*, a London newspaper that in 1733 described a meeting of Liverpool men opposed to Walpole's Excise Tax:

> Last night our merchants met in a body at the Merchants Coffee House, where after drinking His Majesty's and other loyal healths, they ordered the *Daily Courant* of the 15th instant to be burnt, which was accordingly done by the hangman that, in the year 1715, executed the rebels who came to invade our liberties and all that is dear to us.[444]

All of these were considered highly respectable coffeehouses equipped with large newsrooms, but were not suited to the use of travelers, who generally took rooms at coaching inns and taverns instead. In eighteenth-century Liverpool, inns such as the *Woolpack* gradually lost favor among the merchant community as centers of commerce and genteel conversation.

Before 1775, most Liverpool coffeehouses served a motley variety of men, not all of whom were elite overseas merchants and professionals, and some served stronger drink as well as coffee. Less refined men, like former slave-ship captains who had become wealthy merchants, often frequented coffee-houses to rub shoulders with major traders, learn of ship arrivals and departures, insure vessels and cargos, arrange financing, crew vessels, and lodge messages. Of particular interest to merchants in search of market information and general news, was the growing availability of newspapers, pamphlets, and periodicals in the reading-rooms and libraries furnished by the proprietors of many elite coffee-houses for their more literate and affluent clientele. Before the Athenaeum News-Room and Library opened in 1798, there were no public reading-rooms or libraries in Liverpool to meet the voracious appetite of merchants for shipping and general commercial news that coffeehouses and inns alone provided.[445] Because many of the newsrooms found in the better coffeehouses and inns charged admission and were quite expensive, they became "starkly male-dominated spaces" open only to wealthy merchants who required both up-to-date commercial information and sociable relationships with other merchants.[446]

Coffeehouses and inns were also the preferred meeting-places for the host of clubs and societies which had become commonplace in Liverpool by 1750. The associational life of prosperous eighteenth-century towns like Liverpool was rich, expansive, and variegated, as clubs, societies, meetings, and associations of all sorts greatly multiplied in type and number. In addition to the numerous drinking and feasting clubs, there were also a growing number of more formal political associations and reform clubs, philanthropic societies,

---

[441]Nicolas Blundell, *Great Diurnal Diary*, cited in Stewart-Brown, "The Early Coffee Houses of Liverpool," 3; Alan Everitt, "The English Urban Inn, 1560–1760," in *Perspectives in English Urban History*, ed., Alan Everitt (1973), 91–137.

[442]Stewart-Brown, "The Early Coffee Houses of Liverpool," 3, 7, 9; Brooke, 42, 164.

[443]Brooke, 164; Stewart-Brown, "The Early Coffee Houses of Liverpool," 9.

[444]*Cited in* Stewart-Brown, "The Early Coffee Houses of Liverpool," 14.

[445]Brooke, 269; Borsay, 210.

[446]Wilson, 47; Borsay, 210. Borsay notes that the membership roll of Liverpool's subscription library in 1760 lists 145 members, 50 of whom were merchants.

debating clubs, literary and music societies, book clubs, and horticultural societies.[447] For many upwardly mobile Liverpudlians, memberships in such purposeful associations were emblematic of elite social status, while drinking and feasting clubs were far more informal but often equally exclusive.[448] Although short-lived and loosely organized, the social clubs founded by and for merchants and their associates served the useful purpose of bringing men together in a friendly, convivial, and supportive environment conducive to building close commercial relationships, and furthering the mutual pursuit of trade.[449] Much sought after, membership in elite social clubs was often restricted by size, social class, and cost, as a number required the payment of a large fee or annual subscription. However, the pursuit of profitable trading connections was not the sole reason for the rising importance of social clubs. "One of the most commendable activities gentlemen could engage in," Borsay argues,

> and one in which moderation and an even temper were considerable assets, was simply that of meeting and mixing with his fellow human beings. Indeed, sociability was considered one of the foremost civilizing influences…[and] in no case did [a] spirit of fraternity more reveal itself than in the formation of clubs and societies…in which the ties of friendship and good company could be cultivated.[450]

Arising from personal tastes and interests, motivations for joining social clubs could be extremely varied, ranging from simple boredom, a desire to consume strong drink, and fellowship with male friends, to forming new business, social, and business acquaintants, or learning the rules of etiquette. Although many social clubs brought together men from widely varying social and occupational backgrounds under one roof, once admitted to a social club like the Ugly Face Club or the Unanimous Society of Liverpool, all members were adjudged equal within the club. "In such associational settings," Clark argues, "men of diverse ages, occupations, social and marital statuses, and residences could join together in a club or society where diversity was transformed into harmony and friendship."[451] The heterogeneous membership of social clubs arose from the fact that most were short-lived and relied upon the induction of new members to survive rather than intergenerational patrimony between members and their sons. Although pressure to increase membership grew for many social clubs and societies in the eighteenth century, most maintained restrictions on the size of the membership in order to preserve concord and avoid disarray, with less formal clubs generally having smaller, more intimate memberships.

Among the least formal clubs and societies were those devoted solely to gustatory pleasures and ritualized drinking. For one important Liverpool social club, the Ugly Face Club, regular bouts of heavy drinking and eating were customary expressions of masculine sociability and fellowship in which a loyal toast was an obligatory gesture. Raising a toast was accompanied by boisterous, good-natured socializing, and failure to drink was considered petty and ill mannered, and often cost members a symbolic fine.[452] Clark suggests that, in addition to cementing the bonds of masculine sociability, drinking and eating clubs projected the reputation and status of members within the larger community of gentlemen traders and their friends.[453] Membership in the Ugly Face Club, for instance, was a manifestation of the evolving personal relationships between its members, which reflected, in turn, the changed social status of a group of rising merchants and professionals.

Founded at the *Exchange Coffee-house* on January 21, 1743, "Ye Honorable and Facetious Society of Ugly Faces," maintained a small membership of less than forty men, a group largely composed of affluent

---

[447]Corfield, 143; Clark, 134.

[448]Clark, *British Clubs and Societies*, 100.

[449]Wilson, 54; Corfield, 143, Langford, *A Polite and Commercial People*, 100, Nicholas Rogers, "Clubs and Politics in Eighteenth-Century London: The Centenary Club of Cheapside," *London Journal* 11 (1985), 51.

[450]Borsay, 267–268.

[451]Clark, *British Clubs and Societies*, 195.

[452]*ibid*, 163; Brooke, 292.

[453]Clark, *British Clubs and Societies*, 164.

merchants and professionals.[454] As the name of the club suggests, a major requirement for membership in the Ugly Face Club, in addition to being a bachelor and having a facetious disposition, was an ugly face. The first rule of the Ugly Face Club declaimed that "members must feature something odd, remarkable, or droll or out of the way in his phiz: as in the length, breadth, or narrowness thereof; or in his complexion, the cast of his eyes or make of his mouth, lips, chin, etc."[455] Upon admission into this seemingly frivolous fellowship, club recorder and town clerk Francis Gildart sketched often-caustic images of members appearances, including his own. The corpulent Gildart described himself as having a

> "Large[,] Pancake face[,] little, Hollow & Grey eyes[,] short turnip nose[,] large[,] thick under lip which almost meets his nose[,] odd, droll, Sancho Panza phiz [which] gives life and humor to every thing he says[,] therefore sets off a joke to its utmost advantage."[456]

Gildart's descriptions of the physical qualifications of other members were equally scathing. Merchant Peter Holme was depicted as having a "a forehead half his face," merchant Thomas Wycliffe's face was "shriveled; " while merchant Isaac Blackwood had "a sparrow mouth & racked teeth."[457] Such descriptions were a running joke within the club as members took pride in particularly unflattering metaphors for their "Ugly grotesk Phizzies."[458] (See appendix 4.1)

Although the Ugly Face Club was a gentlemen's club whose members were admitted by ballot, a sense of camaraderie and lightness of spirit characterized its rules and operation. In this respect, the rules of the Unanimous Society, founded a decade later in 1753, were quite similar, with the notable exception that candidates for entrance could only be admitted by a unanimous vote of the membership. After a night filled with exuberant toasts, the presidents of both the Ugly Face Club and the Unanimous Society were required to call for a reckoning at the designated hour of 10 o'clock, when each member was to pay his share of the "tavern shott," ordinarily ale, and go home, "or stay longer if he pleases."[459] Members also sponsored lavish entertainments, and laid friendly wagers, the winnings of which were to go towards the "shott."[460] The organization of both clubs put a sophisticated gloss upon a simple desire to drink and socialize, and many club rules were designed to provide funds for the communal "shot," as well as the joint purchase of lottery tickets and elaborate suppers, by specifying the payment of small fines for a litany of trivial infractions. For instance, members of the Ugly Face Club were required to be men of honor who did not utter profanities or play cards or dice, at the "forfeiture of five shillings for each such offense."[461] Upon admission to the Ugly Face Club, new members were expect to drink a "bumper" to its success, or pay a fine, while the rules of the Unanimous Society sought to discourage excessive drinking by members "except [in] his toast."[462] Members of the Ugly Face Club who married were also expected "to forfeit 10 shillings and six pence for the use of the society," a practice common to the Unanimous Society as well.[463] The ninth rule of the Unanimous Society held that if members "do marry, they shall, on the first meeting afterwards, pay unto the president for the time being, the sum of ten shillings and sixpence, which said sum must be paid towards the shott, the first evening of their appearance after such marriage."[464] Members of the Unanimous Society were forbidden to

---

[454]Stewart-Brown, "The Early Coffee Houses of Liverpool," 6; Clark, *British Clubs and Societies*, 134.

[455]*Records of the Ugly Face Society*, 367 UGL/1, Liverpool PRO. Minute and account book," folios 1–2; Index of names, folios 1–3: Rules of the Society, folios.13–20, Listing of members qualifications for admission; Clark, *British Clubs and Societies*, 194; Stewart-Brown, "The Early Coffee Houses of Liverpool," 6.

[456]*Records of the Ugly Face Society*, folios 1–3, Rules of the Society.

[457]*Records of the Ugly Face Society*, folios 13–20, Listing of members qualifications.

[458]*ibid.*

[459]*Records of the Ugly Face Society*, folios 1–3, Rules of the Society, Brooke, 292.

[460]Unanimous Society, 1753–1778, 367/UNA/1, Liverpool PRO; Brooke, 293–294, 517.

[461]*Records of the Ugly Face Society*, folios 1–3, Rules of the Society.

[462]*ibid*; Liverpool Unanimous Society, 1753–1778, 367/UNA/1, Liverpool PRO; Brooke, 292

[463]*Records of the Ugly Face Society*, folios 1–3, Rules of the Society.

[464]Unanimous Society, 1753–1778, 367/UNA/1, Liverpool PRO; Brooke, 292.

come to meetings drunk, or to sing immodest songs "without the consent of the president."[465] Meetings of the Unanimous Society were held at 7 o'clock in the evenings, with members failing to attend at that time assessed a small fine of 1d, a larger fine of 2d. if the member failed to show by 8 o'clock, and a still larger fine of 3d. for those who failed to show at all.[466] Ritualized drinking and good-humored levity fashioned long-lasting bonds of friendship between members of the Ugly Face Club, two-thirds of whom in 1745 were merchants with experience in the slave trade, as well as the Unanimous Society, whose membership included some of the leading slave traders in Liverpool.[467] These were established, successful men, not novice traders or apprentices, upstarts who were not permitted to join either club, although many of the latter were qualified for membership in the Ugly Face Club. Members of both clubs were also conventional men who belonged to a fairly typical sort of social club. These men were fully apart of the evolving urban culture of Liverpool, a literate, enterprising society which united the town's slave traders in intertwining bonds of entrepreneurialism and friendship.[468]

IV

Building upon formal ties of kinship, religious affiliation, and apprenticeship, the informal bonds of friendship and sociability shared by many Liverpool slave traders reflected the evolution of a loosely interconnected but likeminded community of African merchants by the 1740s. In perhaps no other center of the eighteenth-century British slave trade were such informal ties as important to the expansion of the trade as in Liverpool. The relative openness of the Liverpool slave trade, and the eagerness of African merchants to attract outside investment in their ventures, meant that privileged trading connections became increasingly less important to a prosperous career in the African trade. A major factor in the rise of the Liverpool slave trade, this openness also had clear consequences for the community of slave traders as a group, and the construction of slaving partnerships. The informal social and commercial contacts which this disparate group of slavers formed, both in the chains of correspondence they maintained with other men of trade, and in associational venues such as coffee-houses, inns, and social clubs, helped to bridge the differences in social status, occupation, and origins that separated merchants eager to search for profit in the African slave trade. Unlike most other British slaving centers, diversity thus became a strength in the Liverpool slave trade, a shared point of social connection which influenced trading possibilities.

---

[465]Unanimous Society, 1753–1778; Brooke, 292.

[466]Unanimous Society; Brooke, 291.

[467]*Records of the Ugly Face Society*, 367 UGL/1; Unanimous Society, 1753–1778, 367/UNA/1, Liverpool PRO; Brooke, 260–261, 293–298. Slave trading members of the Unanimous Society included: Thomas Golightly, Alexander Nottingham, William Crosbie Sr., William Crosbie Jr., Thomas Tarleton, William Pole, Charles Pole, Thomas Carter, George Case, James Bridge, George Warren Watts, Joseph Brooks Jr., Thomas Hodgson, and John Chorley.

[468]Clark, *British Clubs and Societies*, 194.

Chapter 5

✦

Partners and Partnerships

Modern Liverpudlians are familiar with many eighteenth century slave traders since the city's thoroughfares bear their names. Less is known about their business organizations and those of the host of smaller participants in the trade. This chapter will deal with the many factors that influenced the structure, origin, and composition of Liverpool slaving partnerships in the first three-quarters of the eighteenth century. A number of these arise from the financial and legal realities of overseas trade, including partnership law, commercial practice, assessments of profitability and risk, and capitalization costs and credit. Others emerged specifically from the ties of kinship and association that connected Liverpool Guinea Merchants. While it is not always clear what types of bonds were most crucial in the construction of specific slaving partnerships, it is clear that the African trade served a variety of purposes for different groups of owners. The purpose here is to shed light on these matters. The first four sections discuss legal and financial constraints upon slaving activity. The remainder analyze the types of business organization that emerged and social and market forces affecting their composition.

I

Law has long practiced an important influence upon business organizations and the conduct of trade. Readily made and remade, Liverpool slave-trading partnerships demonstrated not only the importance of kinship and associational ties in eighteenth century overseas trade, but also the variable influence of an evolving law of partnership, general commercial practice, the specific requirements of the trade in African slaves, and the vagaries of business friendship. What business forms were suited to conducting the trade in slaves? Among Liverpool slave traders, the answer to this question depended upon why a man invested in the slave trade, his level of commitment to the trade, and the financial resources he had at his disposal. Unlike the French slave trade, where a highly formalized type of joint stock company called a *société en commandite* had emerged to coordinate the African trade by the early eighteenth century, the evolving structure of the British trade was far more diffuse in composition, more open to outside investment and participation, and less formally organized.[469] In the *société en commandite* investors signed formal contracts of seven years duration, a length of time thought sufficient to permit the books to be closed on a venture.[470] British partnerships had no such temporal restrictions. Viewed with distrust in the King's courts, joint-stock companies were rare in British trade prior to the *Bubble Act of 1720*, and the organizers of private joint-stock companies were often prosecuted at law and heavily fined. In addition to the corporation, which could only be created by an act of parliament, two general forms of business organization governed English commerce before the advent of the limited liability company in the nineteenth century, both of which were found in the Liverpool slave trade after 1695. One was the well-established legal entity of the sole trader, favored by small merchant mariners before 1760 and major slave merchants after 1765, and the other was the far less accepted but nonetheless popular institution of the unincorporated partnership.

A coherent body of laws governing the organization of business hardly existed before the passage of the *Bubble Act* in 1720. The laws of business organization that did exist, some arising from common-law principles and others from late medieval statutory enactments, generally permitted investors to form unincorporated companies, but denied the companies thus formed limited liability or any legal recognition of corporate identity.[471] Largely as a result of the attenuated conflict between the Royal Africa Company, a royally sanctioned slave-trading monopoly that sought to preserve its privileges, and innumerable loose and shifting groups of aggressively entrepreneurial merchants intent upon winning the trade for themselves, the unincorporated partnership, rather than the joint stock company or the chartered corporation, emerged as the *de facto* unit of business organization in the British slave trade in 1712.

Although this evolving form of business organization represented the future of the trade unincorporated, partnerships remained a risky proposition for all involved. In practice, existing law impeded the formation of unincorporated partnerships in two primary ways. Firstly, because a new partner could not legally be brought into a partnership without the approval of the other partners, the ability of investors to transfer partnership shares was constrained. In addition, there were social prohibitions that limited the transferability of partnership shares, for it was also seen as inappropriate for an investor to pressure his partners too forcefully to accept a new man in order to facilitate his departure from the partnership, as many partners were often friends and family.[472] For instance, when the prominent Liverpool merchant Jonathan Blundell sought to sell his one-seventh share in a local sugarhouse in March 1766, his ability to do so was strictly limited by his obligations to his six partners, men who were close business associates and friends. "The herein named Jonathan Blundell," Blundell stipulated in the partnership agreement,

> owner and proprietor of a seventh part of this Haymarket Sugarhouse in Liverpool...by and with the consent and approbation of...Peter Holme, Ralph Earle, William Earle, Thomas Hodgson, Patrick Black and Thomas Lickbarrow, my partners...and in consideration of the sum of two hundred and seven pounds of lawful British money...to me in hand paid by John Sparling of Liverpool...do for myself...grant bargain...assign and convey unto this said John Sparling...all my one seventh part or share of and in the said...Sugarhouse...and also all my one seventh share of all the stock in trade, profits, debts and effects in any wise belonging to me...and the said Jonathan Blundell by and with the consent of my said partners...do hereby nominate and appoint the said John Sparling to become a partner...in the place and stead of the said Jonathan Blundell as fully and effectively to all intents and purposes as if the said John

---

[469]Herbert Klein, *The Atlantic Slave Trade*, 82, Jacob Price, "Transaction Costs: A Note on Merchant Credit and the Organization of Private Trade," in *The Political Economy of Merchant Empires: State Power and World Trade, 1350–1750* ed., James Tracy (1991) 292–293.

[470]Robert Stein, *The French Slave Trade in the Eighteenth Century: An Old Regime Business* (1979), 27–29, 163–166; Ralph Davis, *The Rise of the English Shipping Industry in the Seventeenth and Eighteenth Centuries* (1962) 81–82.

[471]Ron Harris, *Industrializing English Law: Entrepreneurship and Business Organization* (2000), 1*f.*

[472]Davis, *The Rise of the English Shipping Industry,* 102–104.

Sparling had originally been named a partner [and thus] paying, doing, and performing all the covenants and agreements contained in this…Indenture.[473]

At best, Blundell could nominate John Sparling as a partner, but he could not himself make Sparling a partner in the sugarhouse without the consent of his fellow partners. However, at times a partnership had little choice but to accept a change in partners, through death, bankruptcy or fraud, with often-dire consequences for the financial solvency of the partners.

Secondly, the dangers of unlimited liability led many casual investors to shun the unincorporated partnership. A downturn in business, a random disaster such as a fire, or the unexpected death of a partner could ruin all involved in a joint commercial venture. In most ordinary partnerships, all members, whether active or inactive partners were equally liable to the full extent of their individual estates for the debts of the partnership. However, because shipping partnerships were governed by maritime or admiralty law, which was administered in a specialized court of Admiralty, they escaped many of the often onerous legal obstacles which obstructed the formation of more ordinary land-based business partnerships such as the one which owned the Haymarket sugarhouse in Liverpool.[474] Because admiralty law construed a ship as a corporate entity, it limited the liability of the individual shareholder to the amount he or she had invested in the partnership, and did not subject the totality of an investor's estate to an unlimited liability for the financial obligations of the partnership. "All partnership effects," William Earle explained to business associate John Darbyshire in January 1761, "are liable to pay the debts of that partnership, so that I can pay what is unpaid of any voyage…[as] the effects come into my hands as ship's husband."[475] Because admiralty law limited liability to "partnership effects" alone, Davis argues, an investor in a ship "had in practice, though not in legal theory, a safeguard which limited his liabilities."[476] The effective limits which admiralty law placed upon the individual liability of shareholders in ship-owning partnerships made shares in ships attractive investments to a variety of potential investors. However, although shareholders were legally liable for the debts of the partnership, many were never called upon to meet the financial obligations of the partnership.[477]

Despite the very real risk of ruin that faced participants in ordinary unincorporated partnerships, the extent to which a lack of a coherent law of partnerships obstructed English overseas trade is difficult to gauge. Davis suggests that it may have impeded the expansion of commerce by failing to provide unincorporated partnerships with the same type of legal protections for the mobilization of capital that were characteristic of the chartered trading companies.[478] Unlike the great trading companies of the seventeenth and early eighteenth centuries, monopolies such as the *East India Company*, the *Hudson Bay Company*, the *Royal Africa Company*, and the *Levant Company*, powerful organizations whose royal charters stipulated their prerogatives and responsibilities in often minute detail, the formation of unincorporated partnerships was haphazard, ill-defined, and largely unregulated. This made it difficult for them to enter into a number of profitable avenues of trade, such as the slave trade. Kenneth Davies maintains that the inability of government-sanctioned cartels, such as the *Royal Africa Company* or the *Companie du Senegal*, to profit from the slave trade, or even to prevent the intrusion of private slave traders, "made it clear…that competitive private enterprise was the most flexible way of selling slaves and meeting market demand, and perhaps the only way to profit from the trade."[479] The rising importance of unincorporated partnerships paralleled the rapid growth of the English maritime economy after 1660, and represented an organic response to the

---

[473]Article of Partnership for conveying a one seventh share of a Haymarket sugarhouse in Liverpool from Jonathan Blundell to John Sparling, March 31, 1766, D/EARLE/2/2.

[474]Davis, *The Rise of the English Shipping Industry,* 102–104. Ralph Davis notes that Admiralty law created a fictive corporation centered not on the person but on the ship, a corporation that could be sued or arrested for debt or tort.

[475]Earle to John Darbyshire, January 17, 1761, *Letterbook of William Earle*, D/EARLE/2/2, Merseyside Maritime Museum.

[476]Davis, *The Rise of the English Shipping Industry,* 102–104.

[477]Davis, 102–104.

[478]Price, "Transaction Costs…" 292–293.

[479]Davies, *The Royal African Company*, 13.

organizational requirements of overseas trade, particularly in especially uncertain and risky lines of trade such as the traffic in African slaves. Similarly, English trade to the Americas was usually organized around the legally questionable unincorporated partnership. Even if the average merchant or mariner had thought it advantageous to do so, few could afford the expense of petitioning parliament for a royal charter and the likelihood that a charter would be granted was slim. "Despite the negative attitude of the state and the official legal system," Ron Harris argues,

> the business community developed an adequate substitute for the business corporation in the private sphere. This substitute, the unincorporated company, was designed by shrewd businessmen and lawyers, and received from the courts of law the limited degree of recognition for practical functioning.[480]

Because of the memory of the South Sea Bubble, it took more than a century and a half after the rise of the Liverpool slave trade, and nearly forty years after its demise, for limited liability partnerships to obtain legal acceptance. Instead, the law of partnership represented the slow absorption of merchant custom into common law. Although the pragmatism of English law in the seventeenth and eighteenth centuries generally made it more flexible and better able to respond to economic developments than was the case on the continent, English commercial law failed to adapt to the practical, living institution of the African slave trading partnership at its eighteenth century peak.[481] Thus, because of the shortcomings of English law and the requirements of the slave trade, merchant practice and usage, not statute, emerged as the decisive influence in the formation of slaving partnerships.

What differentiated slaving partnerships from other types of ship-owning partnerships? Eighteenth-century ship-owning partnerships were generally composed of small groups of actively engaged investors who earned income by shipping their own goods as well as the goods of others.[482] Thus, partners in shipping ventures did not necessarily seek profits by investing in the cargoes carried in the holds of their ships, but rather from the freighting fees that their ships earned. Besides their own cargoes, most investors in ships had little or no interest in the goods that their ships carried for others. The slave trade, however, represented a major exception to the traditional organization of ship-owning partnerships, a trade in which partners profited from their ownership of both ship and cargo. Davis suggests that the "dissociation" of ship ownership from the management of trade found in the slave trade represented "an important exception to general commercial practice in England."[483] In the slave trade merchants, not ship masters, retained control of both the ship and the cargo it carried, and while captains frequently invested in the slave ships they commanded, or owned slave ships as sole traders, they were more often employees than employers. Although the ownership of both ship and cargo increased the capitalization costs and operating expenses that slaving partners faced when mounting ventures to Africa, it also placed investors fully in charge of their ventures. This permitted slave traders to dispense with the trading and crewing limitations that were frequently imposed by ship-owning partnerships upon their clients, such as stringently legalistic charter-parties that prescribed where a slave trader could trade and for how long.[484] Drawing upon the legal protections of admiralty law, the mixing of trade and transport in the form of the slaving partnership represented a distinctive structural adaptation to the peculiar demands of the transatlantic trade in slaves, an adaptation that enhanced the dynamism, flexibility, productivity, and profitability of the trade in the open commercial environment of Liverpool.

---

[480]Harris, *Industrializing English Law*, 7.

[481]A.H. John, "The London Assurance Company and the Marine Insurance Market of the Eighteenth Century," *Economica* 25 (1958), 129.

[482]Davis, 81–82, 102–104.

[483]*ibid*, 94–96.

[484]Davies, *The Royal African Company*, 197. A charter party was a contract between a ship's owners and parties seeking to charter the vessel which regulated the size of the crew, number of passengers, the cargo to be loaded at each stage of a voyage, places of lading and discharge and the time to be spent at each, freight charges, and demurrage fees for ladings that took longer than permitted.

III

What influenced perceptions of profitability in this, the most dynamic of trades? What factors did a slave merchant *first* examine before investing in the slave trade? When active slave traders, as well as occasional investors, contemplated a new slaving foray, their first considerations were the potential profitability of the venture, their personal associations with other potential investors, and the availability of investment capital. It is not entirely clear what slave merchants expected in terms of profits from their often-varied commercial adventures, or how they measured success. Although it is not always apparent how a slave traders' perceptions of profit colored his involvement in the trade, it seems reasonable to assume that, given the diverse motivations which compelled investors to participate in the slave trade, as well as their varying levels of commitment to the trade, some slave traders viewed profits in terms of annual rates of return, while others focused upon rates of return on a venture basis, depending upon the scale of their involvement in the trade.[485] Although perceptions of what constituted acceptable levels of profit varied by trade, most merchants, regardless of trade, weighed the long-term opportunity costs of participating in a particular trade against the short-run costs, in terms of expenses such as shipping, financing, and insurance, in order to calculate levels of expected profit. "15% profit will never do in the Turkey trade," Levant trader Samuel Bosanquet observed in 1768, "[as] silk hardly even makes more than 5% which with the other 15[%] will give but 20% for 4 or 5% per annum. I can make that in England in time of peace, and I will not run the risk of trade if I can't make 8% at least; indeed, I can make it in more trades than one at this time."[486] While a "bonanza mentality" afflicted many short-term investors who frequently rushed into a trade like slaving, one that was reputed to yield high rates of return on investment *per* voyage, most serious, long-established merchants were more concerned with achieving consistently high annual rates of return than they were in striking it rich with spectacularly profitable individual voyages.[487] While some great trading fortunes arose quickly as the result of lucky strokes, most were the result of "slow and intermittent accruals arising from a shrewd division of a great number and variety of risks...than from a spectacular series of ventures."[488]

In order to plan a marketing strategy in any given year, a slave trader needed to know approximately how profitable his regional African trade was on an annual basis. This might influence where a slave trader bought his slaves, the varieties of trade goods he transported to various African markets, where he sold his slave cargoes in the Americas, the number and type of Guineamen he prepared for sailing, and the cost of insurance. Although the number of ventures that particular traders engaged in varied from year to year, the larger regular traders were often involved in five or more ventures a year, whereas a casual trader might invest in only one slaving venture in his entire trading career. For instance, Liverpool cabinet-maker Josiah Baxendale is listed in the *TSTD* as a partner in only one venture of the *Mary* to Old Calabar in 1761, while general merchant, slave trader, glassmaker, and sugar-baker John Knight averaged four voyages to Africa a year between 1744 and 1774, dispatching eight ships in 1754, seven in 1756, 1759, 1771, and six in 1753

---

[485]David Richardson, "Profits in the Liverpool Slave Trade: The Accounts of William Davenport, 1757–1784," in Roger Anstey and P.E.H. Hair, eds., *Liverpool, the African Slave Trade, and Abolition: Essays to Illustrate Current Knowledge and Research,* (1976), 81f; David Richardson, *The Bristol Slave Traders: A Collective Portrait* (1985), 11–15.

[486]Ralph Davis, *Aleppo and Devonshire Square: English Traders in the Levant in the Eighteenth Century* (1967), 122.

[487]David Richardson, "Profitability in the Bristol-Liverpool Slave Trade," *Revue Français d'Histoire d'Outre-Mer*, 62 (1975), 301–308; Joseph Inikori, "Market Structure and Profits of the British African Trade in the Late Eighteenth Century," *Journal of Economic History*, 41 (1981), 745–776.

[488]Francis Hyde, B.B. Anderson, Sheila Marriner "The Nature and Profitability of the Liverpool Slave Trade," *The Economic History Review* 5 (1953), 371; Anderson and Richardson, "Market Structure and Profits..." 716; Richardson, *The Bristol Slave Traders: Collective Portrait...*" 11.

and 1760.[489] General merchant, slave trader, privateer, insurance underwriter, and banker William Gregson dispatched, on average, three ships a year to Africa, sending seven ships in 1765, and eight in 1771.[490]

Was the slave trade as profitable as some eighteenth-century slave traders thought it was? Was the slave trade generally perceived as an attractive investment? The African slave trade was indeed viewed with great favor by many potential investors, and confidence in the profitability of slave trafficking permeated the merchant community of Liverpool and other centers of the British slave trade. Although much has been written about the profitability of the African trade, it remains unclear what most slave merchants expected in terms of profits, or what led casual investors to view particular slaving ventures as attractive business opportunities. For many eighteenth-century merchants slaving more than met the test of profitability. A captain of Liverpool slavers in the early 1750s, John Newton, remarked in his *Journal* that the slave trade "is, indeed, accounted a genteel employment and is usually very profitable."[491] Aside from the actual profitability of the trade, investment decisions were often based on popular notions of its profitability that may or may not have accorded with economic reality.

Melinda Elder notes that, in Lancaster as in other slaving ports, the African trade enjoyed a growing reputation for profitability before 1740, which resulted in an upsurge of investment and the creation of new trading opportunities for large and small merchants alike. In addition to its growing attractiveness as an investment, Elder suggests that slave trading increasingly spurred investment among casual traders as a speculation that had a "reputation not only for extraordinary rewards...but also for respectability."[492] Contemporaries saw the slave trade as particularly hazardous "for the trader's capital, and for the lives of the seamen employed and the human beings traded and transported as commodities," a trade that was definitely not for "the faint-hearted."[493] A late eighteenth-century Liverpool merchant, not involved in the slave trade, described it as "a commerce of Enterprise and Risk [for which reason] the profits have occasionally been very great."[494] It is clear, however, that Liverpool investors were more interested in the profitability of the African trade than they were in its potential for respectability. In part, this was a result of the relative openness of the Liverpool transatlantic trade to all who possessed the financial means to participate. This openness supported the long-term growth of the slave trade in Liverpool, a recently risen town which lacked many of the commercial, social and political rigidities which impeded trade in other centers. Suffice it to say, Herbert Klein observes, in Lancaster and Liverpool, as well as the other British slaving ports, "there is little question that the thousands of ships that sailed for Africa to engage in the slave trade did so because it was profitable."[495]

In the past two decades, however, the relative profitability of the British slave trade has been much argued, emerging as one of the most controversial topics in the new field of transatlantic studies. Because available sources provide scant evidence regarding annual rates of profit, modern estimates of profitability have been all over the lot. Richardson argues that the belief among most investors concerning the profitability of the slave trade was, to a great extent, over-optimistic, even unjustified, and that the trade was, at best, only moderately profitable. He shows that, in 74 voyages between 1757 and 1784, Davenport earned an overall rate of profit of 10.5%, or 8.1% annually.[496] This was a lower rate of return than the rates suggested by Eric Williams in 1944, and by some more recent observers.[497] Joseph Inikori, for instance, argues that Richardson's estimated annual profit rate of 8.1% is far too low because, as a whole, the average profit rate

---

[489]John Gore, ed., *The Liverpool Directory, For the Year 1766: Containing An Alphabetical List of the Merchants, Tradesmen, and Principal Inhabitants of the Town of Liverpool* (Liverpool: W. Nevett & Co., 1766); *TSTD*.

[490]*TSTD*; Will of Josiah Baxendale, Cabinet-maker of Liverpool, Wills and Inventories, Chester Probate Registry, 1764.

[491]Bernard Martin and Martin Spurrell, eds., *The Journal of a Slave Trader* (1962), 95.

[492]Elder, *The Slave Trade and ... Eighteenth-Century Lancaster*, 27–28.

[493]Joseph Inikori, "Market Structure and the Profits of the British African Trade...," 761.

[494]Inikori, "Market Structure...," 761.

[495]Klein, *The Atlantic Slave Trade*, 98.

[496]Richardson, "Profits in the Liverpool Slave Trade," 11–15, 76; Morgan, *Slavery, Atlantic Trade...*" 40.

[497]Inikori, "Market Structure...," 761f; Stanley Dumbell, "The Profits of the Guinea Trade," *Economic History* 2 (1931), 254–257.

for British business was around 13%.[498] Inikori asserts that the average annual return in his small sample of 24 voyages between 1765 and 1806 was 27%.[499]

However, Inikori's estimates have not been substantiated by the findings of other historians. Roger Anstey maintains that overall profits in the British slave trade were 8.1% between 1761 and 1770, 9.1% between 1771–1780, 13.4% between 1781 and 1790, 13% between 1791–1800, and 3.3% between 1801–1807, yielding an aggregate rate of profit for the period 1761–1807 of 9.5%, which he later revised to 10.2%.[500] In the other centers of the British slave trade, profitability, in terms of annual earnings, seems to have been less than in Liverpool. In Bristol, for instance, Richardson argues that between 1770 and 1792 slave traders earned, on average, profits of only 7.6% per annum, while in London slavers earned an even more modest 6% per annum between 1748 and 1784.[501] Morgan argues that we cannot be certain what eighteenth-century entrepreneurs considered a good profit, or how perceptions of risk influenced investment decisions. He suggests that more cautious investors clearly preferred to place their funds in government financial instruments such as consols, which earned a meager 3.5% rate of return per annum.[502] This represented a conscious acceptance of low annual returns in exchange for significantly lower levels of risk. Such a tradeoff was less acceptable to investors eager to locate investment opportunities that promised higher rates of return. Morgan concludes that, for less risk-averse investors such as this, a return of 8–10% in the slave trade might "appear an attractive alternative satisfactory rate return on capital invested."[503]

No predictable return could ever be safely anticipated from the trade in slaves. As a result, potential investors in slaving ventures often had little idea of how much they stood to profit from an investment in a slave ship before they were called upon to pay their share of the expected costs for the next voyage to Africa. This often placed slaving investors in a bind, as expenses outstripped the income expected from a voyage. The danger of slow returns was amply demonstrated in a January 1761 letter that William Earle sent John Darbyshire, an overextended Birmingham ironmonger and a fellow investor in Earle's slaver *Calypso*. "Yours of the 8th instant I have before me," Earle wrote Darbyshire,"

> [and I] am extremely sorry you had an occasion to make a stop [in payments]…We have no news yet of [Captain] Copeland [and the *Calypso*], I think it long [overdue] & it appears much more so as the *Hector* is arrived here. I am, with offers of my best service to you, Sir, Your humble servant, William Earle.[504]

Still the fact that investors often had to wait for their share of the profits for extended periods did not prevent a significant number of small investors from purchasing shares in new slaving ventures.[505] Eager to count their profits, anticipation of a ship's return was an anxious waiting game for sleeping partners. Managing partners were at least occupied with the laborious task of preparing upcoming ventures, a responsibility that required a serious commitment of time and resources. Slaving ventures required various levels of commitment from all concerned partners, with no guarantee of success.

---

[498]Eric Williams, *Capitalism and Slavery* (1944), 36–39; Inikori, "Market Structure …," 761f; Morgan, *Slavery, Atlantic Trade…*" 42, Anderson and Richardson, "Market Structure and Profits…" 713.

[499]Inikori, "Market Structure …," 761; Richardson, "Profits in the Liverpool Slave Trade…" 15; Anderson and Richardson, "Market Structure and Profits…," 715.

[500]Roger Anstey, "The Volume and Profitability of British Slave Trade, 1761–1807" in Stanley Engerman and Eugene Genovese, eds. *Race and Slavery in the Western Hemisphere* (1976), 3–36; Morgan, *Slavery, Atlantic Trade,* 40.

[501]Hancock, *Citizens of the World:* 423–424; Morgan, *Slavery, Atlantic Trade…*, 40–41 .

[502]Morgan, 42.

[503]Morgan, 42.

[504]Earle to Darbyshire, January 6, 1761, *Letterbook of William Earle.* The *Hector*, a ship owned by *William Gregson & Co.*, departed Liverpool for Bonny on March 8, 1760, four days before the *Calypso*, a larger ship bound for Bonny. *TSTD.*

[505]Peter Mathias "Risk, Credit, and Kinship in Early Modern Enterprise," in *The Early Modern Atlantic Economy*, eds., John McCusker and Kenneth Morgan (2000), 22.

Thus, an investor in a slaving vessel had to come to terms with the inherent unpredictability and riskiness of the African trade. Adam Smith styled overseas trade a "lottery of the sea," a reality that was only too familiar to eighteenth century merchants in all sectors of British overseas trade.[506] For the more than 5,000 slaving vessels that departed Liverpool between 1695 and 1807, risk was an inescapable reality that could not be taken for granted.[507] Richardson suggests that there were no "typical" slave traders or slaving ventures, making no two slaving ventures the same and the unexpected commonplace.[508] Slaving ventures were notoriously protracted affairs in which each stage of the voyage contained potentially serious obstacles to the successful financial outcome of the venture. Two years or more often passed between the initial preparation of a voyage and the sale of the last slave, hogshead of tobacco or sugar, or the maturation of the last bill of exchange arising from the venture.

A profitable slaving venture required commercial judgment of the first order. Relying upon expertise born of long experience, slave merchants had to calculate the timing of voyages to specific African markets to benefit from variable supplies of slaves, estimate New-World demand for slave cargoes from regional African markets, assess the demand for colonial produce in British and European markets, and organize the delivery of trade goods for subsequent ventures.[509] Natural hazards of all kinds, exacerbated by the limitations of eighteenth-century technology, slowed transoceanic communications and imperiled the success of slaving ventures.[510] Intense competition for slaves forced slave merchants to pay great attention to detail in order to avert the risks of prolonged delays in purchasing slaves.[511] Although slave rebellions represented a lesser threat to slaving ventures, slave ships were frequently captured by enemy privateers during times of war, or assaulted by natives on the African coast. Before 1750, many of the vessels lost were under-insured or uninsured, thereby increasing the financial impact.[512] The hazardous disease environment of West Africa, and the rigors of the middle passage, also proved a major threat to both crew and slaves alike, often jeopardizing the success of a venture.[513] The fact that a ship returned to Liverpool was no guarantee of financial success, as variable rates of profit were part of the slave trade. The risk of ruinous loss remained a characteristic feature of slaving, a trade in which small ships plied the great expanse of ocean which connected West Africa with the Americas bearing fragile human cargoes. Each stage of a slaving voyage involved intricate patterns of supply and demand, which shifted over time, as innumerable local and regional factors affected slave prices, ultimately determining where slaves were purchased in Africa, where they were sold in the Americas, the trade goods sent to procure them, and the overall profitability of the transatlantic slave trade.[514]

Liverpool slavers, like most overseas merchants, sought to gain some control over their trade, an elusive goal that forced slave merchants to manage the variety of risks that confronted them. "The merchant…invests his capital in remote and comparatively hazardous concerns," one eighteenth-century writer observed, "he gives long credit, and on single security; he depends sometimes on the conduct of persons resident in distant countries; is liable to the rise and fall of markets, which are often very great; and is, more or less, at the

---

[506]Adam Smith, *The Wealth of Nations*, vol.1, p. 122, cited in Julian Hoppitt, *Risk and Failure in English Business, 1700–1800* (1987) 98.

[507]*TSTD*; David Richardson, "The British Empire and the Atlantic Slave Trade, 1660–1807," in *The Oxford History of the British Empire, vol. II, The Eighteenth Century*, ed., P.J. Marshall, (1998), table 20.2, 446, Morgan, 84–88.

[508]Richardson, *The Bristol Slave Traders: Collective Portrait* (1985) 8; Francis Hyde, B.B. Anderson, Sheila Marriner "The Nature and Profitability of the Liverpool Slave Trade," 372; Richard Sheridan, "The Commercial and Financial Organization of the British Slave Trade, 1750–1807," *Economic History Review* 2 (1958), 252–254

[509]Richardson, *The Bristol Slave Traders…*" 8; Richardson, "The British Empire…," 447.

[510]Mathias, "Kinship…," 17.

[511]Richardson, *The Bristol Slave Traders…*," 8.

[512]Richardson, *Bristol Slave Traders…*" 8.

[513]Philip Curtin, "Epidemiology and the Slave Trade," *Political Science Quarterly*, 83 (1968), 190–216; Stephen Behrendt, "Crew Mortality in the Transatlantic Slave Trade in the Eighteenth Century," in *Routes to Slavery: Direction, Ethnicity and Mortality in the Atlantic Slave Trade*, eds., David Eltis and David Richardson, (1997), 49–71.

[514]Morgan, 9.

mercy of seas and tempests."[515] Reducing the risks of the trade promised both greater profits and higher levels of outside investment. "Not surprisingly," Richardson reasons, "risk-limitation and risk-spreading strategies were an important influence on the organization of the slave trade, particularly outside London."[516] Slave traders sought to avoid risk wherever and whenever possible and, although some varieties of risk were expected and planned for, other less manageable and foreseeable risks were unavoidable in the ordinary conduct of the African trade. In an attempt to introduce a greater degree of consistency in the trade and thus reduce risk, slave traders sought to cut operating costs, achieve speedy returns, and enhance market flexibility. Stephen Behrendt argues that British slavers employed "decision-making strategies" designed to limit risk and manage the complexities of the transatlantic slave trade.[517] Merchants attempted to time voyages in order to coordinate supply and demand in Europe, Africa, and the Americas, because trading "within optimal transaction cycles minimized risks, reduced costs, and maximized the potential for profits."[518] Long before the apogee of the British slave trade at the end of the eighteenth century, Liverpool slavers had come to gain an understanding of, if not a degree of control over, these risks, becoming masters of their complex and noisome trade in the process.

A host of considerations influenced the market calculations of casual and regular slave traders alike. Estimating the profits to be made in a proposed slaving venture, and calculating the profits actually earned, were processes that required differing sets of skills. For most regular slave traders, such calculations were informed by wide slaving experience in one or more specific African slaving regions that many of these men, often-former captains of slave ships, knew from firsthand experience. (See appendix) Perceptions of profit in particular slaving markets ultimately determined where slavers traded. It was in the interest of regular slavers to keep themselves apprised of foreign competition in their specialist markets, to maintain an understanding of the workings of local slave supply systems, and to preserve ready access to supplies of trade goods in England and the continent geared to local slave markets in West Africa.

IV

A merchant's speculative impulse was the motive force in the initiation and construction of slaving partnerships. Entrepreneurship begins with an idea and depends upon the ability to inspire trust, attract investment, and promote "reciprocal transfers" of goods and credit between lenders, suppliers, and customers.[519] The first considerations faced by an entrepreneur contemplating a slave-trading venture were how to raise the necessary funding for the enterprise, and whom to invite into the partnership. How did the founders and managers of slaving partnerships obtain the necessary means to finance ventures? What kind of capital resources did merchants have to invest, and how much of their own financial resources did merchants invest in the trade? Jacob Price maintains that the amount of capital required to set up in business varied from trade to trade.[520] The capital requirements of incorporated trading companies, such as the East India, Levant and Baltic Companies, were generally many times larger than the capitalizations common in the transatlantic trades.[521]

According to Price, the cost of setting up in the Chesapeake trade before 1775 averaged £5,000 to £10,000, while the initial costs in the East India and Levant trades were often far in excess of £10,000.[522] Inflationary pressures caused these costs to rise throughout the eighteenth century. Richardson estimates that

---

[515]T. Gisborne, *An Enquiry into the Duties of Man in the Higher and Middle Classes of Society in Great Britain*; cited in Hoppitt, *Risk and Failure…,"* 96.

[516]Richardson, "The British Empire…,"448.

[517]Stephen Behrendt, "Markets, Transaction Cycles, and Profits: Merchant Decision Making in the British Slave Trade," *The William and Mary Quarterly*, 58 (2001), 173

[518]Behrendt, 173; Hyde, *et al*, "The Nature…," 372.

[519]Avner Offer, "Between the Gift and the Market: The Economy of Regard," *The Economic History Review* 50 (1997), 468.

[520]Jacob Price, *Capital and Credit British Overseas Trade: The View from the Chesapeake, 1700–1776* (1980), 41.

[521]Price, "Transaction Costs…," 278–279.

[522]Price, *Capital and Credit…"* 2, 38; Richardson, "The British Empire…"447; Richardson, *The Bristol Slave Traders…"* 6.

for the British slave trade as a whole, the average cost of preparing a ship for Africa rose from approximately £3,000 at the beginning of the eighteenth century to more than £8,000 by century's end.[523] The average cost of outfitting a slaving venture naturally varied between merchants, as high costs confronted those trading to the distant slave markets of Angola, the Bight of Biafra, and the Bight of Benin, while those trading to the much closer markets of the Upper Guinea coast generally faced lower costs. Annual expenditures also varied throughout the course of a slave trader's career. For example, William Davenport's average *per annum* investments in the African trade were not consistent during his long career, as approximately 75% of his total investment was concentrated in the years 1768–1776.[524] Given an average investment of £750 to £800 per voyage, Richardson calculates that Davenport's investment in slaving between 1748 and 1784, some 160 voyages in all, "must have been" between £120,000 and £130,000, which, in turn, represents an average investment of £3,500 per year during the course of his career.[525] This annual investment figure, Richardson suggests, may have been as high as £7,000 at the height of Davenport's career in the late 1760s and early 1770s, years in which he pioneered the slave trade to the Cameroons.[526] For Bristol slave traders, the average cost of investing in the trade rose from £2,500 in 1710, to £5,000 by the mid-eighteenth century, and to £7,300 in the decade after 1783.[527] For all slave merchants, regardless of their wealth or the scale of their trade, this *per annum* rise in total costs came to be reflected in a gradual increase in capitalization costs for new ventures in both the Liverpool and Bristol trades, the dominant ports in the Atlantic slave trade throughout the eighteenth century. This also contributed to the steady increase in total expenditures in the African trade in the major slave ports. In Liverpool, the average sum invested in the overall slave trade *per annum* rose from £200,000 pounds sterling in 1750, to more than £1 million in 1800, while the corresponding sums invested in the Bristol trade grew from an average of £50,000–60,000 in 1710–1711, to over £150,000 in the 1730s, and to £280,000 between 1788 and 1792.[528] This growing volume of investment seems to suggest that trading opportunities were available to all who wished to invest in the slave trade. However, not all investors were created equal, and some slave traders, those with greater financial resources, slaving expertise or a larger network of contacts in the African trade, were better able to create, and take advantage of, investment opportunities than were lesser men.[529] By the mid-eighteenth century, and probably before, the rising cost of participating in the slave trade presented a significant bar to entry for the small investor.

Laying hands on ready cash was sometimes difficult for even the largest, most well heeled overseas merchants, men who were often heavily concerned in several investments at once. For Liverpool slave traders involved in many lines of trade, manufacturing, and commercial brokerage, overextension was a constant concern. Before the cost of preparing slaving ventures rose during the course of eighteenth century, most slave traders were able to finance ventures from their own resources. Thereafter, securing credit to finance ventures became increasingly important for even the largest trader, becoming a regular part of the trade. Julian Hoppitt observes, "the demand for venture capital was met, in part, by the expansion of credit [as] businesses and prospective businesses could raise only limited funds from friends and relations or, once trading, from profits."[530] Financing a significant portion of a slaving venture through credit held important advantages for slave traders. Borrowing reduced the amount that slave merchants had to contribute from their own funds, lowered the threshold of entry into trade, and allowed novice men of business to expand their

---

[523]Richardson, "The British Empire...,"447.

[524]Richardson, "Profits in the Liverpool Slave Trade: The Accounts of William Davenport, 1757–1784," in *Liverpool, the African Slave Trade, and Abolition*, eds., Roger Anstey and P.E.H. Hair (1976), 64.

[525]Richardson, "Profits...," 64.

[526]Richardson, 66–69.

[527]Richardson, *The Bristol Slave Traders...*," 6.

[528]David Richardson, *Bristol, Africa, and the Eighteenth Century Slave Trade to America*, vol.1, *The Years of Expansion, 1698–1729* (1986) 20–21; David Richardson, *Bristol, Africa, and the Eighteenth Century Slave Trade to America*, vol.4, *The Final Years, 1770–1807*, (1996) 40f.; Morgan, 37–38.

[529]Julian Hoppitt, "The Use and Abuse of Credit in Eighteenth-Century England," in *Business Life and Public Policy: Essays in Honor of D.C. Coleman*, eds., Neil McKendrick and R.B. Outhwaite (1986) 14, 15, 82–83; Offer, 468.

[530]Hoppitt, "The Use and Abuse of Credit..." 72, 133–134.

operations more rapidly than would have been possible otherwise. After 1750, Liverpool slave merchants were purchasing half their cargoes of trade goods on credit.[531]

The proportion of cash and credit used to finance ventures varied by African region. In the Liverpool trade, the greater use of credit in financing ventures was a result, in part, of the southeast movement of the trade from the Upper Guinea Coast, especially Gambia that declined in importance after 1750, to the slave ports of the Niger River delta and Angola. This shift in the regional distribution of the Liverpool trade had two primary effects upon the cost of ventures. Firstly, the purchase of larger cargoes of slaves in the mass markets southeast of the Upper Guinea Coast meant that on average ships had to be larger and heavier than before, and hence more expensive to purchase, outfit, and crew. Because of the peculiarities of the African slave trade, slave traders were unable to reduce shipping costs by chartering vessels rather than purchasing them. Secondly, a steady rise in the price of slaves on the West African coast after the 1750s increased costs, a rise which translated into ever-larger cargoes of trade goods.[532] Thus, the cost of preparing a Guinea venture varied according to the intended number of slaves to be loaded, which, in turn, determined the size, and hence, the cost of the ship.[533]

V

Who were these men who trafficked in human flesh? Who were the largest slave traders in Liverpool, and what differentiated them from their smaller, less prolific colleagues? How did these similarities and differences influence the construction of slaving partnerships? Finally, how did the composition of slaving partnerships change over time? In addressing such important questions, it is necessary to heed Richardson's warning that assumptions about slaving partnerships should be avoided, as "a typical slave trader probably never existed."[534] However, while this is probably true for the slave trade as a whole, it ignores the similarities that characterized vast segments of the Liverpool slave-trading community. As a group, the greatest of Liverpool's slave traders shared a number of characteristics, more so than the much larger group of minor traders. In composition, slaving partnerships could be extremely complex or very simple and straightforward. While the surviving evidence only hints at the often byzantine complexity of many partnership arrangements, *The Trans-Atlantic Slave Trade Database* (*TSTD*) does provide some indication of the diversity of attenuated partnership relationships and connections; this in turn reflected the multiplicity of motivations that prompted individual investors to enter the trade. Slaving ventures served differing purposes for traders at different times, and the formation of partnerships reflected the changing business needs and outlooks of slave traders.

The differing purposes of individual investors are clearly reflected in the varieties of slaving partnerships that emerged in the Liverpool trade. Three general types of slave-trading partnership appeared soon after the advent of the Merseyside slave trade at the beginning of the eighteenth century: partnerships composed of regular traders, those of small, sporadic traders and investors, and sole traders. Each type exemplified an alternative vision of profit, and the variable resources of individual investors. Although smallest in number, the most important type of partnership was that of the regular trader, large-scale investors dedicated to the long-term exploitation of the African trade. Ship-owners who maintained a widespread commercial correspondence in the West Indies and elsewhere, these ambitious men sought to construct an efficient trade in which ships returned year after year to favored slave markets to purchase captive Africans for profitable sale in the New World. By providing the lion's share of the human cargoes that figured so prominently in

---

[531]David Richardson, "West African Consumption Patterns and their Influence on the Eighteenth Century English Slave Trade," in *The Uncommon Market: Essays in the Economic History of the Atlantic Slave Trade*, eds., Henry Gemery and Jan Hogendorn (1979), 315; Richardson, "Profits...," 72.

[532]Richardson, "Prices of Slaves in West and West-Central Africa: Toward and Annual Series, 1698–1807," *Bulletin of Economic Research* 43 (1991), 33f.

[533]Richardson, "The British Empire...,"447, Richardson, *The Bristol Slave Traders...*," 6; David Eltis and David Richardson, "Productivity in the Transatlantic Slave Trade," *Explorations in Economic History* 32 (1995), 467–469n.

[534]Richardson, *The Bristol Slave Traders...*," 6.

transatlantic exchange, regular traders made possible the proper functioning of a system of triangular trade. Committed to this complex pattern of trade, these merchants tended to take a long view of the slave trade as a business, and sought to minimize its costs and risks in order to maximize profits. To these men, profitability in the often-mercurial market in slaves was the product of effective management that promoted a small but steady accrual in annual earnings. Unlike smaller investors, regular traders did not evince a strictly speculative mode of slave trading that focused solely upon short-term gains or by making a large profit. However, the systematic approach of the regular slavers was not limited to the largest traders, and was, in fact, a manifestation of the rational mindset that was characteristic of Liverpool men of business, and their far-flung web of associates throughout the British Isles.

Thus, while every large trader was a regular trader, not every regular trader was a large trader. Even lesser

Table 5.1	*Total Number of Ventures* per *Investor as listed in the* TSTD	
1–10 ventures	11–20 ventures	21–130 ventures
762	113	112

slave traders who were ordinarily casual investors often sought to organize their own partnerships in order to inaugurate long-term African trade. In 1751 and 1753, for instance, the firm of *Edward Lowndes & Co.*, which included Edward Lowndes, his brother Charles, and the up and coming slave merchant John Salthouse, prepared the slaver *Elijah* twice for voyages to Africa, once to the Gold Coast and once to the Windward Coast.[535] While there was nothing unique about these two ventures, they represented something of a departure for Lowndes, a minor slave trader with only sixteen ventures to his credit between 1745 and 1756.[536] Prior to the 1751 voyage of the *Elijah*, Lowndes had invested exclusively with the important 1740s merchant-*cum*-grocer William Whalley, and his cadre of associates including Richard Nicholas, Robert Hallhead, John Welch, and his former apprentice William Davenport.[537] Thereafter, however, he managed half of all the voyages in which he invested. A similar pattern of investment is evident in the trade of other lesser slave traders. Although he participated in fewer overall ventures than Lowndes, the well-connected slave trader Edward Deane managed fully half of his ventures, including two voyages of the *Bridget* in 1746 and 1747 and four voyages of the *Cumberland* between 1748 and 1753, while investing in six ventures with *Foster Cunliffe & Sons*, a major Liverpool firm of tobacco and slave merchants.[538]

These ventures were mere forays into the slave trade when compared to the largest slave traders. Between 1751 and 1753, for instance, John Welch, a major Liverpool slaver from north Lancashire, dispatched five

Table 5.2	*Number of Ventures of the Thirty Largest Traders as listed in the* TSTD				
100–130	90–99	80–89	70–79	60–69	50–59
4	2	1	7	11	5

ventures to Africa, while William James, the largest Liverpool slave trader in the second half of the eighteenth century, averaged seven ventures per year between 1764 and 1775. A number of long-lived partnerships pre-

---

[535]*TSTD*; *Liverpool Memorandum Book (1753)*.

[536]*ibid.*

[537]*ibid.*

[538]*ibid*; *Liverpool Memorandum Book (1753)*.

Table 5.3   *Length of Career of the Thirty Largest Liverpool Slave Traders listed in the* TSTD

Name	Ventures	Career	Length of Career
1) Foster Cunliffe	113	1718–1758	40
2) Robert Armitage	63	1721–1757	36
3) Felix Doran	62	1737–1773	36
4) Arthur Heywood	65	1743–1775	32
5) William Gregson	92	1744–1775	31
6) Samuel Ogden	51	1720–1751	31
7) John Knight	117	1744–1774	30
8) Richard Savage	77	1745–1775	30
9) Benjamin Heywood	61	1745–1774	30
10) John Welch	79	1741–1770	29
11) Samuel Shaw	76	1746–1774	28
12) William Davenport	101	1748–1775	27
13) Jonathan Blundell	72	1748–1775	27
14) Thomas Rumbold	68	1748–1775	27
15) Bryan Blundell	66	1748–1775	27
16) John Crosbie	78	1745–1771	26
17) Edward Parr	54	1744–1768	24
18) John White	60	1750–1774	24
19) William Dobb	69	1745–1768	23
20) William Boates	76	1752–1775	23
21) John Salthouse	70	1752–1775	23
22) William Earle	80	1753–1775	22
23) George Hutton	63	1753–1774	21
24) Thomas Johnson	59	1753–1773	20
25) Robert Green	94	1757–1775	18
26) William James	130	1758–1775	17
27) Thomas Foxcroft	63	1759–1775	16
28) Miles Barber	52	1759–1775	16
29) William Trafford	58	1754–1769	15
30) William Crosbie	67	1757–1771	14

pared ships for repeated trips to Africa, such as "Honeyford's" *Nancy*, a large Bonny trader owned by the major slaver Jonathan Blundell and his associates, which made 19 trips to Africa between 1750 and 1768.[539] This focus on a specific regional slave market was common among long-lived partnerships, and demonstrated the highly organized commercial practices of these slaving firms. As with the group that prepared Blundell's *Nancy*, other important partnership groups also specialized in the Bight of Biafra, such as the owners of the *Duke of Cumberland*, the *Hector*, Gregson's *Nancy*, the *Dalrymple*, the *Chesterfield*, and the *Prince of Wales*, while others sailed exclusively for the Windward Coast, including the *Essex*, the *Rose*, the *Lancashire Witch*, the *Renown*, and the *Apollo*.[540] Other major partnership groups were far less specialized in their African destinations, including the *Knight* and the *Plumper*, both of which traded to the Windward Coast, the Gold Coast, the Bight of Benin, and the Bight of Biafra. Thus, while regional specialization characterized most of the major

---

[539]Will of George Lancaster, or Lancester, mariner now bound out on a Voyage to the Coast of Africa in the Honeyford's *Nancy* belonging to Liverpool, Lancashire, August 29, 1764, PCC: PROB 11/901; *TSTD*.
[540]*TSTD*.

Table 5.4	*Length of Career among the Thirty Largest Slave Traders listed in the* TSTD	
40–30 Years	20–29 Years	14–19 Years
9	15	6

partnerships responsible for the majority of the slaving voyages that departed Liverpool prior to 1775, others sought opportunity in the African slave trade wherever and whenever it could be found.

Despite their ubiquity, regular traders were very much a minority among the nearly 1,000 men who invested in the Liverpool slave trade between 1695 and 1775. Among regular traders, as the table above suggests, only 122 of 987 total investors, or 12%, invested in 21 or more slaving ventures, while only 30, or 3%, invested in 50 or more ventures between 1695 and 1775. Only this latter group can be counted as truly great slavers, men involved dozens of slaving ventures over the course of long careers. The table below indicates that these men had an unrivaled influence on the development in the Liverpool slave trade over an extended period of time. The largest slave traders tended to have the longest slaving careers. As the following table indicates, a number of slave traders such as Robert Armitage, Arthur and Benjamin Heywood, John Knight, and William Gregson, were important figures in the Liverpool slave trade for 30 or more years, while Foster Cunliffe spent 40 years, from the departure of his first ship in 1718 until his death in 1758, preparing ships for the slave markets of West Africa.[541] Kingpins of the Liverpool slave trade, these men were regular traders *par excellence*, ubiquitous dealmakers involved in more than 6 out of every 10 slaving ventures between 1747 and 1775. Among this group of elite traders, the rarest of all were the super-traders, a handful of merchants who participated in more than 90 slaving ventures each, men such as William James, John Knight, Foster Cunliffe, William Davenport, Robert Green, and William Gregson. Much of the growth of the Liverpool trade after the Peace of Paris in 1763 can be attributed to these great traders, especially the upstart James, as well as Davenport and other more established traders.

Although not all of the 30 largest slave traders originated in Liverpool, or its immediate environs, or shared similar social origins, most were contemporaries who knew one another intimately, traded together, or at least knew of each other in the small community of great slave traders. Friendly rivals, these preeminent slave merchants invested with one another, provided commercial services and trade goods, communicated closely in pursuit of common interest, and stood surety for fellow traders when the need arose. Many of these men rose slowly within the community of slave traders, building upon preexisting connections with older, more established African merchants. At the beginning of his slaving career, a fledgling slave merchant often formed life-long attachments with a single mentor, men who provided their *protégé* with *entrée* to the complex world of the African slave trade. In the Liverpool slave trade, mentor relationships grew from master-apprentice associations, kinship ties, and employer-employee connections, most especially those that brought together slaving partners and the captains of ships. Flush with earnings from successful slaving ventures, the captains of many ships managed to overcome the formidable obstacles that faced them to become partners on equal terms with their former employers. (See appendix 5.2)

One such captain, William Boates, began his spectacular rise to the top ranks of Liverpool slave merchants in 1744 as master of the ship *Byrne*, a Bonny trader owned by the eminent Liverpool merchants Thomas Seel and John Knight.[542] After seven voyages to Africa between 1744 and 1756, the last two as part owner, Boates became a full-time trader in partnership with his former employer and mentor John Knight.[543] This was a training period for Captain Billy Boates, an apprenticeship in the vagaries of the slave trade. This apprenticeship with Knight, and the years of partnership that followed, slowly ended after 1763, as Boates

[541]ibid.

[542]*ibid.*

[543]*ibid.*

Table 5.5   *Secondary Investors and their Primary Partners as listed in the* TSTD

Name	Total Career Ventures	Total Ventures with Primary Partners	Primary Partner (s)
1. John Bridge	49	41 (84%)	William Gregson
2. Peter Holme	49	24 (49%)	William Gregson
3. William Rowe	48	26 (54%)	John & William Crosbie
4. John Dobson	46	33 (72%)	Richard Savage
5. Robert Clay	44	24 (54%)	William Dobb
6. Joseph Brown	43	41 (95%)	John Salthouse
	—	30 (70%)	Thomas Foxcroft
	—	27 (63%)	George Hutton
	—	23 (53%)	Thomas Johnson
	—	19 (44%)	John White
	—	16 (37%)	William Dobb
7. Thomas Hodgson	38	27 (71%)	Richard Savage
8. James Lowe	36	29 (80%)	Richard Savage
9. John Tomlinson	34	33 (97%)	John Knight
10. Nehemiah Holland	33	22 (67%)	William Earle
11. Levinius Unsworth	31	10 (32%)	Arthur Heywood
	—	10 (32%)	Jonathan Blundell
12. Patrick Black	30	27 (90%)	William Davenport
	—	21 (70%)	William Earle
13. John Copeland	29	14 (48%)	Richard Savage
14. George Warren Watts	28	12 (43%)	William Davenport
	—	12 (43%)	William Earle
15. Christopher Butler	28	28 (100%)	Francis Ingram
16. Charles Pole	27	19 (70%)	Jonathan Blundell
17. Thomas Ward	25	13 (52%)	William Earle
	—	9 (36%)	Arthur Heywood
18. Edward Chaffers	24	14 (58%)	John & William Crosbie
19. William Jenkinson	22	15 (68%)	William Davenport
20. Robert Jennings	22	16 (73%)	William Davenport
	—	13 (59%)	William Earle
21. Samuel Kilner	21	16 (76%)	Miles Barber
22. John Parker	20	15 (75%)	William Davenport
	—	12 (60%)	William Earle

moved past the certainties of his early career to form links with a new set of partners led by William Gregson. By this time, Boates had emerged as an experienced slave trader, the equal of even the most prolific of Liverpool slave merchants. After 1761, Boates became Gregson's primary partner, joining with him in over 20 slaving ventures to Africa.[544] Thereafter, Boates himself became a mentor to a new group of promising young captains, easing their entry into the ranks of slave traders, much as John Knight had done for him almost two decades before.

---

[544]*ibid.*

Regardless of the scale of their African trade, active traders partnered most often with a smaller group of intimates, while a larger and mixed group of lesser investors followed these elite slave traders in train as sleeping partners. Although smaller investors, men who seldom assumed a managerial role, tended to maintain their relationships with their primary partners, over time they occasionally crossed the aisle to trade with the rivals of their closest partners. This was not necessarily a rejection of their primary partners, but rather a temporary pursuit of apparent trading opportunities. For example, the close relationship between Boates and Knight foundered upon the ambitions of Boates to explore new horizons and expand his trade in slaves. In a similar fashion, in 1769 Richard Hanley left his partnership with Gregson and Boates in order to join a group of minor, nameless investors in the venture of the *Bridson* to Gabon.[545] This was not viewed by Gregson and Boates as a breach of trust, but as an entrepreneurial foray into a promising new slave market. Hanley continued to partner his primary associates in several more voyages to Bonny in the years before the outbreak of the American Revolution in 1775. An investment such as this was not done in secret, as it was understood that commercial advantage often necessitated joining with new partners. After all, business was business. This underlines the fact that the personal associations that undergirded slaving partnerships were subject to the same conflicts and pressures which afflicted all business relationships. Thus, slaving partnerships were seldom, if ever, exclusive arrangements. The impermanence of many partnerships belies the close ties which frequently drew the largest slave traders and their regular investors together, strong personal and professional bonds which united them in common purpose. In the Liverpool slave trade, consequently, centrifugal and centripetal forces produced an often contradictory pattern of partnership that was both flexible and cohesive.

Unlike most of the *Bridson* partners, the regular partners of the largest traders were very often heavily involved in the African trade over the course of several decades. They were ship-owners who, at times, organized ventures that included their primary trading partners as investors. The table below indicates that secondary partners were important figures in the trade of the largest slavers. Peter Holme is an example of one such important but lesser slave trader. In 1750, 1751, and 1752, Holme, a prominent wine and brandy merchant, served as ship's husband in preparing the vessel *Nancy* for Bonny, a partnership that included Holme's primary partner William Gregson, and Gregson's most frequent partner John Bridge.[546] In 1750, Bridge himself managed the preparations for the small Windward Coast trader *Vigilant*, a partnership that included Holme but not Gregson.[547] This pattern of investment resulted not only from the personal relationship between Holme and Bridge, which, for Holme, predated his first partnership with Gregson, but also from the fact that the venture was destined for the Windward Coast, a slave market in which Gregson had little experience or interest.[548] However, Gregson did not begrudge his closest partners the opportunity for profit in what to him was an undesirable market, or curtail his involvement with these men in the slave trade in the decades that followed.

Table 5.6	*Breakdown of Ventures for Traders listed in the* Liverpool Memorandum Book	
50 or more career ventures	30 to 49 Ventures	1 to 19 Ventures
21 (41.2%)	16 (31.4%)	14 (27.4%)

[545]*ibid.* In addition to Hanley, the *Bridson* partners included Captain John Platt, Roger Fisher, John Fisher, Daniel Jones, Edward Bridge, Paul Bridson, John Johnson, and Walter Cahoun.

[546]*Liverpool Memorandum Book of 1753*; *TSTD*; John Gore, ed., *The Liverpool Directory, For the Year 1766*; Articles of Partnership, "for carrying on trade of selling beads, arrangoes, etc," July 24, 1766, Earle Papers, D/EARLE/4/2; Will of Peter Holme, merchant of Childwall, Lancashire, formerly of Liverpool, May 22, 1780, PCC: PROB 11/1065.

[547]*Liverpool Memorandum Book of 1753*; *TSTD*.

[548]*Liverpool Memorandum Book; TSTD.* Peter Holme's first slaving partnership was with John Kennion, trading as *Kennion & Holme*, with whom Holme participated in 20 slaving ventures between 1748 and 1753.

Overall, his most frequent partners were Gregson and Bridge, who joined with him in over twenty voyages, some one-half of his career slaving ventures. The personal and professional relationships Holme formed with these eminent and experienced slave merchants provided him *entrée* to an elite circle of slave traders, and allowed him to establish a reputation as an honest and capable partner. Still, Holme traded with a wide variety of men, often forming transient partnerships with minor traders in order to exploit fleeting market conditions in various slave markets. Nearly 60% of his partners invested with Holme only once, and over 80% invested with him five or fewer times.[549] Holme also used such single-purpose ventures to supply the partnership with the wine and brandy used to barter for slaves in Africa, an important trade he shared with Gregson and Davenport.[550] More importantly, Holme successfully scaled the ladder of personal and professional acceptance, and henceforth became part of a business *milieu* that differentiated him from the common lot of minor slave traders. Slave merchants such as William Gregson, John Welch, William Davenport, Richard Savage, and John Knight, men who traded upon their accumulated expertise, were the gatekeepers of the Liverpool slave trade, eminent figures who admitted ambitious men such as Holme, Boates, and Bridge into the upper echelons of the local slave trade. What took shape was a slave trade that was generally open to a wide range of potential investors, even if the possibility for acceptance by the largest slave merchants was extremely limited. Well-established in the local commercial community, Liverpool's elite slave merchants built a close

Table 5.7	*Numbers of Investors* per *Total Slaving Ventures listed in the* TSTD	
Number of Ventures	Total Investors	Percentage of Total Investors
1–10	762	77%
11–20	113	11%
21–131	112	11%
Totals	987	99%

but not closed community of like-minded businessmen. Ultimately, acceptance was the coin of the realm, a factor that dictated the limits of profitability for the average investor.

What effect did these complex interrelationships have upon the management of slaving ventures? As organizers of many, if not most, slaving ventures between 1695 and 1775, the greatest slave traders often assumed the role of ship's husband, or managing partner, in preparing ships for the African slave markets. However, this was not always the case, for middling and small slavers assumed the role of ship's husband as well. Among the more than 50 slaving partnerships listed in the 1753 edition of the *Liverpool Memorandum Book*, an important commercial guide, smaller slave traders—those with nineteen or fewer career ventures—accounted for nearly one-third. The proportion of such smaller slave traders who participated in the Liverpool slave trade as a whole fluctuated in the years after 1753, and became increasingly important from the mid-to-late 1760s. As the following table shows, the vast majority of investors in the Liverpool slave trade participated in ten slaving ventures or less, suggesting that they sought not so much a sustainable, long-term commerce as windfall profits in particularly promising markets.[551] Only 11% of Liverpool slave traders participated in 20 or more voyages, while 89% participated in 20 or fewer ventures.[552]

---

[549]*TSTD.*

[550]Hyde, et al, "The Nature...," 373; Anderson, *"The Lancashire Bill System...,"* 73.

[551]*ibid.*

[552]*ibid.*

Most ship's husbands were, in fact, the managers of slaving ventures that were small and insignificant. Although these men demonstrated the expertise and courage to organize and manage slaving ventures, most small investors were strictly sleeping partners with little or no interest in taking on the onerous responsibilities that the management of slaving ventures entailed. While ties of kinship and association with the active managers of slaving ventures linked many sleeping partners, these casual investors remained relative strangers to the established merchant community of Liverpool. Davis notes that a sleeping partner invested in a "tangible piece of property, which remained little changed apart from gradual wear and tear, and although he normally paid the fitting-out costs before she sailed, the only substantial liability to be incurred by the ship in her voyages was the wages of the crew, and if the ship were lost the law did not require that wages be paid, even to surviving crew.[553] Sleeping partners were casual participants in slaving voyages, whose ignorance of the African trade was frequently trumped by the capital they could invest in the undertaking.[554] However, for a ship's husband, acceptance of a sleeping partner was not always motivated by financial considerations.

Regardless of his importance in the larger community of Liverpool slavers, or the extent of his trade, a ship's husband was the indispensable link connecting partners with each other, and connecting the partnership with the men who provided necessary goods and services. In many cases, these were the same people. Often the managing partner was the only partner acquainted with all the owners.[555] On the surface, the position of ship's husband was an anomalous one for, despite his integrative role and enormous responsibilities; he received little in the way of remuneration. While Richardson notes that ship's husbands of all degrees of importance received no special privileges, salary, or commissions for discharging their duties, he suggests that they did garner a few indirect benefits.[556] The managing partner was able to distribute largesse to his friends. Given the reciprocal nature of commerce, this created obligations that had to be honored later.[557] In outfitting his ship the *Aston* for Gambia in 1771, for example, John Knight, the ship's husband, relied for the trade goods and ship's stores required for the voyage upon current and former business associates, most of whom had previously invested in at least one slaving venture. Knight purchased pans and swords from John Parr Jr., plumbing and shot from James Aspinall, tobacco from John Dobson, gunpowder from William Penketh, carpentry from Edward Grayson, iron hoops from John Nunes, butter from John Benson and John Postlethwaite, ironmongery from William Earle and Edward Grayson, Manchester textiles from Thomas and John Tipping, brandy from Richard Wickstead, knives and flints from Edward Bate, sails from John Galley, and sugar from his own firm *Knight, Woods & Co.*[558] Regardless of whether any of these men ever partnered him in a slaving venture prior to his death in 1774, Knight had created a debt of honor that these men were obliged to acknowledge.[559]

Among organizers of smaller slaving ventures, the prospect of providing material benefit to friends was a powerful inducement for investment. At the same time, of course, it was understood that mutual self-interest among investors was necessary for the success of a venture. For instance, Roger Fisher, a prominent Liverpool timber merchant and shipwright, organized the voyage of the 48-ton brigantine *Samuel* to the Windward Coast in 1756, a venture that was designed to benefit his friend and frequent partner John Livesley, a house-builder and carpenter of Shaw's Brow, Liverpool, and his associate Nicholas Cross, a timber merchant and cabinet-maker of Poole Lane.[560] Fisher's slaving ventures in the years after the *Samuel* included not only his son John and his son-in-law Peter Hunt, partners in the shipbuilding firm *Roger Fisher & Son*, but also Edward

[553]Davis, 102–104.

[554]Elder, 134–135.

[555]Davis, 105.

[556]Richardson, "Profits...," 67–69, Richardson, *Collective Biography...*," 16–17.

[557]Hyde, et al, "The Nature...," 373; Anderson, *"The Lancashire Bill System...,"* 73.

[558]Invoice of Sundry Merchandize on board the *Aston,* bound for Gambia, 1771, cited in Anderson, "*The Lancashire Bill System,*" 80f.

[559]*TSTD*. Among the men listed, only William Earle, James Aspinall and John Galley invested in slaving ventures with Knight between 1771 and 1775.

[560]*TSTD*; *Liverpool Directory of 1766*; Stewart-Brown, *Liverpool Ships in the 18th Century,* 115–116; Will of John Livesley, house-builder of Liverpool, Wills and Inventories, Chester Probate Registry, Admon., 1769; Will of Nicholas Cross, cabinet-maker of Liverpool, Wills and Inventories, Chester Probate Registry, 1780.

Table 5.8 *Sample of Liverpool Sole Traders listed in the* TSTD

Name	Career Ventures	Solo Voyages	Dates of Solo Voyage (s)	Percentage of Career Ventures
1. William James	130	79	1764–1775	61
2. William Boates	76	18	1765–1775	24
3. Miles Barber	52	16	1762–1772	31
4. Samuel Shaw	76	10	1760–1769	13
5. John Knight	117	6	1763–1773	3
6. Thomas Rumbold	68	3	1766–1768	4
7. James Gildart	37	4	1752–1768	11
8. George Campbell	34	6	1752–1758	18
9. James Clemens	33	3	1761–1774	9
10. Robert Kennedy	23	2	1770–1771	9
11. Samuel Sandys	47	12	1771–1775	25
12. Edward Grayson	21	1	1773	5
13. Thomas Weston	9	4	1761–1766	44
14. John Robinson	7	1	1750	14
15. C. Weatherhead	4	4	1773–1775	100
16. John Scrogham	3	1	1773	33
17. John Gee	2	1	1754	50
18. Henry Pepper	1	1	1739	100
19. Henry West	1	1	1745	100
20. Mark Davis	1	1	1745	100
21. Arthur Higson	1	1	1748	100
22. John Pym	1	1	1748	100
23. William Wright	1	1	1766	100
24. Richard Alcock	1	1	1766	100
25. Alexander Willock	1	1	1770	100
26. Joseph Cazeneau	1	1	1773	100

Mason, a timber merchant and significant slave trader.[561] In addition to the close personal associations that these men shared, Fisher and his associates practiced similar professions, and had much the same financial interests. By contracting with the partnership to provide materials and services, Fisher, as ship's husband, was in a position to benefit himself as well as his partners. Fitting a ship out for a voyage required the services of carpenters and shipwrights, as well as adequate supplies of timber, a lucrative proposition for the owners of the *Samuel*. This suggests that profiting from the sale of slaves was perhaps less important to *Roger Fisher & Co.* than the prospect of more concrete and lucrative business opportunities, such as selling the partnership timber, and providing the carpentry and repair services required to modify the ship for the rigors of the slave trade. Although Fisher invested in seventeen slaving ventures between 1756 and 1771, he was a sporadic trader engaged in small family-oriented business, and no slaving professional. While it is not always clear what motivations lay behind slaving partnerships, the experience of Fisher and his associates suggests that the African trade served a variety of purposes for different groups of owners. They were inexperienced venturers motivated by simple opportunism, whose primary trades—timber merchanting, house-building, and shipbuilding—precluded the construction of any long-term dedication to the African trade.

---

[561] *Liverpool Directory of 1766*; Stewart-Brown, 115–116.

Table 5.9   *Sole Traders as a Proportion of Annual Ventures as listed in the* TSTD

Year	Total Ventures *per* Annum	Total Sole Traders *per* Annum	Percentage
1747	25	9	36
1748	43	5	12
1749	15	1	7
1750	40	2	5
1751	41	3	7
1752	46	2	4
1753	61	2	3
1754	60	3	5
1755	40	3	7
1756	53	2	4
1757	44	2	4
1758	51	4	8
1759	61	2	3
1760	73	3	4
1761	69	2	3
1762	56	3	5
1763	70	3	4
1764	73	3	4
1765	75	7	9
1766	57	9	16
1767	77	8	10
1768	79	15	19
1769	89	13	15
1770	89	24	27
1771	94	20	21
1772	96	19	20
1773	104	25	24
1774	89	32	36

The smallest group of Liverpool slave merchants consisted of sole traders, men who organized ventures on their own account without any partners. (See appendix 5.1) As the following table demonstrates this group was an admixture of regular traders, major participants in the Liverpool slave trade, and small traders, unknown speculators whose interest was to make large profits as quickly as possible with as little capital as possible. However, it is difficult to determine the approximate numbers of sole traders participating in the Liverpool slave trade between 1695 and 1775, because of gaps in the partnership records. These lacunae are particularly evident for the fifty years before 1747 when 60% of partners are unknown.[562] Fortunately, the partnership records become much more complete after 1747, and demonstrate that sole traders were increasingly common in the Liverpool trade in the following three decades. This long-term trend is evident in the following table, which demonstrates this annual increase in the number of sole traders. The total number of Liverpool slaving ventures was one-third greater in 1774 than it was in 1747. During this period there was a marked tendency for individual partnerships to decrease in size.[563] From a high point of between six or seven

---

[562]*TSTD*. The records of slaving partnerships became more accurate over time.
[563]*TSTD*.

Table 5.10 *Significant Upper Guinea Traders as listed in the TSTD*

Name	Senegambia	Windward Coast	Sierra Leone	Total Ventures
1. William James	1	75	4	80
2. John Salthouse	0	46	7	53
3. Thomas Foxcroft	0	45	6	51
4. Robert Green	2	35	10	47
5. Miles Barber	9	3	29	43
6. Thomas Johnson	0	34	8	42
7. George Hutton	0	40	0	40
8. John Knight	30	4	2	36
9. Samuel Shaw	19	9	7	35
10. William Dobb	2	25	8	35
11. John White	0	24	3	27
12. William Earle	1	20	1	22
13. John Crosbie	2	17	1	20
14. William Crosbie	0	17	1	18
15. William Trafford	3	12	2	17

partners *per* ownership group in 1755, the size of slaving partnerships declined to three or four by the early 1770s.[564] (See appendix 5.3, 5.4)

This decline can be attributed to two related factors. Firstly, the regional distribution of the Liverpool trade shifted somewhat from its previous overwhelming concentration upon the Gold Coast, the Bight of Benin, and the Bight of Biafra, to a growing trade with slave markets in Upper Guinea, namely the Windward Coast. This shift was, in part, the result of the operational savings that many slave traders expected to realize by preparing ventures for the far less expensive slave markets of Upper Guinea where increasingly favorable terms of trade made it worthwhile to expand trade to the region. By the mid-1760s, this general region was already familiar to a number of established traders, such as John Knight, who began to barter for slaves in Gambia in 1753, and continued to trade there sporadically until his death in 1774.[565] Secondly, as the table below indicates, new men, including several of the largest, most important Liverpool traders of the 1760s and 1770s, entered Upper Guinea slave markets in a big way after 1765, especially the Windward Coast and Sierra Leone. The most prolific slaver of the period, William James, prepared nearly 60 ventures to the Windward coast, almost three-quarters of all his ventures to this market between 1758 and 1775. A significant

Table 5.11 *Solo Ventures by William James and Miles Barber as listed in the TSTD, 1765–1775*

Name	Upper Guinea	Lower Guinea	West Central Africa
1. William James	58	37	0
2. Miles Barber	34	5	3

Source: TSTD.

---

[564]*ibid.*

[565]*ibid*; Will of John Knight, merchant of Liverpool, Lancashire, December 13, 1774, PCC: PROB 11/1003.

portion of the growth in the Liverpool slave trade during this decade can be attributed to James. Similarly, Miles Barber built up a large trade to Sierra Leone and the Windward Coast after 1765, primarily as a sole trader. The primary benefit of trading in Upper Guinea, in terms of lower costs, were advantages of scale. These advantages were a particular boon to men with the means, predisposition, and confidence to trade slaves on their own account such as William Earle, John Salthouse, Thomas Foxcroft, and George Hutton. Although such a singular mode of trade was not without its risks, it permitted the sole trader to control these risks better, and limit possible losses, assuming complete control. Thus, there were real commercial advantages to be had by going it alone.

VI

The risks of the slave trade were very much in the minds of potential investors, frequently influencing the decision whether or not to invest. However, for both the partnership and the individual investor, an invitation to participate in the slave trade was about more than simply acquiring capital or controlling risk. A value-laden undertaking, the process of assembling a group of dissimilar men into an effective business partnership had an important social dimension. An invitation to join a partnership reflected not only an appreciation of the financial resources a new investor might bring to a venture, it also represented a tacit recognition of his reputation and social standing within the larger commercial community of Liverpool. Because so much was at stake in an African venture, slave merchants often took great care in evaluating new partners, weighing the role they might play in constructing a useful, profitable partnership. Careful consideration of the worth of a potential investor grew from an innate concern for reputation as an unerring guide to character. In considering new partners judgments based primarily upon assessments of reputation were much valued, and accorded great weight. Thus, as self-possessed gentlemen and men of business, slave merchants seldom considered as a partner a man reputed to be dishonest, incautious, or profligate, regardless of his means.

In addition to judging the wealth and worth of prospective partners, slave merchants naturally sought acknowledgement of their social standing within the ranks of their fellow traders. A merchant monitored his relative position in the larger community of traders primarily by including an element of personal criticism and social commentary in business letters, although these observations often took the form of mere gossip. The backhanded compliment was an effective way to relay a negative opinion without being overly harsh. "Mr. John Hunniford is an unexceptionable gentleman," William Earle wrote his brother-in-law in September 1760, "[and while]…his interest & mine are in the same way, I must own [that] I should rather decline being concerned with him, though he is a person [with whom] I have the highest opinion of."[566] The meaning of such mild slights was well understood.

Large and small merchants alike kept regular correspondents apprised of their experiences with, and assessments of, other men in trade. To some degree, a merchant was at the mercy of not only his enemies, but also his friends as well. Business friends depended upon each other to keep their secrets, and to speak well of each other. No merchant, however, was immune to misrepresentation, even by his friends. In December 1760, William Earle, for instance, wrote an unflattering letter to a close London correspondent about the financial misfortunes of his friend and associate John Darbyshire, a Birmingham merchant and ironmonger. "Last post brought me an account [of] John Darbyshire," Earle wrote Joseph Wimpey, "[who] was obliged to lay his affairs before his creditors…I have not liked his proceedings [for] some time."[567] Although Darbyshire quickly emerged from the worst of his financial difficulties a few months later, such commercial gossip could not have bolstered his prospects. By July 1761, however, Earle was inquiring after the financial health of Darbyshire, in order to determine whether he was in a position to invest in slaving ventures again. "I beg you," Earle wrote Richard Rabone, "candidly acquaint me how [Darbyshire's] affairs are likely to be [in the

---

[566]Earle to *John Joseph Bacon & Co.*, September 19, 1760 (*draft letter never sent*)
[567]Earle to *Joseph Wimpey & Co.*, December 30, 1760.

spring], also what your opinion is of Mr. John Humphreys."[568] Despite his friend's tribulations, it is perhaps noteworthy that Earle continued to trade with the financially suspect Darbyshire.[569]

Similarly, Earle often expressed his annoyance with much more significant slave traders than John Darbyshire, writing letters to business associates that were laced with sarcastic innuendo. In quite a lot of these letters, Earle expressed his displeasure with the prominent merchant and former Lord Mayor James Gildart, son and business partner of the illustrious Richard Gildart. Although Earle wrote an associate in February 1761 claiming not to have any connection with Gildart, "either directly or indirectly," both men were partners in the *Baltimore*, a 330 ton slave ship which departed Liverpool in June 1760 bound for Angola.[570] This association with Gildart, which he took care never to repeat, was a tiresome and frustrating experience for Earle. As ship's husband, Gildart was responsible for the management of the ship, a task greatly complicated by the capture of a Dutch ship by the *Baltimore*. This ship, the *Resolute*, was subsequently brought before a prize court where Gildart claimed it on behalf of the owners of the *Baltimore* as a legitimate spoil of war. "As it was agreed," Earle wrote Humphreys,

> Mr. Gildart, who has in his hands all the money arising from sale of the *Resolute's* Cargo… which he consented to the ownery being under an obligation to pay him on the decision of the *Resolute's* trial on appeal. We have had no settlements of said ship. Whenever anything is done you may be assured of being regularly…advised thereof, and my neighbor & intimate friend Charles Lowndes [will]…be paymaster for your 1/16ᵗʰ [share of the *Resolute*].[571]

It thus fell to Gildart to close the books on the voyage of the *Baltimore*, apportion profits arising from the sale of slaves and American produce, and determine each partners' share of the *Resolute*, should she be declared a prize of war. This was not to be, however, and the court ruled that restitution be made to the ship's Dutch owners, and that the *Baltimore* partners refund all profits arising from the capture of the *Resolute*.[572]

While the outcome of this trial cannot be blamed on Gildart, it both embittered Earle and placed him in a difficult financial situation. In addition to the return of the *Resolute* to her owners, the court obligated the owners of the *Baltimore* to pay them compensation, a significant amount of cash that Earle had to lay hands on quickly. "Give me leave to hint to you," Earle wrote Humphreys,

> that there is a long chain of restitutions to be made to the Dutch & when that comes upon [the partners] it must hurt them extremely. I am sorry to acquaint you [that] restitution is ordered… made to the applicants on the *Baltimore's* prize, so that [they] must refund. Never anything so lucky as your knowing me, to be drawn into the *Francis & Baltimore*, [both lost], the former had a great prospect.[573]

This unexpected expense left Earle short in meeting obligations arising from his ongoing slaving activities, a shortfall he hoped to make up, in part, from the proceeds from the sale of the large cargo of Angola slaves which the *Baltimore* had successfully landed in Guadeloupe. Gildart, however, was dilatory in closing the books on the venture and paying each share-holder his division of the profits "I should have replied to [your last letter] some time since," Earle wrote Humphreys in November 1760,"

> but [I] was in expectation of sending you a remittance, which I did flatter myself I could have done long ago…but great…promises be not relied upon, for I have not received as yet one shilling [from Mr. James Gildart], but still have fair promises when it will come. I…[don't

---

[568]Earle to Richard Rabone, July 23, 1761.

[569]Earle to John Darbyshire, January 6, 1761.

[570]Earle to John Humphreys, February 27, 1761, *TSTD*.

[571]Earle to Humphreys, April 23, 1760.

[572]Earle to Humphreys, July 6, 1761.

[573]*ibid.*, July 6, 1761.

need to]…tell [you], in the mean time, [that] it is…hard upon you & me, having advanced all the ready money required for this voyage without any benefit…It is no more than reasonable [that if] Mr. Gildart will not pay us]…he should …[at least] allow interest for the time he has the money in his hands.[574]

Earle clearly resented Gildart for what he saw as his selfishness and incompetence. Earle suggests in his *Daybook* that James Gildart was a difficult and dishonest man who did not honorably fulfill his responsibilities to his fellow partners. In the years thereafter, Earle learned to collaborate men he knew and trusted, rather than to place his fate in the hands of strangers.

VII

The question of trust was of vital importance to the men who formed slaving partnerships. Among the panoply of factors that affected the composition of slaving partnerships, judging a man's reputation was only part of the equation. Davis argues that the many difficulties involved in constructing and altering a partnership were sufficient cause to limit "membership to a small circle, a group of intimates well acquainted with each other's affairs and modes of behavior."[575] Although Davis is speaking about the British shipping industry as a whole, his observation is true for a majority of the slaving partnerships formed in eighteenth century Liverpool. However, this was not the case for all such partnerships. In the Liverpool slave trade, the intensity of personal connections was a major determinant of the social context of partnership. In purely human terms, three gradations of intimacy joined men in the common pursuit of profit in the African trade, a closeness that was often emotional in nature and born of long associations that predated the formation of business ties. As might be expected, variable levels of familiarity gave rise to differing types of partnerships, human links that determined how a partnership was formed, how long it lasted, and how accepting it was of new investors. The ties that formed the closest bonds originated in kinship relationships. Almost as close were those that arose from personal and professional affiliations and friendships. Finally, the least intimate were the non-personal relationships based primarily upon mutual financial interest. The boundaries between these relationships are admittedly indistinct. The types of relationships at the heart of partnership groups suggest that for the individual investor the decision to enter a particular ownership group reflected the variable importance of a host of possible motivations, ranging from familial expectations to purely speculative considerations. Together, this concatenation of intimacy and ambition reveals both the boundaries and possibilities of partnership in the Liverpool slave trade.

Family connections were the basic building blocks for a number of slaving partnerships. Although the decision to undertake a venture to Africa was most often rooted in an awareness of market factors, a multitude of non-market considerations also influenced both the structure of slaving partnerships as well as the conduct of business. In England, it had long been customary for a merchant to turn to his closest kin for both the capital necessary to enter trade, as well as a ready source of partners. This practice was common in the Liverpool slave trade from the beginning, as partnership groups were frequently founded upon close family ties, as well as the economic resources these bonds made available. These factors include not only familial relationships and obligations, but also intimate business associations and expectations of commercial reciprocity that close relationships implied.[576] Thus, ventures were planned in accordance with specific market intentions within the context of a socially constructed notion of commerce.

Many African merchants understood the advantages of kinship ties in organizing long-lived trading relationships better than others did. This recognition was marked in the Liverpool slave trade where distinctive patterns of organization developed among kinship-based slaving partnerships. Complex, overlapping family partnerships played an integrative role that served to consolidate and advance the trade throughout

---

[574]*ibid.*, November 8, 1760
[575]Davis, 102–104.
[576]Mathias, "Risk, Credit, and Kinship in Early Modern Enterprise," 15–17.

Table 5.12 *Partnership Patterns among the 26 Largest Slave Traders listed in the* TSTD

Slave Traders	Total Ventures	Total Partners	Partners with 6/+ ventures with Slaver in column one	Partners with 5/- ventures with Slaver in column one
1. William James	130	38	8 (21%)	30 (79%)
2. John Knight	117	82	22 (27%)	60 (73%)
3. William Davenport	101	112	35 (31%)	77 (69%)
4. Robert Green	93	171	16 (9%)	155 (91%)
5. William Gregson	92	59	21 (36%)	38 (64%)
6. William Earle	80	100	23 (23%)	77 (77%)
7. John Welch	79	59	16 (27%)	43 (73%)
8. John Crosbie	78	84	16 (19%)	68 (81%)
9. Richard Savage	77	79	15 (19%)	64 (81%)
10. William Boates	76	53	9 (17%)	44 (83%)
11. Samuel Shaw	76	35	15 (43%)	20 (57%)
12. Jonathan Blundell	72	53	22 (41.5%)	31 (58.5%)
13. John Salthouse	70	53	16 (30%)	37 (70%)
14. William Dobb	69	54	19 (35%)	35 (65%)
15. Thomas Rumbold	68	82	18 (22%)	64 (78%)
16. William Crosbie	67	71	11 (15.5%)	60 (84.5%)
17. Bryan Blundell	66	32	18 (56%)	14 (44%)
18. Arthur Heywood	65	67	15 (22%)	52 (78%)
19. George Hutton	63	39	15 (38.5%)	24 (61.5%)
20. Thomas Foxcroft	63	41	18 (44%)	23 (56%)
21. Benjamin Heywood	61	70	14 (20%)	56 (80%)

Table 5.12 *Partnership Patterns among the 26 Largest Slave Traders listed in the* **TSTD** *(Continued)*

Slave Traders	Total Ventures	Total Partners	Partners with 6/+ ventures with Slaver in column one	Partners with 5/- ventures with Slaver in column one
22. John White	60	46	18 (39%)	28 (61%)
23. Thomas Johnson	59	50	20 (40%)	30 (60%)
24. William Trafford	58	85	10 (12%)	75 (88%)
25. Edward Parr	54	38	9 (24%)	29 (77%)
26. Miles Barber	52	19	5 (26%)	14 (74%)

Source: TSTD.

the eighteenth century. Such groups included the extended families of Richard Gildart, Foster Cunliffe, John Pemberton Sr., Samuel Ogden, Thomas Tarleton, Samuel Powell, Charles Pole I, John Earle, James Crosbie, Bryan Blundell Sr., Samuel Shaw Sr., and Edward Trafford. Some of these founding groups were particularly extended, connecting several generations of the same family.

The kinship ties which linked successive generations of the Johnson-Gildart family were especially complex. The merchant and political leader Sir Thomas Johnson participated in four slaving voyages between 1700 and 1719, a trade that his son-in-law Richard Gildart Sr. joined in 1714. An organizer and casual partner in nearly 30 ventures between 1714 and 1760, Richard Gildart Sr. often partnered his sons James Gildart Sr. and Captain George Gildart in the firm *Richard Gildart & Sons* from the mid–1730s.[577] Although it is not known whether all of Richard Gildart's sons joined in the slave trade, one of them, Johnson Gildart, invested in 14 ventures between 1734 and 1742, and two others, Thomas and Richard Gildart Jr., participated in one venture each in 1758 and 1748 respectively. Similarly, son-in-law Christopher Whytell invested in one slaving venture in 1744 before his premature death in 1755, and another, Spencer Steers, partnered brother-in-law

Table 5.13 *Familial Trading Patterns of the Heywood Brothers*

Name	Number of Voyages	Number of Partners	Number of partners with 6+/Voyages	Number of partners with 5-/Voyages	Number of Voyages with Brother
1. Arthur Heywood	65	67	15 (22%)	52 (78%)	52/65 (80%)
2. Benjamin Heywood	61	70	14 (20%)	56 (80%)	58/61 (95%)

Source: TSTD.

[577]TSTD.

Table 5.14 *Familial Trading Patterns of the Crosbie & Trafford Brothers*

Name	Number of Voyages	Number of Partners	Number of partners with 6+/Voyages	Number of partners with 5-/Voyages	Number of Voyages with Brother
1. John Crosbie	78	84	16 (19%)	68 (81%)	66/78 (85%)
2. William Crosbie	67	71	11 (15.5%)	60 (84.5%)	67/67 (100%)
3. William Trafford	58	85	10 (17%)	48 (83%)	30/58 (52%)
4. Richard Trafford	32	55	5 (9%)	50 (91%)	30/32 (94%)

Source: TSTD.

James Gildart Sr. in one venture in 1755. Finally, a third generation of Gildarts, James Gildart Jr., continued the family slaving tradition by investing in two ventures in 1772 and 1773.[578]

The involvement of other prominent slave-trading families was equally convoluted. Captain Thomas Tarleton and his brother Captain John Tarleton, for example, the first a captain-partner and the other a captain, organized four slaving ventures together between 1718 and 1721. Some 25 years later, in 1748, their sons, confusingly named John Tarleton and John Tarleton Jr. entered the slave trade together before embarking upon largely separate careers. John Tarleton, the son of Captain Thomas Tarleton, was the better known of the two, becoming a major slave trader with over 40 ventures attributed to him between 1748 and 1775, while also serving as Lord Mayor of Liverpool in 1764. The third generation of Tarletons, Thomas and John Tarleton, both the sons of Alderman John Tarleton, entered the slave trade on their own account after 1775. The generational nature of family slaving groups not only facilitated the rise of slaving dynasties, it promoted the intergenerational transmission of slaving expertise, and restricted membership in most slaving partnerships to a narrow group of kinsmen. Thus, internal consistency was a hallmark of kinship-based slaving partnerships. [579]

The following analysis of the relationships between kinsmen-*cum*-partners—particularly brothers—in ownership groups reveals that, while a number joined with many partners in their ventures, the majority remained in partnership with close kinsmen. Three examples illustrate this point. Brothers Arthur and Benjamin Heywood both participated in a similar number of slaving ventures between 1743 and 1775, and had similar numbers of partners, including their father-in-law Samuel Ogden. However, only fifteen of Arthur's 67 partners and 14 of Benjamin's seventy joined him in more than six ventures. For both the Heywood brothers, this suggests that a small group of partners was involved in the greater part of their slaving ventures. The single greatest partner for both men was his brother, as 80% of Arthur Heywood's ventures included his brother Benjamin, and 95% of Benjamin Heywood's ventures included his brother Arthur.[580]

Family ties were equally pronounced in the slaving firm of *Crosbie & Trafford*, which consisted of two sets of brothers: John and William Crosbie, and William and Richard Trafford. The firm survived the departure of Richard Trafford in 1764 and the death of William Trafford in 1767, and persisted in greatly diminished form

[578] ibid.
[579] ibid.
[580] ibid.

until the early 1770s when John and William Crosbie were declared bankrupts.[581] The roots of this partnership can be traced to John Crosbie's experience as the captain of the slave ship *Blundell*, in the employ of his father James Crosbie and cousin William Blundell, before he joined his father, his cousins Bryan Blundell and Richard Blundell, and Samuel Shaw, as an owner of the Guineaman the *Duke of Cumberland* in 1752.[582] After

Table 5.15	*Davenport and Earle Family Members as Partners listed in the* TSTD[*]		
Name	Family Member in the Slave Trade	Relationship	Number of Ventures Together
1. Christ. Davenport	William Davenport	Brother	14/101
2. Ralph Earle	William Earle	Brother	8/80
3. Thomas Earle	William Earle	Brother	6/80
4. Robert Jennings	William Earle	Brother-in-law	12/80
5. John Copeland	William Earle	Brother-in-law	8/80

[*]*ibid*; William Earle, *Daybook*, D/EARLE/2/2, Will of Robert Jennings, mariner of Liverpool, Wills and Inventories, Chester Probate Registry, 1792; T. A. Earle, 38–45; Richardson, "Profits in the Liverpool Slave Trade…," 61.

the death of James Crosbie in 1755, John Crosbie turned to the Trafford brothers and his brother William the following year, thus laying the foundation of a short-lived but profitable partnership, which dispatched over 60 vessels to Africa between 1757 and 1771.[583] However, within the firm of *Crosbie & Trafford*, brothers traded more with brothers than with their partners.

For example, every venture that William Crosbie participated in included his brother John, while 85% of John Crosbie's ventures included his brother William.[584] Similarly, 94% of Richard Trafford's limited slave trade included his brother William as a partner. The departure of Richard Trafford from the partnership in 1764 explains why little more than half of William Trafford's total ventures included his brother. In the pursuit of trustworthy, reputable business associates, familial intimacies made the Heywood, Crosbie, and Trafford brothers natural partners.

In addition to family members, slave traders formed partnerships with trusted business friends. Usually founded upon close personal and professional relationships of long standing, such unions represented a common organizational type among Liverpool slavers. They took two general forms: one that might be called the Gregson style of partnership, and the other the Davenport-Earle style. A financier and insurance broker, as well as a merchant, Gregson organized ventures with a relatively limited circle of associates. However, he never included family members among his slaving partners. While it is not clear that he had relatives who were capable of investing with him, it is doubtful that he would have partnered them even if he had. Gregson was focused upon running a business that was oriented toward the Bonny trade, and he turned to the same set of experienced partners again and again. Such a specialized business was not amenable to a great deal of variability in the composition of partnership groups.

---

[581]*ibid;* Will of William Trafford, merchant of Liverpool, Wills and Inventories, Chester Probate Registry, 1767; Will of John Crosbie of Liverpool, gentleman, Wills and Inventories, Chester Probate Registry, 1791; *International Genealogy Index; Liverpool Directory of 1766;* Brooke, *Liverpool as it was…,"* 476n, 477; *The Liverpool Memorandum Book; Assignees of Crosbie to Gregory Olive, Indenture of Release of Plantation Premises, Newfoundland,* December 17, 1772, http://ngb.chebucto.org/Articles/1772_indenture.shtml

[582]*ibid;* George Moore to James and John Crosbie, Liverpool 24 December 1755, Manx National Heritage Library MS 501C and MIC 68; cited in Wilkins, 33–34; Will of James Crosbie, merchant of Liverpool, Wills and Inventories, Chester Probate Registry, 1755; Schofield, "The Virginia Trade of the Firm of Sparling and Bolden," 122–123.

[583]ibid.

[584]ibid.

Table 5.16   *Thirty Largest Slave Merchants as listed in the TSTD*

Name	Ventures	Career
1. William James	130	1758–1775
2. John Knight	117	1744–1775
3. Foster Cunliffe	113	1718–1761
4. William Davenport	101	1748–1775
5. Robert Green	94	1757–1775
6. William Gregson	92	1744–1775
7. William Earle	80	1753–1775
8. John Welch	79	1741–1770
9. John Crosbie	78	1745–1771
10. Richard Savage	77	1745–1775
11. William Boates	76	1752–1775
12. Samuel Shaw	76	1746–1774
13. Jonathan Blundell	72	1748–1775
14. John Salthouse	70	1752–1775
15. William Dobb	69	1745–1768
16. Thomas Rumbold	68	1748–1775
17. William Crosbie	67	1757–1771
18. Bryan Blundell	66	1748–1775
19. Arthur Heywood	65	1743–1775
20. George Hutton	63	1753–1774
21. Thomas Foxcroft	63	1759–1775
22. Robert Armitage	63	1721–1757
23. Felix Doran	62	1737–1773
24. Benjamin Heywood	61	1745–1774
25. John White	60	1750–1774
26. Thomas Johnson	59	1753–1773
27. William Trafford	58	1754–1769
28. Edward Parr	54	1744–1768
29. Miles Barber	52	1759–1775
30. Samuel Ogden	51	1720–1751

A somewhat different pattern of partnership characterized the slave trading of both William Davenport and his frequent partner William Earle. Both men, like Gregson, were major slave traders who tended to trade with a limited group of business friends, albeit a larger one than Gregson's. However, there were significant differences in the composition of their slaving partnerships, since both partnered family members in a small number of slaving ventures between 1755 and 1774. Additionally, while both Davenport and Earle tended to trade in some slave markets more than others—Davenport in Old Calabar and the Cameroons, and Earle in Old Calabar and the Windward Coast—they traded in more regional slave markets than Gregson. Both Davenport and Earle traded in seven slaving regions, focusing upon Old Calabar *and* the Windward Coast, while Gregson traded in six, focusing upon Bonny. In these six markets, Gregson dispatched fewer ventures *per* region than did Davenport or Earle. Gregson and his associates specialized in the Bonny trade, while the more entrepreneurial Davenport and Earle did not limit their commercial horizons to such a degree.

VIII

Table 5.17 *Most Productive Partnerships by Ship Name as listed in the* TSTD

Ship Name	Total Voyages	Lifespan of Partnership	Average Ship Tonnage	Slaving Region	Total Partners
1. *Nancy I*	19	1751–1774	118	Biafra	9
2. *Foster*	17	1730–1754	59	Not Specified	5
3. *True Blue*	13	1750–1772	138	Benin	13
4. *Nancy II*	13	1750–1768	100	Biafra	8
5. *Essex*	13	1759–1774	97	Windward	11
6. *Stannage*	12	1721–1739	92.5	Gambia	7
7. *Knight*	12	1752–1774	113	Biafra, Gold Coast	12
8. *Lively*	11	1758–1774	67	Gambia	6
9. *Rumbold*	11	1759–1775	200	Biafra	11
10. *Grace*	10	1733–1748	94	Biafra	5
11. *Swallow*	10	1752–1774	74	Gold Coast	11
12. *Rose II*	10	1758–1774	120	Windward	15
13. *Liverpool Merchant*	9	1731–1741	80	Gambia	1
14. *Willoughby*	9	1733–1746	61	Gambia	2
15. *Pardoe*	9	1737–1753	60	Gambia	2
16. *Duke of Cumberland*	9	1748–1761	150	Biafra	8
17. *Tarleton*	9	1748–1761	111	Biafra	10
18. *Hector*	9	1752–1763	138	Biafra	9
19. *Marquis of Rockingham*	9	1753–1774	84	Gold Coast	6
20. *Lancashire Witch*	9	1761–1773	118	Windward	11
21. *Dalrymple*	9	1762–1773	91	Biafra	14
22. *Chesterfield*	8	1748–1759	130	Biafra	15
23. *Nanny*	8	1758–1765	59	Senegal	3
24. *Ingram*	8	1758–1774	134	Gold Coast	15
25. *Hannah*	8	1759–1771	100	Gold Coast	13
26. *Ranger II*	8	1760–1774	82	Angola	4
27. *Renown*	8	1762–1771	74	Windward	8
28. *Apollo*	8	1763–1775	85	Windward	10
29. *Sally*	8	1764–1775	90	Windward	1
30. *Little Will*	8	1765–1774	80	Windward	1
31. *Hardman*	7	1730–1739	80	Not Specified	3
32. *Princess Anne*	7	1735–1742	84	Not Specified	1
33. *St. George*	7	1740–1748	60	Bonny	12
34. *Bulkeley*	7	1745–1756	99	Windward	10
35. *Fortune*	7	1747–1756	120	Biafra	11
36. *Union*	7	1760–1770	103	Cameroons	13
37. *Kildare*	7	1761–1770	70	Biafra	5
38. *Plumper*	7	1761–1771	104	Windward, Benin	12

Table 5.17   *Most Productive Partnerships by Ship Name as listed in the* TSTD (Continued)

Ship Name	Total Voyages	Lifespan of Partnership	Average Ship Tonnage	Slaving Region	Total Partners
39. *Jenny*	7	1763–1774	70	Biafra	6
40. *Bella*	7	1763–1775	63	Cameroons	11
41. *Robert*	7	1765–1775	106	Windward	17
42. *Kitty*	7	1765–1775	107	Angola	13
43. *Betsey*	7	1768–1774	174	Biafra	1
44. *Brooke*	6	1737–1747	150	Not Specified	2
45. *Barclay*	6	1740–1754	140	Angola, Biafra	9
46. *Lintot*	6	1748–1756	100	Biafra	9
47. *Annabella*	6	1748–1756	80	Windward	5
48. *Stirling Castle*	6	1748–1754	85	Biafra	6
49. *Rainbow*	6	1754–1765	110	Windward, Benin	14
50. *Snapper*	6	1757–1763	52	Sierra Leone	8
51. *Blakeney*	6	1759–1767	70	Windward	4
52. *Portland*	6	1762–1770	100	Windward	10
53. *Society*	6	1763–1773	100	Benin	8
54. *Jenny*	6	1763–1773	70	Biafra	6
55. *Society*	6	1763–1773	100	Gold Coast, Benin	9
56. *Anton*	6	1764–1773	92	Gambia	3
57. *Edward*	6	1764–1772	76	Benin	8
58. *Aston*	6	1764–1773	92	Gambia	3
59. *Blossom*	6	1766–1773	105	Windward	2
60. *Mentor*	6	1766–1773	120	Biafra	10
61. *James*	6	1767–1774	120	Windward	1
62. *Polly*	6	1768–1775	100	Biafra	7
63. *Ellis*	6	1768–1773	135	Biafra	3
64. *Rose I*	5	1726–1733	80	Not Specified	2
65. *Betty*	5	1732–1739	60	Not Specified	3
66. *Pineapple*	5	1735–1741	88	Angola	4
67. *Swan*	5	1748–1757	90	Biafra	9
68. *Ranger I*	5	1750–1756	80	Windward	8
69. *Phoebe*	5	1756–1760	70	Gambia	4
70. *Prince of Wales*	5	1761–1771	200	Biafra	9
71. *Esther*	5	1762–1770	120	Biafra	17
72. *Edgar*	5	1762–1769	150	Biafra, Angola	15
73. *Delight*	5	1763–1769	94	Windward	9
74. *Henry*	5	1763–1769	70	Cameroons	8
75. *Lord Grey*	5	1764–1769	115	Biafra	7
76. *Echo*	5	1764–1770	80	Windward	2
77. *Thomas*	5	1765–1774	96	Angola	8
78. *George*	5	1766–1770	150	Biafra	5
79. *Industry*	5	1766–1771	70	Windward	3

Table 5.17   *Most Productive Partnerships by Ship Name as listed in the* TSTD *(Continued)*

Ship Name	Total Voyages	Lifespan of Partnership	Average Ship Tonnage	Slaving Region	Total Partners
80. *John*	5	1766–1772	80	Windward	4
81. *King of Prussia*	5	1767–1775	100	Cameroons	11
82. *Austin*	5	1767–1774	100	Biafra	5
83. *Captain*	5	1767–1774	140	Windward	2
84. *Friendship*	5	1768–1773	70	Biafra	7
85. *Violet*	5	1768–1774	100	Windward	9
86. *Fox*	5	1769–1775	62	Cameroons	12
87. *Tom*	5	1769–1772	120	Biafra	1
88. *Whim*	5	1769–1773	54	Gabon	3
89. *Little Ben*	5	1769–1773	56	Windward	4
90. *Elizabeth*	5	1770–1774	100	Biafra	1
91. *Gregson*	5	1770–1775	120	Biafra	4

Source: TSTD.

Regional trading specializations were common among slavers. For example, William James, George Hutton, and Thomas Foxcroft looked to the Windward Coast to maintain an ongoing supply of slaves. Similarly the Bonny traders William Gregson and Jonathan Blundell, the Gold Coast specialists Arthur and Benjamin Heywood, and the Benin trader John Welch, established their reputations as slavers in particular African markets, before expanding into other markets.[585] Such specializations permitted the managers of slaving ventures to control better the elements of risk that were an inevitable part of the transatlantic trade in slaves. By bolstering relations in specific African ports, and building regional trading expertise, it improved turn-around times in the largely triangular trade in slaves, and introduced a heightened degree of certainty that improved productivity, encouraged a regular pattern of investment in ventures, and promoted a systematic schedule of sailings.

However, the ebb and flow of market demand for particular types of slaves prompted traders to exploit a variety of African markets throughout their careers. (See appendix 5.5, 5.6) Although he traded primarily on the Windward Coast, William James also organized ventures to the Gold Coast, the Bight of Benin, and Sierra Leone. Extreme specialization did not prevent James from responding to particularly propitious trading opportunities as they presented themselves in regions in which he was a relative stranger. Early in his slaving career, James experimented with various regional slave markets before settling upon the Windward Coast. Like most novice slave traders, he had to prepare a number of ventures to particular slave markets in order to learn how to trade there, a process akin to a regional "learning curve." However, even during this period of testing, James dispatched few ships to the Bight of Benin, Senegambia, the Gold Coast, Sierra Leone, and Angola, and these regions never figured prominently in his planning. After 1766, the patterns that had characterized his trade since 1758 began to diversify and change, as James aggressively entered the high-volume Biafran trade, loading slaves mostly at Bonny. Although James dispatched some thirty slaving ventures to the Bight of Biafra between 1766 and 1774, he never became fixated upon this trade, as did William Gregson and Jonathan Blundell.[586] Despite the growth of his Biafran or "Bite" trade, James remained

---

[585]*TSTD.*

[586]*ibid.*

dedicated to the Windward Coast trade. The Bite trade accounted for less than 27% of his entire trade prior to 1775, whereas the Windward Coast took 60%.[587]

Similarly, John Knight traded to a number of markets early in his slaving career. As the following table demonstrates, Knight was a prolific slaver second only to William James in total slaving ventures before 1775. Despite this, Knight was slow to establish a regional specialization in his first decade, investing in ventures to the Gold Coast, Angola, the Windward Coast, and the Bight of Biafra. However, beginning with the departure of the snow *Nancy* from Liverpool in 1753, a consistent pattern of trade to Gambia characterized much of his early career. Two factors probably made the Gambian trade attractive to Knight. Firstly, it was characterized by slower, piecemeal purchase of slaves in far lesser numbers than the Bight of Biafra. This made the Gambian market in slaves, as well as all markets along the Upper Guinea coast of West Africa, far less expensive, an important consideration for new slave merchants with scant resources. Secondly, when Knight entered the Gambian trade in the early 1750s, it was highly profitable. Its subsequent decline forced Knight to change course. As early as 1752, he partnered William Gregson in the Bonny trader *Hector*, and continued to do so until Knight's death in 1774. This relationship permitted Knight to recreate the regional basis for his trade in slaves. Like William James, Knight initially partnered slave traders more knowledgeable

Table 5.18	*Major Slaving Partners of Gregson over time as listed in the* TSTD		
Partners	Partners Voyages 1748–1762	Partners Voyages 1763–1775	Partners Voyages 1748–1775
1. John Bridge	24 of 30 Voyages	16 of 62 Voyages	40/92=43.5%
2. William Boates	0/30	26/62	26/92=28%
3. Peter Holme	12/30	13/62	25/92=27%
4. Thomas Dunbar	18/30	4/62	22/92=24%
5. John Knight	6/30	9/62	15/92=16%

in the Bite trade than he was, in order to learn its peculiarities. For Knight, the best way to build proficiency in a regional trade was to take advantage of a colleague's expertise before striking out on his own. By 1767, he knew enough about the trade to send his own ship, the *Knight*, to Bonny, a voyage followed by a regular pattern of ventures to Bonny, Old Calabar, and New Calabar. Although Knight continued to participate in the Gold Coast and Benin trades, the Bight of Biafra assumed an ever more dominant position in his trade before 1774.

Unlike Knight, Gregson remained a specialist trader throughout his long slaving career. Of his 92 slaving ventures between 1748 and 1775, 62% were destined for Bonny.[588] Gregson established a pattern of regular trading to Bonny employing a veritable fleet of ships that returned again and again to his favored Biafran port of embarkation. Between 1752 and 1775, the *Hector* sailed to Bonny eight times, the *Polly* six times, the *Gregson* five times, the *Prince of Wales* five times, the *Achilles* four times, the *Lord North* three times, and the *Cerberus* three times.[589] As the following table demonstrates, such multiple voyages were not uncommon. Gregson was dedicated to constructing a virtual slaving assembly line that connected the Bight of Biafra with changing New World slave markets. His singular focus on this trade was the result of insightful market calculation, a market-centered realism that represented, according to David Galenson, "strong evidence of diligent and systematic behavior aimed at profit maximization."[590] To a far greater extent than his slave trading contemporaries in Liverpool, Gregson began and ended his career as a Bonny trader.

---

[587]*ibid.*

[588]*ibid.*

[589]*ibid.*

[590]David Galenson, *Traders, Planters, and Slaves: Market Behavior in Early English America* (1986), 143–146.

Table 5.19   *Major Slaving Partners of James over time as listed in the* TSTD

Slaving Partners	Voyages 1758–1767	Voyages 1768–1775	Voyages 1758–1775
1. Charles Ford	9 of 31 Total Voyages	4 of 99 Voyages	13/130=10%
2. Gill Slater	1/31	11/99	12/130=9%
3. Alex. Nottingham	0/31	11/99	11/130=8%
4. Thos. Spencer Dunn	0/31	11/99	11/130=8%
5. Wm. Ingram	9/31	0/99	9/130=7%
6. Edward Grayson	0/31	9/99	9/130=7%
7. George Evans	0/31	7/99	7/130=5%
8. Capt. Henry Ross	3/31	3/99	6/130=4%

IX

Gregson traded with a variety of partners, including more than fifty smaller ones. However, as the table below reveals, he remained wedded to a relatively small group of important merchants that gradually changed over time. They included John Knight, John Hardman, Thomas Dunbar, William Halliday, Henry Hardwar, Jonathan Blundell, Thomas Case, William Boates, Peter Holme, Richard Savage, and William Earle. Gregson's closest partner, John Bridge, participated in nearly 50% of his total slaving ventures between 1748 and 1775, while other close partners traded with him for briefer periods. For instance, William Boates became an important partner only after 1763, while Thomas Dunbar was only important before 1763.

The relationships that William James formed with his slaving partners differed markedly from Gregson in both size and duration. Between 1758 and 1775, he partnered only 38 men, far fewer than Gregson.[591] Although he participated in 130 ventures, most of James's partners invested with him only a few times. As the following table demonstrates, James had only two partners in his early career—Charles Ford and William Ingram—that he invested with more than twice.[592] These men were relatively unimportant slave traders, and James's association with them ended by 1768. In 1769, James partnered a group of much more prominent slave traders in a few voyages to the Bight of Biafra. They included William Davenport, John Dobson and William Earle. However, James's most important long-term partnership was formed in 1771, and included lesser investors such as Alexander Nottingham, Gill Slater, and Edward Grayson. This partnership loaded trade goods on six ships for eleven voyages to the Bight of Biafra between 1771 and 1774.[593]

Perhaps the greatest difference between the slaving practices of Gregson and James was that James organized 61% of his 130 known slaving ventures as a sole-partner, including fourteen voyages to the Bight of Biafra.[594] In contrast, there is no evidence that Gregson ever participated in any slaving venture as a sole trader. The fact that James was able to finance the greater costs of the Bite trade independently suggests that he had superior financial resources, was more proficient in cutting costs, or was determined to manage the trade as he saw fit. It is also possible that James simply did not have available partners to organize the numbers of ventures he desired. Whatever the reason, he along with John Knight, William Boates, Samuel Shaw, and Miles Barber were the only significant sole-traders among major Liverpool slavers.

---

[591] *TSTD.*

[592] *ibid.*

[593] *ibid.* 64% of these eleven voyages loaded slaves at Bonny, while 36% embarked slaves at Old Calabar.

[594] *ibid.*

Name	Gambia	Bight of Biafra	Bight of Benin	Gold Coast	Windward Coast	Sierra Leone	West Central Africa
1. W. James	1	34	9	7	*75*	4	2
2. R. Green	2	30	1	4	*35*	10	10

Table 5.20 *Regional Distribution in the Trade of James and Green as listed in the* TSTD *(primary slave trading region in italics)*

Another partnership pattern was evident in the Liverpool trade. Those of Robert Green, a Birmingham merchant, differed significantly from both Gregson and James. Green's partners were men whose interest in the slave trade amounted to little more than a desire to profit from a limited number of short-term slaving ventures. For the most part, these unimportant men were not experienced mariners or overseas merchants, but rather a hodgepodge of tradesmen, craftsmen, professionals, gentlemen, and small merchants. They were men of limited means or interest who were attracted to the comparatively inexpensive slave trade to Gambia, Sierra Leone, and the Windward Coast. This trade was conducted on a much smaller scale than the mass slaving operations further south. This region of slave trading greatly influenced both the material requirements for voyages and how partnerships were organized.

The Upper Guinea trade required less expensive trade goods, smaller ships, and fewer crew, the cost of preparing ventures was far less. Not only did smaller ships mean lower capital costs at the outset of a venture, they also cost less to operate. Green's ships, including those that traded to the Bight of Biafra, weighed on average only 80 tons. None of these vessels displaced more than 80 tons, while the *Enterprize*, the *Boscawen*, and the *Thomas* displaced 50 tons, the *Betty* and the *Joseph* 40 tons, and the *John*, the *Jane*, the *William & Edward* a mere 30 tons.[595] By contrast, Gregson's Bonny slavers weighed, on average, 129 tons, with some individual ships weighing as much as 250 tons or more.[596] The average number of crew for these small ships was 13, while a sample of 27 larger ships, mostly Bonny traders 130 tons or more, yielded an average crew size of 37. As a result, the average cost of ventures destined for the Windward Coast was almost £3,000, compared to £7,000 for ventures to Bonny.[597] Unlike the extremely changeable cast of small, sporadic, and short-term investors characteristic of Green's slaving ventures on the Upper Guinea coast, the high costs of the Bonny trade required a regular company of partners willing to invest significant amounts of capital in an ongoing series of ventures. Thus, depending upon the wealth, degree of commitment, and aspirations of investors, the shape of Liverpool slaving ventures could, and did, take many forms.

Much like James, Robert Green, a major but less well-known Liverpool slave trader, primarily specialized in the Windward Coast trade. However, as the following table shows, Green's trade differed from James's in a number of important ways. First, he was more willing to trade in other markets. As the table shows, only 38% of Green's ventures traded on the Windward Coast, while 58% of James's traded there. This pattern that was far less evident in the Bight of Biafra trade, where 32% Green's ventures were dispatched compared to 26% for James.[598] The disparity between their regional slaving patterns is most apparent in West Central Africa where 11% of Green's ships embarked slaves, compared to only 1.5% of James's.[599] This trade to

[595]*ibid.*

[596]*ibid.*

[597]Inikori "Credit Needs of the African Trade," 215.

[598]*ibid.*

[599]*ibid.*

West Central Africa, primarily the Cameroons, meant that the vessels in which Green was an investor visited slave ports south of Cape Three Points, the dividing line between the Upper and Lower Guinea coasts, somewhat more often than did those of James—48% of total voyages versus 41%.[600] In many ways, however, the regional distribution of Green's slave trading is similar to that of a number of other major slave traders, including William James, John Knight, William Earle, and William Davenport. All these traders had a major West African region of specialization.

Secondly, while James regularly partnered a few men, Green seldom invested with the same partners twice. During his slaving career between 1758 and 1775, James drew his partners from an extremely small pool of 38 men.[601] However, Green formed partnerships with an astonishing 171 different investors between 1757 and 1775, including many who were unknown.[602] With the exception of a few scattered ventures with the likes of William James, John Crosbie, William Crosbie, William Trafford, Thomas Rumbold, Felix Doran, William Earle, and Miles Barber, Green tended not to partner major Liverpool slave traders. His partners included an assortment of minor slave traders, men such as John Maine, John Latham, Michael Finch, and Dr. Richard Gerrard.

Far more than Gregson or James, Green partnered men whose limited involvement in the trade was motivated by the common speculative ambitions of middling tradesmen, manufacturers, mariners, and merchants. Ambition was the glue that held such partnerships together. Smaller investors often had little direct connection to the slave trade, and simply sought to take advantage of rising slave markets in Africa and the New World, while others directly profited from the outfitting of slaving vessels, although they were not investors. Among the owners of the Liverpool slaver *Bridson* in 1769, for instance, were two merchant-mariners, a shipwright and his son, two sail-makers, a cooper, and a surgeon-apothecary.[603] To such small men, investing was an experiment, a risky but singular undertaking in which they held great expectations for profit. Many of them never invested in another slaving venture after the unsuccessful voyage of the *Bridson* to Gabon and Barbados. Only two, Roger Fisher and Richard Hanley, had significant previous experience in the slave trade, having invested in fifteen slaving ventures between them. Investing in the *Bridson* was simply a side speculation for these men, and did not involve their normal cast of business associates. To these men, the pursuit of profitable trading opportunities determined both the composition and duration of slaving partnerships.

---

[600] *ibid.*

[601] *ibid.*

[602] *ibid.*

[603] *ibid.; Liverpool Directory of 1766,* The captains and owners of the slaver *Bridson* are listed in the TSTD as follows: Captains: Lancelot Bird, John Platt; Owners: Captain John Platt, Roger Fisher, John Fisher, Daniel Jones, Edward Bridge, Paul Bridson, Richard Hanley, John Johnson, and Walter Cahoun.

Chapter 6

The Trade

The previous chapter demonstrated the diversity of factors that underlay the construction of eighteenth century Liverpool slaving partnerships. The purpose of this one is to examine the nature of slaving and the manner in which the formation of partnerships influenced slave trading in action. Section one will look at how the various attitudes of slavers towards the African trade influenced the composition of partnerships, and the assumptions held by slavers regarding the perceived purposes of the trade. Was the trade viewed as a chance to reap windfall profits, a short-term financial expedient, or an organized, long-term business venture? This perception affected the extent to which slavers were dedicated to the trade, which influenced how long partners intended a partnership to last. Section two examines the social meaning of the partnership share, and what it represented in the context of the traffic in slaves. Section three traces the changing relationships between partners in the preparation of a slaving venture. Finally, section four investigates how expectations of reciprocity and obligation shaped the trading relationships that facilitated trade. Slave traders greatly valued close business and personal associations and saw them as commercially beneficial.

I

A slaving venture was born of the ambition of men to profit in the marketplace for slaves. The continuing pursuit of profit had enormous consequences for the practical management of ventures in the African trade. When opportunities beckoned in the slave markets of West Africa or the Americas, ever-vigilant merchants took notice. The prospect of profit invariably incited a scramble that spread like an epidemic among rival slavers, for the ships which departed Liverpool and arrived in Africa first had the best chance of buying the best slaves at the best prices. However, good fortune in Africa did not ensure a successful voyage across the Atlantic. This required that the captain speedily traverse the middle passage, manage slave mortality, and arrive in the New World ahead of rival vessels. Thereafter, profit was a matter of exploiting the right contacts among local slave factors, selling the slaves at a profit, and returning safely to Liverpool with the proceeds of the voyage. Throughout the eighteenth century, Liverpool slave traders struggled to respond decisively to market opportunities, attempting to avoid miscalculations that could spell ruin. Slave traders used complex human and material resources, including ships, trade goods, personal relationships, reputable partners, social status, able captains and crews, capital and credit, brokerage services, market knowledge, and managerial skill. Successful slave trading required the ability to coordinate these complex elements every time a ship slipped its moorings on the Mersey and embarked upon the long journey to Africa and the Americas.

This expertise was available to many men, but was not easy to acquire or master. Would-be traders had many opportunities to gain competence in the African trade, as captains, investors, factors, financiers, brokers, or suppliers. Not every type of slave trader, however, required the same degree of proficiency in the trade to be successful. The managing partner of a long-lived firm required skills that were different from those of the short-term speculator. Whereas active slave traders were professionals exercising judgment and skill, their small-scale counterparts were often gamblers running under-funded schemes. The 1761 voyage of the tiny 10-ton schooner *Hesketh* illustrates how little some owners were willing to invest as does the 1757 voyage of the 30-ton brig *Whydah*, a fifteen year old vessel built in Virginia.[604] These were much smaller than most slave ships.[605] Similarly, some owners used cheap, old ships, such as the 38-year-old *Ann & Betty*, the 21-year old *Nelly*, and the 20-year-old *Glory*, vessels that could be bought at auction by men anywhere in England for very little.[606] In many cases, purchasers purposely acquired decrepit ships like the *Oldham* and the *Lydia*, which were frequently sold or condemned in the Americas for unseaworthiness after disembarking slaves.[607] It is possible that these ships were never intended to return to Liverpool, a marketing tactic that relieved owners of the necessity of preparing return voyages. Because they were disposable vessels they cost less to refurbish and outfit, and were thus cheaper to operate. More importantly, lower costs meant that each investor was called upon to contribute less capital to the venture, an inducement for lesser men to try their luck in the African trade. Such ventures did not need to earn much in order to cover costs, providing investors with enhanced prospects of profit. However, slave trading on the cheap had serious drawbacks. Smaller or older ships were more often wrecked at sea, more vulnerable to attack by African natives, less able to defend themselves against privateers during times of war, and susceptible to elevated rates of slave mortality while on the African coast and during the middle passage. Given the minimal investment, it mattered less whether such ships were lost or greater numbers of African captives perished.

In addition to providing these practical benefits and disadvantages, a minimalist approach to slaving influenced the marketing of slaves. Because many organizers of minor schemes lacked real experience of the trade, their forays to Africa were often haphazard propositions, based upon unsound estimations of the slave market. These men knew the risk but were willing to hazard the trade in hopes of striking it rich. Such investors did not require a great deal of familiarity with the slave trade in order to succeed. Investors in poorly capitalized ventures were free of the necessity of thinking ahead, of anticipating market trends in order to prepare a ship properly for its next voyage to Africa. In contrast, the maintenance of a constant trade required that active partners pay close attention to fluctuations in the demand for slaves over a long period in order to plan a venture properly. These ongoing market calculations determined where slave ships traded, the number and price of slaves purchased, the type and amount of trade goods assembled, the size and type of ship used, and the specialized experience of the men employed to captain the vessel. Investors in long-term partnerships generally relied upon the same ship's husbands voyage after voyage, repeatedly reinvested some of their profits in the ongoing venture, regularly purchased goods from the same suppliers, and replaced ships when needed. The much more limited market objectives of the slaving gamblers rendered these considerations moot. For them, either a venture succeeded or it did not.

In a fundamental way, the internal cohesiveness of a slaving partnership reflected the extent to which the individual partners were dedicated to the trade, which, in turn, influenced how long partners intended a

[604]TSTD

[605]*ibid.;* Walter Minchinton, Characteristics of British Slaving Vessels, 1698–1775," *Journal of Interdisciplinary Studies* 20 (1989); 60–65; Christopher French, "Eighteen-Century Shipping Tonnage Measurements," *The Journal of Economic History* 33 (1973), 435–436.

[606]*ibid.;* Marshall Smelser and William Davisson, "The Longevity of Colonial American Shipping," *American Neptune* 33 (1973), 16–17.

[607]ibid.

partnership to last. Consequently, there was a close relationship between the longevity of slaving partnerships and the perceived purposes of the trade. However, while most slaving partnerships, large or small, retained a significant degree of internal consistency, most long-term partnerships did experience some turnover in membership. Death, old age, and financial discomfiture took a steady toll on partnerships. The slaving careers of several noteworthy traders, including Sir Thomas Johnson, James Pardoe, William Penketh, John and William Crosbie, were cut short by bankruptcy.[608] Death claimed other active slave traders, such as Foster Cunliffe, John Knight, Thomas Johnson, William Pownall, and John Gorell.[609] Still, many slaving partnerships were composed of the same men over long periods without replacement from outside the original ownership group. For example, the initial owners of the *Nancy* in 1751 included Thomas Kendall, Jonathan Blundell, Henry Townsend, Levinius Unsworth, William Benson, Samuel Shaw, James Crosbie, and Charles Pole.*[610]* This assortment remained unchanged until 1754, when the deaths of James Crosbie and Henry Townsend permitted a new member, Captain John Hunniford, to join the group. Hunniford was master of the *Nancy* during four voyages to Bonny between 1751 and 1756 before becoming a partner. Assuming an important role in the management of the *Nancy*, Hunniford remained a partner until his death in the mid-1760s.[611] Two other partners, or their heirs, left the partnership at about the same time as Hunniford: Levinius Unsworth, who died in 1757, and Thomas Kendall, who died in 1765.[612] New investors replaced these men, Captain James Waddington, who had succeeded Hunniford as captain in 1756, Bryan Blundell, brother of Jonathan Blundell, and William Crosbie Jr., grandson of James Crosbie.[613] The fact that the Blundells and Crosbies were relatives further narrowed the ownership group. At the time when these new men became partners, another long time investor, William Benson, left, probably having died some time after 1765. Reduced to six partners from the original eight, a new partnership group took form by 1767. Composed of James Waddington, Jonathan Blundell, Bryan Blundell, Samuel Shaw, William Crosbie Jr., and Charles Pole, it persisted until the outbreak of the American Revolution in 1775. By this point, four of six partners were kinsmen, a factor which worked to ensure the cohesiveness of the ownership group over the course of two decades.

As suggested in chapter five, slaving minimalists were a diverse group of individuals whose participation in the slave trade was merely a sideline. Far less organizationally cohesive than their professional rivals, these traders had fewer kinship ties. This diversity was revealed most clearly in their occupational background. Although some of them were well known in the Liverpool slave trade, many were far more obscure. They included lawyers, surgeons, apothecaries, ropers, coopers, tanners, bakers, and brewers.[614] Among the owners of the 1768 voyage of the 60-ton sloop *Billy* to the Windward Coast were a shipbuilder and his son-in-law, a sail-maker,

---

[608]Michael Power, "Councillors and Commerce in Liverpool, 1650-1750," *Urban History* 24 (1997), 306, 308; Melinda Elder, *The Slave Trade and the Economic Development of Eighteenth-Century Lancaster* (1992), 135; Maurice Schofield, "Chester Slave Trading Partnerships," *Transactions of the Historic Society of Lancashire and Cheshire* 130 (1981), 188; L.M. Angus-Butterworth, "Liverpool Glassmaking, 1696–1939" *Glass* 24 (1947), 290; Bill of Sale in St. John's, Assignees of Crosbie to Gregory Olive, Release of Premises, Plantation Premises, Newfoundland, December 17, 1772 http://ngb.chebucto.org/Articles/1772_indenture.shtml, accessed 5/2/2004. A fuller accounting of these proceedings are available in the records of the Bankruptcy Court.

[609]John Tyler, Foster Cunliffe and Sons: Liverpool Merchants in the Maryland Tobacco Trade, 1738–1765," *Maryland Historical Magazine* 73 (1978), 249; Richard Brooke, *Liverpool as it was during the Last Quarter of the Eighteenth Century, 1775–1800* (1853) 239,Will of Foster Cunliffe of Liverpool, Lancashire, May 19, 1758, PCC: PROB 11/837; *Liverpool Directory of 1766*, Will of John Knight, merchant of Liverpool, Lancashire, December 13, 1774, PCC: PROB 11/1003; Will of Thomas Johnson of Liverpool, esquire, Wills and Inventories, Chester Probate Registry, 1771; Ronald Stewart-Brown, *Liverpool Ships in the Eighteenth Century* (1932), 117, 119–122, Will of William Pownall of Liverpool, esquire, Wills and Inventories, Chester Probate Registry, Admon., 1768.

[610]TSTD.

[611]Will of George Lancaster or Lancester, mariner now bound out on a Voyage to the Coast of Africa in the Honeyford's *Nancy* belonging to Liverpool, Lancashire, August 29, 1764, PCC: PROB 11/901.

[612]Will of Levinus (*sic*) Unsworth, merchant of Liverpool, Wills and Inventories, Chester Probate Registry, 1757; Will of Thomas Kendall, merchant of Liverpool, Wills and Inventories, Chester Probate Registry, 1765.

[613]Maurice Schofield, "The Virginia Trade of the Firm of Sparling and Bolden, of Liverpool, 1788–99," *Transactions of the Historical Society of Lancashire and Cheshire* 116 (1964), 122.

[614]TSTD.

a cooper, a ship's captain, an ironmonger, a boat-builder, and a Birmingham merchant-*cum*-slaver.[615] In many cases, such partnerships assume the appearance of a hurriedly assembled venture organized by close friends over a tankard of ale or bowl of coffee. While the owners of the *Billy* were mostly friends and acquaintances, other ships were owned largely by kinsmen-speculators. For example, the owners of the 40-ton schooner *Talbot* included Captain John Clare, and his brothers Thomas and Joseph Clare, while the owners of the 80-ton snow *Lydia* included John, Thomas, Peter, and Samuel Touchet, partners in the elite Manchester firm *Touchet & Sons*, major manufacturers of inexpensive textiles for the transatlantic trade.[616] Like their smaller rivals, the largest slave traders frequently engaged in short-lived ventures as sleeping partners or active managers.

II

On December 30, 1760, William Earle wrote to the Manx merchant John Joseph Bacon to request assistance and to invite him to join in a proposed slaving venture to the Windward Coast. "This is to beg your interest in the purchase of the privateer lately brought into Douglas, [Isle of Man]," Earle asked Bacon,

> [As] the under mentioned gentlemen have a...scheme for her & an unexceptionable man as captain for Africa. She is proposed to be [divided] in 6 [shares]. Your interest I will engage to take care of if you are inclined to make one of the members. The whole capital is not proposed to exceed £2,400, if the ship [can be had] anywhere about £450, but would not miss her for £500 & above, that sum the gentlemen are not willing to go unless she has some valuable materials which we are not at present acquainted with. In this case, leave it to your own prudence & I am, Sir, Your most Humble servant,
>
> William Earle.
> [Investors]
> The Captain (John Davies)
> Mr. William Davenport
> Mr. Charles Cooke
> Mr. Samuel Winstanley
> William Earle
> & 1/5 open or else 1/5ths.[617]

Not randomly nor lightly made, such an invitation to purchase a share in a slaving venture entailed the possibility not only of great profit, but also of crippling loss and financial ruin. Davis observes that the tradition of selling parts in a venture was "international and of very great antiquity," and not strictly limited to maritime ventures.[618] By 1750, this old practice was characteristic of the transatlantic trade, where shareholding in a large number of ships held great advantages.[619]

---

[615]ibid; Liverpool Directory of 1766.

[616]*TSTD; Liverpool Directory of 1766;* Will of John Clare, merchant of Liverpool, Wills and Inventories, Chester Probate Registry, August 9, 1802; Will of Joseph Clare, Sadler of Liverpool, Wills and Inventories, Chester Probate Registry, June 6, 1810; Will of Thomas Clare, merchant of Liverpool, Wills and Inventories, Chester Probate Registry, September 23, 1816; Thomas Truxes, ed., *Letterbook of Greg & Cunningham, 1756–1757* (2001) 64n; Stanley Chapman, "British Marketing Enterprise: The Changing Roles of Merchants, Manufacturers, and Financiers, 1700–1860," *Business History Review* 53 (1979), 209; Elder, *The Slave Trade... of Eighteenth-Century Lancaster,* 26; Will of John Touchet, merchant of Manchester Limd, Wills and Inventories, Chester Probate Registry, Admon., 1794.

[617]Earle to Bacon, December 30, 1760, D/EARLE/2/2; TSTD. It was common for a partnership to purchase a ship, often a captured vessel, for use in the slave trade.

[618]Davis, *The Rise of the English Shipping Industry,* 82–87.

[619]*ibid,* 82–85.

How were partnership shares sold, and who sold them? Effective control of a venture was ordinarily vested in the men who founded the proposed partnership group, men who intended to purchase a particular ship that was suitable for the demands of specific African slave markets, and who had a general idea of how much they were willing to spend to prepare the vessel for the coast. In order to finance the proposed venture and spread the risk, the members of a founding group approached their respective circles of family, business associates, and friends and offered them shares in the venture. Because large ships were more expensive to outfit and operate than smaller ones, the size of a ship had a bearing upon the number of parts in which the ownership shares in proposed ventures were divided. Davis maintains that the smallest ships often had single owners or were divided into only two, three or four parts, but few ships of more than a hundred tons had such small owning groups.[620] Thus, the number of shares available to potential new partners depended upon where the founding partners intended to trade, a factor that determined the size of the ship required for the slave trade in specific African regions.

Although ownership shares were generally divided in fourths and distributed equally amongst the primary partners, individual partners often further reduced their shares by sub-dividing them and selling pieces to other interested merchants. Because shares in a ship were readily transferable by bill of sale, a fragmented, and largely invisible, pattern of investment in ventures became common in ports such as Liverpool.[621] Popular within slaving partnerships, the practice of sub-dividing ownership shares made additional capital resources available, and frequently brought in new partners with low-cost access to necessary supplies, such as trade goods and ships provisions, that were required for a profitable slaving venture. This practice also attracted individuals with little experience of the slave trade, men who had little to say regarding the management of ventures. The partners in a slaving venture, regardless of the size of their ownership share, were assigned a portion of the overall expense of preparing a ship for Africa. In the case of the Birmingham merchant and ironmonger John Darbyshire, for instance, this share, or division, could be met by forwarding cash, proffering bills of exchange, paying for goods on credit, or supplying materials himself. This produced often-complex patterns of financing in the preparation of slaving vessels for Africa. "I received a letter from Mr. Rumbold," Earle wrote Darbyshire in October 1760,

> [and an] order from you concerning his 1/2 of 1/8th [share] in the *Calypso* with you. You know [that] I have not charged anything in the division with you but 1/8 of my disbursement, which I paid so that you & Mr. Rumbold must make a sub-division of the 1/8 & then each party knows who they are to pay. It seems that he has paid you 1/2 disbursement & 1/2 Halliday & Dunbar's bill for arms. Nothing remains but yours & his discharging the 13 last articles in the division, no matter to the concerned who pays it so [long as] it is discharged. I shall as you direct, credit your account £29-10-3½ the insurance with Mr. Samuel Shaw & debit Mr. Rumbold's account with the same as also be accountable to him for 1/16 remittance & call upon if should have occasion at any time to collect any money for his 1/16 from you.[622]

It is likely that John Darbyshire was sold a part-share in the slaver *Calypso* not so much because he was a skilled slaver, but rather because he was an ironmonger who could pay for at least a part of his division with alternative capital resources such as ironmongery. The partnership arrangement between Rumbold and Darbyshire was further complicated when the financially strapped Darbyshire sold a portion of his part share to a third man, the merchant Richard Rabone. "I have to desire you will by return of post," Earle wrote Rabone in January 1761,

> Send me an account of the 1/8 division of the *Calypso* betwixt Mr. John Darbyshire & you, as also what money he has paid & what money you have paid, what bills he has to pay & what

---

[620]*ibid*, 82–85.

[621]*ibid*, 102–104.

[622]Earle to Darbyshire, October 5, 1760.

bills you have to pay on account of the division & what insurance is done upon her besides the £500 I did for 1/8.[623]

The extent of this *sub rosa* market in ownership shares is a matter of speculation, for part-owners are never listed in the available partnership records. Although both Darbyshire and Rabone are mentioned in the *Daybook of William Earle* as part owners of the *Calypso*, neither appears in the *Transatlantic Slave Trade Database* as members of the ownership group.[624]

As a species of property that was both liquid and transferable, ownership shares in slaving ventures became a common feature in the wills of slave merchants. When a merchant drafted a will he included his partnership interests in commercial ventures in the inventory, along with all other holdings of land and property. The will of Richard Houghton, a prominent Liverpool merchant and ship-owner, was granted probate on August 11, 1712, and listed "cargoes provided for the ship *Loyalty* for a voyage to Maryland, the ship *Planter* for a voyage to Virginia, some part of which ships belong to me."[625] Because shares were valuable commodities, the executors of merchant estates were often dilatory in liquidating those that came into their possession in the hopes of extracting the fullest possible benefit from the initial investment. Shareholders habitually bequeathed their ownership interests to sons and other heirs, who, in turn, maintained the family stake in slave trading partnerships of the deceased. Liverpool merchant and ironmonger Peter Rigby noted in his will that "I give and bequeath all such share and shares and interests as I shall hold at my decease in any vessel and vessels, and the cargo and cargoes thereof then upon any voyage or voyages in any vessel and vessels then at home unto my son William and my daughter Catherine equally."[626]

The continuing value of shares meant that in a number of cases, prominent traders continued as participants in slaving partnerships years after their death. Foster Cunliffe, John Hardman, William Pownall, and John Gorell, for instance, all died before or after a slaving venture in which they had interest departed Liverpool for Africa, but each remained partners, albeit silent ones. As the head of the merchant firm *Foster Cunliffe & Sons*, Foster Cunliffe was listed on the ownership roll of the slave ship *Young Foster* for two years after his death in January 1758, primarily because his ownership share was vested in a family firm whose sole management passed directly to his sons Ellis and Robert. In his 1756 will, Foster Cunliffe specified that none of his just debts, funeral expenses, or probate charges were to be paid from the common property "in any partnership I am or hereafter shall be…engaged in," and that such property should pass to his family.[627] Similarly, the prominent merchant and politician John Hardman, who died suddenly in 1755 while serving in Parliament, remained a listed owner of several ships after his death, including: the Gregson slaver *Nancy*, which departed Liverpool four times between 1756 and 1761; the Heywood slaver *Hardman*, which made two voyages to the Gold Coast in 1756 and 1761, and the *Esther*, which also sailed for the Gold Coast in 1760.[628] In the *Esther*, the long-dead Hardman joined with the merchant ship-builders John Gorell and William Pownall, business partners both of whom died as members of active slave trading partnerships. The late Gorell continued as an owner of two slave ships, the *Anton* and the *Union*, for three years after his death in 1761, while Pownall remained an owner of the *Union* for three years after his death in March 1767.[629] Despite its risks, the heirs of slave traders fully recognized the continuing possibilities for profit in the slave trade, a realization that motivated them to cling to the ownership shares they inherited until they could be sold to best advantage.

---

[623]Earle to Rabone, January 16, 1761.

[624]*TSTD*. The owners of the *Calypso* are listed in the TSTD as William Earle, Richard Powell, Thomas Rumbold, Peter Leay, Maurice Melling, William Farrington, Captain John Copeland, and Edmund Lyon.

[625]Ronald Stewart-Brown, ed., *Cheshire Sheaf*, (1930), Appendix, 140.

[626]Will of Peter Rigby, merchant and ironmonger of Liverpool, Lancashire, July 4, 1795, PCC: PROB 11/1264.

[627]Will of Foster Cunliffe of Liverpool, Lancashire, May 19, 1758, PCC: PROB 11/837.

[628]*TSTD*.

[629]Ronald Stewart-Brown, *Liverpool Ships in the Eighteenth Century* (1932), 117, 119–122; Will of William Pownall of Liverpool, esquire, Wills and Inventories, Chester Probate Registry, Admon., 1768.

III

The practical concerns that made slave trading so complicated are well illustrated by the voyage of the 100-ton brigantine *Prince Vada*.[630] On December 22, 1760, the 100-ton brigantine *Prince Vada* cleared customs at Liverpool and set out upon an arduous three-month voyage to Angola, arriving at the slave markets of Malembo on March 31, 1761.[631] After three difficult months of bargaining with local slave dealers, the master of the *Prince Vada*, Captain John Clifton, assembled a cargo of 197 slaves, and departed Angola in late June or early July, 1761 for "the latitude of Barbadoes or Tobago."[632] After a middle passage that lasted 80 days or more, the *Prince Vada* made landfall at Barbados sometime in the late summer of 1761, before proceeding on to her principal port of disembarkation at St. Kitts, where the bulk of her surviving 180 slaves were sold over the course of two or three months. After her human cargo had been sold, and a return freight of sugar, coffee, or cotton loaded, the *Prince Vada* left St. Kitts early the next year and successfully returned to Liverpool some three months later on April 12th, 1762. From beginning to end, the *Prince Vada's* venture took 476 days, 100 of which comprised the first leg of her voyage from Liverpool to Angola. Given this and the mean average middle passage for Liverpool slavers from 1696–1775 of 78.81 days, one can deduce that it took perhaps 90–105 days for the *Prince Vada* to assemble her cargo and about the same length of time to sell her slaves in Barbados and St. Kitts.[633]

These raw facts provide some indication of the intentions of the *Prince Vada's* owners on her voyage to Malembo. In terms of the Angola trade, the "market plan" for the *Prince Vada* was somewhat limited. At 100 tons, the *Prince Vada* was some 24% smaller than the average tonnage of 132.32 tons for Liverpool ships in the Angola trade. The limited ambitions of the owners were also reflected in the customs declaration for the *Prince Vada*, made prior to her departure from Liverpool. This indicates that the owners sought to purchase only 250 slaves, or about two-thirds as many as the average venture to Angola. Since the *Prince Vada* departed Liverpool in late December, it is possible that her owners hoped to beat their competitors to market, and by so (6.1 Map—The Voyage of the *Prince* Vada) doing obtain the highest possible prices for their smaller cargo of slaves.[634]

A detailed account of the voyage can be drawn from the business correspondence of William Earle, the ship's husband. In some 267 letters written over the course of nineteen months between January 13th, 1760 and September 23rd, 1761, Earle established and maintained relationships with over 80 different business correspondents, ranging from West Indian slave factors and London moneymen, to Manx fish traders, Italian bead merchants, and an African chief. This wide-ranging web of communication reflected both the scope and diversity of William Earle's business interests throughout the Atlantic world. His letters provide valuable insight into how slave traders did business, acquired the information they needed to make informed market decisions, and related to one another. Earle's "business friends" kept him apprised of important developments in the trade, pointed him towards profitable opportunities, and assisted him in turning vague intentions into concrete schemes. An inveterate letter writer, Earle was an astute and conscientious man of business whose correspondence betrays an active mind diligently plumbing the possibilities of profit in the expanding Atlantic world. The state of the slave markets in Africa, the creditworthiness and reputation of possible business associates, the availability of suitable ships, captains, and investment capital, prevailing insurance rates, discount rates for bills of exchange, and current prices for sugar, cotton, dyewood, glass beads, brass pots, Indian textiles and a multitude of other goods, were only a portion of the many commercial concerns that Earle discussed in a steady stream of correspondence. Earle's insightful use of the information he gathered goes a long way towards explaining his extraordinary success as a slaver.

---

[630]The itinerary of the voyage can be deduced from entries in the TSTD.

[631]TSTD.

[632]William Earle to John Clifton, January 20, 1761, *Letterbook of William Earle*, D/EARLE/2/2, Merseyside Maritime Museum; *The Trans-Atlantic Slave Trade Database* on CD-ROM (TSTD).

[633]TSTD.

[634] *ibid.*

Map 6.1 *The Voyage of the* Prince Vada

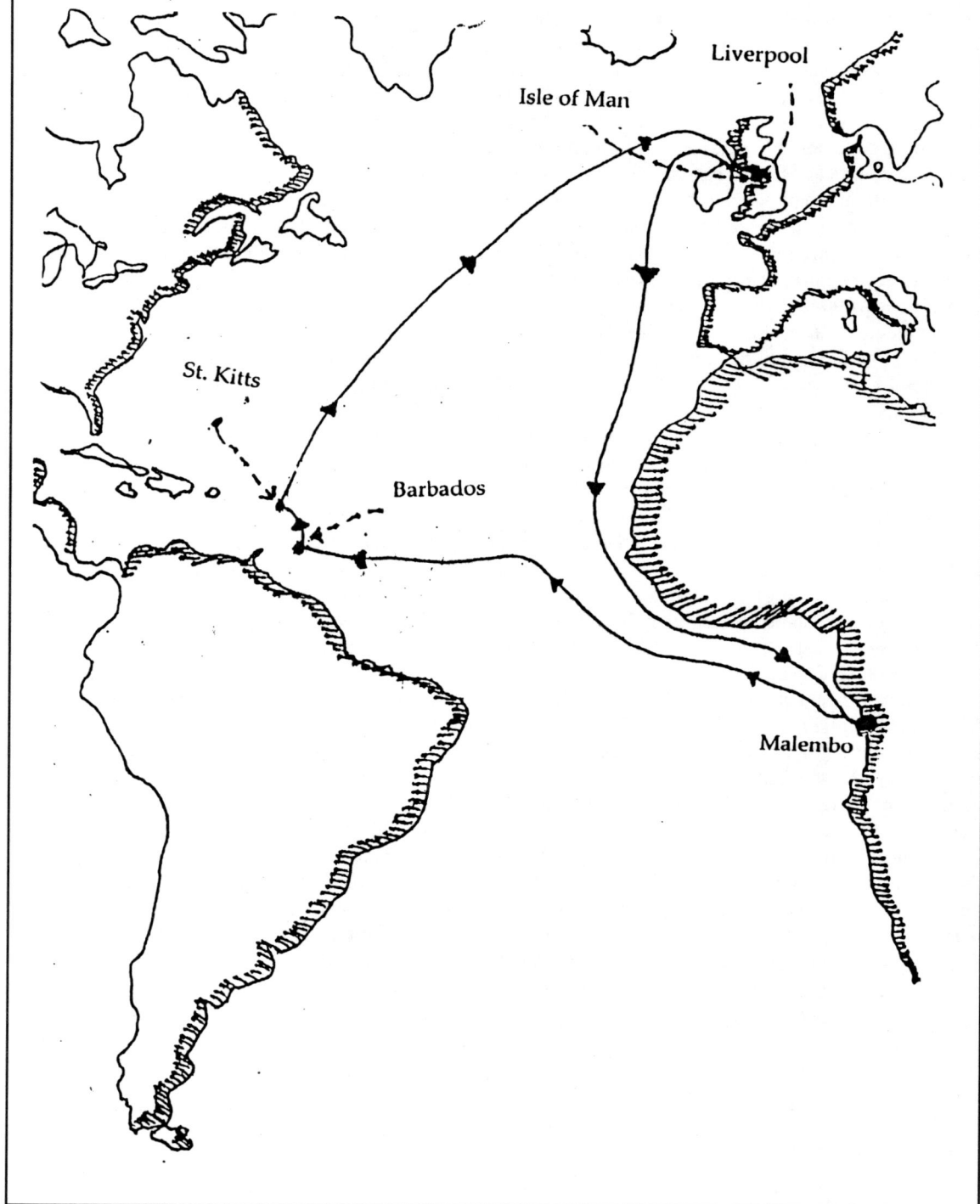

Timely communication was a key factor influencing slavers in their assessments of the potential profitability of ventures. Acquiring eagerly sought-after market news, such as the price of slaves, sugar, and other commodities, and acting upon this information before competitors, often determined the relative success of a voyage, or even whether a voyage was mounted at all. Informal social contacts formed one source of news. By the 1750s insurance offices, churches, the Customs office, charitable and convivial societies, the Company of Merchants Trading to Africa, town hall, and coffee houses emerged as important venues for the exchange of information and the conduct of business.[635] Eighteenth-century Liverpool slave traders increasingly came to rely upon highly personalized networks of business correspondence to fathom the complexities of their trade. While Liverpool slavers often demonstrated a singular talent for anticipating changes in the slave markets, allocating both their efforts and resources accordingly, the necessity of conducting business over great distances challenged their ability to respond effectively to the often-unpredictable realities of the African trade, making the acquisition of reliable information essential.

Collecting market information was never easy. There was often a time lag between learning of favorable markets and putting ships to sea. This makes it difficult for the historian to discern what news impelled the race to market. This is the case with regard to December 1772, when eleven ships departed Liverpool bound primarily for the markets of Upper Guinea, eight of which cast off the same day, December 23rd.[636] What particular scraps of news drove these ships to Africa is not clear, and may have differed greatly. The competitive pressures that propelled these and other ships to embark upon this hazardous trade compounded the fears of the men involved, investors willing to gamble all in hopes of great rewards. However, such great expectations were no guarantee of success.

By maintaining their own resident agents in the West Indies prior to the 1750s, Liverpool slavers were better able to acquire information on the state of New World slave markets. These agents were slavers in training, merchant apprentices learning the business as supercargoes and captains. Increasingly, however, large firms of resident commission agents, based primarily in London, such as *Turner, Hilton & Briscoe*, and *Thomas Hibbert & Co.*, came to dominate the slave factorage business in the British Plantations in the years after 1750, becoming, in effect, clearinghouses of valuable market information. Earle made quite clear in his letters the great value he placed upon maintaining an active, friendly, and honorable correspondence with such firms in assuring the sale "of [our] Negroes to our best advantage."[637] These West Indian correspondents assumed a variety of functions. In addition to their role in the sale of slaves, Earle clearly relied upon West Indian firms for assessments of the state of the slave markets in the plantations, information that proved useful in planning ventures to Africa. In a letter dated November 27th, 1760 to Samuel Carter, a partner in the Barbadian firm of *Carter & Woodhouse*, Earle stated that he was "greatly obliged...for the Jamaica and Guadeloupe Markets for Negroes" which Samuel Carter had evidently provided him some time earlier.[638]

Earle's instructions to his captains indicate the importance of West Indian contacts in determining where slaves were sold. A request for a "state of the market" was a common feature of Earle's West Indian correspondence, news which he requested be passed on to the masters of his ships. In July 1760, Earle addressed a "letter of government" to Captain John Copeland, the master of the slave ship *Calypso*, advising him that the "Jamaica & Guadeloupe Markets [are] Very good for Ibo Negroes [from Bonny] that have greatly the preference to Angola's," and recommended that he consider bypassing his intended port of call at Barbados, and selling his nearly 400 Bonny slaves at Jamaica.[639] At Barbados, Captain Copeland discovered that his Bonny slaves were indeed selling for less than what Earle had reported in Jamaica. As a result, the captain of the *Calypso* sailed on to Kingston to arrange for the sale of his cargo with Jamaican slave factors that represented his employers' interests. Provided that such letters of government reached the captains of slave

---

[635]A. H. Arkle, "The Early Coffee Houses of Liverpool," *Transactions of the Historic Society of Lancashire and Cheshire* 64 (1912), 3, 7–8f.

[636]*TSTD*.

[637]Earle to *Sparling & Bolden*, February 20, 1760, *Daybook of William Earle*.

[638]Earle to Samuel Carter November 27, 1760.

[639]Earle to John Copeland, July 25, 1760.

ships in sufficient time, slave traders enjoyed some small degree of flexibility in deciding where a cargo of slaves would ultimately be sold.

At their inception, slaving ventures, like that of the *Prince Vada*, took shape from a considered assessment of the costs and benefits of arranging financing, acquiring and outfitting a ship, loading a cargo of African trade goods, procuring insurance, hiring and providing for a captain and crew, and making provision for the sale of a possible return cargo of colonial produce. From these many discrete and contingent assessments, the promoters of slaving ventures formulated "schemes" or market plans that reflected the perceived relationships between supply and demand, real and opportunity costs, and the overall possibilities of profit in mounting a voyage. Such formulations were not only marketing plans; they represented sober statements of commercial intent cast in current market terms, serving as critically important blueprints from which ventures were prepared. The ultimate success of a scheme was dependent upon the development of such market plans, strategies that attempted to forecast the availability and price of slaves at various points of purchase in West Africa, the demand for slaves in the plantations, and the market for sugar and other staple goods in the West Indies, Britain, and Europe. Because of the risks of the African trade, especially during wartime, such a plan was as realistic an appraisal of the probabilities of the success of a particular venture as promoters could put forward.

The risks were explained to potential investors who often imperfectly understood the hazards and rewards of the slave trade. Because they were highly speculative in nature, slaving ventures required ready access to substantial expertise in the management of risk. In a fundamental way, the joining of investor capital with such expertise made an expansive and profitable slave trade possible, and was a primary function of the slaving specialist. The voyage of the *Prince Vada*, for instance, probably grew out of business contacts forged by William Earle with Manx traders in the Shetland fish trade, and originated with one such trader, John Joseph Bacon and his circle of business associates centered on the Isle of Man. However, Bacon, like the vast majority of the nearly 1000 known participants in Liverpool slaving partnerships between 1695 and 1775, was a casual investor unversed in the slave trade, a man who lacked the practical experience necessary to analyze the often regionally divergent market for slaves in West Africa. Bacon, like many other expectant investors, often turned to slaving professionals like Earle to remedy this want of knowledge. Sometime before September 1760, Bacon proposed to Earle the creation of a partnership to send a ship to the Windward Coast for a cargo of slaves. In his reply to Bacon on September 2, 1760, Earle expressed an interest in Bacon's projected scheme, but foresaw "some Difficulties & Inconveniences...in the way of Promising Success at this time."[640]

Earle saw problems with three major aspects of Bacon's scheme: the difficulty of purchasing a suitable and reasonably priced ship, the currently high cost of insurance for ships and goods employed in the African trade, and the decision to send a ship to the Windward Coast. Earle counseled Bacon that he did not know of any ship then available that was suitable for the Windward trade that did not require some degree of alteration, "a little of which", Earle lamented, "amounts to a [great] Deal of money."[641] Because he was perpetually in search of slave ships for his own use, and had many close contacts familiar with the market for ships, Earle could speak with authority on this facet of Bacon's proposed endeavor. A further obstacle, Earle continued, also stood in the way of success. Because of the ongoing war with France, and the substantial loss of Liverpool slave ships to the depredations of French privateers, insurance rates had skyrocketed after 1756. Normally 7–7 1/2% or less, Earle advised Bacon that insurance coverage could not be had "at this time [for] under 20% the Middle Risque."[642] Since each partner in the venture was responsible for covering his own partnership share in ship and cargo, such high rates were considerable disincentives to investment. More importantly, however, Earle questioned the entire market rationale underlying Bacon's projected scheme. Drawing upon informed observation, experience, and an extended network of correspondence, Earle provided Bacon with an astute analysis of the state of the slave market on the Windward Coast. Earle cautioned that because "there

---

[640]Earle to Bacon, September 2, 1760.

[641]*ibid.*

[642]*ibid*; A.H. John, "The London Assurance Company and the Marine Insurance Market of the Eighteenth Century," *Economica* 25 (1958), 127.

Map 6.2   *West African Slaving Regions*

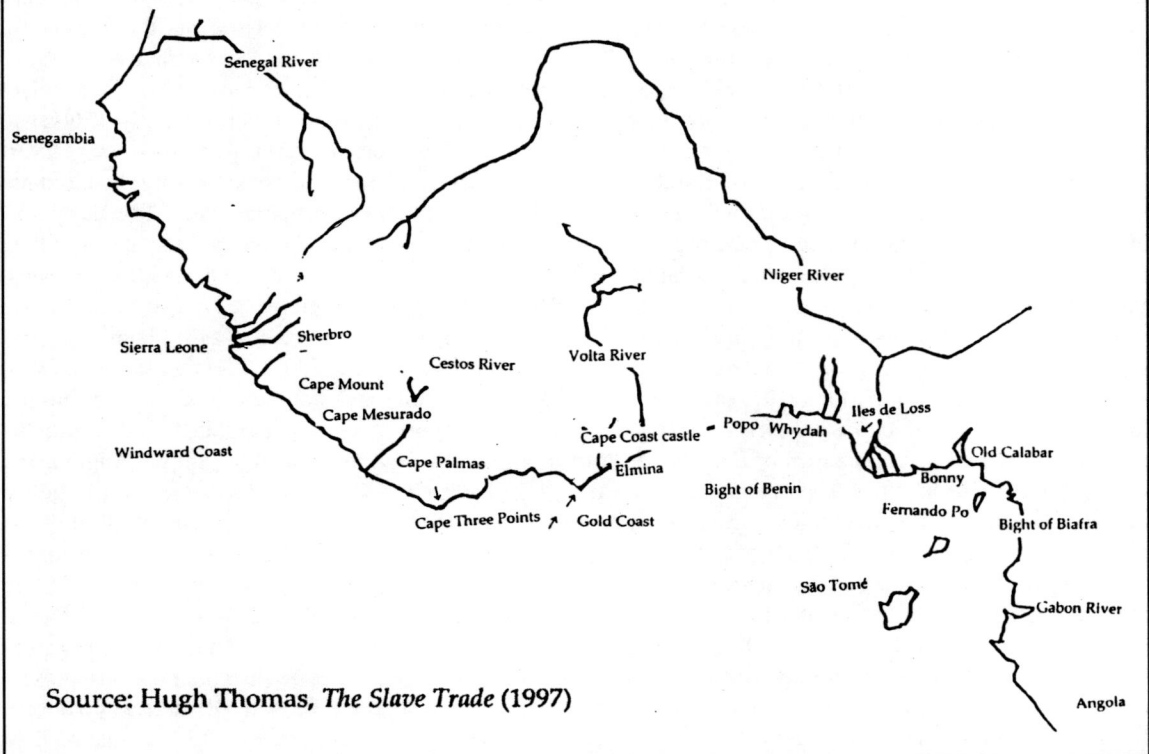

Senegal River

Senegambia

Sierra Leone   Sherbro
Cape Mount   Cestos River   Volta River   Niger River

Cape Mesurado
Windward Coast   Cape Palmas   Cape Coast castle   Popo Whydah   Iles de Loss
Elmina   Old Calabar
Cape Three Points   Gold Coast   Bight of Benin   Bonny
Fernando Po   Bight of Biafra
São Tomé   Gabon River
Angola

Source: Hugh Thomas, *The Slave Trade* (1997)

are a number of Vessels gone & going to the Windward Coast," increased demand there had "advanced" the price of slaves.[643] Earle shrewdly noted that such price increases "must Always be the case when a number of Ships are upon the coast."[644] Enough though Earle was to propose a Windward Coast venture to Bacon some months later, at this time the overall thrust of his advice was to dissuade Bacon from considering this stretch of coast at all.[645]

Earle's assessment of the slave markets elsewhere in West Africa was equally gloomy. He suggested that a cargo of trade goods suitable for the Sierra Leone trade might be assembled, but that "Slaves must be Bought Dearer there...[than on]...the ports of the coast."[646] Generally, Sierra Leone was never a significant region of slave embarkation for Liverpool traders, and only 6.6% of all voyages between 1695 and 1775 traded in Sierra Leone.[647] Procuring proper cargoes for Popo, or other points along the Slave Coast, was even more problematic.[648] In addition, Earle advised Bacon "I believe a Cargo might be got for Sierra Leone but not for Popo for Mr. [William] Boates can't get a cargo for the *Peggy*."[649] What Earle neglected to tell Bacon in this letter may be as significant as what he did mention. Although 61% of Earle's trade in slaves between 1748 and 1775 was centered in the Bight of Biafra, he made no reference to Bacon of the "Bite

---

[643]*ibid.*

[644]*ibid.*

[645]*ibid.*

[646]*ibid.*

[647]ibid.

[648]Earle to Bacon, September 2, 1760.

[649]*ibid.*

trade" as a possible alternative to the Windward Coast, nor did he mention Angola, the slave market that was eventually decided upon as the focus of marketing efforts.[650] While the motivations underlying Earle's failure to suggest Biafra are not clear, he may have been unwilling to damage his own interests in the "Bite" by sending another ship to trade there. Earle's failure to suggest Angola, however, is easier to comprehend. While a Liverpool Guineaman may have been dispatched there as early as 1700, Angola was the destination for only 5.9% of Liverpool slave ships prior to 1775, and may not have seemed a viable alternative at first.[651] To many merchants, sheer distance made Angola an unpopular destination. The eventual decision to select Angola may have been influenced by information that Earle received some time in the summer of 1760 as to the "great Demand Every Where for Negroes."[652] Ethnicity was an important factor in the (6.2 Map—West African Slaving Regions) marketing of slaves, and may have inclined Earle to consider Angola. Colonial planters had decided preferences as to which slaves were best suited to their particular needs. The rice plant-ers of South Carolina, for instance, preferred slaves from Senegambia and the Windward Coast because they had long experience in rice cultivation, but had little use for Ibos or Angolans.[653] While Chesapeake tobacco planters were less concerned with the ethnic origins of their slaves, many preferred Senegambians, and to a lesser extent, Angolans.[654] Such considerations influenced Earle's calculations for, as he later informed one correspondent, "a cargo of 450 Angolans [in] Virginia [that had] averaged £32–5 [a head] & a Cargo of Windwards[,] mostly children[,] [that had sold] at £35–6."[655] While it is not clear where Earle initially intended to sell the *Prince Vada's* cargo, a favorable market for Angolan slaves in Virginia, together with his friendly ties with the Virginia firm of *Sparling & Bolden*, eventually led him to send the ship to Angola, and then possibly on to Virginia. The *Prince Vada's* clearance from customs in Liverpool lists the West Indies as the ship's destination, a fact which may have reflected Bacon's preferences, but not necessarily Earle's. At the conclusion of his analysis, Earle offered Bacon the considerable advantage of his services in outfitting a ship for whichever African market he finally decided upon, that is, if Bacon chose to "run the risque."[656] In any case, Earle made it abundantly clear that the future of the venture was entirely in the Manxman's hands.

By mid-October 1760, however, John Bacon's vague business proposal of two months before began to take shape as a partnership group was established, a ship was procured, and an African market was chosen. As was shown in the previous chapter, partnerships tended to be relatively short-lived, *ad hoc* creations, forming and reforming around and between multiple, overlapping investment groups often dominated by a few major slave traders. Slaving partnerships were, in effect, temporary companies of varying longevity that were created for a specific purpose. Two general patterns of partnership are discernible in the Liverpool slave trade: one exhibiting a primarily familial pattern of connection, and another that was more associational, and non-familial. In a sample of 55 Liverpool slave traders active between 1696 and 1775, 40% demonstrated a more clearly familial pattern of connection in the composition of slaving partnerships, while 60% typically formed partnerships that were more associational in nature.[657] Although his father John Earle, an ironmonger and former Lord Mayor of Liverpool, was a pioneer of the slave trade in the 1710s, William Earle tended to form slave-trading partnerships that were more associational than familial in composition, partnerships that grew out of his experiences as a captain of slaving vessels between 1748 and 1750. This type of associational connection was especially evident in Earle's relationship with William Davenport, a major slave trader with whom Earle collaborated in some 38 slaving ventures between 1750 and 1775.[658] Bonds of affiliation and association became ever more important after 1750 in the composition of partnership groups.

---

[650]Draft letter, Earle to Bacon, October 10, 1760.

[651]*TSTD.*

[652]Earle to Samuel Carter, November 27, 1760.

[653]Peter H. Wood, *Black Majority: Negroes in Colonial South Carolina from 1670 through the Stono Rebellion* (1974), 179n, 250–1.

[654]Phillip D. Morgan, *Slave Counterpoint: Black Culture in the Eighteenth-Century Chesapeake and Lowcountry* (1998), 62–64ff.

[655]Earle to Carter, November 27, 1760.

[656]*ibid.*

[657]*TSTD.*

[658]*ibid.*

The composition of the *Prince Vada* partnership reflected its Manx origins, William Earle's circle of business associates, and the overriding importance of expertise in preparing slaving ventures. Of the eight members of the *Prince Vada* "Ownery" or partnership listed in *The Trans-Atlantic Slave Trade* database, three—John Joseph Bacon, Hugh Cosnahan, and William Quayle—were from the Isle of Man, while the rest, Earle, Davenport, Patrick Black, William Hayes, and Robert Jennings were primarily Liverpool-based merchants and mariners.[659] (See appendix 6.6) It is not clear whether Bacon meant to give control of his enterprise to Earle and Davenport, but this is what soon happened. While Bacon may have resented his involvement in the scheme, Davenport's experience as a slaver could not be denied. Together, Earle's group could muster well over 30 years of experience in the trade by 1760. Earle, Black, and Hayes all had experience as ship's captains in the African trade, while Davenport was a general merchant involved in no less than 101 slaving ventures between 1748 and 1775. Davenport had been apprenticed as a grocer to the prominent slave trader William Whaley in 1741, a line of trade that gave him practical experience in the provisioning of Guineamen.[660]

Davenport was also a prominent wine and bead merchant of Harrington Street, Liverpool, and had a long connection with the Earle family in the Mediterranean trade.[661] While less is known about the commercial experience of Jennings, he was probably a general merchant with some limited involvement as an investor in the slave trade prior to 1760. Unlike Bacon, Cosnahan, and Quayle, Earle's associates "were conversant in the [African] trade," a fact which virtually guaranteed William Earle the dominant management role in the enterprise.[662] Perhaps this is what Bacon had intended all along, for on September 23, 1760, Earle "[took] upon [himself] the Direction of the Vessel" as ship's husband.[663] For Bacon, this could not have been a much-unexpected development. After all, Bacon had approached Earle precisely because of his understanding of the African trade, and should not have been surprised that Earle expected to manage the project. The tone of Earle's letter to Bacon, however, suggests that Bacon raised some objections to Earle's involvement of his Liverpool friends in the scheme without his let or leave. Earle had taken it upon himself to offer Davenport an interest in the venture, even consulting with an "intimate" friend about the possibilities of obtaining a suitable ship.[664] Far from weakening Bacon's financial interest in the enterprise, Earle's high-handed reliance upon his own circle of associates greatly improved the venture's prospects for success by offering new avenues of investment, and a wider field of expertise. As a result, the capital resources of Bacon and his fellow Manx Men were more profitably employed. Bacon did not make much of an issue of Earle's actions, perhaps realizing that the enterprise was in capable hands. Bacon apparently became a "sleeping partner" without much resistance.

Ship's husbands, or managing partners, offered important advantages in both the financing and organization of slaving projects. The explosive growth of the Liverpool slave trade after 1750 greatly increased the trade's capital requirements, forcing slavers to look outside their trade, and outside Liverpool, for alternative sources of financing.[665] While the slave trade promised lucrative returns, its uncertainty and complexity was a major obstacle to investment, as was the smallness of Liverpool's banking community. The ship's husbands facilitated investment by permitting "sleeping partners" to purchase shares in projected ventures safely without the necessity of personal oversight or even active involvement. As noted above, shares could, in turn, be subdivided and sold to other investors. After 1750, investment poured into the Liverpool slave trade from

[659]*ibid.*; Frances Wilkins, Manx Slave Traders: A Social History of the Isle of Man's Involvement in the Atlantic Slave Trade (1999), 9, 45, 50, 57–58.

[660]David Richardson, "Profits in the Liverpool Slave Trade: The Accounts of William Davenport, 1757–1784," in *Liverpool, the African Slave Trade, and Abolition*, eds., Roger Anstey and P.E.H. Hair (1976), 61.

[661]Richardson, "Profits in the Liverpool Slave Trade," 61.

[662]Earle to Bacon, September 23, 1760.

[663]*ibid.*

[664]*ibid.*

[665]Richardson, "Profits in the Liverpool Slave Trade," 61.

Table 6.1	*Average Month of Departure for Slave Ships as listed in the* TSTD, *1695–1775*	

Month	Frequency	Percentage
January	102	4.5
February	130	5.8
March	161	7.2
April	176	7.8
May	197	8.8
June	214	9.5
July	244	10.9
August	285	12.7
September	197	8.8
October	176	7.8
November	120	5.3
December	145	6.5
Total	2147	95.7

divergent sources through out Britain, primarily Lancashire and the Midlands.[666] As the scale of the trade grew after the 1740s, slavers increasingly turned to London money markets to finance their operations.[667] Earle's demonstrate, large London merchant houses, like those of William Hogg, Anthony Merry, and Joseph Wimpey, provided him a range of financial services, from lines of credit and insurance policies to current accounts and other sources of capital. Long lines of trade credit became increasingly important after 1750, but slavers also used their own financial resources. Although Liverpool slavers had a wider variety of capital resources after 1750, profits from previous slaving ventures remained perhaps the single greatest source. The slave traders themselves, for the most part, met the growing capital needs of their trade.

The main outlays for slaving ventures included the cost of suitable cargoes of African trade goods, the purchase or charter of a ship and its outfit, insurance, and crew wages and provisions. Various forms of credit usually financed the enormous expense of assembling a cargo of trade goods, while the actual outfitting of the ship, including the cost of shackles and manacles for restraining slaves, was paid for in cash by the partnership as a whole. Four factors determined the selection of a suitable vessel: rigging, tonnage, cost, and availability. The fact that Bacon wanted a particular ship placed constraints upon Earle's planning of the voyage. While it is difficult to trace his calculations in this regard, Earle seems to have adopted a market strategy that focused upon securing a small ship, and purchasing fewer slaves. As noted before, it is possible that Earle planned to beat his competitors to market by departing from Liverpool some six-months earlier than was usually the case, and offering his slaves for sale when supply was low. As the table shows, a larger proportion of ships left port in late spring and summer months than in either the late fall or winter. This type of "first-to-market" strategy was dependent upon an accurate reading of the supply and demand for slaves in the plantations. A smaller, faster ship leaving port early could expect to arrive in the West Indies well before other ships, and could rely upon market timing rather than cargo size or volume to assure a successful venture.

Earle had given an indication of his thinking in an analysis he sketched for Bacon in early September 1760. Earle warned Bacon that at that late date in the slaving season, "Their [was] a great Risque of Small Vessels getting to Market [first]."[668] While the *Prince Vada* cannot be considered a small ship, Earle may have intended to use her much like the nimble sloops, schooners, and ketches that many slavers employed to win

---

[666]B.L. Anderson, "The Lancashire Bill System and its Liverpool Practitioners, in *Trade and Transport: Essays in Economic History in Honor of T.S. Willan*, eds., W.H. Chaloner, Barrie Ratcliffe (1977), 60–62f.

[667]D.M. Joslin, "London Private Bankers, 1720–1785," *The Economic History Review* 7 (1954), 167, 175–176.

[668]Earle to Bacon, September 2, 1760.

the race to market.[669] (See appendix 6.3) This strategy was not without its risks, however. Less heavily armed, sloops, ketches, schooners, and other smaller vessels were far more susceptible to capture during wartime, as became apparent after the outbreak of the Seven Years' War. Despite this vulnerability, smaller vessels had advantages that made them attractive alternatives to the larger vessels typically used in the slave trade. They were less expensive to purchase, insure, outfit and man, and promised lower rates of slave mortality during the middle passage.[670] This depended, however, upon whether these small ships could run the gauntlet of enemy privateers, the dangers of storm, and slave insurrection. Since news concerning the slave markets in West Africa and the plantations quickly lost its validity, slave traders frequently made use of smaller, faster vessels to capitalize upon market information before it became obsolete. Although this market-based practice of dispatching smaller ships was not how Liverpool slavers typically did business, it was successfully employed by small and large traders alike, and was not necessarily a "small trader" strategy.

The acquisition of the ship later renamed the *Prince Vada* provides further evidence of the importance of affiliation and association in the structuring of slaving partnerships. Earle's correspondence suggests that the circumstances of her purchase clear, but provides one possible explanation. Davenport's participation in the venture arose from the fact that Earle had earlier consulted him regarding the availability of the *Mercury*, an older ship built in the plantations that may already have been a veteran of the slave trade.[671] Although many Guineamen were chartered from ship-owning partnerships that specialized in providing vessels for the slave trade, the *Prince Vada* was probably purchased using the cash proceeds of the partnership. Bacon expressed an interest in purchasing the *Mercury*, and asked Earle whether the ship would cost less than £580, a price Earle considered "Dear."[672] When Earle asked for Davenport's assistance in arranging the purchase of the *Mercury*, his friend initially refused to assist the Manxmen unless he was compensated, for "he would never be concerned with foreigners without a commission."[673] This suggests that Earle had enlisted his friend to act as an intermediary in the purchase of the *Mercury*, or some other suitable vessel, thus laying the groundwork for Davenport's further involvement in the scheme. It was perhaps asking too much of Davenport, Earle noted, to expect him to undertake the purchase of this vessel unless "with a View of being Directly to Oblige… Friends," namely Earle himself.[674] To Davenport, Bacon and his circle were men whose *bona fides* as slave traders were unknown. Earle's arguments may have been a tactic to impress his novice partners with how the slaving experience of both Davenport and himself, suggesting that their guidance was crucial to the success of the venture. This apparently did the trick, and the Manxmen yielded effective control to Earle. Although the *Mercury* became the joint property of the partnership upon her purchase, and was not owned by any one slave trader or his firm, Earle, as ship's husband, was free to outfit and provision her as he saw fit.

Even before the acquisition of the *Mercury* had been finalized, Earle began gathering a cargo of trade goods suitable for Angola. His knowledge of the slave markets was vital in this regard. Although owners and captains had some leeway in deciding where they sold their slaves, they had far less flexibility as to where slaves were purchased once a ship sailed. The assortment of trade goods assembled for a particular voyage reflected the trading requirements at the proposed point of slave purchase, and became part of the overall marketing plan for the venture. Liverpool slave captains almost always acquired slaves at their intended African destinations. Of the 2242 known slave voyages that originated in Liverpool between 1696 and 1775, 66.9% of slaves were purchased at the intended region, while only 8% purchased slaves in more than one region of purchase.[675] (See appendix 6.1, 6.2) Because West African slave dealers had differing tastes, and often expected a particular assortment of trade goods for barter, cargoes of African goods had to be carefully

---

[669]*TSTD*. 20.2% of all vessels weighed 60 tons or less, 32.3% weighed between 65 and 90 tons, and 46.7% weighed 100 tons or more.

[670]*ibid*. Using the data from the *TSTD*, the correlation between ship tonnage and estimated slave mortality is significant at the 0.01 level; Herbert Klein and Stanley Engerman, "Long-Term Trends in African Mortality in the Transatlantic Slave Trade," *Slavery and Abolition* 18 (1997), 36, 44–45.

[671]The TSTD lists several ships built in the 1740s and 1750s named *Mercury* that may have become the *Prince Vada*.

[672]Earle to Bacon, September 19, 1760.

[673]*ibid*.

[674]*ibid*.

[675]*TSTD*. There are, of course, many Liverpool slave vessels whose region of purchase is unknown.

chosen. Iron bars weighing twelve to thirteen kilograms, and measuring three feet in length, were the most typical currency of account between the Senegal River and the Gold Coast.[676] Gold dust was widely used as currency on the Gold Coast, while gold dust and an assortment of copper and brass objects were traded in the Bight of Benin. In the slave markets of the Bight of Biafra, the types of currencies used varied widely, ranging from copper bars and horseshoe-shaped manillas to cowry shells, swatches of cloth, glass beads, and other items.[677] Slave dealers also had widely differing expectations as to the quality and type of goods to be offered in trade, expectations that had to be clearly understood by slavers before they placed orders with their suppliers. These cargoes might include calicos from Manchester, carpet, silk, and textiles imported from India, shoes, clothing, cutlery, tools, swords, muskets, gunpowder, beads, glassware, pottery, copper rods, iron bars, brass kettles, manillas, neptunes, iron furnaces, jewelry, soap, salt, foodstuffs, wine, and brandy.[678] Before trading began, it was also customary to pay the local chief "*coomey*," a fee for the privilege of doing business in his lands, and to provide *dashee*, the various gifts bestowed upon the chief and his men to ensure good will and speed the process of slave purchase. At Earle's intended destination in Angola, the recipient of this largesse was Prince Vada, the chief of Malembo, in whose honor the *Mercury* had been renamed. In Prince Vada's realm, glass beads of particular hues and designs were much prized as a medium of exchange, and these preferences were reflected in the cargo gathered for the *Prince Vada*. A proper selection of beads was crucial, for, as Earle warned one supplier, "[the] want of [the correct] assortment [of beads] may ruin a voyage."[679] With only a month to assemble a cargo before the scheduled November 1760 departure, Earle did not enjoy the luxury of time. The venture had only been agreed upon in September 1760, forcing Earle to work quickly in order to ready the ship for sea. Short notice made it difficult for suppliers to find and deliver the correct assortment of beads, textiles, and other goods that Earle had ordered, goods essential to the success of the scheme.

In early October 1760, Earle, and his set of associates within the *Prince Vada* partnership, feverishly began ordering the trade goods required for the scheme, applying to their own networks of friends to supply them speedily. Because he had less than a month to get the ship ready for departure in October 1760, fellow partner Patrick Black assisted Earle in ordering goods. Whether Black acted as a commission agent for the entire partnership group or not, such close personal and trade relationships as existed between Earle and him may have resulted in a blurring of the respective roles of ship's husband and sleeping partner. This was especially the case with Earle, Davenport, and Black, men who shared long associations and possessed wide experience in the slave trade as ship's husbands and captains. As ship's husband for the *Prince Vada*, Earle acted much like the chairman of an executive committee of experienced slavers, delegating important responsibilities to trusted men as circumstances warranted. Whether this reflected common practice in the management of slaving enterprises, or arose from the hurried nature of the *Prince Vada*'s preparation, is unclear. However, unlike many of his partners in the Shetland fish trade, whom he denigrated in a number of letters, Earle was confident that his *Prince Vada* partners could be trusted to organize the venture properly and serve the interests of the partnership as a whole. His friends, Davenport and Black in particular, were well known in the trade and prepared the cargoes for many Guineamen.

Bacon's expectations of profit in the outfitting of the voyage were soon dashed. One of the primary attractions of investing in slaving partnerships was the lucrative prospect of outfitting the ship or supplying the trade goods, provisions, and financial services that the undertaking required. Few, if any, investors were slave traders alone. It was common practice for the partners in slaving ventures, or their friends, to act as suppliers in outfitting ships and arranging cargoes, or to serve as commission agents, factors, or brokers in providing goods and services on behalf of their associates. Partners in slaving ventures, and merchants generally, had an expectation that they or their friends would be consulted first by their partners, before outsiders or strangers, in preparing a ship and its cargo. This was viewed almost as a right of partnership. Earle gave voice to it

---

[676]Philip Curtin et al, *African History*, (1978), 226.

[677]Curtin, 226–7.

[678]Earle to Bacon, September 19, 1760; Philip Curtin, *African History*, 226f; Gomer Williams, *History of the Liverpool Privateers and Letters of Marque with an Account of the Liverpool Slave Trade* (1897) 539.

[679]Earle to Peter Abraham Lucard, September 19, 1760; Williams, *History of the Liverpool Privateers…,"* 545–546.

in the spring of 1760, after French privateers took Bacon's ship, the *George & Betty*. "If you Replace your Vessel," Earle remarked to his Manx friend, "I shall be obliged to you for the Installation of the Ironmongery & Smiths [work,]…[and] will make [it] a point to oblige you."[680] As the owner of an ironworks on Redcross Street in Liverpool, Earle frequently provided the ironmongery required in the outfitting of ships in which he was a partner, or for ships in which his business associates had an interest.[681] While Liverpool slavers maintained a far-flung network of suppliers, ranging from Italian and Dutch bead merchants, French vintners, and Swedish gun manufacturers, to more local sources of supply in Liverpool, Manchester, Birmingham, and Sheffield, personal contacts between experienced slavers and their friends and suppliers structured the preparation of many slave ships.

These expectations of privilege, however, also contained the seeds of conflict between partners, as was the case with the people who owned the *Prince Vada*. They represented the temporary union of two separate circles of merchants, each with differing interests, relationships, and levels of expertise in the slave trade. Earle was presented with the choice of favoring either his occasional partners in the Shetland fish trade or his closest friends and associates in Liverpool. The preparations undertaken for the *Prince Vada* demonstrate that this did not present much of quandary. Although Bacon expected that his own circle of "business friends" would be permitted to supply at least part of the cargo, Earle expressed doubts as to whether he or his friends possessed sufficient knowledge of the African trade to procure the proper assortment of trade goods. "It is very Immaterial," Earle reasoned in a letter to Bacon in late September 1760, "whether you or I order [the cargo] from your friend [in Holland] but as it chiefly consists of a Variety of Beads I should rather apprehend it Best to order the goods from a person…conversant in [the African] trade."[682] As a specialist in the slave trade, Earle well understood the dangers implicit in allowing amateurs to assume an active role in the preparation of a ship, regardless of how they construed their partnership privileges. Because of his misgivings, Earle compelled Bacon to establish his friends' credentials in the slave trade, to prove, in effect, that they knew what they were doing. "Let me know," Earle insisted of Bacon, "who of your Friends have served Guinea cargoes & the goods shall be ordered from them."[683] When finally assembled, however, the cargo ordered for the *Prince Vada* was furnished more by Earle's regular network of suppliers, than Bacon's. Earle evidently ordered an excessive amount of goods from multiple sources both to insure that the required items would be delivered in time and to appease Bacon by ordering token goods from his friends as well. This may have seemed poor management to Bacon, who feared that an outsized cargo would overload the ship and tax Captain Clifton's ability to dispose of it in trade. "If he misses the enemy," Earle later asserted to Bacon, "[Clifton] is extremely well Laid for a Voyage [but] It is not my fault the Cargo is so Large [but] make no doubt Clifton will find room to lay it all out…He has…Room for 400 [slaves, but] If he brings in but 350 it will[,] as Slaves sell [well] abroad, be a Lucky Hit."[684] Earle ordered a variety of trade goods from a wide circle of suppliers: beads from Peter Lucard; textiles from William and James Manson, James Wetherhead, John Welch, Folliott Powell, Samuel Robinson; knives from the Manson brothers and Joseph and Benjamin Broomhead; cannons from Thomas Jordan; butter and beef from David Giball; and brandy, wine, claret, green and black tea, vinegar, soap, and "A Sow and Pigg" from Eleazer Ward.[685] These men were merchants based primarily in Manchester, Birmingham, and Liverpool. While Earle sought to "oblige" his friends whenever

---

[680]Earle to Bacon, April 7, 1760.

[681]John Gore, ed., *The Liverpool Directory, For the Year 1766: Containing An Alphabetical List of the Merchants, Tradesmen, and Principal Inhabitants of the Town of Liverpool* (Liverpool: W. Nevett & Co., 1766)

[682]Earle to Bacon, September 23, 1760.

[683]*ibid.*

[684]Earle to Bacon, February 12, 1761.

[685]Earle's feverish efforts to prepare the ship on time are revealed in the volume of correspondence in this *Daybook*: Earle to Lucard, September 19, 1760, Earle to *Knipe & Pennridge*, October 8, 1760; Earle to *Tennant & Massenbird*, October 8, 1760; Earle to *William & James Manson*, October 8, 1760; Earle to Folliott Powell, October 8, 1760; Earle to Samuel Robinson, October 8, 1760; Earle to *William & James Manson*, October 11, 1760; Earle to Bacon, October 10, 1760; Earle to Joseph & Benjamin Broomhead, October 23, 1760; Earle to David Giball, October 26, 1760; Earle to Folliott Powell, October 30, 1760; Earle to James Weatherhead, November 1, 1760; Earle to *Tennant & Massenbird*, November 1, 1760; and, Earle to Eleazer Ward, December 18, 1760.

Map 6.3 *Sources of Supply for the* Prince Vada

Whitehaven

Isle of Man

Lancaster

Leeds

Liverpool · Manchester

Chester

Sheffield

Birmingham

London

Bristol

Source: **Penelope Corfield, *The Impact of Towns* (1982)**

possible as ship's husband he was entirely within his rights to acquire goods from whomever and from wherever he chose, providing the price was right. Because they lacked any demonstrable experience in the slave trade, Bacon and his group could assert no real management role in organizing the *Prince Vada's* (Map 6.3 Sources of Supply for the *Prince Vada*, Source: Penelope Corfield, *The Impact of Towns* 1982) voyage that Earle did not mean for them to have. Bacon, Cosnahan, and Quayle no doubt profited less from their partnership perquisites than they had initially anticipated.

In his accounting of the expenses incurred by the partnership in readying the *Prince Vada*, Earle estimated that the cash outlay for the ship's outfit cost a total of £1327, including £730 for the purchase and alteration of the ship, and £597 for wage advances and ship's provisions. The cargo of textiles, knives, beads, Spanish Brandy, and wine cost the partnership £2571, for a combined total of £3898 for both outfit and cargo.[686] This

---

[686]Earle to Bacon, October 20, 1760.

amount was closer to what Earle had anticipated.[687] In addition, Earle took the liberty of insuring Bacon's interest in the *Prince Vada* and her cargo with two Liverpool firms, *Gill Slater, Charles Caldwell & Co.*, and *Matthew Ford, William Gregson & Co.* "I have taken this upon myself", Earle informed Bacon, "[and] if I have done wrong...I will get the policys Cancell'd."[688] While it is difficult to ascertain what contacts Bacon may have already had with these insurance firms, it seems evident that Earle drew upon his own extensive business connections to purchase Bacon's policy from Liverpool men and fellow slave traders. This is more than mere coincidence. Although slavers purchased insurance from a variety of sources in Liverpool, London, and elsewhere, the desire to "oblige" friends must have practiced a powerful influence. While this may have been a matter of convenience on the part of Earle, it was also a reflection of the alternating bonds of obligation that informed Earle's relationship with Bacon and his Liverpool friends.

The expense of assembling and providing for the *Prince Vada's* crew was also considerable. Among the expenditures listed in Earle's accounting of the ship's outfit, wage advances cost £200, £397, or 10% of the total outlay, was expended in the purchase of 5 tons of bread, 22 tons of shelled barley and split peas, 5 tons of "Pease & Beans," 2 tons of "Flower", and an unspecified amount of salt, cheese, oatmeal, and other necessaries.[689] While no final accounting of the *Prince Vada's* voyage has survived, additional crew-related expenditures, such as wages, crimpage, and transportation expenses, undoubtedly increased overall costs. Labor requirements were effected more by the size of the ship and the number of cannons it mounted than by the number of slaves to be loaded or the intended point of slave purchase. The most important single factor affecting the variability in the size of slaving crews was the need to mount additional guns during wartime. Although a correlation existed between the number of crewmen on board a ship at departure from Liverpool and the number of slaves the owners intended to purchase, it reflects the size of the ship rather than the number of slaves.[690] Larger crews were needed to sail bigger ships. In the first three quarters of the eighteenth century, Liverpool slaving crews ranged in size from the six carried on a number of sloops, schooners, and ketches of 30 tons or less, small vessels that could only mount a few guns, to the 80 carried onboard the 200-ton *Sarah Frigate* in 1749.[691] For all lines of trade between 1650 and 1775, crews ranged in size from two or three for small coasters to a hundred or more for large East Indiamen, but averaged around 8 or 9.[692] Between 1696 and 1775, the average crew complement for Liverpool slave ships of all sizes was just over 23.[693] Moreover, the distinctive nature of the African trade determined both the character and composition of these larger crews. Only a portion of the 49,464 crewmen known to have departed Liverpool onboard slaving vessels during this period were seamen employed to sail the ships. Perhaps as much as half were landsmen engaged to control the slaves. While *The Trans-Atlantic Slave Trade* database does not specify what proportion of the *Prince Vada's* 25 were landsmen, her crew was slightly smaller than the 29 that typically manned vessels of her size.[694] It is possible that the partnership chose to hire a smaller crew for financial reasons, or was limited by insurance considerations from employing a larger crew. Whatever the reason, Earle was not happy.[695] Four days before the ship cleared customs, he and Bacon were still disputing the details of manning the ship. While Earle had "waged a cooper" and admitted that "Men [were] plentiful here [in Liverpool]," he hoped Bacon would procure "3 or 4 servants" on the Isle of Man to supplement the 25 man crew already recruited.[696] "Our commission," Earle complained, "[means] that we must Take [only] 25 men."[697] The size of

---

[687]*ibid*, February 12, 1761.

[688]*ibid*, October 31, 1760.

[689]*ibid*, October 20, 1760.

[690]*TSTD*.

[691]*TSTD*.

[692]Peter Earle, *Sailors: English Merchant Seamen, English Merchant Seamen, 1650–1775* (1998), 8; Minchinton, "British Slaving Vessels," 69–71.

[693]*TSTD*.

[694]*ibid*.

[695]*ibid*.

[696]Earle to Bacon, December 18, 1760, Earle to Bacon, December 25, 1760.

[697]*ibid*.

the ship and crew formed fixed variables in Earle's marketing plans, inflexibilities that he sought to transcend with his superior understanding of the slave markets.

Although Earle says little about how the *Prince Vada's* crew was obtained in his letters, traditional means were probably used to man the ship. Ship's crews were normally procured in three main ways. Seamen could apply directly to the ship's captain, they could investigate the available positions listed at seamen's taverns, or they could be "crimped." For a fee, crimps, or procurement agents, regularly scoured the taverns, and other places frequented by English seamen in the eighteenth century, on behalf of merchants and mariners in need of crewmen. These sailors were generally impressed into service. Many crewmen were drawn from the dregs of society, and landsmen in particular had a reputation for drunkenness and violence. Earle himself did not hold a high opinion of Guinea sailors. "I would always Recommend Humanity," Earle observed to Francis Lowndes, captain of the *Baltimore*, "but I think that may be over acted with Respect to Seamen as very few of them have any Gratitude, but on the contrary after the most kind usage they will distress you the first Opportunity that Offers."[698] While William Earle's account of the *Prince Vada's* outlay makes no mention of expenditures for crimpage, these costs may have been substantial. Outlays for William Earle's privateer *Enterprize* in 1779 clearly records the cost of "crimpage...pilotage, and boatage" for three voyages at over £91, and lists over £645 in cash advances, as well as £221 in wages paid to the captain, and over 90 officers, seamen, landsmen, and apprentices.[699]

While the *Prince Vada* was ready by mid-November 1760 at the latest, unfavorable weather conditions delayed her departure. This unforeseeable development, together with a desire to reward his friends in Virginia, led Earle to consider an alteration in the market plan for the entire venture. In payment for past favors, Earle had promised to send the *Prince Vada's* cargo of slaves to the Virginia firm of *Sparling & Bolden*, but the delay made this pledge difficult to keep. "[The *Prince Vada* has]...long...[been]...detained by Contrary winds," Earle cautioned his associates in the Chesapeake, "and [I] am Afraid she will be too late for Virginia, being thrown past the time Usual for a favorable Current to get up the Coast of Angola."[700] In the early spring of 1760, Earle had promised *Sparling & Bolden* the schooner *Industry's* cargo of Calabar slaves, but had been forced by wartime conditions to divert the ship elsewhere.[701] He now felt obliged to deliver the *Prince Vada's* cargo to his friends in Virginia, and swore that he would send the ship their way if possible. The *Prince Vada*, Earle reassured *Sparling & Bolden*,

> is a thing that Sails Incomparable well and has now the Benefit of a fine Wind, and if is so lucky to get into the Latitude of Tobago by the first day of July, I have ordered her to proceed directly to you[.] If not[,] She is to go to Guadeloupe. There is a probability if [she] has a Good passage out[,] of her doing it in that time[,] which I am very Anxious She Should[,] being very desirous to throw Something in your way[,] which I think I am[,] in Gratitude for the favors I have Received from you[,] Bound to do.[702]

His friends in Virginia had assisted him in the past, and Earle hoped they would continue to do so in the future.

Attenuated lines of communication, the vagaries of wind and tide, and the uncertainties of war limited Earle's ability to influence the *Prince Vada's* ultimate destination once she was at sea. After the ship set out from the Mersey, her fate was largely in the hands of her master, Captain John Clifton. A captain's abilities as a mariner, and his familiarity with the slave trade, were of critical importance in the success of all slaving ventures. Captains were well rewarded for their knowledge and efforts. William Boates, Ambrose Lace, and other captains grew rich in the slave trade, eventually becoming slave traders themselves. While a crewman's meager wages were largely customary, captains were well positioned to negotiate for additional

---

[698]Earle to Francis Lowndes, August 18, 1760.

[699]Williams, *History of the Liverpool Privateers...*, 661–664.

[700]Earle to *Sparling & Bolden*, January 24, 1761.

[701]*ibid*, April 3, 1760.

[702]*ibid*, January 24, 1761.

advantageous privileges in addition to their wages. Although they were well paid, the proceeds from the sale of "privilege" slaves, coast commissions, primage, and other lucrative bonuses formed the major part of their compensation. Experienced and capable captains like John Clifton were much in demand and expected to be amply rewarded. While Earle needed good men to sail his ships, he did not always trust the honesty of slave factors or the judgment of captains. "They have played a cunning game Lately at Barbadoes", Earle confided to London friends, "by persuading...Ignorant captains to agree with them at a certain price & have taken the benefit of the sale to themselves."[703] In their search for profit, captains were even known to take their ships on long, unplanned diversions in order to trade on their own account, malfeasance that could greatly delay a ships return to Liverpool. Much as slavers were themselves, captains were men on the make who were often unreasonable in their demands for privilege. Slavers fully expected this. Fearful that Clifton would demand too much, Earle urged Bacon to give him "a Lesson not to be too Expecting as to privilege or any unnecessary materials [.]"[704] Apparently, however, Earle had less reason to complain about Captain Clifton than perhaps he first feared.

Earle's letters also suggest that a market of sorts existed for captains among Liverpool slave traders. One prominent firm of slavers, *Crosbie & Trafford*, used the promise of a larger ship in an attempt to recruit William Hindle, Earle's former apprentice and captain of his ship the *Industry*. "I don't care to part with so Valuable a Man as I have Experienced [him] to be", Earle wrote of Hindle, "for his Knowledge in the Bite Trade puts him in competition with any man."[705] Skilled captains were so important that even before the details of a voyage had been settled, slavers routinely purchased or chartered ships for particularly skillful or experienced men. Slavers did not so much send ships to Africa, as they sent captains.

While many captains were employees recruited by reputation alone, others were no mere hired hands. A significant number of captains were connected to partnership groups by bonds of family or apprenticeship, or were themselves partners. Among Earle's captains in 1760, John Copeland, captain of the *Calypso*, was his brother-in-law, while others, like William Hindle, had been apprentices. Many prominent mid-eighteenth-century slave traders first entered the trade as ship's captains, including William Earle himself. Between 1696 and 1775, the average sailing career for captains who later became partners was a little over two years.[706] Earle, for instance, captained two ships, the *Lucy* and the *Chesterfield*, during three voyages between 1748 and 1750, and in the last, he was also a partner. His experiences suggest that a career pattern existed for at least some Liverpool slave traders. Young apprenticed slavers began their careers as supercargoes or resident slave factors in the plantations, becoming ship's captains and, in many cases, partners in slaving ventures. Slavers without maritime backgrounds, like William Davenport, Jonathan Blundell, and John Backhouse, relied upon family connections, or drew upon contacts formed during merchant apprenticeships, to gain entrance into the trade. These career patterns built upon and added to a pool of practical slaving knowledge that allowed men like Earle and Davenport to excel in an unforgiving trade.

A Manx associate of Bacon, Clifton's role as captain had been a key element of the *Prince Vada* scheme from the very beginning. While Earle had expressed qualms about many aspects of Bacon's proposed venture, he exhibited no similar reservations about Clifton's qualifications. "Mr. Clifton is a Man I have a very great opinion of," Earle informed Bacon in September 1760, "[and the choice of the best possible point of purchase on the Windward Coast] I submit to [him]."[707] Because partners rarely attended the purchase and sale of slaves, captains became the active, "on-the scene" managers of slaving ventures. This was reflected in the captain's relationship with the ship's husband. The managing partners commonly gave the captains of slave ships detailed letters of instruction prior to departure. These outlined where slaves were to be purchased, the slave factors to be contacted in the plantations, and the ideal selling prices of slave cargoes. Although important guides, letters of instruction reflected market conditions only at the time they were written, requiring ship's husbands to grant captains a wide degree of latitude in interpreting instructions as conditions

---

[703]Earle to *Hilton, Turner & Briscoe*, July 7, 1760.

[704]Earle to Bacon, September 23, 1760.

[705]*ibid*, October 10, 1760.

[706]*TSTD*.

[707]Earle to Bacon, September 2, 1760.

warranted. The changes in the market plan for the *Prince Vada* occasioned by her delay in departure gives a good example of the flexibility required in such instructions. A month after the *Prince Vada* left Liverpool, Earle contacted Clifton to discover whether a voyage to Virginia was still possible. "As you have had a fine wind & fair whether Since you left", Earle wrote Clifton on January 20th, 1761, "we may be in Expectation of your having a Good passage up the Coast of Angola & a Quick dispatch."[708] Earle recommended that if Clifton were able to assemble a cargo of slaves quickly in Angola and sail the *Prince Vada* to the vicinity of Barbados or Tobago by July 10th, 1761, he should proceed directly to Norfolk, Virginia, and "there apply to Messrs. Sparling & Bolden" to arrange for the sale of his cargo.[709] The tenor of these amended instructions suggests that Virginia was not the *Prince Vada's* intended destination, and that Earle had altered his objectives in mid-voyage in hopes of taking advantage of a robust demand for Angolan slaves in Virginia. Earle reminded Clifton that the Virginia market favored "Grown people", and that if he thought he could "leave Angola Seas [in time] to Compass this Scheme," he must "Assort [his] Cargo differently" to reflect changed market requirements.[710] Earle's revised scheme, however, died aborning. The loading of slaves proved difficult and took upwards of three months. As a result, Clifton was not able to depart Malembo in sufficient time to reach Barbados by early July. Although he knew as early as May 1761 that his Virginia scheme could not be accomplished, his desire to oblige his friends in Virginia led Earle to continue to promise them *Prince Vada's* cargo as late as August 1761. Perhaps *Sparling & Bolden* suspected that they would never see the *Prince Vada* or her cargo, but it was important for them to know that Earle had intended to "throw something" their way.

An important and oft-stated theme of William Earle's correspondence was his concern for a "quick dispatch", which he saw as "the Life of Everything."[711] Captains were urged to assemble their African cargoes as quickly and expeditiously as possible, and to dispose of them in the plantations without delay. Earle saw quick dispatch as a financial necessity, for the length of a voyage determined how long it took for bills of exchange to reach Liverpool.[712] "It is very Hard upon People in Trade", Earle protested to his brother-in-law in April 1760, "to Lye so long out of their Money[.]"[713] An extended period of slave purchase on the African coast also exposed the ship and its crew to a damaging and deadly tropical environment, increased slave mortality, and the heightened possibility of conflict with native African populations. One estimate based on 158 Liverpool voyages between 1770 and 1775 suggests that crew mortality rates may have been as high as 32%, the majority of deaths occurring in Africa.[714] Long purchases had equally dire consequences for slaves. Levels of slave mortality prior to departure from Africa are not well known, and are not well represented in total mortality rates. While 71, 827 captive Africans are known to have died in Liverpool ships during the middle passage between 1696 and 1775, a great many also died while being enslaved.[715] Earle demonstrated no real concern for the welfare of slaves, but as a merchant, he understood that dead slaves were not good business. Earle also understood that a ship's arrival in the New World did not end the threat to its cargo. In his instructions to Captain Clifton, Earle made it clear that he saw a quick dispatch of the *Prince Vada's* cargo in the plantations as essential to success. "Long purchases," Earle complained to a Jamaican firm of slave factors, "make Sickly ships & unless one would Expect Slaves to Spring & grow like Mushrooms[,] it is not to be Expected...that it should be otherwise."[716]

In order to speed the *Prince Vada's* progress and insure a quick dispatch, Earle lodged a series of letters of introduction and instruction with major firms in Barbados, St. Kitts, and Guadeloupe, to which Clifton

---

[708]Earle to John Clifton, January 20, 1761.

[709]*ibid.*

[710]*ibid.*

[711]Earle to Isaac Dove, April 22, 1761.

[712]Ian Duffy, *Bankruptcy and Insolvency in London during the Industrial Revolution* (1985), 229–230.

[713]Earle to John Copeland, April 26, 1760.

[714]Stephen Behrendt, "Crew Mortality in the Transatlantic Slave in the Eighteenth Century" in *Routes to Slavery: Direction, Ethnicity and Mortality in the Atlantic Slave Trade*, eds., David Eltis and David Richardson, 60–1.

[715]*TSTD.*

[716]Earle to *Kenyon & Southworth*, April 22, 1761.

was to apply for the sale of his slaves. Although Earle continued to suggest in his instructions that the *Prince Vada* proceed to Virginia, he also forwarded Clifton a "State of the Market" in slaves at St. Kitts which had been sent him by a local firm in Basseterre.[717] Earle made his general intentions clear, but left it for Clifton to decide the *Prince Vada's* final destination.

Wharton, Douglas & Co. of St. Kitts was not a firm that Earle had much familiarity with before 1761. Fellow slave trader Felix Doran recommended this firm to Earle as one that would "do the best in their Power [to] give [a] quick dispatch."[718] Earle introduced himself to *Wharton's & Douglas* in a letter dated May 18th, 1761, asking them for their assistance in selling his Angolans. "By Recommendation of Mr. Felix Doran" Earle informed them,

> I have addressed to you the *Prince Vada*, who I Expect will be in the West Indies in...July Next[.] She is to call [first] at Barbados for Orders, [and] you will please to forward the Enclosed [letter] to your Friends [*Fisher & Davis*] in Barbados with a letter to Captain Clifton and advise him the State of your Market for Slaves and the prospect of a freight there [,] in doing which you will Oblige.

What led Clifton to sell his slaves in St. Kitts is unknown, but we can surmise that the market information that met him in Barbados offered the prospect of concluding an already long voyage at St. Kitts with profit and dispatch. While it is not known whether Clifton ever attempted to sell his cargo at Barbados or Guadeloupe, Earle instructed him to "sit down with" *Roger Smith & Co.* of Barbados and Guadeloupe, "provided they will agree to the following terms...to Engage to turn your Cargo out [and] give you a Quick dispatch."[719] Depending upon the proportion of bills and produce they proposed to offer Clifton in payment for his cargo, Earle suggested terms to *Roger Smith & Co.* "which...[he thought]...Very Moderate Considering how Slaves have Sold."[720] Clifton was instructed to sell his cargo of slaves at between £25 to £27 per head, and to accept a payment that was one-half freight, and one-half bills of exchange. As to a return cargo, Earle desired "But Little Sugar & that good [and] Cotton & Coffee for the Remainder."[721] Above all, Earle hoped for a quick dispatch, requesting that *Smith & Co.* "not keep the Captain in suspense" if terms could not be reached "as he...[had]...other Houses to call upon."[722] Clifton's instructions left the final terms of payment to his discretion. These instructions were just as qualified and contingent as those specifying where he should sell his slaves and to whom. "I have made [Clifton's] Limits Low", Earle advised *Roger Smith & Co.*, "But that is no Rule for Sale [and if] they Turn out More [it] is to the advantage of the owners."[723] Earle cautioned Clifton to make his "Bargain sure", and to procure good bills at short dates. [724] If attempts to dispose of the cargo in Guadeloupe proved unavailing, Earle directed Clifton to proceed to the Leewards and "put [his] cargo into the hands of *Messrs. Wharton & Douglas*" at St. Kitts, where he succeeded in selling his 180 remaining slaves some time in the late summer or early fall of 1761.[725] Although the terms of this sale are not well known, they were informed by Earle's thorough understanding of market trends, an awareness sharpened both by his slave trading savvy and an extensive information gathering network.

In the nearly five hundred days between her departure from Liverpool and successful return in April 1762, the *Prince Vada* absorbed only a portion of Earle's time. As a general merchant, he was involved in a range of commercial activities from selling fish in Ireland, Italy and Spain to supplying ivory and a host of

---

[717]Earle to Clifton, May 18, 1761.

[718]*ibid.*

[719]Earle to Clifton, June 8, 1761.

[720]Earle to *Roger Smith & Co.*, June 8, 1761.

[721]*ibid.*

[722]*ibid.*

[723]*ibid.*

[724]Earle to Clifton, June 8, 1761.

[725]*ibid.*

other "vendible goods" to merchants through-out Britain.[726] However, it was the slave trade that engrossed most of his waking hours. Besides managing the *Prince Vada* and maintaining close contacts with Captain Clifton, making arrangements for the payment of the *Prince Vada's* outlay, and attending to his skittish Manx partners, Earle was deeply involved as ship's husband in preparing two upcoming slaving ventures: the *Mentor*, for a voyage to Whydah in November 1761, and the *Seahorse*, for a journey to the Windward Coast in the summer of 1762. Earle was also responsible for the management of two other ships already at sea, the *Calypso*, and the *Industry*. Although less demanding of his time, Earle had more casual interests in six other Guineamen that departed Liverpool between April 1759 and October 1762.[727] While Earle was not ship's husband for the *Chesterfield*, the *Francis*, the *Baltimore*, the *Lyme*, the *Minerva*, or the *Dalrymple*, these vessels represented significant investments that required close attention. The capture of the *Chesterfield*, the *Calypso*, the *Industry*, and the *Lyme* by French privateers, and the wreck of the *Francis* off the Canary Islands, greatly complicated his management duties, forcing Earle to reassure his jittery Manx partners that the *Prince Vada* had so far escaped 'the shoals of privateers" that threatened the ship and its prospects for a successful voyage.[728] However, the loss of these ships further weakened the tenuous bonds that held the *Prince Vada* partnership together by making manifest the real dangers inherent in the Guinea trade. Both Hugh Cosnahan and William Quayle attempted to sell part of their interest in the voyage to the partnership to Earle, which he rejected as "not Convenient."[729] Having lost ships before, Earle understood better the level of risk involved in sending Guineamen to Africa, a hard lesson Bacon, Cosnahan, and Quayle were just beginning to learn. Earle's multiplicity of interests in the slave trade represented a calculated strategy designed to lessen the hazards of an already risky trade, oblige his friends, and draw upon the expertise of the larger community of slavers.

The enormous variability and unpredictability of the slave trade shaped Earle's perception of his role as a slave trader. No two voyages were ever the same, and nothing could be taken for granted in preparing ships for departure. Almost a quarter of Liverpool ships dispatched to Africa between 1695 and 1775 failed to return home.[730] A fast ship, a capable captain, and an ample cargo of trade goods were essential elements of any slaving venture, but no guarantees of success. From his office on Redcross Street in Liverpool, Earle could do little to insure a good market for his slave cargoes, or protect his ships from hurricanes or privateers. While there were limits as to what Earle could do to lessen the risks intrinsic to the trade, the *Prince Vada* venture demonstrates that he was not totally powerless to influence the outcome of a voyage. Ready access to market information made it possible for Earle and other slavers to manage risk more effectively than ever before. The advent of a rudimentary system of communications had a revolutionary impact upon the conduct of business.[731] The steadily increasing volume of transatlantic commerce after 1675 not only "Americanized" British trade, it transformed the context and scope of commercial relationships.[732] For the first time, slave merchants were able to establish and maintain close connections with a host of overseas business contacts. Firms such as *Sparling & Bolden* and *Kenyon & Southworth* provided Earle with timely market information that greatly enhanced his ability to anticipate changes in the price and demand for slaves and West Indian produce. Earle passed along what he learned to his captains, guiding them towards friendly firms of slave factors and promising New World markets. Although the technical infrastructure of eighteenth-century transatlantic communication was primitive and the information it provided incomplete and often out-of-date, it presented slavers with a resource that became critically important in the ordinary conduct of trade.

---

[726]Earle to Joseph Carter, September 13, 1760; Earle to Joseph & Benjamin Broomhead, April 7, 1760.

[727]*TSTD*

[728]Earle to *Sparling & Bolden*, March 6, 1761.

[729]Earle to Bacon, February 20, 1761.

[730]*TSTD*. 77% of Liverpool ships dispatched to Africa between 1695 and 1775 successfully returned home.

[731]Ian Steele, *The English Atlantic, 1675–1740: An Exploration of Communication and Community* (1986), 213–228.

[732]Kenneth Morgan, *Slavery, Atlantic Trade, and the British Economy, 1660–1800* (2000), 1*f.*

IV

Earle's prolific letter-writing reveals the expectations of reciprocity and obligation that shaped mercantile relationships and created highly personal attachments that facilitated trade for "People who have Large Connections abroad[.]"[733] He greatly valued such close associations, as his persistent attempts to reward the firm of *Sparling & Bolden* for past favors indicate. Because such friendships were so commercially beneficial, wayward behavior that jeopardized them was viewed as more than merely unsociable; it was, to use Earle's term, "unmercantile."[734] Earle's treatment of his Manx partners, however, suggests that a somewhat different etiquette frequently governed behavior within the slaving partnership itself. The perils of the Guinea trade made it the province of experts like William Davenport, Patrick Black, and William Earle himself. Similarly, the trading acumen of the captain was essential to the success of a venture. His own experiences as a ship's captain made it clear to Earle that the success of a voyage was often directly related to the degree of discretion given a ships captain. Men such as John Clifton, William Hindle, and John Copeland, knew the trade and Earle had no difficulty in allowing them a significant supervisory role. The same could not be said of Earle's Manx partners. Although the *Prince Vada* scheme originated with John Joseph Bacon, his major contribution to the voyage ended with his choice of captain. Earle determined nearly every aspect of the marketing plan for the venture, from the selection of a likely African market, to the purchase of a cargo of trade goods, to the choice of West Indian produce to be accepted in payment for his slaves. Bacon, Cosnahan, and Quayle were experienced managers accustomed to overseeing their own affairs, and Earle's domination of their joint venture may not have sit well with them. Bacon invested in thirteen other Guineamen between 1761 and 1775, none of which were managed by William Earle or William Davenport. While Hugh Cosnahan invested in one additional slaving project, the voyage of the *Douglas* to Bonny in April 1762, fellow Isle Men managed this undertaking. William Quayle never participated in the slave trade again. Earle's masterful actions as ship's husband for the *Prince Vada* grew from his intimate knowledge of slave markets, and were necessary for the success of the enterprise. In Earle's estimation, acceding to the advice of old hands in the trade was only common sense. In his negotiations for a return freight with the experienced Jamaican slave factor Thomas Southworth, Earle counseled his young former apprentice Isaac Dove to "Make a fast friend of him" and listen to his recommendations. "Be governed by his Advice", Earle cautioned Dove, "in that as well as other matters you are not thoroughly acquainted with."[735] As important as ties of affiliation and association were in the construction of slaving partnerships, expertise was the key to authority and prominence in the trade.

---

[733]Earle to John Humphreys, July 6, 1761.

[734]Earle to John Finch, February 12, 1761.

[735]Earle to Dove, December 8, 1760.

Conclusion

The purpose of this study is to demonstrate the ways in which the social and commercial bonds formed by slave merchants underpinned the growth of their trade and manner in which they traded slaves. More than any other city on the Atlantic periphery, the rise of Liverpool is attributable to the character of the town's slave-trading community. Historians, however, have not viewed social factors in the evolution of transatlantic trade. There are exceptions to this emphasis. The work of David Hancock, David Richardson, and Melinda Elder has explored the role of social factors in the emergence of the British slave trade.

While the formation and composition of Liverpool slaving partnerships has not been a focus of recent scholarship, the *Transatlantic Slave Trade Database* promises to shed light on the social dimension of the Liverpool slave trade. This neglect lies in the fact that while many aspects of Liverpool slave trade have been examined in detail by a succession of scholars, the questions asked center upon general interpretations of the slave trade, such as the scale of the trade, its regional distribution, the evolution of the trade in the Americas, and slave mortality. These broader questions have not borne directly upon the composition of slave trading community Liverpool, or how patterns of partnership influenced their commerce in African slaves. This study attempts to remedy this deficiency.

The Glorious Revolution allowed merchants to dominate Liverpool for most of the eighteenth century. This permitted them to remove the restraints that had hindered commercial enterprise. As a result, Liverpool merchants achieved self-awareness as an interest group, and joined together to promote their common interests. Trade became the focal point of town government, and newly influential merchants became the lords of Liverpool. This liberation was the result of the expansion of Liverpool's maritime trade after 1700, and the pursuit of profit unlocked a world of commercial, political, and social opportunity for an increasingly diverse group of men.

A major feature of this study is the impact of the openness of the African trade upon the social composition of the Liverpool slave trading community. Any investor with enough funds could trade for slaves in Africa, regardless of social position. This differed from Bristol where an elite group of merchants monopolized the slave trade for much of the eighteenth century. Thus, the rise of the Liverpool slave trade can be attributed, in part to the appearance of a diverse group of slaving entrepreneurs after 1700.

Certainly, there are strong indications that by 1730 that a slaving elite had begun to take shape in Liverpool. This group included prominent old Liverpool families. However, such families did not monopolize the opportunities for profit that transatlantic commerce in tobacco, sugar, or slaves offered. Birth, kinship, and social status alone were not sufficient to insure success in trade. While kinship ties and privileged relationships remained the essential building blocks of many merchant fortunes, the involvement of less-rooted men in Liverpool trade after 1700 suggests that by the mid-eighteenth century an ongoing process of social and commercial liberalization had altered the composition of the Liverpool mercantile community. The Liverpool slave-trading community was thus an amalgam of long established merchant families and new men in search of both profit and social connection.

Migration to Liverpool had an important affect upon the construction of the Liverpool slaving community. The rapid growth of Liverpool trade after 1700 attracted a diverse group of men eager to establish themselves as merchants, mariners, professionals, tradesmen, and craftsmen. This exodus increased in numbers in the late seventeenth and early eighteenth centuries when many young men journeyed to Liverpool from elsewhere in Britain. The emergence of Liverpool as a leading port of the transatlantic slave trade can be traced back to this migration. The Liverpool slave trade was thus built upon the ingenuity and labor of both native-born and immigrant entrepreneurs, and was an important factor in the rise of Liverpool.

In many ways, the openness of the Liverpool slave trade can be traced to a general loosening of traditional social practices and institutions that had restricted access to trade for many merchants. The new men of trade often had little interest in the traditional structure of town society. These men did not come to Liverpool to become town fathers, but rather to make a fortune in trade. While many of them were considered outsiders by the merchant elite, these entrepreneurs transcended their often modest origins to become the real powers in the Liverpool slave trade.

Bibliography

MANUSCRIPT SOURCES

The Daybook of William Earle, 23 Jan 1760–23 Sept 1761, Earle MS, D/EARLE/2/2, Merseyside Maritime Museum, Liverpool.

Partnership Papers, 1763–1836, Earle Papers, D/EARLE/4/1-2, Merseyside Maritime Museum.

Accounts of John Tarleton, 1748–1771, Tarleton MS, 920 TAR 2/2–19 (2), Liverpool PRO, Picton Library.

Plan of the Ancient Town and Harbour of Liverpool, with the Ownership of Property, about 1670, Macdonald & Macgregor, Liverpool, (No Date), Liverpool PRO, Picton Library.

Liverpool Political Pamphlets, 1727–1754, 920 PLU 35, Liverpool PRO, Picton Library.

Liverpool Memorandum Book or Daily Packet (1753), Liverpool PRO, Picton Library.

Corporation Minute Books, MF2/2–5, Liverpool PRO, Picton Library.

Committee Book of the African Company of Merchants Trading from Liverpool, 1750–1820, Liverpool PRO, Picton Library.

Extracts from Liverpool Town Books, 1727–1755, 352 CLE/TRA 2/1/8–9, Liverpool PRO, Picton Library.

Papers relating to the Mayoralty of Foster Cunliffe, 1729–1731: Petitions to Foster Cunliffe as Mayor from debtors in Prison, 8 December 1729–20 June 1730, MD72/116, Liverpool PRO, Picton Library.

Apprenticeship Enrollment Book, 352/CLE/REG/4/1, Liverpool PRO, Picton Library.

(no date, no author given, but presumed to be William H. Wakefield) *The Case Family of Prescott & Liverpool, Pedigree of Case of Thingwall, Lancashire*, Wakefield MSS, 2 of 3, 942/WAK33/103/10, Liverpool PRO, Picton Library.

(no date, no author given, but presumed to be William H. Wakefield) *Our Old Families*, Wakefield MSS, 2 of 3, 942/WAK33/10, Liverpool PRO, Picton Library.

S. Hazard, J. Marshall, R. White, The Apprentice's Monitor; or, INDENTURES IN VERSE, shewing what they are bound to do (1795) No, 27 Queen-Street, Cheap-Side, and No. 4, Aldermary Church Yard; Piccadilly, London.

Records of the Ugly Face Society, 367 UGL/1, Liverpool PRO. Minute and account book," folios 1–2; Index of names, folios 1–3: Rules of the Society, folios.13–20, Listing of members qualifications for admission, Liverpool PRO, Picton Library.

Rate Assessment Book for the Parish of Liverpool (1743), Liverpool PRO, 920/PLU/pt. 51.

Slave Ship Returns, 1771–1774: Peet Papers Concerning the Slave Trade, 1910, D-514/1/8xiii, Sidney Jones Library, Liverpool University.

WILLS

Chester Probate Registry, National Archives, DocumentsOnline.

Will of Josiah Baxendale, Cabinet-maker of Liverpool, Wills and Inventories, Chester Probate Registry, 1764.

Will of Patrick Black, mariner of Liverpool, Wills and Inventories, Chester Probate Registry, Admon., 1776.

Will of John Blackburn of Blakelyhurst, Lancashire, Esquire, Wills and Inventories, Chester Probate Registry, Admon., 1766.

Will of Roger Brooke, merchant of Liverpool, Wills and Inventories, Chester Probate Registry, 1753.

Will of John Brooks of Liverpool, gentleman, Wills and Inventories, Chester Probate Registry, 1779.

Will of Clayton Case, merchant of Liverpool, Wills and Inventories, Chester Probate Registry, 1779.

Will of John Clare, merchant of Liverpool, Wills and Inventories, Chester Probate Registry, August 9, 1802.

Will of Joseph Clare, Sadler of Liverpool, Wills and Inventories, Chester Probate Registry, June 6, 1810.

Will of Thomas Clare, merchant of Liverpool, Wills and Inventories, Chester Probate Registry, September 23, 1816.

Will of James Crosbie, merchant of Liverpool, Wills and Inventories, Chester Probate Registry, 1755.

Will of John Crosbie of Liverpool, gentleman, Wills and Inventories, Chester Probate Registry, 1791.

Will of Nicholas Cross, cabinet-maker of Liverpool, Wills and Inventories, Chester Probate Registry, 1780.

Will of Thomas Galley, boat-builder of Liverpool, Wills and Inventories, Chester Probate Registry.

Will of John Goad, merchant of Liverpool, Wills and Inventories, Chester Probate Registry, 1773.

Will of Robert Jennings, mariner of Liverpool, Wills and Inventories, Chester Probate Registry, 1792.

Will of Thomas Johnson of Liverpool, esquire, Wills and Inventories, Chester Probate Registry, 1771.

Will of Thomas Kendall, merchant of Liverpool, Wills and Inventories, Chester Probate Registry, 1765.

Will of John Livesley, house-builder of Liverpool, Wills and Inventories, Chester Probate Registry, Admon., 1769.

Will of John Okill, timber merchant of Liverpool, Wills and Inventories, Chester Probate Registry, 1773.

Will of William Pownall of Liverpool, esquire, Wills and Inventories, Chester Probate Registry, Admon., 1768.

Will of John Renshaw, roper of Liverpool, Wills and Inventories, Chester Probate Registry, 1742.

Will of Richard Savage of Liverpool, esquire, Wills and Inventories, Chester Probate Registry, 1793.

Will of John Seddon, anchorsmith of Liverpool, Wills and Inventories, Chester Probate Registry, 1759.

Will of Thomas Seel, merchant of Liverpool, Wills and Inventories, Chester Probate Registry, 1755.

Will of John Touchet, merchant of Manchester Limd, Wills and Inventories, Chester Probate Registry, Admon., 1794.

Will of William Trafford, merchant of Liverpool, Wills and Inventories, Chester Probate Registry, 1767.

Will of Levinus (*sic*) Unsworth, merchant of Liverpool, Wills and Inventories, Chester Probate Registry, 1757.

Prerogative Court of Canterbury and related Probate Jurisdictions: Will Registers, National Archives, DocumentsOnline.

Will of Jonathan Brooks of Liverpool, Lancashire, February 9, 1787, PCC: PROB 11/1150.

Will of Joseph Brooks of Liverpool, Lancashire, May 6, 1788, PCC: PROB 11/1165.

Will of Foster Cunliffe of Liverpool, Lancashire, May 19, 1758, PCC: PROB 11/837.

Will of Sir Ellis Cunliffe of Saint George Hanover Square, Middlesex, November 28, 1767, PCC: PROB 11/933.

Will of Sir Robert Cunliffe of Chester, Cheshire, November 27, 1778, PCC: PROB11/1047.

Will of Richard Gildart of Liverpool, Lancashire, February 23, 1770, PCC: PROB 11/955.

Will of Peter Holme, merchant of Childwall, Lancashire, formerly of Liverpool, May 22, 1780, PCC: PROB 11/1065.

Will of John Knight, merchant of Liverpool, Lancashire, December 13, 1774, PCC: PROB 11/1003.

Will of Peter Rigby, merchant and ironmonger of Liverpool, Lancashire July 4, 1795, PCC: PROB 11/1264.

Will of Patrick Savage, October 29,1695, PCC: PROB 11/427239.

Will of Samuel Shaw, December 10, 1781, PCC: PROB 11/1085.

Will of John Welch, merchant of Leck, Lancashire, March 16, 1780, PCC: PROB 11/1063.

Will of Christopher Whytell, merchant of Liverpool, Lancashire, July 3, 1755, PCC: PROB 11/817.

Will of George Lancaster, or Lancester, mariner now bound out on a Voyage to the Coast of Africa in the Honeyford's *Nancy* belonging to Liverpool, Lancashire, August 29, 1764, PCC: PROB 11/901.

PRINTED SOURCES

Primary Sources

Robert Dickinson, ed., *Parish Registers of St. Nicholas, Liverpool*, Lancashire Parish Record Society, vol. 101, part 2, 1705–1725, Liverpool PRO, Picton Library.

John Gore, ed., *The Liverpool Directory, For the Year 1766: Containing An Alphabetical List of the Merchants, Tradesmen, and Principal Inhabitants of the Town of Liverpool* (Liverpool: W. Nevett & Co., 1766).

Harry Hignet, "Extracts from Bryan Blundell, his Journal," http://www.cronab.demon.co. uk/hig.htm, p. 1.

Paul Martin, *The Slave Trade as a Business Enterprise with Particular Reference to Liverpool* (1969) 326.1/ MAR, Liverpool PRO.

Sir Edward Moore, *The Moore Rental, 1667–1668,* ed., Thomas Heywood (1847).

The Norris Papers, ed., Thomas Heywood, in *Remains Historical and Literary Connected with the Palatine Counties of Lancaster and Chester*, vol. 9, (1846).

Selected Burial Records of the Parish of Liverpool at our Lady and St. Nicholas, March 26, 1705–October 1725; Selected Marriage Records of the Parish of Liverpool at Our Lady and St. Nicholas, April 1705–January 1725, *The Cheshire Sheaf, History of Cheshire*, vol. 11 (1882).

Sir James Picton, *Selections from the Municipal Archives and Records, from the 13th to the 17th Century Inclusive* (1883).

The Liverpool Memorandum Book; Assignees of Crosbie to Gregory Olive, Indenture of Release of Plantation Premises, Newfoundland, December 17, 1772, http://ngb.chebucto.org/Articles/1772_indenture.shtml.

Arthur Wardle Transcript, *"Some Inhabitants of Liverpool: 1700–1704,"* MD 168 Liverpool PRO

Secondary Sources

Agnew, Jean. *Belfast Merchant Families in the Seventeenth Century.* 1995.

Anderson, Bruce. "The Lancashire Bill System and its Liverpool Practitioners: The Case of a Slave Merchant," in *Trade and Transport: Essays in Economic in Honor of T.S. Willan*, ed., W.H. Chaloner and Barrie Ratcliffe, 1977.

Anderson, D. "Blundell's Collieries, The Progress of the Business," *Transactions of the Historical Society of Lancashire and Cheshire* 116 (1965): 59–116.

Anstey, Roger. "The Volume and Profitability of British Slave Trade, 1761–1807" in Stanley Engerman and Eugene Genovese, eds. *Race and Slavery in the Western Hemisphere,* 1976.

Arkle, A. H. "The Early Coffee Houses of Liverpool," *Transactions of the Historic Society of Lancashire and Cheshire* 64 (1912): 1–16.

Aughton, Peter. *Liverpool: A People's History.* 1990.

Bailey, F.A. "Early Coalmining in Prescot, Lancashire," *Transactions of the Historical Society of Lancashire and Cheshire,*" 99 (1949): 1–20.

Bailey, F.A. and T.C. Barker. in "The Seventeenth-Century Origins of Watch making in South-West Lancashire," in *Liverpool and Merseyside: Essays in the Economic and Social History of the Port and its Hinterland*, ed. J.R. Harris, 1969.

Baines, Thomas. *History of the Commerce and Town of Liverpool, and of the Rise of Manufacturing Industry in the Adjoining Counties*, 1852.

Barker T.C. "Lancashire Coal, Cheshire Salt, and the Rise of Liverpool," *The Transactions of the Historical Society of Lancashire and Cheshire*, 111 (1951): 83–101.

Barker T.C. "The Failure of Sir Thomas Johnson," *Transactions of the Historical Society of Lancashire and Cheshire* 105 (1953): 203–204.

Bass, R.D. *The Green Dragon.* 1957.

Behrendt, Stephen. "Crew Mortality in the Transatlantic Slave in the Eighteenth Century" in *Routes to Slavery: Direction, Ethnicity and Mortality in the Atlantic Slave Trade*, eds., David Eltis and David Richardson, 1997.

Behrendt, Stephen. "Markets, Transaction Cycles, and Profits: Merchant Decision Making in the British Slave Trade," *William and Mary Quarterly*, 58 (2001): 171–204.

Black, Arthur *et al. The Changing Face of Liverpool, 1207–1727*, 1981.

Bonfield, Lloyd. "Affective Families, Open Elites, and Strict Family Settlements in Early Modern England," *Economic History Review* 29 (1986): 341–354.

Borsay, Peter. *The English Urban Renaissance: Culture and Society in the Provincial Town, 1660–1770.* 1989.

Borsay, Peter. "The London Connection: Cultural Diffusion and the Eighteenth Century Provincial," *London Journal* 19 (1994): 21–35.

Brewer, John. "Commercialization and Politics," in *The Birth of a Consumer Society: The Commercialization of Eighteenth Century England*, ed., Neil McKendrick, John Brewer, and J.H. Plumb. 1982.

Brooke, Richard. *Liverpool as it was During the Last Quarter of the Eighteenth Century, 1775–1800.* 1853.

Brooks, Christopher. "Professions, Ideology, and the Middling Sort in the Late Sixteenth and Early Seventeenth Centuries," in *The Middling Sort of People: Culture, Society, and Politics in England, 1550–1800*, eds., Jonathan Barry and Christopher Brooks, 1994.

Brooks, Christopher. "Apprenticeship, Social Mobility, and the Middling Sort, 1550–1800," in Jonathan Barry and Christopher Brooks, eds., *Middling Sort of People: Culture, Society, and Politics in England, 1550–1800*, 1994.

Angus-Butterworth, L.M. "Liverpool Glassmaking, 1696–1939" *Glass* 24 (1947): 290–1.

Cain, P.J. and A.G. Hopkins. "Gentlemanly Capitalism and British Expansion Overseas: The Old Colonial System, 1688–1850," *Economic History Review* 39 (1986): 501–525.

Carlos Ann M. and Jamie Kruse. "The Decline of the Royal African Company: Fringe Firms and the Role of the Charter," *Economic History Review* 49 (1996): 291–313

Chapman, Stanley. "British Marketing Enterprise: The Changing Roles of Merchants, Manufacturers, and Financiers, 1700–1860," *Business History Review*, 53 (1979): 205–234.

Clark, Peter and Paul Slack. *English Towns in Transition, 1500–1700.* 1976.

Clark, Peter. *British Clubs and Societies, 1580–1800: The Origins of an Associational World.* 2000.

Clemens, Paul G.E. "The Rise of Liverpool, 1665–1750," *Economic History Review* 29 (1976): 211–225.

Copley, Stephen. "Commerce, Conversation, and Politeness in the Early Eighteenth-Century," *The British Journal for Eighteenth-Century Studies* 18 (1995): 63–77.

Corfield, Penelope. *The Impact of English Towns, 1700–1800.* 1982.

Coward, Barry. *Social Change and Continuity: England, 1550–1750.* 1997.

Curtin, Philip. "Epidemiology and the Slave Trade," *Political Science Quarterly*, 83 (1968): 190–216.

Curtin, Philip *et al. African History.* 1978.

Davies, K.G. *The Royal African Company.* 1957.

Davis, Ralph. *The Rise of the English Shipping Industry in the Seventeenth and Eighteenth Centuries.* 1962.

Davis, Ralph. "English Foreign Trade, 1700–1774," *Economic History Review* 15 (1962): 285–303.

Davis, Ralph. *Aleppo and Devonshire Square: English Traders in the Levant in the Eighteenth Century.* 1967.

Defoe, Daniel. *A Tour Through The Whole Island of Great Britain* (1724–6) ed., Pat Rogers. 1978.

Dickinson, H. T. *The Politics of the People in Eighteenth-Century Britain.* 1994.

Dresser, Madge. "Squares of Distinction, Webs of Interest: Gentility, Urban Development and the Slave Trade in Bristol *c.* 1673–1820," *Slavery and Abolition* 21 (2000): 21–47.

Dresser, Madge. *Slavery Obscured: The Social History of the Slave Trade in an English Provincial Port.* 2001.

Duffy, Ian. *Bankruptcy and Insolvency in London during the Industrial Revolution*, 1985.

Earle, T. Algernon. "Earle of Allerton Tower," *Transactions of the Historical Society of Lancashire and Cheshire*, 42 (1890): 15–76.

Earle, Peter. *Sailors: English Merchant Seamen, English Merchant Seamen, 1650–1775.* 1998.

Elder, Melinda. *The Slave Trade and the Economic Development of Eighteenth-Century Lancaster*, 1992.

Eltis David and David Richardson. "Productivity in the Transatlantic Slave Trade," *Explorations in Economic History* 32 (1995): 465–484.

Estabrook, Carl. *Urbane and Rustic England: Cultural Ties and Social Spheres in the Provinces, 1660-1780.* 1998.

Fiennes, Celia. *The Journeys of Celia Fiennes* ed. Christopher Morris, 1947.

Fishwick, H. "Notes on the Hardman Family," *The Transactions of the Historical Society of Lancashire and Cheshire*, 42 (1890): 77–80.

French, Christopher. "Eighteenth-Century Shipping Tonnage Measurements," *The Journal of Economic History* 33 (1973): 434–443.

French, Christopher. "Crowded with Traders and Great Commerce: London's Domination of English Overseas Trade, 1700–1775," *London Journal*, 17 (1992): 27–35.

Friedrichs, Christopher. *Urban Politics in Early Modern Europe.* 2000.

Galenson, David. *Traders, Planters, and Slaves: Market Behavior in Early English America.* 1986.

Gauci, Perry. *The Politics of Trade: The Overseas Merchant in State and Society, 1660–1720.* 2001.

Gnosspelius, Janet and Stanley Harris. "John Moffat and St. Peter's Church, Liverpool," *Transactions of the Historical Society of Lancashire and Cheshire* 130 (1981): 1–14.

Grant, Alexander. "The Cooper in Liverpool," *Industrial Archeology Review*, 1 (1976): 28–36.

Grubb, Farley and Tony Stitt. "The Liverpool Emigrant Servant Trade and the Transition to Slave Labor in the Chesapeake, 1697–1707: Market Adjustments to War," *Explorations in Economic History* 31 (1994): 376–405.

Hancock, David. *Citizens of the World: London Merchants and the Integration of the British Atlantic Community, 1735–1785.* 1995.

John Handley, "Local Initiatives for Economic and Social Development in Lancashire, 1689–1731," *Parliamentary History* 9 (1990): 14–37.

Harris, Ronald. *Industrializing English Law: Entrepreneurship and Business Organization.* 2000.

Hockedy, Doreen M. "Bound for a New World: Emigration of Indentured Servants Via Liverpool to America and the West Indies, 1697–1707," *Transactions of the Historical Society of Lancashire and Cheshire* 144 (1995): 115–135.

Holt, Ann. *Walking Together: A Study in Liverpool Nonconformity, 1688–1938.* 1938.

Hoppitt, Julian. "The Use and Abuse of Credit in Eighteenth-Century England," in *Business Life and Public Policy: Essays in Honor of D.C. Coleman,* eds., Neil McKendrick and R.B. Outhwaite, 1986.

Hoppitt, Julian. *Risk and Failure in English Business, 1700–1800.* 1987.

Julian Hoppitt, *A Land of Liberty? England, 1689–1727.* 2000.

Horn, James *Adapting to a New World: English Society in the Seventeenth Century Chesapeake.* 1994.

Hoskins, W.G. "English Provincial Towns in the Early Sixteenth Century," in *The Early Modern Town,* ed. Peter Clark, 1976.

Hughes, John. *Liverpool Banks and Bankers.* 1906.

Hunt, Margaret. *The Middling Sort: Commerce, Gender, and the Family in England, 1680–1780.* 1996.

Hutton, Ronald. *The Rise and Fall of Merry England: The Ritual Year, 1400–1700.* 1994.

Hyde, Francis, Bradbury Parkinson and Sheila Marriner, "The Nature and Profitability of the Liverpool Slave Trade," *The Economic History Review,* (1953): 368–377.

Hyde, Francis. *Liverpool and the Mersey: An Economic History of a Port, 1700–1970.* 1971.

Inikori, Joseph. "Market Structure and Profits of the British African Trade in the Late Eighteenth Century," *Journal of Economic History,* 41 (1981): 745–776.

Inikori, Joseph. "Measuring the Unmeasured Hazards of the Atlantic Slave Trade: Documents Relating to the British Trade," *Cahiers D'Etudes Africaines* 36 (1996), 55–56.

Jackson, Gordon. *The Trade and Shipping of Eighteenth Century Hull.* 1975.

Jarrett, Derek. *England in the Age of Hogarth.* 1986.

Jarvis, Rupert. "The Illicit Trade with the Isle of Man, 1671–1765," *Transactions of the Historical Society of Lancashire and Cheshire* 58 (1945): 245–267.

Jarvis, Rupert. "The Head Port of Chester; and Liverpool, its Creek and Member," *Transactions of the Historical Society of Lancashire and Cheshire* 102 (1950): 69–84.

John, A.H. "The London Assurance Company and the Marine Insurance Market of the Eighteenth Century," *Economica* 25 (1958): 126–141.

Joslin, D.M. "London Private Bankers, 1720–1785," *The Economic History Review* 7 (1954): 160–179.

Kahl, W.F. "Apprenticeship and the Freedom of the London Livery Companies, 1690–1750," *Guildhall Miscellany*, 7 (1956): 17–20.

Kirby, Joan. "Restoration Leeds and the Aldermen of the Corporation, 1661–1700," *Northern History*, 22 (1986): 123–174.

Kishlansky, Mark. *A Monarchy Transformed: Britain, 1603–1714.* 1996.

Klein, Herbert and Stanley Engerman, "Long-Term Trends in African Mortality in the Transatlantic Slave Trade," *Slavery and Abolition* 18 (1997): 37–49.

Krauseman Ben-Amos, Ilana. "Failure to Become Freemen: Urban Apprentices in Early Modern England," *Social History* 16 (1991): 155–171.

Kurlansky, Mark. *Salt: A World History.* 2002.

Langford, Paul. *A Polite and Commercial People: England, 1727–1783.* 1989.

Langford, Paul. *Public Life and Propertied Englishman, 1689–1798.* 1991.

Langton, John. "Coal Output in South-West Lancashire, 1590–1799," *Economic History Review*, 25 (1972): 28–54.

Littler, Dawn. "The Earle Collection: Records of a Liverpool Family of Merchants and Shipowners," *Transactions of the Historical Society of Lancashire and Cheshire* 146 (1996): 93–106.

Lucas, Paul. "A Collective Biography of Students and Barristers of Lincoln's Inn, 1680–1804: A Study in the 'Aristocratic Resurgence' of the Eighteenth Century," *Journal of Modern History* 46 (1974): 227–261.

Averill Mackenzie-Grieve, *The Last Years of the English Slave Trade: Liverpool, 1750–1807.* 1941.

Marriner, Sheila. *The Economic and Social Development of Merseyside.* 1982.

Martin, Bernard and Martin Spurrell, eds., *The Journal of a Slave Trader.* 1962.

Mathias, Peter. "Risk, Credit, and Kinship in Early Modern Enterprise," in *The Early Modern Atlantic Economy*, eds., John McCusker and Kenneth Morgan. 2000.

McLoughlin, George. *A Short History of the Liverpool Infirmary, 1749–1824.* 1978.

Minchinton, Walter. "Bristol—Metropolis of the West in the Eighteenth Century," *Transactions of the Royal Historical Society* 4 (1953–4): 69–89.

Walter Minchinton, Characteristics of British Slaving Vessels, 1698–1775, "*Journal of Interdisciplinary Studies* 20 (1989), 53–81

Morgan, Gwenda and Peter Rushton, "The Magistrate, the Community and the Maintenance of an Orderly Society in Eighteenth-Century England," *Historical Research* 76 (2003): 54–77.

Morgan, Kenneth. ed., *An American Quaker in the British Isles: The Travel Journals of Jabez Maud Fisher, 1775–1779.* 1992.

Morgan, Kenneth. "Business Networks in the British Export Trade to North America, 1750–1880," in *The Early Modern Atlantic Economy*, eds., John McCusker and Kenneth Morgan. 2000.

Morgan, Kenneth. *Slavery, Atlantic Trade, and the British Economy, 1660–1800.* 2000.

Morgan, Phillip D. *Slave Counterpoint: Black Culture in the Eighteenth-Century Chesapeake and Lowcountry.* 1998.

Mowser, Bruce. "Iles de Loss as a Bulking Center in the Slave Trade," *Revue Francais d'Histoire d'Outre-Mer* (1996): 77–90.

Muir, Ramsay and Elizabeth Platt, *History of the Corporation of Liverpool.* 1906.

Muir, Ramsay and Edith Platt, *History of Municipal Government in Liverpool.* 1906.

Muir, Ramsay *A History of Liverpool.* 1907.

Muir, Ramsay, Henry Young, and Harold Young, *Bygone Liverpool.* 1913.

Mullett, Michael. "The Politics of Liverpool, 1660–88," *Transactions of the Historical Society of Lancashire and Cheshire*, 124 (1972): 31–56.

Neeson, J.M. *Commoners: Common Right, Enclosure, and Social Change in England, 1700–1820.* 1993.

Offer, Avner. "Between the Gift and the Market: The Economy of Regard," *The Economic History Review* 50 (1997): 450–476.

Oxley, G.W. "The Permanent Poor in South-West Lancashire under the Old Poor Law," in *Liverpool and Merseyside: Essays in the Economic and Social History of the Port and its Hinterland*, ed., J.R. Harris, 1969.

Parkinson, C.N. *The Rise of the Port of Liverpool.* 1952.

Peet, Henry. "Liverpool in the Reign of Queen Anne: 1705–1708: From a Rate Assessment Book of the Town and Parish, Giving one of the earliest known lists of Inhabitants, with their respective holdings, by Street: with an Appendix containing Inscriptions from the Monuments and Windows of the Parish Churches, and Abstracts of Several Wills, *Transactions of the Historical Society of Lancashire and Cheshire* 59 (1907): 3–177.

Peet, Henry. "St. Nicholas Church, Liverpool: Its Architectural History," *Transactions of the Historical Society of Lancashire and Cheshire*, 65 (1913): 12–46.

Perkin, Harold. *The Origins of Modern English Society, 1780–1880.* 1969

Phythian-Adams, Charles. "Ceremony and the Citizen: The Communal Year at Coventry, 1450–1550," in *The Early Modern Town*, ed., Peter Clark. 1976.

Pitt-Rivers, Julian. "The Kith and Kin," in Jack Goody, ed., *The Character of Kinship.* 1973.

Platt, Edith "Sir Thomas Johnson," *Transactions of the Historical Society of Lancashire and Cheshire*, 52 (1900): 147–164.

Power, Michael. "Councillors and Commerce in Liverpool, 1650–1750," *Urban History* 24 (1997): 301–323.

Power, Michael. "Politics and Progress in Liverpool, 1660–1740," *Northern History* 35 (1999): 120–138.

Price, Jacob. *Capital and Credit British Overseas Trade: The View from the Chesapeake, 1700–1776*, 1980.

Price, Jacob. "Transaction Costs: A Note on Merchant Credit and the Organization of Private Trade," in *The Political Economy of Merchant Empires: State Power and World Trade, 1350–1750* ed., James Tracy. 1991.

Price, Jacob. "The Great Quaker Business Families of Eighteenth Century London," in *Overseas Trade and Traders: Essays on some Commercial, Financial, and Political Challenges Facing British Atlantic Merchants, 1660–1775.* 1996.

Gordon Reed, *Introduction to the Earle Collection*, D/EARLE/1, Merseyside Maritime Museum

Richardson, David. "Profits in the Liverpool Slave Trade: The Accounts of William Davenport," in *Liverpool, the African Slave Trade, and Abolition*, eds., Roger Anstey and P.E.H. Hair. 1976.

Richardson, David. "West African Consumption Patterns and their Influence on the Eighteenth Century English Slave Trade," in *The Uncommon Market: Essays in the Economic History of the Atlantic Slave Trade*, eds., Henry Gemery and Jan Hogendorn, 1979.

Richardson, David. *The Bristol Slave Traders: A Collective Portrait.* 1985.

Richardson, David. *Bristol, Africa, and the Eighteenth Century Slave Trade to America*, vol.1, *The Years of Expansion, 1698–1729.* 1986.

Richardson, David. "The Eighteenth-Century British Slave Trade: Estimates of its Volume and Coastal Distribution in Africa," *Research in Economic History* 12 (1989): 151–195.

Richardson, David. "Slave Exports from West and West-Central Africa, 1700–1810: New Estimates of Volume and Distribution," *Journal of African History*, 30 (1989): 1–22.

Richardson, David. "Prices of Slaves in West and West-Central Africa: Toward and Annual Series, 1698–1807," *Bulletin of Economic Research* 43 (1991): 21–56.

Richardson, David. *Bristol, Africa, and the Eighteenth Century Slave Trade to America*, vol.4, *The Final Years, 1770–1807*, 1996.

Richardson, David. "The British Empire and the Atlantic Slave Trade, 1660–1807," in *The Oxford History of the British Empire, vol. II, The Eighteenth Century*, ed., P.J. Marshall. 1998.

Richardson, David. "Profitability in the Bristol-Liverpool Slave Trade," *Revue Francais d'Histoire d'Outre-Mer*, 62 (1975): 301–308.

Rideout, Eric H. "The Old Custom House, Liverpool," *Transactions of the Historical Society of Lancashire and Cheshire* 79 (1927): 3–73.

Rogers, Nicholas. "Clubs and Politics in Eighteenth-Century London: The Centenary Club of Cheapside," *London Journal* 11 (1985): 46–70.

Rogers, Nicholas. "The Middling Sort in Eighteenth Century Politics," in *The Middling Sort of People: Culture, Society, and Politics in England, 1550–1800*, eds., Jonathan Barry and Christopher Brooks, 1994.

Sacks, David. *The Widening Gate: Bristol and the Atlantic Economy, 1450–1700*. 1991.

Schochet, Gordon. *The Authoritarian Family and Political Attitudes in Seventeenth Century England: Patriarchalism in Political Thought*. 1988.

Schofield, Maurice. "The Virginia Trade of the Firm of Sparling and Bolden, of Liverpool, 1788–99," *Transactions of the Historical Society of Lancashire and Cheshire* 116 (1964): 117–165.

Schofield, Maurice. "The Slave Trade from Lancashire and Cheshire Ports Outside Liverpool, c. 1750–c.1790," *Transactions of the Historical Society of Lancashire and Cheshire* 126 (1977): 30–73.

Schofield, Maurice. "Chester Slave Trading Partnerships," *Transactions of the Historic Society of Lancashire and Cheshire* 130 (1981): 187–190.

Schofield, Maurice. "Shoes and Ships and Sealing Wax: Eighteenth-Century Lancashire Exports to the Colonies," *Transactions of the Historical Society of Lancashire and Cheshire* 135 (1986): 61–82.

Schofield, Maurice. "A Good Fortune and a Good Wife: The Marriage of Christopher Hassell of Liverpool, Merchant, 1765," *The Transactions of the Historical Society of Lancashire and Cheshire* 138 (1989): 85–111.

Schofield, Maurice. "Lancashire Shipping in the Eighteenth Century: The Rise of A Seafaring Family," *Transactions of the Historical Society of Lancashire and Cheshire* 140 (1991): 1–31.

Serjeant, W.R. "The Tarleton Papers: A Merchants Accounts," *The Liverpool Libraries, Museums, and Arts Committee Bulletin*, 6 (1956): 29–33.

Sharpe, J.A. *Early Modern England, A Social History, 1550–1760*. 1987.

Shaw, George. "History of the Liverpool Directories, 1766–1907," *Transactions of the Historical Society of Lancashire and Cheshire* 58 (1907): 113–162.

Sheridan, Richard. "The Commercial and Financial Organization of the British Slave Trade, 1750–1807," *Economic History Review* 11 (1958): 249–263.

Singleton, F. J. "The Flax Merchants of Kirkham," *Transactions of the Historical Society of Lancashire and Cheshire* 126 (1977): 73–108.

Slack, Paul. *The English Poor Law, 1531–1782.* 1990.

Smelser, Marshall and William Davisson, "The Longevity of Colonial American Shipping," *American Neptune* 33 (1973): 16–19.

Smith, Adam. *The Theory of Moral Sentiments*, eds., D.D. Raphael and A.L. Macfie. 1976.

Steele, Ian. *The English Atlantic, 1675–1740: An Exploration of Communication and Community.* 1986.

Stein, Robert. *The French Slave Trade in the Eighteenth Century: An Old Regime Business.* 1979.

Stewart-Brown, Ronald. "The Tower of Liverpool, with some notes on the Clayton Family of Crooke, Fulwood, Adlington, and Liverpool," *Transactions of the Historical Society of Lancashire and Cheshire* 61 (1909): 41–82.

Stewart-Brown, Ronald. "The Townfield of Liverpool, 1207–1807," *Transactions of the Historical Society of Lancashire and Cheshire*, 68 (1916): 24–72.

Stewart-Brown, Ronald. "Early Coffee Houses of Liverpool," *Transactions of the Historical Society of Lancashire and Cheshire*, 68 (1916): 1–16

Stewart-Brown, Ronald. "The Pool of Liverpool," *Transactions of the Historical Society of Lancashire and Cheshire*, 82 (1930): 88–135

Stewart-Brown, Ronald. "Tarleton of Fazakerley, Aigburth, Liverpool, and Bolesworth Castle," *The Cheshire Sheaf* (1930): 193–206.

Stewart-Brown, Ronald. *Liverpool Ships in the Eighteenth Century: Including the King's Ships Built there, with Notes on the Principal Shipwrights* (1932)

Stone, Lawrence. *The Family, Sex, and Marriage in England.* 1977.

Sweet, Rosemary. *The English Town, 1680–1840: Government, Society, and Culture.* 1999.

Swett, Katharine. "The Account Between Us: Honor, Reciprocity and Companionship in Male Friendship in the Later Seventeenth Century," *Albion*, 31 (1999): 45–67.

Tadmor, Naomi. *Family and Friends in Eighteenth Century England: Household, Kinship, and Patronage.* 2001.

Tattersfield, Nigel. *The Forgotten Trade: Comprising the Log of the Daniel & Henry of 1700 and Accounts of the Slave Trade from the Minor Ports of England, 1698–1725.* 1991.

Thomas, E.G. "The Old Poor Law and Maritime Apprenticeship," *Mariner's Mirror* 63 (1977): 153–161.

Trumbach, Randolph. *The Rise of the Egalitarian Family: Aristocratic Kinship and Domestic Relations in Eighteenth-Century England.* 1978.

Truxes, Thomas. *Irish-American Trade, 1660–1783.* 1988.

Truxes, Thomas ed. *Letterbook of Greg & Cunningham, Merchants of New York and Belfast.* 2001.

Tyler, John W. "Foster Cunliffe and Sons: Liverpool Merchants in the Maryland Tobacco Trade, 1738–1765," *Maryland Historical Magazine,* 78 (1978): 246–277.

Wardle, Arthur. "Sir Thomas Johnson: His Impecuniosity and Death," *Transactions of the Historical Society of Lancashire and Cheshire,* 90 (1938): 181–195.

Wardle, Arthur. "The Opening of the First Liverpool Dock, 1715," *Transactions of the Historical Society of Lancashire and Cheshire,* 93 (1941): 128–130.

Wardle, Arthur. "Some Glimpses of Liverpool during the first half of the Eighteenth Century," *Transactions of the Historical Society of Lancashire and Cheshire,* 93 (1941): 145–157.

Wardle, Arthur. "The Customs Collection of the Port of Liverpool," *Transactions of the Historical Society of Lancashire and Cheshire,* 99 (1949): 31–40.

Whyman, Susan. "Land and Trade: The Case of John Verney, London Merchant and Baronet, 1660–1720," *London Journal* 22 (1997): 16–32.

Whyman, Susan. *Sociability and Power in Late-Stuart England: The Cultural Worlds of the Verneys, 1660–1720.* 1999.

Wilkins, Frances. *Manx Slave Traders: A Social History of the Isle of Man's Involvement in the Atlantic Slave Trade.* 1999.

Williams, Gomer. *History of the Liverpool Privateers and Letters of Marque with an Account of the Liverpool Slave Trade.* 1897.

Wilson, Kathleen. *The Sense of the People: Politics, Culture, and Imperialism in England, 1715–1785.* 1998.

Wilson, R.G. *Gentlemen Merchants: The Merchant Community in Leeds, 1700–1830.* 1971.

Wokeck, Marianne S. *Trade in Strangers: The Beginnings of Mass Migration to North America.* 1999

Wood, Peter H. *Black Majority: Negroes in Colonial South Carolina from 1670 through the Stono Rebellion.* 1974.

Wrigley, E.A. "Urban Growth and Agricultural Change: England and the Continent in the Early Modern Period," *Journal of Interdisciplinary History,* 15 (1985): 37–56.

Wunderli, Richard. "Evasion of the Office of Alderman in London, 1523–1672," *London Journal* 15 (1990): 3–18.

Zahedieh, Nuala. "Making Mercantilism Work: London Merchants and Atlantic Trade in the Seventeenth Century," *Transactions of the Royal Historical Society*, 9 (1999): 143–158.

Appendix

Chapter 2

2.1 LORD MAYORS OF LIVERPOOL, 1695–1775 (SLAVE TRADERS IN ITALICS)

1695.	Sir Thomas Johnson Jr.
1696.	William Preeson
1697.	James Benn
1698.	Thomas Sweeting
1699.	Cuthbert Sharples
1700.	Richard Norris
1701.	Thomas Bickesteth
1702.	John Cockshutt
1703.	*John Cleveland*
1704.	William Hurst
1705.	William Webster
1706.	Sylvester Moorcroft
1707.	James, Earl of Darby
1708.	John Seacome
1709.	*John Earle*
1710.	*George Tyrer*
1711.	James Townsend
1712.	Edward Tarleton
1713.	Thomas Core
1714.	*Richard Gildart*
1715.	William Squire
1716.	*Foster Cunliffe*
1717.	Richard Kelsall
1718.	Josiah Poole
1719.	Thomas Fillingham

1720.	Henry Taylor
1721.	*Bryan Blundell*
1724.	John Goodwin
1725.	William Marsden
1726.	Thomas Bootle *(resigned)*
1727.	*John Hughes*
1728.	*Bryan Blundell*
1729.	*Foster Cunliffe*
1730.	*George Tyrer*
1731.	*Richard Gildart*
1732.	Thomas Brereton
1733.	William Pole
1734.	James, Earl of Derby
1735.	*Foster Cunliffe*
1736.	*Richard Gildart*
1737.	*George Norton*
1738.	*Robert Armitage*
1739.	Thomas Steers
1740.	*Henry Trafford (died in office)*
1741.	William Carr
1742.	*Edward Trafford*
1743.	*John Brooks*
1744.	*Owen Pritchard*
1745.	James Blomfield
1746.	*Joseph Bird*
1747.	Thomas Shaw
1748.	Joseph Clegg
1749.	Joseph Davies
1750.	*James Gildart*
1751.	*Edmund Rigby*
1752.	Henry Winstanley
1753.	*James Crosbie*
1754.	*Charles Goore*
1755.	*Spencer Steers*
1756.	*Richard Hughes*
1757.	*William Goodwin*
1758.	*Robert Cunliffe*
1759.	*Lawrence Spencer*
1760.	*John Blackburn*
1761.	*William Williamson*
1762.	*William Gregson*
1763.	*George Campbell*
1764.	*John Tarleton*
1765.	*John Crosbie*
1766.	*Thomas Johnson*
1767.	*William Pownall (died in office)*
1768.	*Matthew Strong*
1769.	*Ralph Earle*
1770.	*John Sparling*
1771.	Thomas Wilson
1772.	*Thomas Golightly*

1773.	*John Parr*
1774.	*Peter Rigby*

Source: Thomas Baines, *History of the Commerce and Town of Liverpool, and of the Rise of Manufacturing Industry in the Adjoining Counties*, (1852); Richard Brooke, *Liverpool as it was During the Last Quarter of the Eighteenth, 1775–1800*, 1853; Henry Peet, *Liverpool in the Reign of Queen Anne* (1908).

2.2 LIVERPOOL BAILIFFS, 1695–1775 (SLAVE TRADERS IN ITALICS)

1695.	Richard Norris, Levinius Houston
1696.	Cuthbert Sharples, William Reynolds
1697.	Joseph Briggs, John Crane
1698.	John Cockshutt, John Lady
1699.	Robert Shields, James Kennion
1700.	J. Gibbons, Sylvester Moorcroft
1701.	John Crompton, John Proctor
1702.	John Seacome, William Webster
1703.	Charles Diggles, Joseph Eaton
1704.	Peter Hull, Robert Benson
1705.	*John Earle*, John Fells
1706.	William Squire, Thomas Cooke
1707.	Josiah Poole, Henry Clarke
1708.	*Foster Cunliffe*, John Wainwright
1709.	Francis Goodrich, Henry Taylor
1710.	Edward Tarleton, John Hughes
1711.	Richard Kelsall, Thomas Kendrick
1712.	William Braddock, *Richard Gildart*
1713.	*John Hughes (?)*, John Murray
1714.	Thomas *Fillingham*, John Litherland
1715.	Edward Ratchdale, Samuel Richardson
1716.	Richard Aspinall, William Marsden
1717.	James Halsall, *George Norton*
1718.	*Robert Armitage, John Goodwin*
1719.	John Scarisbrick, Thomas Steers
1720.	Edward Beckwith, *Henry Trafford*
1721.	*John Goodwin*, George Taylor
1722.	William Furnival, William Carr
1723.	Robert Hornby, James Shaw
1724.	*Charles Pole*, Peter Rainford
1725.	Robert Hornby, James Shaw
1726.	John Martindale, Robert Whitfield
1727.	Josiah Poole, *Foster Cunliffe*
1728.	*George Tyrer*, Thomas Blease
1729.	Robert Whitfield, *William Pole*
1730.	John Martindale, Edward Litherland
1731.	Thomas Steers, Philip Wilcox
1732.	*Edward Trafford, Robert Dixon*
1733.	*John Brooks, Owen Pritchard*
1734.	*George Tyrer, John Hughes (?)*
1735.	John Scarisbrick, *Bryan Blundell*

1736.	*Johnson Gildart*, James Brookfield
1737.	George Wilkinson, William Hornby
1738.	*Joseph Bird*, Thomas Shaw
1739.	Joseph Clegg, Joseph Davies
1740.	*James Gildart*, William Barlow
1741.	*Edmund Rigby*, Henry Winstanley
1742.	*George Gildart, Thomas Ball*
1743.	Edward Forbes, Robert Mercer
1744.	James Kelsall, William Penketh
1745.	*Spencer Steers*, Robert Fillingham
1746.	Lawrence Spencer, William Hornby
1747.	*Charles Goore*, James Kelsall
1748.	*James Crosbie, Richard Cribb*
1749.	*John Ashton*, William Hornby
1750.	*Ellis Cunliffe, Richard Blundell*
1751.	*William Goodwin, Matthew Strong*
1752.	*Robert Cunliffe, Richard Hughes*
1753.	*Scrope Colquitt*, Oliver Castland
1754.	William Armitage, Laurence Carr
1755.	*Richard Trafford, John Blackburn*
1756.	*George Campbell*, James Jackson
1757.	*Joseph Manesty, John Parr*
1758.	*Thomas Johnson*, Ralph Peters
1759.	Joshua Jackson, *John Williamson*
1760.	*Robert Armitage, William Gregson*
1761.	*Roger Parr, Ralph Earle*
1762.	*John Crosbie, William Pownall*
1763.	*Peter Rigby, William Boates*
1764.	*Jonathan Blundell, Edward Parr*
1765.	*James Bridge*, Thomas Wilson
1766.	*William Crosbie, Henry Trafford II*
1767.	William Pickering, *John Hughes*
1768.	*Richard Powell, John Sparling*
1769.	*William Pole, John Parr*
1770.	*John Brown, Thomas Golightly*
1771.	*Thomas Birch, Thomas Earle*
1772.	*Thomas Rumbold*, Richard Stratham
1773.	*James Clemens, Dr. Richard Gerrard*
1774.	John Colquitt, *James Gildart*
1775.	*William Crosbie Jr., George Case*

Source: Thomas Baines, *History of the Commerce and Town of Liverpool, and of the Rise of Manufacturing Industry in the Adjoining Counties*, (1852); Richard Brooke, *Liverpool as it was During the Last Quarter of the Eighteenth, 1775–1800*, 1853; Henry Peet, *Liverpool in the Reign of Queen Anne* (1908).

Appendix

Chapter 4

4.1 DESCRIPTIONS OF MEMBERS OF THE UGLY FACE CLUB

John Tarleton, Draper:
"Hollow eyed, long nose, very thin lips, wide mouth, no upper teeth. An odd effeminate way & grim. Smack faced."

John Williamson, Merchant:
"Ruff face[,] Bleary eyes[,] flowing like two fountains[,] Monstrous long nose[,] Hooked like an eagles beak[,] Pretty large mouth."

John Parr, Sr., Merchant:
"Broad Punch-like face[,] Flat nose[,] Wide nostrils[,] Large mouth[,] Thick Lips[,] Stern looks[,] Hideous Grin."

Capt. Nicholas Southworth:
"A fine yellow guinea complexion[,] Large nostrils, Negro nosed[,] Hollow forehead[,] Long....chin[,] on the whole resembles Thom Thumb in a puppet show"

The Honorable Walter Sherby of the City of London
"Aged about twenty two years; of a death like UNFINISHED

Thomas Widdens of Wirral, Merchant.
"A Long.....phiz Pig eyed, long nose[,] long chin. Resembles the picture of Capt. Flash in the *London Magazine* of April 1747"

George Mercer, Merchant
"A round face[,] tallow complexion[,] Bushy eyebrows[,] bottle nose[,] little or no chin[,] wide mouth[,] blubber lipped[,] a monkey like grin. On the whole a well qualified member"

Robert Moss Esq., Chancellor at law
"A long....visage[,] lantern jaws[,] hollow pigs eyes[,] large nose[,] a prodigious wide mouth[,] especially when he laughs. Looks like a Grub street poet half-starved"

Lewis August Young of Liverpool, M.D.
"A large Carbuncle Potato nose, fine bushy Eye Brows[,] an agreeable facetious Grin, wide Mouth when he laughs[,] carries the shape of the Moon at a Quarter Old, on the whole a face fitting a member of this society"

William Tunball, of Tortola Merchant, September 9, 1749
"A Mahogany Complexion, carved face, Negro Teeth[,] lantern jawed & sharp monkey chin & wt ones seldom sees in [the] same person/gray eyes & black eye brows/a fine grin & every way an excellent member"

Peter Holme, Merchant of Liverpool, November 13, 1749
"A pale complexion with a forehead half his face[,] squinting pig eyes[,] sharp hooked-nose[,] wide mouth[,] narrow teeth[,] long chin[,] queer grin, [as a member], eminently well qualified."

Captain James Stewart of Liverpool, July 23, 1750
"A mahogany complexion[,] deep furrowed cheeks[,] a hawks bill nose[,] a sharks mouth[,] a blinkered Japanezy Grin[,] ...fit & qualified in every feature for this honorable Society."

Captain William. Hayes of Liverpool, July 7, 1750
"A Numidian complexion[,] platter face[,] pig eyes[,] bottle nose[,] shark? mouth[,] prominent chin & ...shorter Sancho Panchopean features

Captain Thomas Marsden of Liverpool, November 26, 1750
"*Vide* his brother John Marsden page 26 his qualifications but larger nose & less chin

Mr. John Woods, of Liverpool, architect, July 22, 1751
"A stone colored complexion, a dimple on his Attic Story, the Pilasters of his face fluted, tortoise eyed--a prominent nose, wild grin, & face altogether resembling a badger at times, though smaller than Sir Christopher Wren's or Inigo Jones's"

Arthur Hamilton, Merchant in Liverpool, September 25, 1752
"A Covent Garden Complexion[,] A fine Prominent nose with a scar on the bridge[,] a shark mouth with ragged lips[,] Lantern Jaws: a facetious grin: upon the whole well Qualified"

Thomas Wycliffe, Merchant in Liverpool, January 22, 1753
"A Ghost like Complexion[,] Goggle Eyed[,] a fine shriveled face, a Marl Pitt in his chin[,] tumors in his cheeks[,] Bushy Eye brows: on the whole a picture of a hard winter with a ghastly grin"

Isaac Blackwood, Merchant in Liverpool, January 22, 1753
"Sharp Nose, Large Eye Brows[,] Double Chin, his nose and chin meets together like a pair of Nut Crackers[,] Chub cheeks[,] thin lips[,] a sparrow mouth & racked teeth[,] a Dish face[.] Affect is grim."

Richardson Douglas, Merchant in Drury Lane October 31, 1753
"A Good...Blunt face [,] Mace Horn Look [,] Irregular set of Features [,] Facetious Grin [,] Hutton lipped [,] Irregular set of Teeth [,] Freckled face."

John Kennion Esq. of Kingston in Jamaica, January 26, 1756
"A Jewish phiz and Negro grin[,] a Dutch Dark Countenance[,] Sank cheek[,] large mouth[,] Black Bushy Eyebrows and well Qualifies for a member."

The Reverend Mr. Thomas Mallory LLB April 28, 1756
"Of the Vicar of Bray type[,] well set off with a pipe[,] a merry grin[,] a roguish eye, white eyebrows[,] A good smoker and well qualified for chaplain to the club."

Captain William Boates, Liverpool, April 28, 1756
"A Phuged face: a turtle nose, pig Eyes[,] sallow complexion much jontured by going to Africa; ghastly grin: freckled face & upon the whole well Qualified"

Thomas Hodgson, merchant and Doctor of Music [1756]
"A Razor bill nose [,] Jewish eyes [,] a face long chin....UNFINISHED

Mr. Robert Armitage, Merchant, Liverpool, January 14, 1757
"A fine Razor bill nose [,] small pig eyes: an irregular set of Teeth [,] a Comical grin & a farmer's Countenance & a Claret like bluster[,] on the whole a good Member"

Mr. Thos. Hodgson of Leghorn, November 3, 1757
"A forehead as round as a flask, an olive eye, a nose resembling a chest of Florence, a tongue like an anchovy, a facetious Grin, on the whole a proper member"

Mr. John Reilly, Merchant of Dublin, November 3, 1757
"A fine Claret complexion, a hedge hog forehead, fine Bushy eyebrows, a bottled nose, a good facetious grin, on the whole duly qualified"

Source: Records of the Ugly Face Society, 367 UGL/1, Liverpool PRO. Minute and account book, folios 1–2; Index of names

Appendix

Chapter 5

Table 5.1	*Numbers of Sole Traders in the Liverpool Slave Trade, 1695–1775*		
Year	Number of Ventures	Sole Traders	Percentage
1747	25	9	36%
1748	43	5	12%
1749	15	1	7%
1750	40	2	5%
1751	41	3	7%
1752	46	2	4%
1753	61	2	3%
1754	60	3	5%
1755	40	3	7%
1756	53	2	4%
1757	44	2	4%
1758	51	4	8%
1759	61	2	3%
1760	73	3	4%
1761	69	2	3%
1762	56	3	5%
1763	70	3	4%
1764	73	3	4%
1765	75	7	9%
1766	57	9	16%
1767	77	8	10%
1768	79	15	19%
1769	89	13	15%
1770	89	24	27%
1771	94	20	21%

Table 5.1   *Numbers of Sole Traders in the Liverpool Slave Trade, 1695–1775 (Continued)*

Year	Number of Ventures	Sole Traders	Percentage
1772	96	19	20%
1773	104	25	24%
1774	89	32	36%
1775	32	9	28%

Source: TSTD.

Table 5.2   *Proportion of Merchants/Partners versus Captain/Partners* per *Number of Ventures*

	Total Number of Partners	Total Merchant/Partners	Total Current Captain/ Partners or Partners with experience as Captain
1–10	762	572 (75%)	192 (25%)
11–20	113	83 (73%)	30 (27%)
21–131	112	79 (70.5%)	33 (29.5%)
Totals	987	732 (74%)	252 (26%)

Source: TSTD.

Table 5.3   *Numbers of Partners in Liverpool Slaving Ventures per Year, 1747–1775*

Year	Voyages	1–3	4–6	7–9	10 & over	Not specified
1747	25	14	8	2	1	—
1748	43	9	22	9	2	1
1749	15	6	6	3	—	—
1750	40	11	18	10	1	—
1751	42	15	19	7	1	—
1752	45	11	23	11	—	—
1753	61	14	35	9	1	2
1754	60	14	33	13	—	—
1755	40	8	21	10	1	—
1756	52	7	29	15	1	—
1757	44	6	26	10	2	—
1758	54	15	22	15	2	—
1759	59	20	30	11	—	—
1760	72	20	33	19	—	—
1761	69	21	31	16	1	—
1762	56	16	25	17	2	—
1763	69	22	27	17	1	2
1764	74	30	25	18	1	—
1765	75	33	22	16	3	1
1766	56	24	20	9	2	1

Table 5.3 Numbers of Partners in Liverpool Slaving Ventures per Year, 1747–1775 (Continued)

Year	Voyages	1–3	4–6	7–9	10 & over	Not specified
1767	76	36	21	16	2	1
1768	78	41	24	13	—	—
1769	88	38	33	17	—	—
1770	90	41	40	17	2	—
1771	94	47	25	21	1	—
1772	96	49	35	10	2	—
1773	99	50	27	17	5	—
1774	85	49	23	9	4	—
1775	32	17	9	2	1	3

Source: TSTD.

Table 5.4 Size of Liverpool Slaving Partnerships per Year as listed in the TSTD, 1747–1775

Year	Ventures	1	2	3	4	5	6	7	8	9	10+	NS
1747	25	9	1	4	3	2	3	1	1	0	1	0
1748	43	5	2	2	4	8	10	2	5	2	3	1
1749	15	1	3	2	2	2	2	1	2	0	0	0
1750	40	2	5	2	7	9	3	6	1	1	0	0
1751	41	3	1	10	4	7	8	3	4	0	1	0
Total	*164*	*20*	*12*	*20*	*20*	*23*	*26*	*13*	*13*	*3*	*5*	*1*
1752	46	2	1	6	8	4	11	5	6	0	0	0
1753	61	2	5	6	11	7	17	3	5	1	1	2
1754	60	3	5	6	5	17	11	6	5	2	0	0
1755	40	3	1	4	5	8	6	5	3	2	0	0
Total	*207*	*10*	*12*	*22*	*29*	*36*	*45*	*19*	*19*	*5*	*1*	*2*
1756	53	2	2	3	6	12	11	13	2	1	1	0
1757	44	2	0	4	6	8	12	6	2	1	2	0
1758	51	4	4	7	10	7	5	10	0	1	2	0
1759	61	2	4	12	11	4	11	5	4	4	0	0
Total	*209*	*12*	*10*	*26*	*23*	*31*	*39*	*34*	*8*	*7*	*5*	*0*
1760	73	3	6	11	9	6	18	13	5	1	0	0
1761	69	2	7	10	12	9	12	10	3	3	0	0
1762	56	3	4	5	10	4	11	11	3	3	2	0
1763	70	3	8	12	11	8	8	5	11	1	0	0
Total	*268*	*11*	*25*	*38*	*42*	*27*	*49*	*39*	*22*	*8*	*2*	*0*
1764	73	3	11	15	13	5	7	9	5	4	1	0
1765	75	7	10	16	8	6	8	6	7	3	3	1
1766	57	9	8	7	11	5	4	4	3	2	0	1
1767	77	8	17	7	4	11	6	5	9	2	1	1
Total	*282*	*27*	*46*	*45*	*36*	*27*	*25*	*24*	*24*	*11*	*5*	*3*

Table 5.4 *Size of Liverpool Slaving Partnerships* per *Year as listed in the TSTD, 1747–1775 (Continued)*

Year	Ventures	↔————Number of Partners *per* Venture————↔										
		1	*2*	*3*	*4*	*5*	*6*	*7*	*8*	*9*	*10+*	*NS*
1768	79	15	11	15	7	8	9	4	7	2	0	0
1769	89	13	10	15	7	9	9	6	8	3	0	0
1770	89	24	11	6	10	11	9	6	8	3	2	0
1771	94	20	11	16	10	7	8	11	6	4	1	0
Total	*351*	*72*	*43*	*52*	*34*	*35*	*35*	*27*	*29*	*12*	*3*	*0*
1772	96	19	12	19	11	13	11	5	5	0	2	0
1773	104	25	6	19	17	5	5	10	4	3	5	0
1774	89	32	5	12	10	6	7	4	4	1	1	0
1775	32	4	4	2	6	2	1	0	2	0	1	9
Total	*321*	*80*	*27*	*52*	*44*	*30*	*24*	*19*	*15*	*4*	*9*	*9*
Totals	1802	232	175	255	228	209	243	175	152	50	30	15

Source: TSTD.

Table 5.5 *Distribution of the Regional Trade of the 26 Largest Liverpool Slave Traders, 1744–1775*

Name	Gambia	Sierra Leone	Wind. Coast	Gold Coast	Bight of Benin	Bight of Biafra	West Central Africa	Not Spec.
1. W. James	1	4	75	7	9	34	2	—
2. J. Knight	30	2	4	19	17	42	2	10
3. Davenport	8	2	4	1	5	50	30	—
4. R. Green	2	0	35	4	1	30	10	1
5. W. Gregson	1	0	6	16	9	52	10	1
6. W. Earle	1	1	20	5	4	48	2	—
7. J. Welch	1	1	7	5	18	24	6	14
8. J. Crosbie	2	1	17	3	1	39	14	1
9. R. Savage	2	1	12	31	13	20	4	—
10. W. Boates	1	0	4	27	15	37	2	—
11. S. Shaw	19	7	9	0	1	35	5	2
12. J. Blundell	2	2	3	1	0	53	14	—
13. Salthouse	0	7	46	6	4	9	1	1
14. W. Dobb	2	8	25	5	9	16	4	1
15. Rumbold	10	4	7	6	11	27	5	—
16. W. Crosbie	0	1	17	3	1	31	14	—
17. B. Blundell	14	4	4	0	0	32	14	1
18. A Heywood	4	3	11	21	2	14	7	5
19. G. Hutton	0	0	40	3	1	9	3	0
20. T. Foxcroft	0	6	45	4	2	9	0	0
21. B Heywood	3	4	10	24	2	12	6	2

Table 5.5 *Distribution of the Regional Trade of the 26 Largest Liverpool Slave Traders, 1744–1775 (Continued)*

Name	Gambia	Sierra Leone	Wind. Coast	Gold Coast	Bight of Benin	Bight of Biafra	West Central Africa	Not Spec.
22. J. White	0	3	24	3	11	18	3	0
23. T. Johnson	0	8	34	7	3	7	1	0
24. W Trafford	3	2	12	3	1	24	13	0
25. E. Parr	1	1	5	5	16	18	5	2
26. M. Barber	9	29	3	2	1	2	5	1

Source: TSTD. Due to gaps in the record, Foster Cunliffe, Felix Doran, Samuel Ogden, and Robert Armitage are excluded.

Figure 5.6 *Primary Trading Regions for the Leading Liverpool Slave Traders, 1695–1775*

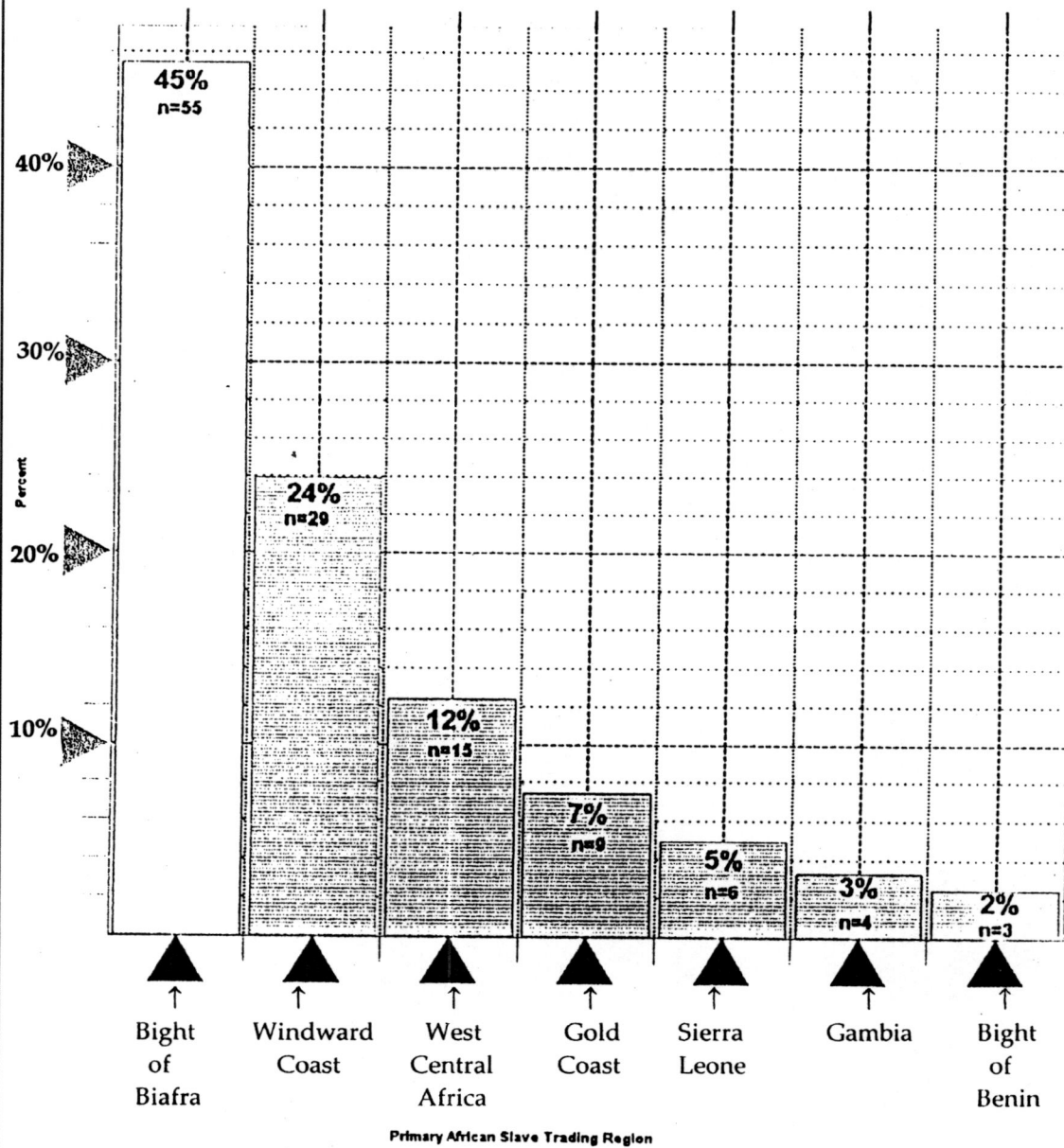

Source: TSTD.

Appendix

Chapter 6

Table 6.1	*Intended* versus *Actual Regions of Slave Embarkation, 1695–1775*								
Intended Points↓	↓Actual Points→								
	Sene-gambia	Sierra Leone	Wind-ward Coast	Gold Coast	Bight of Benin	Bight of Biafra	Angola	Not Speci-fied	Total
Sene-gambia	90	1	7	2	1	—	—	12	113
Sierra Leone	1	88	18	4	1	—	—	8	120
Windward Coast	15	14	344	21	9	5	1	36	445
Gold Coast	—	2	5	112	4	7	—	5	135
Bight of Benin	1	3	3	7	99	2	2	13	130
Bight of Biafra	4	2	4	5	3	418	5	17	460
Angola	—	2	2	2	1	1	—	8	16
Not Specified	27	5	5	21	4	32	21	450	565
Total	138	117	388	174	122	465	29	549	1984

Source: TSTD. The Cameroons and Gabon are not included in Angola.

Table 6.2 *Number of Slaves Intended to Purchase by Points of Embarkation, 1695–1775*

Gambia, Not specified	195.98
Sierra Leone, Not specified	229.56
Iles de Loss, Sierra Leone	218.04
Bananas Islands, Sierra Leone	196.00
Sherbro, Sierra Leone	151.43
Windward Coast, Not specified	214.82
Gold Coast, Not specified	244.81
Anomabu, Gold Coast	313.29
Whydah, Bight of Benin	399.30
Benin, Bight of Benin	317.27
Popo, Bight of Benin	198.82
Bonny, Bight of Biafra	417.21
Old Calabar, Bight of Biafra	341.12
New Calabar, Bight of Biafra	318.00
Angola, Not specified	389.83
Cameroons, Not specified	226.96
Gabon, Not specified	191.94

Source: TSTD.

Table 6.3 *Annual Distribution of Ship Tonnages in the Liverpool Slave Trade, 1747–1775*

Year	Total Ventures	10–70 Tons	71–139 Tons	140 Tons +	Not Specified
1747	25	7/28%	11/44%	7/28%	0/—
1748	42	11/26%	25/59%	5/12%	1/2%
1749	18	2/11%	9/50%	6/33%	1/5%
1750	40	14/35%	22/55%	4/10%	0/—
1751	41	15/36%	21/51%	5/12%	0/—
1752	45	17/38%	25/56%	3/6%	0/—
1753	61	20/33%	29/47%	10/16%	2/3%
1754	60	24/40%	31/52%	4/6%	1/2%
1755	40	16/40%	20/50%	4/10%	0/—
1756	53	22/41	30/57%	1/2%	0/—
1757	44	19/43%	18/41%	6/14%	1/2%
1758	51	20/39%	23/45%	7/14%	1/2%
1759	61	20/33%	27/44%	13/21%	1/2%
1760	72	27/37%	29/40%	16/22%	1/1%
1761	69	2435%	30/43%	15/22%	0/—
1762	56	17/30%	27/48%	12/21%	0/—
1763	70	24/34%	35/50%	9/13%	2/3%
1764	73	22/30%	38/52%	13/18%	0/—
1765	75	21/28%	40/53%	12/16%	2/3%
1766	57	15/26%	34/60%	8/14%	0/—

Table 6.3		*Annual Distribution of Ship Tonnages in the Liverpool Slave Trade, 1747–1775 (Continued)*			
Year	Total Ventures	10–70 Tons	71–139 Tons	140 Tons +	Not Specified
1767	77	22/29%	45/58%	9/12%	1/1%
1768	78	18/23%	50/64%	10/13%	0/—
1769	88	28/32%	47/53%	13/15%	0/—
1770	90	24/27%	57/63%	9/10%	0/—
1771	94	24/25%	54/57%	15/16%	1/1%
1772	96	28/30%	54/56%	13/13%	1/1%
1773	104	29/28%	55/53%	16/15%	4/4%
1774	88	27/31%	37/42%	20/23%	4/4%
1775	32	7/22%	15/47%	9/28%	1/3%

Source: TSTD.

Figure 6.4   *Number of Liverpool Slaving Ventures per Year, 1747–1775*

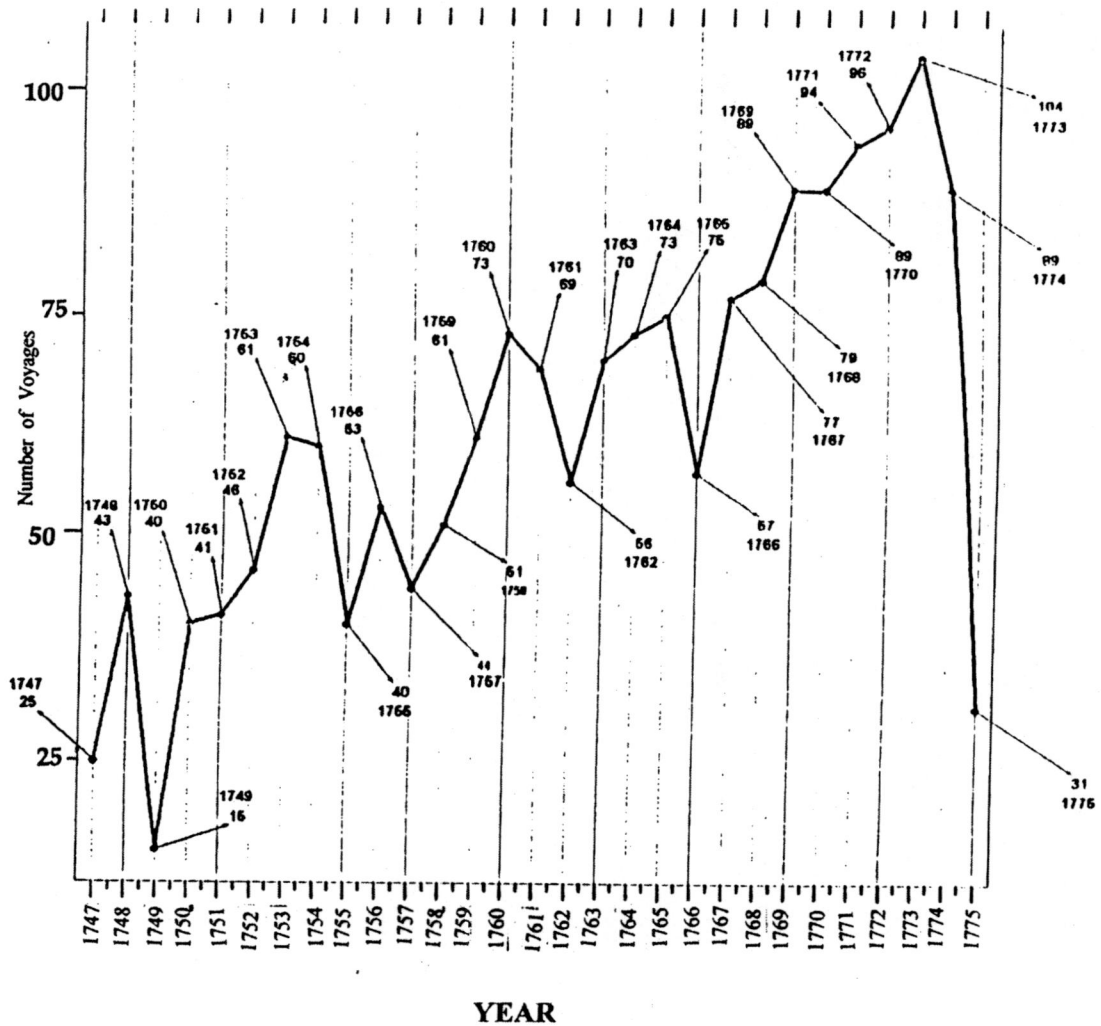

Number of Voyages (y-axis): 25, 50, 75, 100

YEAR (x-axis): 1747, 1748, 1749, 1750, 1751, 1752, 1753, 1754, 1755, 1756, 1757, 1758, 1759, 1760, 1761, 1762, 1763, 1764, 1765, 1766, 1767, 1768, 1769, 1770, 1771, 1772, 1773, 1774, 1775

Data labels shown on the chart:
1747 25; 1748 43; 1749 15; 1750 40; 1751 41; 1752 46; 1753 61; 1754 60; 1755 53; 1756 40; 1757 44; 1758 51; 1759 61; 1760 73; 1761 69; 1762 56; 1763 70; 1764 73; 1765 75; 1766 57; 1767 77; 1768 79; 1769 89; 1770 89; 1771 94; 1772 96; 1773 104; 1774 89; 1775 31

YEAR

Source: TSTD.

6.6 A *Prince Vada* Partners

All Liverpool slaving voyages listed below were extracted from the *Transatlantic Slave Trade* database and were assigned a number based upon the year and month of departure from Liverpool. For example, the *Prince Vada* was the 1,092nd venture to leave Liverpool between 1695 and 1775, and is therefore listed below as *Prince Vada/*1092)

1. William Earle (1721–1788) Alderman John Earle's fourth and youngest surviving son, William Earle was a Guinea captain, general merchant, slave trader, and ironmonger of Redcross Street, Liverpool, and the Brick House in West Derby Village. (*Liverpool Directory of 1766;* T. Algernon Earle, "Earle of Allerton Tower," *The Transactions of the Historical Society of Lancashire and Cheshire,* 42 (1890), 45). In 1753, William Earle married Anne Winstanley (died-1789) daughter of Thomas and Mary Hosken, and the widow of Samuel Winstanley. William Earle had three sons with Anne Winstanley, Thomas Earle of Spekelands, (1754–1822), Ralph Earle (1756–1767), William Earle of Everton, (1760–1839), and one daughter, Mary Earle (1758–1831). (T. Algernon Earle, 45) Anne Winstanley Earle had two married sisters, Catherine Jennings and Elizabeth Copeland, and a niece Ann Copeland, who was also her daughter-in-law. (T. A. Earle, 45) Although William Earle was a major overseas trader between 1751 and the outbreak of the American Revolution, and was elected a member of the Liverpool Chamber of Commerce in 1774, he was not involved in public affairs in Liverpool to any great extent. (T. A. Earle, 45) Some of William Earle's ships, like the *Thomas & Mary,* were involved in the Levant trade to Italy and elsewhere in the Mediterranean, others, like the *Apollo,* the *Minerva,* the *Lyme,* the *Industry,* the *Chesterfield,* the *Calypso,* the *Bacchus,* the *Friendship,* and others, were involved in the slave trade to Africa and British America, while others like the *Susannah Christina,* were employed in the Shetland fish and other trades. William Earle was a partner with Peter Holme, Thomas Hodgson, Ralph Earle, Thomas Earle, William Davenport, and John Copeland in a firm "for carrying on trade of selling beads, arrangoes, etc." (Partnership Agreement, July 24, 1766, *Letterbook of William Earle,* D/EARLE/2/2) William Earle made his sons partners at an early age, and when his brother Thomas Earle died in April 1781 his business was amalgamated with his own. (T.A. Earle, 45f) In 1781, William Earle allowed his son Thomas to manage the family business at age 27, and William Earle went into semi-retirement, dying seven years later at age 67. A major slave trader, William Earle is listed in the *TSTD* as a captain or partner in 83 slaving ventures between 1748–1775, three as captain between 1748–1751:

> *Lucy/490 (1748)*—William Earle—**Owner (s):** Peter Pemberton, Robert Patten, John Brownall, Christopher Pearson
>
> *Chesterfield/530 (1750)*—William Earle—**Owner (s):** Robert Hallhead, William Whalley, John Clayton, Edward Lowndes, Peers Legh, John Williamson, William Davenport
>
> *Chesterfield/583 (1751)*—William Earle—**Owner (s):** Robert Hallhead, William Whalley, John Clayton, Edward Lowndes, Peers Legh, John Williamson, William Davenport
>
> *Grampus/713 (1753)*—John Maddock—**Owner (s):** William Earle, Nathaniel Bassnett, Samuel Smith, Robert Armitage, Edward Cropper, Alexander Talbot, William Davenport, Captain John Maddock
>
> *Chesterfield/739 (1754)*—Patrick Black—**Owner (s):** William Earle, John Williamson, John Gorell, William Pownall, William Davenport, Thomas Moseley, Captain Patrick Black
>
> *Grampus/774 (1755)*—John Corbett, John Maddock—**Owner (s):** William Earle, Nathaniel Bassnett, Samuel Smith, Robert Armitage, Edward Cropper, Alexander Talbot, William Davenport, Captain John Maddock
>
> *Lyme/780 (1755)*—Nehemiah Holland—**Owner (s):** John Knight, John Sanforth, Thomas Mears, William Earle, Joseph Kitchingham, Captain Nehemiah Holland
>
> *Tom/817 (1756)*—Joseph Anderton, Thomas Hughes—**Owner (s):** William Earle, John Williamson, John Gorell, William Pownall, William Davenport, Christopher Davenport, Patrick Black, Thomas Falkner, Jack Home
>
> *Chesterfield/819 (1756)*—Patrick Black—**Owner (s):** William Earle, John Williamson, John Gorell, William Pownall, William Davenport, Thomas Moseley, Captain Patrick Black
>
> *Lyme/881 (1757)*—John Farrar, Nehemiah Holland—**Owner (s):** John Knight, John Sanforth, Thomas Mears, William Earle, Joseph Kitchingham, Captain Nehemiah Holland
>
> *Grampus/884 (1757)*—John Corbett—**Owner (s):** William Earle, Nathaniel Bassnett, Samuel Smith, Robert Armitage, Edward Cropper, Alexander Talbot, William Davenport, John Maddock
>
> *Chesterfield/892 (1757)*—Patrick Black, Joseph Hesketh—**Owner (s):** William Earle, John Williamson, John Gorell, William Pownall, William Davenport, Thomas Moseley, Captain Patrick Black

Prince of Bevern/911 (1758)—Nathaniel Dickinson—**Owner (s):** William Earle, John Blackburn, William Farrington, Richard Powell, Maurice Melling, John Darbyshire, Peter Leay

Chesterfield/978 (1759)—James Hesketh—**Owner (s):** John Williamson, William Earle, John Gorell, William Pownall, Christopher Davenport, Thomas Middleton, Captain James Hesketh

Lyme/986 (1759)—John Hogan—**Owner (s):** John Knight, John Sanforth, Thomas Mears, William Earle, Joseph Kitchingham, Nehemiah Holland

Industry/1010 (1759)—William Hindle—**Owner (s):** William Earle, William Davenport, Patrick Black, Richard Powell, William Farrington, Thomas Rumbold

Francis/1029 (1760)—Nathan Dickinson, Thomas Onslow—**Owner (s):** Captain Thomas Onslow, William Ingram, Robert Green, William Earle

Calypso/1037 (1760)—John Copeland—**Owner (s):** William Earle, Richard Powell, Thomas Rumbold, Peter Leay, Maurice Melling, William Farrington, Captain John Copeland, Edmund Lyon

Baltimore/1054 (1760)—Francis Lowndes—**Owner (s):** James Gildart, Charles Lowndes, Captain Francis Lowndes, Edmund Lyon, William Williamson, William Earle, Henry Hardwar

Lyme/1060 (1760)—John Hogan—**Owner (s):** John Knight, John Sanforth, Thomas Mears, William Earle, Joseph Kitchingham, Nehemiah Holland

Minerva/1086 (1760)—John Farrar—**Owner (s):** Rothwell Willoughby, John Knight, Joseph Kitchingham, William Earle, William Boates, Nehemiah Holland, Robert Clay, Francis Willoughby

Prince Vada/1092 (1760)—John Clifton—**Owner (s):** William Davenport, John Joseph Bacon, William Quayle, Hugh Cosnahan, Patrick Black, William Hayes, Robert Jennings, William Earle

Seahorse/1142 (1761)—Elias Glover—**Owner (s):** Edward Seddon, Nehemiah Holland, Thomas Ward, Samuel Salisbury, William Earle

Mentor/1158 (1761)—John Copeland—**Owner (s):** Peter Leay, Richard Powell, Charles Cooke, William Earle, Edmund Lyon, Maurice Melling, William Farrington, Ralph Earle, Captain John Copeland

Dalrymple/1206 (1762)—James Berry—**Owner (s):** William Davenport, William Earle, Patrick Black, Samuel Linekar

Seahorse/1209 (1762)—Elias Glover—**Owner (s):** Edward Seddon, Nehemiah Holland, Thomas Ward, Samuel Salisbury, William Earle

Jupiter/1245 (1763)—Michael Connor—**Owner (s):** William Earle, Maurice Melling, Robert Green, Captain Michael Connor

Dalrymple/1274 (1763)—James Berry—**Owner (s):** William Davenport, William Earle, Patrick Black, Samuel Linekar

Friendship/1276 (1763)—John Jones—**Owner (s):** William Earle, Richard Powell, Peter Leay, Ralph Earle, William Davenport, John Copeland

Apollo/1289 (1763)—Elias Glover—**Owner (s):** William Earle, Edward Seddon, Nehemiah Holland, Thomas Ward, John Hogan, Thomas Birch, Thomas Johnson, Captain Elias Glover

Little Britain/1323 (1764)—John Clare—**Owner (s):** William Davenport, William Earle, Patrick Black, William Strickland, John Reilly, Edward Cropper, (*Thomas?*) Carter

Sisters/1336 (1764)—Joseph Caton—**Owner (s):** William Davenport, Ralph Earle, Patrick Black, William Moss, Peter Leay, John Parker, John Copeland, William Earle

Dalrymple/1373 (1765)—Alexander Allison, James Berry—**Owner (s):** William Davenport, William Earle, Patrick Black, Robert Jennings, William Jenkinson, Captain James Berry, Thomas Kelly, Ambrose Lace

Friendship/1385 (1765)—John Jones—**Owner (s):** William Earle, Richard Powell, Peter Leay, Ralph Earle, William Davenport, John Copeland

Dispatch/1396 (1765)—John Ritchie—**Owner (s):** Peter Holme, William Boates, William Earle, John Kennion

Apollo/1416 (1765)—Elias Glover—**Owner (s):** William Earle, Edward Seddon, Nehemiah Holland, Thomas Ward, John Hogan, Thomas Birch, Thomas Johnson, Captain Elias Glover

Dalrymple/1453 (1766)—Alexander Allison—**Owner (s):** William Davenport, William Earle, Patrick Black, Robert Jennings, William Jenkinson, James Berry, Thomas Kelly, Ambrose Lace

Friendship/1464 (1766)—John Jones, Owen Williams—**Owner (s):** William Earle, Richard Powell, Peter Leay, Ralph Earle, William Davenport, John Copeland

Little Britain/1466 (1766)—Captain Fazakerley, Henry Madden—**Owner (s):** William Davenport, William Earle, Patrick Black, William Strickland, John Reilly, Edward Cropper

Apollo/1510 (1767)—Elias Glover—**Owner (s):** William Earle, Edward Seddon, Nehemiah Holland, Thomas Ward, John Hogan, Thomas Birch, Thomas Johnson, Captain Elias Glover

Dispatch/1540 (1767)—John Ritchie—**Owner (s):** William Earle, Peter Holme, Thomas Hodgson Jr., William Boates, John Copeland, Ralph Earle, Thomas Earle

Dalrymple/1579 (1768)—Alexander Allison, Patrick Fairweather—**Owner (s):** William Davenport, William Earle, Patrick Black, Robert Jennings, William Jenkinson, James Berry, Thomas Kelly, Ambrose Lace

Ann/1597 (1768)—John Davies—**Owner (s):** Robert Kennedy, William Earle, John Maddrell, Robert Jennings, Michael Finch, Captain John Davies

Polly/1601 (1768)—John Kendall—**Owner (s):** William Gregson, John Knight, William Earle, Captain John Kendall

Apollo/1614 (1768)—Elias Glover, Edward Fisher—**Owner (s):** William Earle, Edward Seddon, Nehemiah Holland, Thomas Ward, John Hogan, Thomas Birch, Thomas Johnson, Captain Elias Glover

Dispatch/1650 (1768)—John Ritchie—**Owner (s):** William Earle, Peter Holme, Thomas Hodgson Jr., William Boates, John Copeland, Ralph Earle, Thomas Earle

Dobson/1682 (1769)—John Potter—**Owner (s):** Christopher Hassell, William Davenport, John Dobson, Charles Ford, William James, William Earle

Lord Cassills/1690 (1769)—John Tittle—**Owner (s):** Robert Kennedy, William Earle, Captain John Tittle

Delight/1705 (1769)—William Millroy, John Barber—**Owner (s):** William Earle, Thomas Parker, Edward Seddon, William Millroy, Nehemiah Holland, James Cotter

Apollo/1725 (1769)—Edward Fisher—**Owner (s):** William Earle, Edward Seddon, Nehemiah Holland, Thomas Birch, Thomas Ward, George Warren Watts, William Dennison, Thomas Johnson

Mars/1726 (1769)—Francis Holland—**Owner (s):** William Earle, Edward Seddon, Nehemiah Holland, Thomas Birch, Thomas Ward, George Warren Watts, William Dennison, Thomas Johnson

Polly/1728 (1769)—John Kendall—**Owner (s):** William Gregson, John Knight, William Earle, Captain John Kendall

Dalrymple/1755 (1770)—Patrick Fairweather—**Owner (s):** William Davenport, William Earle, Patrick Black, Robert Jennings, William Jenkinson, James Berry, Thomas Kelly, Ambrose Lace

Swift/1764 (1770)—John Simes—**Owner (s):** William Davenport, William Earle, William Jenkinson, John Parker, Robert Jennings, Ambrose Lace, Patrick Black

Dispatch/1773 (1770)—John Ritchie—**Owner (s):** William Earle, Peter Holme, Thomas Hodgson Jr., William Boates, John Copeland, Ralph Earle, Thomas Earle

Dobson/1807 (1770)—John Potter—**Owner (s):** Christopher Hassell, William Davenport, John Dobson, William James, William Earle

Bacchus/1811 (1770)—John Barber—**Owner (s):** William Earle, Edward Seddon, Nehemiah Holland, William Dennison, Thomas Ward, Thomas Johnson, George Warren Watts

Fox/1817 (1770)—John Beard—**Owner (s):** Christopher Hassell, John Dobson, William Davenport, William Earle, William James, Charles Ford

Mars/1821 (1770)—Francis Holland—**Owner (s):** William Earle, Edward Seddon, Nehemiah Holland, Thomas Birch, Thomas Ward, George Warren Watts, William Dennison, Thomas Johnson

Polly/1851 (1771)—John Kendall—**Owner (s):** William Gregson, John Knight, William Earle, Captain John Kendall

Dalrymple/1862 (1771)—Patrick Fairweather—**Owner (s):** William Davenport, John Parker, Patrick Black, William Earle, William Jenkinson, Robert Jennings, Christopher Davenport

Apollo/1873 (1771)—Edward Fisher—**Owner (s):** William Earle, Edward Seddon, Nehemiah Holland, Thomas Ward, George Warren Watts, William Dennison

Mentor/1891 (1771)—John Ritchie, Captain Bruce, James Downie—**Owner (s):** William Earle, Thomas Hodgson, Ralph Earle, Thomas Earle, Peter Holme, Captain John Ritchie, Hindley Leigh

Swift/1900 (1771)—William Setton—**Owner (s):** William Davenport, Christopher Davenport, Patrick Black, Robert Jennings, William Jenkinson, John Parker, William Earle, Ambrose Lace

Mars/1922 (1771)—Francis Holland—**Owner (s):** William Earle, Edward Seddon, Nehemiah Holland, Thomas Birch, Thomas Ward, George Warren Watts, William Dennison, Thomas Johnson

Polly/1951 (1772)—John Kendall—**Owner (s):** Captain John Kendall, William Gregson, John Knight, William Earle, George Case, Jonathan Blundell, James Aspinall

Bacchus/1952 (1772)—Peter Morris—**Owner (s):** William Earle, Nehemiah Holland, George Warren Watts, Thomas Ward, William Dennison, Thomas Earle, Thomas Hodgson

Swift/1955 (1772)—James Sharp—**Owner (s):** William Davenport, Christopher Davenport, Patrick Black, Robert Jennings, William Jenkinson, John Parker, William Earle, Ambrose Lace

Dalrymple/2002 (1772)—Patrick Fairweather—**Owner (s):** William Davenport, John Parker, Patrick Black, William Earle, William Jenkinson, Robert Jennings, Christopher Davenport

Apollo/2013 (1772)—Edward Fisher—**Owner (s):** William Earle, Edward Seddon, Nehemiah Holland, Thomas Ward, George Warren Watts, William Dennison

Dreadnought/2016 (1772)—John Cooper—**Owner (s):** William Davenport, John Parker, William Earle, Patrick Black, Robert Jennings, William Jenkinson, Ambrose Lace, Edward Chaffers

Laurel/2045 (1773)—Joseph Matthews—**Owner (s):** John White, Thomas Foxcroft, Edward Grayson, William Earle, John Salthouse, James Welch, Joshua Rose, Captain Joseph Matthews, Folliott Powell

Dalrymple/2063 (1773)—Patrick Fairweather—**Owner (s):** William Davenport, Christopher Davenport, Ambrose Lace, Edward Chaffers, Patrick Black, Robert Jennings, William Jenkinson, Thomas Gaskell, Richard Middleton, William Earle, John Parker

Bacchus/2067 (1773)—William Hayman, John Nevin, John Barber—**Owner (s):** William Earle, Nehemiah Holland, John Finch, William Dennison, Thomas Hodgson Jr., George Warren Watts, Thomas Earle

King George/2088 (1773)—James Sharp, James Grundy—**Owner (s):** William Davenport, Patrick Black, Ambrose Lace, Edward Chaffers, Robert Jennings, John Perkins, William Earle

Mars/2090 (1773)—Francis Holland—**Owner (s):** William Earle, Edward Seddon, Nehemiah Holland, Thomas Birch, Thomas Ward, George Warren Watts, William Dennison, Thomas Johnson

Swift/2101 (1773)—William Setton—**Owner (s):** William Davenport, Christopher Davenport, Patrick Black, Robert Jennings, William Jenkinson, John Parker, William Earle, Ambrose Lace

Neptune/2104 (1773)—Hugh Ashcroft—**Owner (s):** William Earle, Nehemiah Holland, George Warren Watts, Michael Finch, William Dennison, Thomas Earle, Thomas Hodgson

Polly/2150 (1774)—John Kendall—**Owner (s):** Captain John Kendall, William Gregson, John Knight, William Earle, George Case, Jonathan Blundell, James Aspinall

Dreadnought/2161 (1774)—John Cooper—**Owner (s):** William Davenport, John Parker, William Earle, Patrick Black, Robert Jennings, William Jenkinson, Ambrose Lace, Edward Chaffers

Apollo/2182 (1774)—John Forsyth—**Owner (s):** William Earle, Edward Seddon, Nehemiah Holland, Thomas Ward, George Warren Watts, William Dennison

Laurel/2189 (1774)—Joseph Matthews, James Waddington—**Owner (s):** John White, Thomas Foxcroft, Edward Grayson, William Earle, John Salthouse, James Welch, Joshua Rose, Captain Joseph Matthews, Folliott Powell

Polly/2234 (1775)—John Kendall—**Owner (s):** Captain John Kendall, William Gregson, John Knight, William Earle, George Case, Jonathan Blundell, James Aspinall

2. William Davenport (1725–1797) William Davenport is listed in the *Liverpool Directory of 1766* as a merchant of Drury Lane, Liverpool, and as senior partner in *William Davenport & Co.*, wine merchants of Harrington Street. Davenport was apprenticed to the Liverpool grocer and slave trader William Whalley, and was admitted a freeman of Liverpool in 1749. (David Richardson, "Profits in the Liverpool Slave Trade: The Accounts of William Davenport, 1757–1784," in *Liverpool, the African Slave Trade, and Abolition*, eds., Roger Anstey and P.E.H. Hair (1976), 61) Although Davenport was an eminent Liverpool merchant, he neither held political office in his adopted town, nor did he become a freeman of the Liverpool Company of Merchants Trading to Africa, and like his brother Christopher Davenport, he never married. At his death in 1797, he was buried at St. Nicholas, Prescott. With the exception of William James, John Knight, and Foster Cunliffe, William Davenport was the most prolific slave trader in Liverpool between 1695 and 1775. Born in Red Lion Square, London, William Davenport was a son of Cheshire gentleman Davies Davenport, and grandson of Monk Davenport. Davies Davenport was christened in Prestbury, Cheshire on March 14, 1695, and married Penelope Ward (1700–1737) of Carpesthorne, Cheshire at Kensington, Middlesex on October 19, 1721. (*International Genealogy Index*) A member of Gray's Inn and the Inner Temple, Davies Davenport lived in London after his marriage, where his wife bore him eleven children; including: John Davenport (born and died in 1722), Davies Davenport Jr. (1723–1758), Ann Davenport (born and died in 1724), William Davenport (1725–1797), Phillip Davenport (1726–1727), Penelope Davenport (1728–1741), Richard Davenport (1729–1799) Christopher Davenport (1730–1793), Thomasina Davenport (1732–1766), Thomas Davenport (1733–1786), later a resident of York, and Charles Davenport (1735–1767). (*International Genealogy Index*) After William Davenport's mother Penelope died on November 11, 1737, his father returned to Cheshire, where he died three years later. In a number of business pursuits, including the slave trade, William Davenport's most frequent partners were William Earle, Christopher Davenport, and Patrick Black. Davenport was a partner with Peter Holme, Thomas Hodgson, Ralph Earle, Thomas Earle, William Earle, and John Copeland in a firm "for carrying on trade of selling beads, arrangoes, etc." (Partnership Agreement, July 24, 1766, D/EARLE/2/2) William Davenport is listed in the *TSTD* as a partner in 101 slaving ventures between 1748–1775, a figure which rose to 160 career voyages before his retirement in the mid-1780s. (Richardson, 64)

Chesterfield/481 (1748)—Patrick Dwyer, John Jenkins—**Owner (s):** Robert Hallhead, William Whalley, John Clayton, Edward Lowndes, Peers Legh, John Williamson, William Davenport

St. George/494 (1748)—John Grayson—**Owner (s):** Robert Hallhead, William Whalley, John Knight, Edward Lowndes, Peers Legh, Ralph Whalley, William Davenport, Captain John Grayson

Chesterfield/530 (1750)—William Earle—**Owner (s):** Robert Hallhead, William Whalley, John Clayton, Edward Lowndes, Peers Legh, John Williamson, William Davenport

Chesterfield/583 (1751)—William Earle—**Owner (s):** Robert Hallhead, William Whalley, John Clayton, Edward Lowndes, Peers Legh, John Williamson, William Davenport

Orrell/609 (1752)—Samuel Lacer, John Whiteside, James Griffin—**Owner (s):** Robert Hallhead, William Whalley, William Davenport, George Clowes

Chesterfield/660 (1753)—Patrick Black—**Owner (s):** Robert Hallhead, William Whaley, John Clayton, Edward Lowndes, Peers Legh, John Williamson, William Davenport

Charming Nancy/689 (1753)—Samuel Sachaverell—**Owners (s):** William Davenport, Lawrence Spencer, Thomas Rumbold, Thomas Foulkes, Christopher Davenport

Charming Nancy/714 (1754)—Samuel Sachaverell—**Owner (s):** William Davenport, Lawrence Spencer, Thomas Rumbold, Thomas Foulkes, Christopher Davenport

Chesterfield/739 (1754)—Patrick Black—**Owner (s):** William Earle, John Williamson, John Gorell, William Pownall, William Davenport, Thomas Moseley, Captain Patrick Black

James/753 (1754)—Isaac Hyde, John Hyde—**Owner (s):** William Davenport, Lawrence Spencer, Thomas Foulkes, James Campbell, Thomas Rumbold

Charming Nancy/811 (1755)—Thomas Dickson, Samuel Sachaverell—**Owner (s):** William Davenport, Lawrence Spencer, Thomas Rumbold, Thomas Foulkes, Christopher Davenport

Tom/817 (1756)—Joseph Anderton, Thomas Hughes—**Owner (s):** William Earle, John Williamson, John Gorell, William Pownall, William Davenport, Christopher Davenport, Patrick Black, Thomas Falkner, Jack Home

Chesterfield/819 (1756)—Patrick Black—**Owner (s):** William Earle, John Williamson, John Gorell, William Pownall, William Davenport, Thomas Moseley, Captain Patrick Black

Charming Nancy/841 (1756)—Samuel Sachaverell—**Owner (s):** James Campbell, Lawrence Spencer, William Davenport, Christopher Davenport, Thomas Rumbold, Captain Samuel Sachaverell, Robert Cheshire, John Maine

Raccoon/855 (1756)—Thomas Hughes—**Owner (s):** William Davenport, Thomas Marsden, John Perkins, John Maddock, Edward Cropper

Grampus/884 (1757)—John Corbett—**Owner (s):** William Earle, Nathaniel Bassnett, Samuel Smith, Robert Armitage, Edward Cropper, Alexander Talbot, William Davenport, John Maddock.

Chesterfield/892 (1757)—Patrick Black, Joseph Hesketh—**Owner (s):** William Earle, John Williamson, John Gorell, William Pownall, William Davenport, Thomas Moseley, Captain Patrick Black

Polly/906 (1757)—John Corbett, Edward Lloyd—**Owner (s):** William Davenport, John Maddock, John Kelly, Thomas Rumbold, Thomas Rigby

Calveley/946 (1758)—Thomas Hughes—**Owner (s):** William Davenport, Thomas Rumbold, John Maddock, Thomas Marsden, Edward Cropper, John Gorell, William Pownall

Industry/1010 (1759)—William Hindle—**Owner (s):** William Earle, William Davenport, Patrick Black, Richard Powell, William Farrington, Thomas Rumbold

Eadith/1056 (1760)—Thomas Jordan—**Owner (s):** William Davenport, Thomas Kelly, Patrick Black, Captain Thomas Jordan, Ambrose Lace, Samuel Winstanley

Prince Vada/1092 (1760)—John Clifton—**Owner (s):** William Davenport, John Joseph Bacon, William Quayle, Hugh Cosnahan, Patrick Black, William Hayes, Robert Jennings, William Earle

Union/1094 (1760)—Thomas Hughes—**Owner (s):** William Davenport, John Gorell, William Pownall, Thomas Rumbold, John Maddock, Edward Cropper, John Perkins

Tyrell/1102 (1761)—William Hindle, McNeale—**Owner (s):** John Maine, James Gildart, William Davenport, Christopher Davenport, William Gardner, William Hayes

Middleton/1128 (1761)—William Metcalf—**Owner (s):** Thomas Falkner, William Davenport, Roger Parr, Patrick Black, Captain William Metcalf

Charles/1144 (1761)—John Davies—**Owner (s):** William Davenport, Charles Cooke, Samuel Winstanley, Thomas Kelly, John Maddock, Captain John Davies

Eadith/1156 (1761)—Thomas Jordan, Captain Rabine—**Owner (s):** William Davenport, Thomas Kelly, Patrick Black, Captain Thomas Jordan, Ambrose Lace, Samuel Winstanley

Union/1196 (1762)—Thomas Hughes—**Owner (s):** William Davenport, John Gorell, William Pownall, Thomas Rumbold, John Maddock, Edward Cropper, John Perkins

Dalrymple/1206 (1762)—James Berry—**Owner (s):** William Davenport, William Earle, Patrick Black, Samuel Linekar

Delight/1230 (1763)—William Richardson—**Owner (s):** Thomas Rumbold, William Davenport, John Kitchingham, Thomas Parker, Christopher Davenport

Dalrymple/1274 (1763)—James Berry—**Owner (s):** -William Davenport, William Earle, Patrick Black, Samuel Linekar

Friendship/1276 (1763)—John Jones—**Owner (s):** William Earle, Richard Powell, Peter Leay, Ralph Earle, William Davenport, John Copeland

Union/1301 (1764)—Thomas Hughes—**Owner (s):** William Davenport, John Gorell, William Pownall, Thomas Rumbold, John Maddock, Edward Cropper, John Perkins

Delight/1312 (1764)—William Richardson—**Owner (s):** Thomas Rumbold, William Davenport, John Kitchingham, Thomas Parker, Christopher Davenport

Little Britain/1323 (1764)—John Clare—**Owner (s):** William Davenport, William Earle, Patrick Black, William Strickland, John Reilly, Edward Cropper, (*Thomas?*) Carter

Sisters/1336 (1764)—Joseph Caton—**Owner (s):** William Davenport, Ralph Earle, Patrick Black, William Moss, Peter Leay, John Parker, John Copeland, William Earle

William/1357 (1764)—William Patten—**Owner (s):** William Davenport, William Jenkinson, John Maddock, James Chapman

Dalrymple/1373 (1765)—Alexander Allison, James Berry—**Owner (s):** William Davenport, William Earle, Patrick Black, Robert Jennings, William Jenkinson, Captain James Berry, Thomas Kelly, Ambrose Lace

Friendship/1385 (1765)—John Jones—**Owner (s):** William Earle, Richard Powell, Peter Leay, Ralph Earle, William Davenport, John Copeland

Union/1402 (1765)—Thomas Hughes—**Owner (s):** William Davenport, William Pownall, Edward Cropper, Thomas Carter, John Perkins, Thomas Kelly, Captain Thomas Hughes, Charles Ford

Active/1408 (1765)—Francis Lowndes, **Owner (s):** Captain Francis Lowndes, Thomas Johnson, William Dobb, Peter Rigby, John Salthouse, Rossendale Allen, William Davenport, Christopher Hassell, Charles Ford

Dalrymple/1453 (1766)—Alexander Allison—**Owner (s):** William Davenport, William Earle, Patrick Black, Robert Jennings, William Jenkinson, James Berry, Thomas Kelly, Ambrose Lace

Friendship/1464 (1766)—John Jones, Owen Williams—**Owner (s):** William Earle, Richard Powell, Peter Leay, Ralph Earle, William Davenport, John Copeland

Little Britain/1466 (1766)—Captain Fazakerley, Henry Madden—**Owner (s):** William Davenport, William Earle, Patrick Black, William Strickland, John Reilly, Edward Cropper

William/1478 (1766)—John Eccles—**Owner (s):** William Davenport, William Jenkinson, John Maddock, James Chapman, John Perkins, Thomas Hughes, Charles Woods, William Jenkinson, Richard Middleton, Francis Lowndes

Union/1507 (1767)—Thomas Hughes—**Owner (s):** William Davenport, William Pownall, John Perkins, Charles Ford, Thomas Cropper Jr., Thomas Kelly, John Maddock, John Yates, Captain Thomas Hughes

Dobson/1513 (1767)—Francis Lowndes—**Owner (s):** Christopher Hassell, William Davenport, John Dobson, Charles Ford, Captain Francis Lowndes, John Copeland

Good Intent/1533 (1767)—James Gardner—**Owner (s):** Christopher Hassell, John Dobson, William Davenport, John Copeland, Francis Lowndes

King of Prussia/1560 (1767)—Samuel Richardson—**Owner (s):** Thomas Staniforth, Alexander Nottingham, Joseph Taylor, Felix Doran, William Pole, Charles Martin, Bryan Blundell, William Davenport

Neptune/1578 (1768)—John Potter—**Owner (s):** William Davenport, William Jennings, Robert Jennings, John Parker, Patrick Black, Thomas Kelly

Dalrymple/1579 (1768)—Alexander Allison, Patrick Fairweather—**Owner (s):** William Davenport, William Earle, Patrick Black, Robert Jennings, William Jenkinson, James Berry, Thomas Kelly, Ambrose Lace

Plumper/1586 (1768)—Joseph Matthews—**Owner (s):** John White, Thomas Foxcroft, Samuel Woodward, William Davenport, George Warren Watts, Edward Grayson, John Salthouse, Joseph Brown

William/1599 (1768)—John Eccles—**Owner (s):** William Davenport, William Jenkinson, John Maddock, James Chapman

Union/1624 (1768)—Thomas Hughes—**Owner (s):** William Davenport, William Pownall, John Perkins, Charles Ford, Thomas Cropper Jr., Thomas Kelly, John Maddock, John Yates, Captain Thomas Hughes

Dobson/1682 (1769)—John Potter—**Owner (s):** Christopher Hassell, William Davenport, John Dobson, Charles Ford, William James, William Earle

King of Prussia/1688 (1769)—Samuel Richardson—**Owner (s):** Thomas Staniforth, Alexander Nottingham, Joseph Taylor, Felix Doran, William Pole, Charles Martin, Bryan Blundell, William Davenport

Fox/1692 (1769)—William Brodie, Patrick McLain—**Owner (s):** Christopher Hassell, John Dobson, William Davenport, William James, Charles Ford

Hector/1713 (1769)—Nonus Park—**Owner (s):** William Davenport, Ambrose Lace, John Washington, Edward Chaffers, Henry Trafford, William Rowe, Captain Nonus Park

William/1724 (1769)—John Eccles—**Owner (s):** William Davenport, Francis Lowndes, Richard Middleton, Christopher Hassell, Thomas Hughes

Plumper/1729 (1769)—William Batty—**Owner (s):** John White, Thomas Foxcroft, Samuel Woodward, William Davenport, George Warren Watts, Edward Grayson, John Salthouse, Joseph Brown, Joseph Matthews

Andromache/1730 (1769)—James Sharp—**Owner (s):** William Davenport, Ambrose Lace, John Washington, Edward Chaffers, Henry Trafford, Nonus Park, William Rowe

Dalrymple/1755 (1770)—Patrick Fairweather—**Owner (s):** William Davenport, William Earle, Patrick Black, Robert Jennings, William Jenkinson, James Berry, Thomas Kelly, Ambrose Lace

Swift/1764 (1770)—John Simes—**Owner (s):** William Davenport, William Earle, William Jenkinson, John Parker, Robert Jennings, Ambrose Lace, Patrick Black

Union/1772 (1770)—John Peers, Thomas Hughes—**Owner (s):** William Davenport, William Pownall, John Perkins, Charles Ford, Thomas Cropper Jr., Thomas Kelly, John Maddock, John Yates, Captain Thomas Hughes

Dobson/1807 (1770)—John Potter—**Owner (s):** Christopher Hassell, William Davenport, John Dobson, William James, William Earle

Fox/1817 (1770)—John Beard—**Owner (s):** Christopher Hassell, John Dobson, William Davenport, William Earle, William James, Charles Ford

Hector/1847 (1771)—Nonus Park—**Owner (s):** William Davenport, Ambrose Lace, John Washington, Edward Chaffers, Henry Trafford, William Rowe, Captain Nonus Park

King of Prussia/1856 (1771)—Samuel Richardson—**Owner (s):** Thomas Staniforth, Alexander Nottingham, Joseph Taylor, Felix Doran, William Pole, Charles Martin, Bryan Blundell, William Davenport

Dalrymple/1862 (1771)—Patrick Fairweather—**Owner (s):** William Davenport, John Parker, Patrick Black, William Earle, William Jenkinson, Robert Jennings, Christopher Davenport

Andromache/1869 (1771)—James Sharp—**Owner (s):** William Davenport, Ambrose Lace, John Washington, Edward Chaffers, Henry Trafford, Nonus Park, William Rowe

Plumper/1883 (1771)—Joseph Matthews—**Owner (s):** John White, Thomas Foxcroft, Samuel Woodward, William Davenport, George Warren Watts, Edward Grayson, John Salthouse, Joseph Brown

Swift/1900 (1771)—William Setton—**Owner (s):** William Davenport, Christopher Davenport, Patrick Black, Robert Jennings, William Jenkinson, John Parker, William Earle, Ambrose Lace

Fox/1902 (1771)—John Peers—**Owner (s):** William Davenport, Christopher Davenport, Thomas Gaskell, Richard Middleton, Thomas Hughes, John Perkins, John Richardson

Swift/1955 (1772)—James Sharp—**Owner (s):** William Davenport, Christopher Davenport, Patrick Black, Robert Jennings, William Jenkinson, John Parker, William Earle, Ambrose Lace

May/1960 (1772)—John Simes—**Owner (s):** Robert Kennedy, John Parker, William Davenport

Will/1970 (1772)—James Spencer—**Owner (s):** Francis Ingram, James Perkins, William Davenport, Christopher Butler

Thomas/1977 (1772)—Edward Lyon—**Owner (s):** James Clemens, Robert Kennedy, William Davenport

Dalrymple/2002 (1772)—Patrick Fairweather—**Owner (s):** William Davenport, John Parker, Patrick Black, William Earle, William Jenkinson, Robert Jennings, Christopher Davenport

Dreadnought/2016 (1772)—John Cooper—**Owner (s):** William Davenport, John Parker, William Earle, Patrick Black, Robert Jennings, William Jenkinson, Ambrose Lace, Edward Chaffers

Patty/2018 (1772)—John Forsyth—**Owner (s):** Edward Chaffers, William Rowe, William Davenport, Ambrose Lace, John Parker

Badger/2019 (1772)—John Peers, Peter Potter—**Owner (s):** William Davenport, Thomas Hughes, John Jackson, Thomas Gaskell, Richard Middleton, John Galley, Robert Jennings, Christopher Davenport

Hector/2029 (1773)—Edmund Doyle, William Griffiths—**Owner (s):** William Davenport, Ambrose, John Washington, Edward Chaffers, Henry Trafford, William Rowe, Nonus Park

Fox/2031 (1773)—Samuel Lang—**Owner (s):** William Davenport, Christopher Davenport, Thomas Gaskell, Richard Middleton, Thomas Hughes, John Perkins, John Richardson

Favorite/2056 (1773)—William Berry, John Hollingsworth—**Owner (s):** Alexander Nottingham, Thomas Case, Clayton Case, Thomas Staniforth, William Pole, William Davenport, Charles Martin, Joseph Taylor, George Warren Watts, Felix Doran

Andromache/2057 (1773)—James Benn Rowe, Edward Dugan—**Owner (s):** William Davenport, Ambrose Lace, Edward Chaffers, William Rowe, John Fletcher, John Parker

Dalrymple/2063 (1773)—Patrick Fairweather—**Owner (s):** William Davenport, Christopher Davenport, Ambrose Lace, Edward Chaffers, Patrick Black, Robert Jennings, William Jenkinson, Thomas Gaskell, Richard Middleton, William Earle, John Parker

King of Prussia/2066 (1773)—John Smale—**Owner (s):** Thomas Staniforth, Alexander Nottingham, Joseph Taylor, Felix Doran, William Pole, Charles Martin, William Davenport, George Warren Watts, Thomas Case, Clayton Case

Charles/2070 (1773)—William Hurst—**Owner (s):** Alexander Nottingham, Thomas Staniforth, Thomas Case, Clayton Case, Joseph Taylor, William Pole, William Davenport, Charles Martin, Felix Doran, George Warren Watt

King George/2088 (1773)—James Sharp, James Grundy—**Owner (s):** William Davenport, Patrick Black, Ambrose Lace, Edward Chaffers, Robert Jennings, John Perkins, William Earle

Swift/2101 (1773)—William Setton—**Owner (s):** William Davenport, Christopher Davenport, Patrick Black, Robert Jennings, William Jenkinson, John Parker, William Earle, Ambrose Lace

Sam/2129 (1774)—Samuel Richardson—**Owner (s):** Thomas Staniforth, Alexander Nottingham, Felix Doran, Thomas Case, Clayton Case, Joseph Taylor, William Davenport, Charles Martin, William Pole, George Warren Watts

Nancy/2134 (1774)—Nehemiah Brettargh—**Owner (s):** William Davenport

Fox/2136 (1774)—Robert Mitchell—**Owner (s):** William Davenport, Christopher Davenport, Thomas Gaskell, Richard Middleton, Thomas Hughes, John Perkins, John Richardson

Badger/2152 (1774)—Peter Potter—**Owner (s):** William Davenport, Thomas Hughes, John Jackson, Thomas Gaskell, Richard Middleton, John Galley, Robert Jennings, Christopher Davenport

Favorite/2159 (1774)—William Berry, John Hollingsworth—**Owner (s):** Alexander Nottingham, Thomas Case, Clayton Case, Thomas Staniforth, William Pole, William Davenport, Charles Martin, Joseph Taylor, George Warren Watts, Felix Doran

Mary/2160 (1774)—John Barkley—**Owner (s):** Robert Kennedy, John Parker, William Davenport

Dreadnought/2161 (1774)—John Cooper—**Owner (s):** William Davenport, John Parker, William Earle, Patrick Black, Robert Jennings, William Jenkinson, Ambrose Lace, Edward Chaffers

Charles/2188 (1774)—William Hurst—**Owner (s):** Alexander Nottingham, Thomas Staniforth, Thomas Case, Clayton Case, Joseph Taylor, William Pole, William Davenport, Charles Martin, Felix Doran, George Warren Watts

King of Prussia/2207 (1774)—John Smale—**Owner (s):** Thomas Staniforth, Alexander Nottingham, Joseph Taylor, Felix Doran, William Pole, Charles Martin, William Davenport, George Warren Watts, Thomas Case, Clayton Case

Badger/2217 (1775)—Peter Potter, Ford—**Owner (s):** William Davenport, Thomas Hughes, John Jackson, Thomas Gaskell, Richard Middleton, John Galley, Robert Jennings, Christopher Davenport

Sam/2237 (1775)—Samuel Richardson—**Owner (s):** Thomas Staniforth, Alexander Nottingham, Felix Doran, Thomas Case, Clayton Case, Joseph Taylor, William Davenport, Charles Martin, William Pole, George Warren Watts

3. Patrick Black (died-*c.*1776) Captain Patrick Black is listed in the *Liverpool Directory of 1766* as a merchant of Hanover Street, Liverpool. Patrick Black was the son of John Black of Belfast, Ireland, and brother of Robert Black, a partner in *Ross, Black & Christian,* prominent merchants of Castletown, Isle of Man. (Frances Wilkins, *Manx Slave Traders* (1999), 56–58) Patrick Black was a close associate of William Earle and William Davenport in the African trade, and is listed in the *TSTD* as a captain and/or partner in 34 slaving ventures between 1753–1774, four as a captain between 1753–1757, and 30 as an owner between 1754–1774. (Will of Patrick Black, mariner of Liverpool, Wills and Inventories, Chester Probate Registry, Admon., 1776)

Chesterfield/660 (1753)—Patrick Black—**Owner (s):** Robert Hallhead, William Whalley, John Clayton, Edward Lowndes, Peers Legh, John Williamson, William Davenport

Chesterfield/739 (1754)—Patrick Black—**Owner (s):** William Earle, John Williamson, John Gorell, William Pownall, William Davenport, Thomas Moseley, Captain Patrick Black

Chesterfield/819 (1756)—Patrick Black—**Owner (s):** William Earle, John Williamson, John Gorell, William Pownall, William Davenport, Thomas Moseley, Captain Patrick Black

Chesterfield/892 (1757)—Patrick Black, Joseph Hesketh—**Owner (s):** William Earle, John Williamson, John Gorell, William Pownall, William Davenport, Thomas Moseley, Captain Patrick Black

Industry/1010 (1759)—William Hindle—**Owner (s):** William Earle, William Davenport, Patrick Black, Richard Powell, William Farrington, Thomas Rumbold

Eadith/1056 (1760)—Thomas Jordan—**Owner (s):** William Davenport, Thomas Kelly, Patrick Black, Captain Thomas Jordan, Ambrose Lace, Samuel Winstanley

Prince Vada/1092 (1760)—John Clifton—**Owner (s):** William Davenport, John Joseph Bacon, William Quayle, Hugh Cosnahan, Patrick Black, William Hayes, Robert Jennings, William Earle

Middleton/1128 (1761)—William Metcalf—**Owner (s):** Thomas Falkner, William Davenport, Roger Parr, Patrick Black, Captain William Metcalf

Eadith/1156 (1761)—Thomas Jordan, Captain Rabine—**Owner (s):** William Davenport, Thomas Kelly, Patrick Black, Captain Thomas Jordan, Ambrose Lace, Samuel Winstanley

Dalrymple/1206 (1762)—James Berry—**Owner (s):** William Davenport, William Earle, Patrick Black, Samuel Linekar

Dalrymple/1274 (1763)—James Berry—**Owner (s):** William Davenport, William Earle, Patrick Black, Samuel Linekar

Little Britain/1323 (1764)—John Clare—**Owner (s):** William Davenport, William Earle, Patrick Black, William Strickland, John Reilly, Edward Cropper, Thomas Carter

Sisters/1336 (1764)—Joseph Caton—**Owner (s):** William Davenport, Ralph Earle, Patrick Black, William Moss, Peter Leay, John Parker, John Copeland, William Earle

Dalrymple/1373 (1765)—Alexander Allison, James Berry—**Owner (s):** William Davenport, William Earle, Patrick Black, Robert Jennings, William Jenkinson, James Berry, Thomas Kelly, Ambrose Lace

Dalrymple/1453 (1766)—Alexander Allison—**Owner (s):** William Davenport, William Earle, Patrick Black, Robert Jennings, William Jenkinson, James Berry, Thomas Kelly, Ambrose Lace

Little Britain/1466 (1766)—Captain Fazakerley, Henry Madden—**Owner (s):** William Davenport, William Earle, Patrick Black, William Strickland, John Reilly, Edward Cropper

Neptune/1578 (1768)—John Potter—**Owner (s):** William Davenport, William Jennings, Robert Jennings, John Parker, Patrick Black, Thomas Kelly

Dalrymple/1755 (1770)—Patrick Fairweather—**Owner (s):** William Davenport, William Earle, Patrick Black, Robert Jennings, Ambrose Lace, Patrick Black

Lord Cassills/1832 (1771)—Henry Madden, Samuel McCutcheon—**Owner (s):** Robert Kennedy, Patrick Black, John Clowes, Wingfield Harding

May/1848 (1771)—John Simes—**Owner (s):** Robert Kennedy, Patrick Black, John Parker, John Clowes

Dalrymple/1862 (1771)—Patrick Fairweather—**Owner (s):** William Davenport, John Parker, Patrick Black, William Earle, William Jenkinson, Robert Jennings, Christopher Davenport

Swift/1900 (1771)—William Setton—**Owner (s):** William Davenport, Christopher Davenport, Patrick Black, Robert Jennings, William Jenkinson, John Parker, William Earle, Ambrose Lace

Swift/1955 (1772)—James Sharp—**Owner (s):** William Davenport, Christopher Davenport, Patrick Black, Robert Jennings, William Jenkinson, John Parker, William Earle, Ambrose Lace

Dalrymple/2002 (1772)—Patrick Fairweather—**Owner (s):** William Davenport, John Parker, Patrick Black, William Earle, William Jenkinson, Robert Jennings, Christopher Davenport

Dreadnought/2016 (1772)—John Cooper—**Owner (s):** William Davenport, John Parker, William Earle, Patrick Black, Robert Jennings, William Jenkinson, Ambrose Lace, Edward Chaffers

Dalrymple/2063 (1773)—Patrick Fairweather—**Owner (s):** William Davenport, Christopher Davenport, Ambrose Lace, Edward Chaffers, Patrick Black, Robert Jennings, William Jenkinson, Thomas Gaskell, Richard Middleton, William Earle, John Parker

King George/2088 (1773)—James Sharp, James Grundy—**Owner (s):** William Davenport, Patrick Black, Ambrose Lace, Edward Chaffers, Robert Jennings, John Perkins, William Earle

Swift/2101 (1773)—William Setton—**Owner (s):** -William Davenport, Christopher Davenport, Patrick Black, Robert Jennings, William Jenkinson, John Parker, William Earle, Ambrose Lace

Lord Cassills/2133 (1774)—John Simes—**Owner (s):** Robert Kennedy, Patrick Black, John Clowes, Wingfield Harding

Dreadnought/2161 (1774)—John Cooper—**Owner (s):** William Davenport, John Parker, William Earle, Patrick Black, Robert Jennings, William Jenkinson, Ambrose Lace, Edward Chaffers.

4. Robert Jennings (died-*c*.1792) Brother-in-law of both William Earle and John Copeland Jr., and possibly from Cumberland, Robert Jennings is listed in the *Liverpool Directory of 1766* as a merchant of Frederick Street, Liverpool. (T. A. Earle, 46) Robert Jennings is listed in the *TSTD* as a captain and/or partner in 26 slaving ventures between 1748–1775, three as captain, one as captain/partner, and 22 as a partner. (Will of Robert Jennings, mariner of Liverpool, Wills and Inventories, Chester Probate Registry, 1792)

Pym/467 (1748)—Robert Jennings, Robert Dillon—**Owner (s):** John Pym

Cavendish/632 (1752)—Robert Jennings—**Owner (s):** Hugh Ball, Richard Nicholas, James Pardoe, Charles Lowndes, John Chorley, William Whalley, Benjamin Heywood

Nicholas/796 (1755)—Robert Jennings—**Owner (s):** Richard Nicholas, William Rowe, John Gorell, John Leather, George Mort, William Pownall, Thomas Johnson, Rossendale Allen, Thomas Park, Captain Robert Jennings

Mac/929 (1758)—Edward Cropper Jr., Wilfred Inman—**Owner (s):** Captain Edward Cropper Jr., William Reid, Edward Cropper Sr., Robert Jennings

Molly/1033 (1760)—Edward Cropper Jr.—**Owner (s):** Thomas Hodgson, Edward Cropper Sr., Captain Edward Cropper Jr., Charles Cooke, Robert Jennings, Robert Kennedy

Prince Vada/1092 (1760)—John Clifton—**Owner (s):** William Davenport, John Joseph Bacon, William Quayle, Hugh Cosnahan, Patrick Black, William Hayes, Robert Jennings, William Earle

Molly/1170 (1762)—Richard Dutery—**Owner (s):** Thomas Hodgson, Edward Cropper Sr., Edward Cropper Jr., Charles Cooke, Robert Jennings, Robert Kennedy

Waree/1182 (1762)—Blackburn Willock—**Owner (s):** Thomas Hodgson, Edward Cropper Sr., Edward Cropper Jr., Charles Cooke, Robert Jennings, Robert Kennedy

Nancy/1287 (1762)—John Davies—**Owner (s):** Charles Cooke, Edward Cropper, Robert Kennedy, Robert Jennings, Robert Clay, Captain John Davies

Waree/1322 (1764)—William Brookbank—**Owner (s):** Thomas Hodgson, Edward Cropper, Edward Cropper Jr., Charles Cooke, Robert Jennings, Robert Kennedy

Dalrymple/1373 (1765)—Alexander Allison, James Berry—**Owner (s):** William Davenport, William Earle, Patrick Black, Robert Jennings, William Jenkinson, Captain James Berry, Thomas Kelly, Ambrose Lace

Dalrymple/1453 (1766)—Alexander Allison—**Owner (s):** William Davenport, William Earle, Patrick Black, Robert Jennings, William Jenkinson, James Berry, Thomas Kelly, Ambrose Lace

Dalrymple/1579 (1768)—Alexander Allison, Patrick Fairweather—**Owner (s):** William Davenport, William Earle, Patrick Black, Robert Jennings, William Jenkinson, James Berry, Thomas Kelly, Ambrose Lace

Ann/1597 (1768)—John Davies—**Owner (s):** Robert Kennedy, William Earle, John Maddrell, Robert Jennings, Michael Finch, Captain John Davies

Dalrymple/1862 (1771)—Patrick Fairweather—**Owner (s):** William Davenport, John Parker, Patrick Black, William Earle, William Jenkinson, Robert Jennings, Christopher Davenport

Swift/1900 (1771)—William Setton—**Owner (s):** William Davenport, Christopher Davenport, Patrick Black, Robert Jennings, William Jenkinson, John Parker, William Earle, Ambrose Lace

Swift/1955 (1772)—James Sharp—**Owner (s):** William Davenport, Christopher Davenport, Patrick Black, Robert Jennings, William Jenkinson, John Parker, William Earle, Ambrose Lace

Dalrymple/2002 (1772)—Patrick Fairweather—**Owner (s):** William Davenport, John Parker, Patrick Black, William Earle, William Jenkinson, Robert Jennings, Christopher Davenport

Dreadnought/2016 (1772)—John Cooper—**Owner (s):** William Davenport, John Parker, William Earle, Patrick Black, Robert Jennings, William Jenkinson, Ambrose Lace, Edward Chaffers

Badger/2019 (1772)—John Peers, Peter Potter—**Owner (s):** William Davenport, Thomas Hughes, John Jackson, Thomas Gaskell, Richard Middleton, John Galley, Robert Jennings, Christopher Davenport

Dalrymple/2063 (1773)—Patrick Fairweather—**Owner (s):** William Davenport, Christopher Davenport, Ambrose Lace, Edward Chaffers, Patrick Black, Robert Jennings, William Jenkinson, Thomas Gaskell, Richard Middleton, William Earle, John Parker

King George/2088 (1773)—James Sharp, James Grundy—**Owner (s):** William Davenport, Patrick Black, Ambrose Lace, Edward Chaffers, Robert Jennings, John Perkins, William Earle

Swift/2101 (1773)—William Setton—**Owner (s):** William Davenport, Christopher Davenport, Patrick Black, Robert Jennings, William Jenkinson, John Parker, William Earle, Ambrose Lace

Badger/2152 (1774)—Peter Potter—**Owner (s):** William Davenport, Thomas Hughes, John Jackson, Thomas Gaskell, Richard Middleton, John Galley, Robert Jennings, Christopher Davenport

Dreadnought/2161 (1774)—John Cooper—**Owner (s):** William Davenport, John Parker, William Earle, Patrick Black, Robert Jennings, William Jenkinson, Ambrose Lace, Edward Chaffers

Badger/2217 (1775)—Peter Potter, Captain Ford—**Owner (s):** William Davenport, Thomas Hughes, John Jackson, Thomas Gaskell, Richard Middleton, John Galley, Robert Jennings, Christopher Davenport

5. William Hayes A William Hayes is listed in the *TSTD* as a captain and/or partner in nine slaving ventures between 1752–1761, five as captain, one as captain/partner, and three as partner:

Elizabeth/610 (1752)—William Hayes—**Owner (s):** Samuel Shaw, John Backhouse, Bryan Blundell, William Blundell, Richard Blundell, James Crosbie

Elizabeth/668 (1753)—William Hayes—**Owner (s):** Samuel Shaw, John Backhouse, Bryan Blundell, William Blundell, Richard Blundell, James Crosbie

Elizabeth/742 (1754)—William Hayes—**Owner (s):** Samuel Shaw, John Backhouse, Bryan Blundell, William Blundell, Richard Blundell, James Crosbie

Judith/838 (1756)—Samuel Murdock, William Hayes—**Owner (s):** John Welch, Edward Parr, John Howard, Nicholas Southworth, John Cheshire

Judith/904 (1757)—William Gill, William Hayes—**Owner (s):** John Welch, Edward Parr, John Howard, Nicholas Southworth, John Cheshire, John Gorell

Beaver/995 (1759)—William Hayes—**Owner (s):** William James, William Ingram, Captain William Hayes

Beaver/1087 (1760)—James Sanders—**Owner (s):** William James, William Ingram, William Hayes

Prince Vada/1092 (1760)—John Clifton—**Owner (s):** William Davenport, John Joseph Bacon, William Quayle, Hugh Cosnahan, Patrick Black, William Hayes, Robert Jennings, William Earle

Tyrell/1102 (1761)—William Hindle, Captain McNeale—**Owner (s):** John Maine, James Gildart Sr., William Davenport, Christopher Davenport, William Gardner, William Hayes

6. John Joseph Bacon (died-*c.*1809) A prominent Manx merchant and supplier of Guinea cargoes, Bacon is listed in the *TSTD* as a partner in fourteen slaving ventures between 1760–1775. (Will of John Joseph Bacon of Douglas, Isle of Man, August 26, 1809, PCC: PROB 11/1501)

Prince Vada/1092 (1760)—John Clifton—**Owner (s):** William Davenport, John Joseph Bacon, William Quayle, Hugh Cosnahan, Patrick Black, William Hayes, Robert Jennings, William Earle

Rumbold/1308 (1764)—Michael Finch, Captain Walker—**Owner (s):** Captain Michael Finch, John Joseph Bacon, Thomas Rumbold, William Snell

Rumbold/1387 (1765)—Michael Finch—**Owner (s):** Captain Michael Finch, John Joseph Bacon, Thomas Rumbold, William Snell

Rumbold/1474 (1766)—Evan Livesay—**Owner (s):** Michael Finch, John Joseph Bacon, Thomas Rumbold, William Snell

Hare/1662 (1769)—Thomas Looney, William Chapman—**Owner (s):** Thomas Rumbold, Thomas Falkner, John Joseph Bacon, John Simmons, Michael Finch, Thomas Looney

Rumbold/1674 (1769)—Michael Finch—**Owner (s):** Thomas Rumbold, John Joseph Bacon, Captain Michael Finch, John Simmons

Rumbold/1766 (1770)—Michael Finch—**Owner (s):** Thomas Rumbold, John Joseph Bacon, Captain Michael Finch, John Simmons

Hare/1842 (1771)—William Chapman—**Owner (s):** Thomas Rumbold, Thomas Falkner, John Joseph Bacon, John Simmons, Michael Finch, Thomas Looney

Rumbold/1865 (1771)—John Thompson—**Owner (s):** Thomas Rumbold, John Joseph Bacon, Michael Finch, John Simmons

Rumbold/1959 (1772)—John Thompson, Thomas Sarrat—**Owner (s):** Thomas Rumbold, John Joseph Bacon, Michael Finch, John Simmons

Venus/1969 (1772)—William Dennison—**Owner (s):** Thomas Rumbold, Michael Finch, Captain William Dennison, John Joseph Bacon, John Simmons

Venus/2122 (1773)—William Dennison—**Owner (s):** Thomas Rumbold, Michael Finch, Captain William Dennison, John Joseph Bacon, John Simmons

Rumbold/2139 (1774)—Michael Finch, Robert Sayers—**Owner (s):** Thomas Rumbold, John Joseph Bacon, John Simmons

Rumbold/2228 (1775)—Robert Sayers—**Owner (s):** Thomas Rumbold, John Joseph Bacon, Michael Finch, John Simmons.

7. Hugh Cosnahan (died-1799) Merchant of Douglas, Isle of Man specializing in the importation of Holland goods from Rotterdam for Liverpool Guineamen. Hugh Cosnahan married Eleanor Finch, daughter of Philip Finch, who bore him fifteen children, six of whom survived to adulthood. His brother-in-law was Michael Finch, a Manx-born Guinea captain and merchant. Unlike many Manx-based merchants involved in supplying the Guinea trade, Cosnahan remained on the Isle of Man after the Act of Revestment in 1765 ended this trade, and served as a member of the House of Keys, the Manx legislative assembly, from 1777 to 1799. (Wilkins, 58) Cosnahan was also involved in the Shetland fish trade with William Earle in 1760–1761. (*Daybook of William Earle*, D/EARLE/2/2) Hugh Cosnahan is listed in the *TSTD* as a partner in two slaving ventures in 1760 and 1762:

Prince Vada/1092 (1760)—John Clifton—**Owner (s):** William Davenport, John Joseph Bacon, William Quayle, Hugh Cosnahan, Patrick Black, William Hayes, Robert Jennings, William Earle

Douglas/1177 (1762)—Michael Finch, **Owner (s):** Captain Michael Finch, John Maine, William Stewart, Robert Green, James Bates, Hugh Cosnahan, Daniel Jones, Thomas Smith, James Campbell.

8. William Quayle (died-*c.*1785) A prominent merchant of Douglas, Isle of Man, William Quayle was a smuggler and an active participant in the Manx depot trade which supplied visiting Guineamen with trade goods. Thomas Truxes notes that "Quayle's extensive involvement with Rotterdam merchants and the close ties between Douglas and ports in France, particularly Lorient and Bordeaux, suggest a peripheral role in the Dutch trade with the French West Indies *via* the neutral Islands." (Thomas Truxes, ed., *Letterbook of Greg & Cunningham, 1756–1757* (2001), 65*n*) In addition, Truxes suggests that Quayle developed close ties with the expatriate community of Irish merchants in Douglas that had "roots in Belfast, Dublin, and Waterford."

(Truxes, 66n) William Quayle is listed in the *TSTD* as a partner in one voyage of the slaver *Prince Vada* in 1760:

> ***Prince Vada/1092 (1760)***—John Clifton—**Owner (s):** William Davenport, John Joseph Bacon, William Quayle, Hugh Cosnahan, Patrick Black, William Hayes, Robert Jennings, William Earle

Printed in the United States
119788LV00003B/3-16/P

9 781934 269251